A growing number of adolescents do not have a supportive and trusting relationship with an adult in a birth, foster, adoptive, or chosen family. Through a variety of circumstances, they are literally or functionally "alone." Yet like all adolescents, they need routine and sometimes specialized health care. This book is a collection of essays, case studies, and guidelines that describe the demographic, philosophical, medical, legal, and developmental framework in which these youth and health care staff confront medical decision making. The authors address questions of consent, confidentiality, access to care, and the right to refuse or demand care. The emphasis throughout is on the real-world experience of adolescents as they struggle to overcome the challenges of being alone. Professionals who work with these adolescents cannot replace their absent or disinterested families but can fulfill the critical role of trusted adult advisor.

Jeffrey Blustein is Associate Professor of Bioethics at Albert Einstein College of Medicine, Bronx, New York, and Adjunct Associate Professor at Barnard College of Columbia University.

Carol Levine joined the United Hospital Fund in New York City in October 1996 as director of a new project, Families and Health Care. She also continues to direct The Orphan Project: Families and Children in the HIV Epidemic.

Nancy Neveloff Dubler is the Director of the Division of Bioethics, Department of Epidemiology and Social Medicine, Montefiore Medical Center, and Professor of Bioethics at the Albert Einstein College of Medicine, Bronx, New York.

The Adolescent Alone
Decision Making in Health Care
in the United States

Edited by

JEFFREY BLUSTEIN
Montefiore Medical Center

CAROL LEVINE
United Hospital Fund

NANCY NEVELOFF DUBLER
Montefiore Medical Center

CAMBRIDGE
UNIVERSITY PRESS

PUBLISHED BY THE PRESS SYNDICATE OF THE UNIVERSITY OF CAMBRIDGE
The Pitt Building, Trumpington Street, Cambridge, United Kingdom

CAMBRIDGE UNIVERSITY PRESS
The Edinburgh Building, Cambridge CB2 2RU, UK   http: //www.cup.cam.ac.uk
40 West 20th Street, New York, NY 10011-4211, USA   http: //www.cup.org
10 Stamford Road, Oakleigh, Melbourne 3166, Australia

© Cambridge University Press 1999

First published 1999

Printed in the United States of America

Typeface Times Roman 10/12.5 pt   *System* QuarkXPress™   [HT]

A catalog record for this book is available from the British Library

Library of Congress Cataloging-in-Publication Data

The adolescent alone: decision making in health care in the United States/edited
by Jeffrey Blustein, Carol Levine, Nancy Neveloff Dubler.
      p. cm.
ISBN 0 521 65240 5 (hbk.). — ISBN 0-521-65891-8 (pbk.)
1. Teenagers—Medical care—United States—Decision making.
2. Behavioral assessment of teenagers—United States.   I. Blustein. Jeffrey.
II. Levine, Carol.   III. Dubler, Nancy Neveloff.
RJ102.A366 1999
362.1'0835'0973—dc21   98-48330
CIP

ISBN 0 521 65240 5 hardback
ISBN 0 521 65891 8 paperback

To the memory of Andy Boxer, our friend, colleague, and contributor to this volume, whose life and work exemplified respect and concern for adolescents alone.

Contents

Contributors

Aylin Atillasoy
Ethnographer
National Development Research
  Institutes, Inc.

Jeffrey Blustein
Bioethicist
Montefiore Medical Center
Associate Professor of Bioethics
Albert Einstein College of Medicine

Andrew M. Boxer
Assistant Professor and Director
The Evelyn Hooker Center for Gay and
  Lesbian Mental Health
Department of Psychiatry
The University of Chicago

Michael C. Clatts
Principal Investigator
National Development Research
  Institutes, Inc.

Judith A. Cook
Professor of Sociology in Psychiatry
Director
National Research and Training Center
  on Psychiatric Disability
The University of Illinois at Chicago

Susan Coupey
Professor of Pediatrics
Albert Einstein College of Medicine
Associate Director
Division of Adolescent Medicine
Montefiore Medical Center

Francine Cournos
Professor of Clinical Psychiatry
Columbia University
New York State Psychiatric Institute

Cathy Cramer
Adolescent Health Care Consultant

W. Rees Davis
Project Director
National Development Research
  Institutes, Inc.

Nancy Dubler
Director
Division of Bioethics
Montefiore Medical Center
Director
Bioethics Consultation Service
Montefiore Medical Center
Professor of Bioethics
Albert Einstein College of
  Medicine

Abigail English
Project Director
Adolescent Health Care Project
National Center for Youth Law

Linda Freeman
Assistant Professor
Columbia University
Children's Aid Society

ix

Donna C. Futterman
Director
Adolescent AIDS Program
Montefiore Medical Center
Associate Professor of Pediatrics
Albert Einstein College of Medicine

Deborah J. Hillman
Therapist/Freelance Editor

Gilbert Herdt
Professor
Department of Psychology
Committee on Human Development
The University of Chicago

Neal D. Hoffman
Assistant Professor of Pediatrics
Albert Einstein College of Medicine
Montefiore Medical Center, Division of
    Adolescent Medicine

Nancy Leffert
Research Scientist
Search Institute

Betty Wolder Levin
Professor
Department of Health and Nutrition
    Sciences
Brooklyn College, City University of
    New York

Carol Levine
Executive Director
The Orphan Project
Director
Families and Health Care Project
United Hospital Fund

Peter Millock
Nixon, Hargrave, Devans, and Doyle LLP

Jonathan D. Moreno
Emily Davie and Joseph S. Kornfeld
    Professor of Biomedical Ethics
Director of the Center for Biomedical
    Ethics
University of Virginia

Susan Newcomer
Statistician (demography)
National Institutes of Health
Center for Population Research

Michael Pawel
Executive Director
August Aichhorn Center for Adolescent
    Residential Care
Associate Clinical Professor of Psychiatry
Columbia University College of
    Physicians and Surgeons

Anne C. Petersen
Senior Vice President for Programs
W.K. Kellogg Foundation

Audrey Smith Rogers
Epidemiologist
Pediatric, Adolescent, and Maternal
    AIDS Branch
National Institute of Child Health and
    Human Development
National Institutes of Health

Kenneth Schonberg
Director
Division of Adolescent Medicine
Montefiore Medical Center
Professor of Pediatrics
Albert Einstein College of Medicine

Luis H. Zayas
Associate Professor
Graduate School of Social Service
Fordham University

Foreword

Angela R. Holder

The current political agenda to "enhance family values" presupposes the existence of a *family,* usually envisioned as a mommy, a daddy, and one or more children who are sufficiently affluent to own a computer on which the children can, if sufficiently computer literate, find sexual material. This agenda not only ignores but completely denies the existence of an adolescent prostitute thrown out of his family when his parent discovers that he is gay and who keeps himself from starving by *becoming* sexual material. Where are the "family values" for a sixteen-year-old girl living on the street to escape sexual and physical abuse at home? As this book points out, there are approximately 200,000 adolescents who are permanent residents of the streets and about 1,500,000 adolescents who spend some time on the streets, as runaways or throwaways, because they are orphans, or because they are members of homeless families. Three-fourths of children in foster care require urgent mental health referrals and few receive them.

These young people need medical care, in addition to their many other needs, and this book will help those health care providers who must assist them. Part I of the book consists of chapters detailing the nature of the problems of the adolescent who is alone (including those who theoretically have a parent, but whose parents are unwilling or unable to exercise parental responsibilities), the legal issues involved in their care, the psychosocial issues that are peculiar to their circumstances, their health problems, and the effect of being an orphan or gay on the adolescent's decision-making capacity. Part II consists of nine real cases presented to health care providers with essays on the most effective means of helping these young people. Part III of the book is a set of suggested guidelines for health care providers who must treat the adolescent who is alone.

This excellent book will serve two purposes. First, it offers concrete advice to those who must meet the young persons' health needs. Probably more important, however, I wish it could be made required reading for the politicians, both state and federal, who deny that this population even exists in our nation and do nothing to provide the services they need. Congress funds "abstinence-only" sex education in public schools when 38 percent of ninth graders and 68 percent of twelfth graders report that they have had sexual intercourse and 25 percent of the girls report some

Angela R. Holder is Clinical Professor of Pediatrics (Law) at Yale University School of Medicine.

sort of sexual abuse. If politicians read this book, they might finally realize that they are legislating for a world that in millions of instances has never existed and start trying to find solutions instead of worsening the problem. If the case studies in this book (which are drawn from actual situations) do not convince the readers of the desperate situations in which millions of our adolescents find themselves, nothing will.

Introduction
The Adolescent Alone: "You Got Nobody in Your Corner"

Carol Levine, Jeffrey Blustein, and Nancy Dubler

Imagine the waiting room of an adolescent health clinic at an urban medical center. Some patients are accompanied by a parent, another adult, or a friend. Most of these adolescents see the doctor alone, but occasionally they ask the accompanying person to come into the office for a post-examination discussion. Other patients come to the clinic alone, tell no one about the visit, and do not ask for outside advice or help in making decisions about medical treatment.

Tammy, for example, a fifteen-year-old, has lived a few months at a time with various relatives since her mother died of AIDS two years ago. She has had asthma since childhood and the stress of her recent past has exacerbated her illness. No one in her family seems aware of her declining health or that she needs continuing support to adhere to her medication regimen. Seventeen-year-old Robert, on the other hand, does not even have an unconcerned relative; he has been living in shelters and on the streets since he left home after his mother's latest boyfriend issued an ultimatum: "Either he goes or I go." Robert has had several episodes of sexually transmitted diseases; he has finally agreed to an HIV antibody test. He has no close friend or relative to talk to should the result be positive. James, sixteen years old, left home after a fight with his parents over his announcement that he is gay. He has been drinking heavily and tried to commit suicide once. A counselor at the health clinic has convinced him to see a doctor for psychiatric evaluation. James has no one to help him sort out the options for in-patient or out-patient treatment. Amelia, fourteen years old, lives with her elderly grandmother who speaks no English. She believes that Amelia's rapid weight loss is caused by Amelia's spiritual impurity, and has been treating her with traditional medicine. A teacher has convinced Amelia to visit the clinic, where extensive testing has been recommended. Amelia is sure her grandmother will not approve, and she herself does not know what to believe.

These are a few of a special group of adolescents – we call them *unsupervised* or *alone.* This is a book about the ethical and legal issues that arise in their encounters with the medical care system. These youth are "alone" because they do not have a supportive relationship with an adult in a birth, foster, adoptive, or chosen family.

1

There is no trusted adult who is consistently available to guide and monitor their passage to adulthood and to help them evaluate medical options and make appropriate decisions. In the past several years clinicians, researchers, and other service providers and policy analysts have become increasingly aware of such adolescents. Their numbers have increased, as later chapters will show; in addition, their health care needs have become more complex, for example, because of the emergence of AIDS as a major threat to youth.

The book is the result of a project that was supported by grants from the Fan Fox and Leslie R. Samuels Foundation and the American Foundation for AIDS Research. The editors were the project coordinators. Nearly all the authors were participants in the project; a few were invited later to expand our scope. The project undertook an analysis of the ethical issues that practitioners were confronting with their adolescent patients and clients who faced health care decisions largely without adult guidance. Practitioners found that the prevalent legal and ethical principles were inadequate.

One problem is that the existing principles are ambiguous about adolescents, who are in transition from childhood to adulthood. Even the age range defining adolescence varies according to the setting, the professional methodology, and the purpose of the definition. The authors in this volume have selected different age ranges as appropriate to their discussions. Competent adults are legally and ethically empowered to make decisions for themselves based on their values and preferences, their personal experiences, their religious beliefs, the availability of alternatives, their level of pain and suffering, and, increasingly, on the economic consequences that follow from their decisions. For children the equivalent principle is that parents make medical decisions on their behalf. Children, especially young children, are assumed to have neither the cognitive skills nor the mature judgment to make complex choices that may have far-reaching health consequences. Parents are empowered to make medical decisions because they are assumed to be in the best position to determine the best interests of their child, they know and love the child, and they can interpret medical options in light of their family history and values. Moreover, they have to share the consequences of the decision, which may affect not only one youngster but also siblings and other family members. Parents, through public or private insurance, are also the primary source of payment or eligibility for medical care. For the majority of families, and for the majority of decisions, this paradigm works well enough. Certainly no other authority – medical, legal, or other professional – has the same privileged status as the parent in our society.

But the paradigm has clear limits. First, it is best suited to infants and young children, not adolescents. In general, adolescents have achieved a degree of intellectual and emotional maturity that surpasses that of young children, yet they are not fully adult. Another limitation, now recognized in state statutes, is that adolescents need some medical services, such as treatment for sexually transmitted diseases, for which parental consent or even notification may present serious barriers. The most important limitation, in terms of the population addressed in this volume, is that the model assumes the presence of at least one parent who has a stable, nurturing, and supportive relationship with the child. The lack of such a parent or other adult is precisely what makes these adolescents alone.

In the traditional schema for decision making for children, parents do not stand alone. In making difficult health decisions for children, generally a therapeutic alliance emerges among the pediatrician or the adolescent medicine physician, the parents, and the child. As the child matures through adolescence, adults gradually incorporate his or her participation and preferences. More or less together they choose among the alternative plans for treatment or – occasionally in the case of terminal illness – nontreatment..

Because of the state's *parens patriae* obligations to protect the welfare of children, the state, through the courts and the child welfare system, may also play a role. The trigger to invoking the power of the state is a judgment by a physician or other care provider that the child is suffering from or is at risk for "medical neglect." Parents, physicians, and the state each have rights, duties, and obligations in making medical decisions for children. However, the boundaries may be unclear or disputed.

Adolescents alone are unsettling precisely because they do not fit the established pattern. We began by thinking that we were discussing rare cases – orphaned, abandoned, homeless, "street kids," youth in prison or detention centers, outcasts of family and society. They were the epitome of *the other.* We quickly saw, however, that many adolescents, while not literally alone, are functionally alone. Throughout the discussions among the editors and authors, and in the working meetings that produced the chapters in this book, we asked, who are these youth? How did they come to be "alone"?

There are many answers. Some of these young people have been orphaned because their caregiving parent died of AIDS, other diseases, drug use, or violence. Some are functionally alone because their parent or grandparent or other nominal caregiver is mentally ill or addicted to drugs or alcohol, or is simply overwhelmed by poverty or other pressures. Some gay and lesbian youth have been ostracized by their families. Some adolescents have run away from homes where adults physically or sexually abused them. Some are in foster care, where they may have both biological and foster parents but no one to trust with private information and concerns. Others have parents or other adults who drift in and out of their lives, promising support, occasionally providing it, but withdrawing it at will and often when the youth needs it most.

Some adolescents alone are involved with their families but live apart from them for economic or other reasons. Some are recent immigrants to the United States, living in extended families where they are the only ones who speak English. These adolescents, caught between two cultures, with very different concepts of disease, medicine, and decision making, may be surrounded by loving family but alone in the modern medical setting. Some adolescents do not *appear* to be alone – that is, several adults may claim to represent the young person's interests – but these adults have neither legal guardianship nor continuous relationships. The involvement of many adults, none with clear parental authority or responsibility, may engender conflict or ambivalence rather than support.

As the chapters and cases in the book illustrate, adolescents alone do not fit into a single category. Some of the youth described in this book have been cast outside society's boundaries of acceptability. Through the dismal circumstances of their lives, they have become "the other." In Chapter 8, Michael Clatts and colleagues eloquently describe the struggles and feelings of youth who are truly alone. But "the other" also looks more familiar. In Chapter 9 on adolescents in in-patient settings, Betty Levin moves toward this end of the spectrum. The youngsters she describes have adults in their lives but the social dislocation and poverty they have experienced jeopardize what might otherwise be supportive relationships.

There is an even broader range to be considered. Adolescents alone are not confined to poverty-stricken areas or city streets. Health care providers everywhere may encounter such youths in their offices, managed care plans, school clinics, or hospitals. These youths' aloneness may, in fact, be harder to recognize because they do not have the distinguishing characteristics of youth who live on the streets. Examples are lesbian or gay youth still establishing their sexual identity or youth whose parent's addiction to drugs or alcohol is concealed by the trappings of middle-class conventionality.

What does it mean to be alone? One of the youths interviewed in Clatts's study put it eloquently: "You're by yourself, you got nobody in your corner, nobody sticking behind you, no type of support." The needs of this group of adolescents are complex and urgent. When there is "nobody in your corner, nobody sticking behind you," the transition to adulthood is often marked by insecurity, instability, and outright danger. In conventional adult terminology, these adolescents are sometimes called *hard to reach* or even *unreachable*. Yet they must not be ignored or abandoned. Although many of their most pressing needs lie outside the health care arena, their contacts with supportive health care providers may offer an opportunity to obtain a measure of the acceptance and support they have not received from their parents. Most have experienced traumatic childhoods that have brought them to adolescence with a host of prior losses. Adults have failed them repeatedly. Their adolescent years may be the last chance for many to attempt to achieve a productive and healthy adulthood.

The following sections of this introduction briefly discuss the societal changes that have influenced the growth of this population, some developmental issues, the philosophical underpinnings of concepts of parent–child relationships and adolescence, and the main themes that emerge from the chapters and case studies.

Changes in Family Structure and Functioning

What has happened to produce this growing number of unsupervised youth? Although *family* is an enduring concept, what the term means in any given society at any given time may vary considerably. As Donzelot (1979) pointed out, the family is not a "point of departure . . . a manifest reality, but . . . a moving resultant, an uncertain form whose intelligibility can only come from studying the system of relations it maintains with the sociopolitical level." Families are, in other words, social as well as biological constructs.

We believe that a definition of family that is congruent with contemporary American life should be broad but not unlimited. If everyone counts as family, then family loses its special meaning. If only a few count as family, then our understanding of family is impoverished. What separates family from friends and strangers is not just blood or legal ties but an emotional quality of commitment, continuity, and stability. The essential characteristics of these relationships are permanence (at least in intention), commitment to mutuality of various forms of economic, social, and emotional support, and a level of intimacy that distinguishes this bond from other, less central attachments.

Using these parameters, Levine (1991) provides a good working definition of family:

> Family members are individuals who by birth, adoption, marriage, or declared commitment share deep personal connections and are mutually entitled to receive and obligated to provide support of various kinds to the extent possible, especially in times of need.

This definition, written with adults in mind, speaks of a level of reciprocity that children are not able to provide because they are dependent on others for their most basic needs and nurturing. The deep personal connections and commitments that define family, however, are typified by parents' responsibilities toward their children. A group of adults who took good care of each other but neglected their children would not, by this definition, be fulfilling the obligations that are essential to family.

Throughout the world families are changing in ways that put at risk one of their most basic functions: nurturing, socializing, and supporting the children that are born into them or come to depend on them. A Population Council report (Bruce, Lloyd, and Leonard 1995) outlines several relevant global trends:

- As a result of decreasing fertility rates and the dispersal of family members, families and households are generally getting smaller. There are fewer people in family support networks to take care of children and other dependents.
- Even though families have fewer children, the burden on working-age parents to support older and younger dependents has increased. Children become independent at later ages and require more educational investment to prepare them to become self-sufficient. When women marry, they tend to do so at later ages.
- Multiple marriages are common, creating a complex set of relationships for children and an "uncertain claim on parents' attention and income." Many children do not live with both parents, and do not receive adequate emotional attention and economic support from either or both parents. The proportion of female-headed households has increased.
- Women's participation in the formal labor force has increased while men's has declined, placing more economic responsibility on women, not just women who are heads of households. At the same time, men have not balanced their decreased economic opportunities and responsibilities with an increase in child-rearing responsibility.

One far-reaching result of these large-scale trends is that children's well-being is often jeopardized because of their family's adverse economic circumstances.

These global trends are evident in the United States. According to the 1990 U.S. Census, 73 percent of children under age eighteen are living with two parents, a decline from 1960 of 88 percent (Roberts 1995). These two-parent families may not both be biological parents. Of all children in two-parent families, a little more than half are being reared by both biological parents. One in three African-American children living in a two-parent household is living with a biological mother and a stepfather.

The number of single-parent families has increased dramatically since 1970, when there were 3.8 million families, or 12.9 percent of all families, headed by a single parent. In 1991, the number had tripled to 10.1 million, or 29 percent of all families with children. In almost 90 percent of these families the single parent was the mother. More than half (55 percent) of the African-American children in the U.S. today are being raised by one parent, arguably the largest percentage since slavery. In 1960 that percentage was 22 percent. In the same three decades the percentage of white children living with one parent tripled to 19 percent.

In 1970 nearly 400,000 babies were born to single mothers; in 1989 that number had more than doubled to more than a million, or 27 percent of all births. Although the increase in never-married women with children is particularly steep among educated and professional women, an estimated 47 percent of families headed by single mothers live in poverty, compared to 8.3 percent of two-parent families. The number of unmarried couples grew from 523,000 in 1970 to 3 million in 1991, with an estimated 40 percent of these couples having children.

These complex changes are the result of many interacting economic, political, cultural, and personal factors. We reject simplistic and moralistic views that look backward to a golden age that never was when families lived problem-free as long as everyone, especially women and children, stayed in place. Families come in many different shapes and sizes: "blended" families of divorced and remarried partners with children; lesbian or gay couples or single women or men with biological, foster, or adopted children; grandparents raising grandchildren; aunts and uncles raising nieces and nephews; oldest children raising younger siblings; and an array of other combinations of individuals, both adults and children. Such alliances are often viewed as abnormal, but this is a skewed and narrow view, even of American families. As one commentator remarked, "*Leave It to Beaver* was not a documentary" (Coontz 1993).

Diversity in family structure, greater control of reproduction, and more varied educational and economic opportunities for women do not by themselves create problems for children. Nor does poverty, except for extreme deprivation, always threaten family commitments. Children can be nurtured and supported in diverse family structures and through difficult economic and family situations, as long as there are adults who love them, remain committed to caring for them, and are capable of doing so. It is clear, however, that changes in family life, especially those brought about by economic deprivation and shifts in the labor market, have not been addressed by policies and programs that attend to the needs of dependent children. Family structures that do not fit a particular legal, social service, or medical outlook are at a disadvantage in dealing with those systems. Although families have changed, systems have not.

It is also clear, as the chapters and case studies in this volume show, that for a variety of individual and systemic reasons – substance abuse being arguably the most destructive – some parents and other adults have failed to act as protectors of their children. They have abandoned them literally and emotionally, ignored their needs for supervision and guidance, and acted inconsistently and unpredictably. As these children grow to adolescence, many enter the category we have identified as unsupervised or alone. In many aspects of their lives, the traditional parent–child relationship, in which the parent acts as supportive nurturer, has never worked. If that is the case, the paradigm will not work in the health care setting.

Adolescent Development and the Search for New Paradigms

The emergence of this new category of adolescents presents challenges to prevailing paradigms of family decision making and principles of medical ethics. Adolescents in general have always been at the margins of these paradigms, presenting clinicians and parents with often difficult decisions in judging a young person's capacity to make autonomous choices. Testing those limits is one of the tasks of adolescence. Adolescents alone stretch the margins even further, giving clinicians more discretion, perhaps, but also more qualms about the extent to which it is ethically justifiable and clinically prudent to allow adolescents to make their own health care decisions.

From a developmental perspective, adolescents are in the final stage of becoming adults and are functioning independently of their parents. This is a major step for at least two reasons. First, although the adolescent has been taking small steps toward independence almost since birth, full independence is contrary to the major assumptions and habits of the adolescent's lifetime. Second, childhood has become, through experience and concrete evidence, a familiar place, whereas adulthood has been glimpsed only vicariously and is still uncharted territory.

All children are engaged in the process of developing their own unique identities and becoming autonomous persons, but adolescents have reached the stage where they need, want, and should be encouraged to test their decision-making skills in making the increasingly important decisions in their lives. They have also reached the stage where their basic cognitive skills are likely to be substantially similar to those of adults, even though they lack the experience of adults. Moreover, adolescents have a well-developed system of preferences and values. These values may to some extent reflect the special pressures of adolescence, especially the need for peer approval, and if so may evolve as the adolescent matures. Nevertheless, they are the contemporaneous system by which the adolescent defines himself or herself and the foundation from which the more refined set of adult preferences, values, and behaviors will grow.

Adolescence is also a time of sexual awakening. The internal forces driving this powerful force, whether encouraged or discouraged by culture and family, may be overwhelming. Although American culture has increasingly acknowledged, and through advertising and the media even encouraged, adolescent sexuality, society also expresses stern disapproval of sexual activity. It is often sexual activity, as well as disease, that brings young people to the health care system.

Many authors in this volume address the complex questions concerning unsupervised adolescents' capacity to consent to or refuse medical treatment and recommend practical ways of involving adolescents in their own health care decisions. In order to put these specific concerns in a broad ethical context, the next section discusses the main themes and concepts that have appeared in philosophical writings about adult–child relations, childhood, and adolescence.

Philosophical Background

In order to place the concerns of this book in a larger ethical context, it is necessary to examine the main concepts and themes that have appeared in philosophical writings about childhood, adolescence, and adult–child relations. Most adolescents grow up in families and, in the contemporary ethics literature on family relationships, questions about the grounds and limits of parental authority are often asked with adolescents in mind. In addition, although philosophers have not addressed the specific problems posed by the group studied in this book, namely unsupervised adolescents, the substantial literature on ethical issues in childhood occasionally has considered whether and how far the analysis extends to adolescents.

Philosophical writing on the ethical foundations of family life has a distinguished history, although, for the most part, interest in the moral aspects of parent–child relations has been subordinated to more general political concerns. Among writers of the modern period like Bodin, Hobbes, and Filmer, the family served as a focal point of debate on the nature and justification of political authority. To be sure, the relationship between familial and political institutions was not a totally new concern in this period; indeed, it had been a recurring theme of social and political philosophy since Plato's *Republic* and Aristotle's *Politics*. But the emphasis in the modern period on parental authority definitely reoriented thinking about the family and gave new prominence to issues of obedience and discipline in family life. In contrast to the ancient Greeks, parental authority was not regarded merely as something to be reflected on or understood or as one element of a larger problem of family–state relations, but as something on which to focus moral judgment.

After Locke's devastating critique of patriarchalism in *Two Treatises on Civil Government,* (1690) and in no small measure due to its influence, philosophers who wrote on the family became less preoccupied with larger normative questions about the political organization of society, although their views on these matters certainly influenced their thinking about the family. Rousseau and Kant, for example, wrote at length on the moral and intellectual education of children, emphasizing individual autonomy as the goal of both endeavors. And although interest in the foundations of parent–child relationships waned somewhat in the philosophical writing of the first part of this century, in recent years moral philosophers have increasingly turned their attention to questions about the interpretation and justification of parental authority.

The following propositions are commonly accepted by philosophers of the family. First, parental authority cannot be justified only, or even primarily, in terms of the interests of parents. There is some disagreement about the extent to which parents' own interests may be legitimately served by the exercise of authority over their children, but no one seriously argues that parental authority exists solely for the benefit of parents. Rather, parental authority is for the good of children, and justified only to the extent that children cannot yet be presumed able to make decisions for themselves. Second, parental authority, if justified at all, must encourage and adjust to the developing capacity of children for independent judgment. It must be aimed at bringing children to the point where they no longer require continual adult protection and supervision, and can care for themselves, at which point parental authority properly ceases.

Adolescence, however, poses special problems. It both challenges our beliefs about the appropriateness of parental authority and complicates our understanding of its scope. Indeed, over the past three decades, an expanding body of professional literature has questioned our traditional assumptions about the boundaries of adolescent decision making in general and health care decision making in particular. Contemporary moral philosophy's contribution to this rethinking of adolescence has principally consisted of asking questions about the rights of young people, and about whether and to what extent the arguments that secure adult rights apply to adolescents as well. Philosophers, of course, are not the only ones who have been attracted to the language of rights. Appeals to children's rights have also played a significant political and rhetorical role. At the same time, there is a significant undercurrent of ambivalence in our society about where to set the general limits of children's legal rights and about whether adolescents should be considered children or adults for purposes of deciding what rights they have. This ambivalence reflects an underlying uncertainty about the moral status of young people, a subject that requires and has received close philosophical examination.

In order to clarify what is at issue in debates about the rights of children and adolescents, it is useful to begin with some basic distinctions that appear in philosophical discussions of moral rights. The rights that concern us here are *claim rights* rather than *liberty rights,* although some philosophers may define these terms differently. Claim rights can themselves be divided into negative rights to noninterference and positive rights to services, and imply corresponding obligations on the part of others. The negative claim rights are held against "the world at large" and imply obligations of all others not to interfere with the right holder in the exercise of his or her right; hence, they are called general obligations. The positive claim rights (for example, children's rights to food and shelter) are held against some specific individuals (their parents) and imply obligations only on their part to meet certain needs of the right holder; hence they are called special obligations. This principle that every claim right implies a corresponding duty is referred to in the literature as the correlativity of rights and duties thesis. Liberty-rights, by contrast, are simply liberties or permissions (the right to apply to a particular college or for a job); they are equivalent to a lack of obligations in their possessors, and imply no obligations whatever in others.

A further issue concerns the primary function of claim rights, and this can be explained in either of two ways. To quote philosopher L. W. Sumner (1987), "The interest conception treats rights as devices for promoting individual welfare. . . . On the other hand, the choice conception treats rights as devices for promoting freedom or autonomy." The former depicts right holders as "passive beneficiaries," the latter as "active managers." Although the interest conception can be thought of as incorporating the choice conception, the interest people have in being free and autonomous agents argues for interpreting them as distinct conceptions.

The prevailing view in the philosophical literature is that children have a number of positive claim rights, including the means for ensuring survival and healthy physical growth, affectionate care by adults, and an education that equips them to participate in the life of adult society. These rights can be straightforwardly justified on welfare grounds. The water gets murkier, however, when we consider whether the choice conception can be applied to children to yield additional rights. Arguably children are entitled to some measure of autonomy during childhood, and not just because, as future autonomous adults, they currently have an interest in developing capacities for self-determination. (This argument is based on the interest conception.) But the key question is the extent to which and the matters about which children should be allowed to make decisions for themselves. With young children the answer seems clear enough: the rights that are most important for them are positive claim rights, which do not accommodate much moral room for independent decision making. But over the course of adolescent development, the conditions for actually possessing rights to make certain decisions for oneself are normally satisfied, and there is a blurring of the bright line separating young children from mature adults with respect to the possession of rights.

Not all philosophers agree that the interest conception of rights should be the dominant one, even among young children. Some so-called child liberationists, such as John Holt and Howard Cohen, have taken a radically different view (Holt 1974). Child liberationists argue in part that, with respect to the possession of legal rights, children make up an oppressed group and are, in this respect, like women and members of certain racial minorities. But liberationists are not just concerned about legal rights: whether explicitly or implicitly, they rest their claims about legal rights on other claims relating to the *moral* rights of children – specifically, that children have all the moral rights of adults. This sweeping liberationist position has struck many commentators as extremely implausible, and philosophers have responded to it with assorted versions of what might be called "the argument from incompetence." The classic statement of this position is found in Locke:

> To inform the Mind, and govern the Actions of their yet ignorant Nonage, till Reason shall takes it place, and ease them of that Trouble, is what the Children want, and the Parents are bound to. . . . Whilst [Man] is in an Estate, wherein he has not *Understanding* of his own to direct his *Will,* he is not to have any Will of his own to follow: He that *understands* for him, must *will* for him too; he must prescribe to his Will, and regulate his Actions. (Locke 1963)

Similarly, the utilitarian philosopher Jeremy Bentham argued:

> The feebleness of infancy demands a continual protection. The complete development of its physical power takes many years; that of its intellectual faculties is still lower . . . . Too sensitive to present impulses, too negligent of the future, such a being must be kept under an authority more immediate than that of the laws. (Bentham 1838–1843)

A fuller statement of the incompetency argument goes like this. In order to exercise liberty, individuals must have autonomy, that is, be able to make decisions on their own. They can only do this if they have relevant knowledge and understanding, sufficient experience to predict the consequences of their actions, knowledge of their own interests, and the ability to act voluntarily. Young children, however, are deficient in these experiences and abilities. Hence, they do not have the same moral rights as adults.

As stated, this is a rather crude argument and certainly some qualifications and refinements are in order. It is fair to say, however, that most philosophers who have written about children are in broad agreement with this position. But if the sweeping liberationist posture seems untenable for this reason, a narrowly circumscribed liberationist position, one confined to adolescents, is perhaps not so easy to dismiss. Here the debate between the liberationists and their so-called protectionist opponents – those who emphasize that children have rights to assistance and care from adults rather than rights to self-determination – becomes more complicated and interesting. (For further discussions, see Purdy 1992.)

One reason this more focused liberationist position is harder to dismiss than the sweeping one is that scepticism about the reality of older children's current immaturity seems more warranted than scepticism about the current immaturity of younger children. The immaturity of young children seems to be a necessary and inevitable feature of human development, although it is possible that changes in child-rearing practices can affect their capacities for independent decision making. If youngsters were given more freedom to act independently and were expected to take responsibility for the consequences of their actions, we might find them not as immature as we have supposed. But the extent to which their apparent inability to act maturely can be significantly altered by changes in our behavior toward them seems to be severely constrained by ineradicable features of biological maturation. In contrast, the capacities of adolescents for mature decision making seem to be more heavily influenced by adult expectations and rearing practices. As social scientists have pointed out, not every society regards adolescence as a distinct stage of human development (Keniston 1976). Many cultures do not recognize an extended period of preparation for adulthood beyond early childhood; young people are expected to take on adult roles much earlier than they do in our society, and they appear to function adequately in the adult world of their society. Of course, we cannot infer that adolescence does not exist as a distinct developmental stage from the failure of some societies to recognize it as such. However, awareness of other cultural practices and their consequences should at least occasion some scepticism about our own society's views of child development. Perhaps our adolescents would demonstrate a greater capacity for independent decision making if we gave them the opportunity to do so.

Some (moderate) adolescent liberationists are satisfied if they can persuade us to take a less rigid view of human development than that which our culture usually assumes. But others go further, maintaining that our current treatment of adolescents retards and deforms their development, thereby preventing them from realizing at a much earlier age their potential for mature choice and conduct. According to this view, our practices *create* immaturity – they do not *respond to* necessary features of human development.

Clearly this view presupposes social consensus on the indicators of maturity. Anthropologists report extreme variability in how cultures define maturity and adulthood, both with respect to the rights and responsibilities that characterize adulthood and the age at which persons achieve adult status (Group for the Advancement of Psychiatry 1968). It is possible to understand the strong liberationist claim this way: According to our society's criteria of functional maturity, adolescents are (relatively) immature. However, it is only because of our failure to treat them as the equals of adults that they fail to satisfy these criteria to the extent that they do.

Some might cite the case of unsupervised adolescents as a counterexample to this liberationist thesis. They might argue that, although these adolescents have significantly greater independence than so-called normal adolescents who must still answer to their parents to some degree, unsupervised adolescents do not generally display greater maturity. Indeed, they frequently display less. But, even granting this – and that is not the position taken here – the liberationist has a ready response to the objection. The liberationist can claim, indeed any reasonable liberationist must claim, that adolescents will mature more rapidly if they are granted the freedom to act independently, but only in the context of other concurrent social changes. The result would be very different in the case of unsupervised adolescents, the liberationist maintains, if their entrance into responsible adulthood were supported and facilitated by wide-ranging changes in social practices that affect them.

Despite this effective rejoinder, the liberationist view remains unconvincing. To describe the immaturity of adolescents as a social construction is to make an empirical claim, which must be tested by empirical means, such as large-scale experimental trials comparing different child-rearing strategies, as well as social and legal practices affecting youth. The outcome of these trials, assuming their feasibility, naturally cannot be known in advance, and until we can tease out the respective contributions of nature and nurture, a moderate liberationist view of adolescents is the only sensible one to adopt. Human development is contingent on a variety of factors, and contemporary thinking generally concedes that both variable environmental and relatively invariable psychological and biological factors play a significant causal role. Although it is foolish to ignore the extent to which children and young people are shaped by the influences to which they are exposed, neither should it be supposed that they are infinitely malleable and that, under favorable social conditions, they would function well in adult society if they were freed of adult-imposed controls.

Finally, it should be noted that while philosophers have performed an important service in pressing the issue of adolescent rights, the issue of rights refers to only one dimension of value in the relationships that make up the family. Adolescents often live in their parents' home and continue to be materially dependent on them well after they have acquired adult moral rights, and these circumstances should be considered when there is a question of parental infringement of their rights to freedom. What adolescents may gain by having their rights acknowledged must be balanced against possible serious damage to other values such as love, trust, and loyalty in relation to their parents. Unsupervised adolescents, of course, do not have relationships of this sort with their parents, but a similar caution about the need to balance their rights against other values is in order. For even if unsupervised adolescents do not have *parents* to whom they can turn for guidance and emotional support, other opportunities for forming trusting and supportive relationships with adults may be available and should not be overlooked. Health care providers and others who interact with unsupervised adolescents during periods of stress or crisis must bear this in mind.

Themes of Adolescence and Medical Decision Making

This book is divided into three parts. The first contains essays authored by experts in the fields of adolescent medicine and adolescent development, psychiatry, epidemiology, ethics, law and anthropology. The second is a series of case studies with commentaries, and the third is a set of ethics guidelines for practitioners.

Part I provides information and concepts essential to understanding the complex demographic, societal, legal, and medical framework in which adolescents alone are confronted with health care decisions. It also contains a moving personal essay by psychiatrist Francine Cournos on growing up an orphan in foster care and the impact of that experience on emotional development and decision making (Chapter 6). This essay is not only important in its own right but also in reminding us that, in contrast to other more exotic areas of inquiry, we have all been adolescents. Many who criticize "today's kids" would probably rather not revisit their own teenage years. A post-adolescent college student once commented to his parents: "I'd like to explain to you why I was so silent for the last five or six years of growing up; adolescence is very embarrassing."

To a greater or lesser degree every adolescent is or feels alone. There may be occasional discussions with friends or family, and perhaps some sharing with teachers or mental health professionals, but many critical events are anguished over in solitude. Experiments with relationships and behaviors are part of the task of being an adolescent. They provide the raw material from which personality, preferences, and goals are shaped. But shaping the raw material is often a turbulent and confusing process.

Adolescents live in a continuum of settings, opportunities for education and employment, and availability of financial and material support. In their opening chapter, Audrey Rogers and Susan Newcomer define the category of adolescence, most commonly set at ages ten to nineteen, the middle years between childhood and adult status during which individuals undergo dramatic psycho-social-physical changes at substantially different rates. Clearly the attempt to discuss any such variable category in fixed terms risks overgeneralizing.

However, key characteristics of the group emerge from this overview. By the year 2000, 31 percent of adolescents in the United States will be nonwhite; current estimates indicate that 7 million high-risk youth have only a limited potential for becoming productive adults because of serious problems at home or school; HIV infection may be as high as 8 to 21 percent among certain subgroups of adolescents at risk. Of the youth who are HIV positive, the vast majority have histories of sexual-risk behavior. Many are without health insurance, although most have access to specialized clinics. But, in this age of managed care and the health consumer revolution, many such "boutique" clinics are disappearing. The notion that the indigent could always rely on the public health system is increasingly challenged as publicly supported clinics and hospitals fail to meet the fiscal and organizational demands of managed care companies. It is worth noting that before 1995 the academic medical centers controlled 5 percent of the hospital beds in the country, but provided more than 50 percent of the uncompensated care. Savvy street youth often knew how to access care from this endangered resource.

Nancy Leffert and Anne Peterson expand the discussion in Chapter 2 by identifying and analyzing markers of adolescent physical, psychosocial, and contextual development that may be affected in degree or in timing by the traumatic circumstances that leave adolescents without adult guidance or a secure, predictable environment. There is a wide variety in the changes that accompany adolescent development, such as different relationships in family, school, and peer group. The impact of these changes may be more stressful when the adolescent lacks adult support or is in the midst of family crisis, such as homelessness. Extremely deprived environments may inhibit cognitive and psychosocial development and make the adolescent alone vulnerable to peer and adult pressure to engage in high-risk sexual and drug-using behavior. At the same time, resiliency, exhibited through coping skills and other protective behaviors, may help adolescents through troubled times. Health care providers, Leffert and Petersen advise, can help increase adolescents' capacity to make decisions by providing a supportive, anxiety-reducing atmosphere.

In Chapter 3, Neal Hoffman provides a comprehensive survey of adolescent health problems essential to understanding the chapters and case studies and commentaries that discuss specific medical decisions. Synthesizing a wealth of recent data, Hoffman sketches a picture of a segment of the adolescent population with a variety of chronic and acute unmet health care needs. Remarkably, health care providers discuss the risks of sexually transmitted diseases to sexually active youth in only 1 percent of office visits. In an era of HIV infection, it is hard to conceive of a more inadequate match of needs and services.

This chapter also destroys the myth that all adolescents are healthy and have little need for the health care system. The reality is that adolescents are at risk for traumatic injuries, broken bones, fractured spines and serious burns (think of the risks of working at fast-food counters). They are beset with mental health problems and with depression, and suicide attempts are not rare in the population. It is sobering to realize that 30 percent of the completed suicides are by gay and lesbian youths and that 90 percent of nicotine-addicted adults began smoking as adolescents.

Prenatal care and abortion are central to the health of young women who are pregnant; these services are diminishing. Access to specialized oncology care is important for youth with cancer; many childhood cancers actually have a reasonable rate of cure if care is timely and consistent. We often think of the chronically ill older adult but rarely think that chronicity is a problem of youth. Hoffman describes adolescents with sickle cell disease, asthma, cystic fibrosis, and hemophilia and shows how these conditions become the defining characteristics of the youth's life. The differences in decision making between acute and chronic conditions is a theme that recurs in many authors' work.

Abigail English, in a particularly elegant and nuanced discussion in Chapter 4, untangles the thickets in the legal landscape of adolescent health care that has been articulated by case law and statute over the last several decades. Historically parents have had extensive authority over their minor children until those children reached the age of majority or became legally emancipated through marriage, service in the armed forces, or living apart and managing their own affairs. Although few adolescents are legally emancipated, many are living in circumstances that affect their legal status as well as their access to health care. Providers struggle with uncertainty about the capacity of minors to consent on their own for health care, as well as their obligation to maintain confidentiality of medical information. Access to care often requires an independent ability to pay; English describes the currently available array of funded programs, noting that managed care will alter the landscape. Some barriers to care are specifically legal, and others have legal underpinnings. English cautious that removing these barriers, while essential to improving adolescent health, will require concerted advocacy by a broad range of actors.

Jeffrey Blustein and Jonathan Moreno tackle the daunting task of creating a morally coherent framework for the decision of an adolescent to accept or refuse care. This intermediate time of life, neither child nor adult, has always been troubling for care providers and ethicists. Given the variability in underlying intelligence, emotional sophistication, developmental success, relationship to parents and authority figures, and character, how can we have rules about the moral appropriateness of choosing? The law, as Abigail English points out, has created an ostensibly clear framework: parents decide for their nonadult children. This framework is punctured by small and huge exceptions: minors can give consent for treatment of sexually transmitted diseases and can obtain contraception and consent for abortion in certain states and under certain circumstances. Can moral analysis be as variable and quixotic as the law?

Blustein and Moreno construct a theory based not solely on the usual analysis of the concept of decisional capacity but also on the notion of *enduring characteristics* that support the concept and fact of a self. Valid consent, they argue, presupposes a self that can articulate values to apply in the process of choosing. Further – but appropriately – complicating the discussion, the authors opt for a concept of *decision-specific* capacity and reject a mechanically imposed *absolute* standard for empowering choice. As with adults, whose capacity can also vary based on age, intelligence, experience, and disability, Blustein and Moreno argue that after the age of fourteen or fifteen, there should be a presumption that the adolescent has the ability to provide ethically adequate informed consent. This presumption of capacity presents care providers with the space in which to balance the obligations of self-determination and beneficence.

They also argue that an additional obligation for adolescent providers is not only to respect autonomy but to actively engage in autonomy-promoting activities. This obligation of active intervention in the decision-making process is one of the morally significant features of the provider role. As part of this obligation they highlight the notion of informed consent as a "process," not merely an event. It is by engaging the adolescent over time in this process, by using the contacts for discussion, education, and support, that providers fulfill the obligation of advocacy.

Whereas these are generic statements applicable to the evaluation of moral capability of all adolescents, there are special considerations for the adolescent alone. For adolescents alone, care providers must create a characterological and personal profile from available data about the time of abandonment, the emotional effects of such wrenching events, and the ancillary supports that were available and might have filled the void. This youth-specific evaluation must precede decisions about the moral acceptability of various decisions and must consider issues of self-esteem, control of drives and impulses, temporal perspective, cognitive abilities and development of trust – a full agenda for the time-constrained, overworked professional dealing with the adolescent alone. Unrealistic? Maybe. But absolutely essential to distinguish those youth who can provide morally valid informed consent from those who must be protected from their ill-considered or self-destructive behaviors. Respecting the appearance of autonomy without the substance turns respect for persons into abandonment.

Chapter 6, as already noted, introduces personal experience and self-examination into the discussion. Francine Cournos describes how she and her siblings became orphaned and how, "while acting like a miniature adult," she hid the "very needy child who suffered from depression, distrust of adults, an inability to make any new intimate connections, and a tremendous loss of a sense of structure."

This personal insight makes her review of the impact of parental death particularly rich. She explores the notion of trauma, the silent companion of every adolescent alone, and argues that events can trigger self-examination and growth or destruction of trust and the collapse of earlier developmental accomplishments. Feelings of helplessness and meaninglessness hover at the outskirts of conscious and unconscious existence.

Following an elegant review of the psychological, psychiatric, and analytic literature on the adolescent alone, Cournos reflects on her childhood experience. Remembering the experience of having a needle removed from her foot and the rational and irrational threads of thought and emotion this event provoked, she writes:

> Adolescents who are alone have a terrible dilemma. They have a developmental need to break away from their parents, but their parents have beaten them to the punch. They need continuous adult involvement, but it feels like the wrong time to begin again. This may result in an exaggeration of the normal adolescent posture of simultaneously wanting and refusing help.

In Chapter 7, Andrew Boxer, Judith Cook, and Gilbert Herdt address a poorly understood group of adolescents alone – the population of gay and lesbian youth who self-identify as gay during their teenage years. They point out that consideration of the homoerotic as a part of the human condition is politically charged and controversial within medicine and public health as well as within society. Because of the stigma attached to gay gender orientation and behavior, the process of constructing a gay or lesbian identity carries with it the danger of isolating experiences.

The authors' prospective longitudinal study of a cohort of gay adolescents in Chicago, using individual interviews and anthropological ethnographic research, provides the basis for observations on and generalizations about growing up gay. The authors assert that self-identification as a gay person occurs at about age sixteen but is based on desires and fantasies that may go back to the preadolescence age of nine. Sexual development, they note, is an ongoing process rather than a set of stages. Furthermore, some heterosexual activity is compatible with a developing gay gender identity. Given society's general attitude about gay persons, it is not surprising that the investigators found discrepancies between the mental health profile of gay youth and their heterosexual counterparts.

Nevertheless, the authors end on a hopeful note:

> The narratives of the youth reveal the very opposite of stereotypes that portray the murky past of the closeted, shameful, homosexual mythology. These youth gener-

ally regarded themselves as pioneers of a new generation whose special nature affords an insight into the timeless struggle to be human. Far from being mentally disturbed, sexually fixated, or anti-social, as studies in the past have portrayed such youth, we found them to be courageous, intelligent, and healthy adolescents grappling with the many challenges involved in coming out so early in the life course.

At the same time, many of these youth are functionally alone because ashamed and punitive parents have withdrawn love and support.

The last two chapters in this section and the cases that follow focus on the lived existence of youth on their own. The reality is emotionally compelling, intellectually challenging, and morally complex. Michael Clatts and his co-authors have worked among homeless youngsters in New York City, a population among the most impoverished of any specially identified group. The authors estimate that as many as two million youth in the United States are homeless at any time with some 200,000 residing as permanent residents of the streets. They comment that:

> . . . it is apparent that large numbers of youth have become part of the population living on and from the streets, a social and economic environment in which they are dependent upon the vagaries of the street economy. This is a precarious and often violent world in which these young people do what they can to stay afloat. Often this means exchanging sex for money, food, shelter, and drugs.

Not surprisingly, these youth are exceptionally vulnerable to disease and poor health outcomes, including high rates of STDs, tuberculosis, HIV, pregnancy, and abortion. Despite their numbers, little is known about the reasons for this degree of homelessness and about the consequences for these youth. Chapter 8 reviews existing data and new ethnographic studies, and examines the lives of these youngsters from the perspectives of freedom and independence, the sense of loss and depression, the harshness and violence of everyday life on the streets, the struggle with hunger and exhaustion, the effect of watching others get sick and die from AIDS, the lack of trust even among peers, and the tremendous barriers that confront these youth when they try to leave life in the streets. In richly evocative quotations the authors confront the reader with these sad and troubled lives. This shameful portrait of adult neglect – this is, after all, the rich United States, not a poor developing nation – leaves us with admiration for the outreach workers who forge connections with these youth and link them with increasingly scarce health and counseling services.

Part I closes with a gripping chapter by Betty Levin. An anthropologist, she spent part of a recent sabbatical year as an observer on the adolescent service and the Neonatal Intensive Care Unit of a large urban medical center. Her observations provide an excellent intellectual bridge from the adolescent alone to the huge number of adolescents who, while not formally alone, have fragile, undependable adult support systems.

Levin notes that none of the youngsters whom she observed was technically alone. However, the vast majority were part of chaotic families where the guardians had such serious problems that they "were not able to provide appropriate support." Therefore, in many ways, these adolescents were alone. This assertion is clearly supported by the stories in this section and by the case studies that follow in the next section. Having explored the emotional, intellectual, and moral development of youth, readers can see how these youngsters are left to the kindness and decisions of strangers. The real deciders about medical care are the providers themselves who not only sift and structure the choices but basically direct the result.

In the cases Levin describes, there appears to be scant scrutiny, by adolescent or family member, of the risks, benefits, and alternatives to care. Rather, random relationships and emotional needs substitute for a rational process of consideration and consent. Even in involved families the barriers of class and education mean that physicians basically make the decisions. Physicians are not riding roughshod over families. Rather, families and adolescents in Levin's study consider that these are *medical* decisions, in which they do not expect to participate. This is not a trivial finding. It provides one more example of the lack of fit between the theory of informed consent and its reality. Especially where there are imbalances of race, class, gender, education, and ethnicity, the doctors call the shots. Whatever papers are signed and permissions are given, it is the care providers who decide.

It has been long recognized but rarely discussed that the norm of informed consent is honored for all patients – adult or child – more in the breach than in the observance. In most cases the physician or care team decides what care is appropriate and presents their conclusion to the patient and sometimes family – and then the patient agrees. The instances of disagreement make legal cases and sometimes headlines, but they are the rarity in medical practice. Dialogue, choice, and preferences are all goals to which care providers aspire. Most decision-making processes, however, fall far short of reaching this level of discussion and collaboration. If this is the case for adults, and we submit that it is, then the model of the adolescent alone choosing an option for care without parental or other adult involvement is just one more step on a continuum. Once the power of physicians as decision makers has been acknowledged, distinctions among patients are diminished. In this sense, then, the adolescent alone is just like most of us, whatever our age, education, income, or experience.

This awesome reality imposes stringent additional ethical obligations on the medical care professionals involved in any case. The theory of the allocation of decision-making authority in medicine assumes that there is an informal system of checks and balances in which the physician proposes and advises and the patient and family question and choose. But if that is not the case, and Levin's chapter indicates the shortcomings of the model, then care providers must challenge each other to arrive at the best care for the patient. They must struggle to discover and apply the values of the patient and to arrive at an ethically justifiable decision.

Part II contains nine cases followed by commentaries authored by scholars in adolescent medicine and development, law, ethics and public policy. These are real stories about real people, with only names and identifying characteristics changed.

In some cases there are several commentaries; in others only one. The purpose of the commentaries is to bring a multidisciplinary analysis to the cases. No attempt has been made to bring the authors into agreement or to give them a single point of view. Although readers might wish for a neat resolution, this does not often occur. In this way the cases are true to life.

The third and final section of the book brings us back to the initial concept that animated this project. This project began as an attempt to create ethics guidelines for health care providers who treat adolescents in all the categories we have defined as *alone.* The guidelines distill, although do not necessarily agree with, the many points of view expressed by project participants who became authors in this volume. Like other ethics guidelines, these are not legal rules nor regulations that carry sanctions. Rather, they present salient ethical principles and practices that should be considered in individual decision making. They are intended to be flexible and to encourage reflection, while at the same time recommending the outer bounds of permissibility and the inner bounds of ethical requirement.

This project, and the resulting book, has been an intellectual and emotional journey for the editors and authors. We have seen how the most vulnerable among us are both different from and like everyone else. We invite readers to share the milestones and detours that have brought us to this juncture.

References

Bentham, J. (1838–1843). *The Works of Jeremy Bentham.* Ed. John Bowring. Edinburgh: W. Tait.

Bruce, J., C. B. Lloyd, and A. Leonard (1995). *Families in Focus: New Perspectives on Mothers, Fathers, and Children.* New York: The Population Council.

Cohen, H. (1980). *Equal Rights for Children.* Totowa, NJ: Littlefield.

Coontz, S. (1993). The way we never were: American families and the nostalgia trap. In S. Roberts, *Who We Are: A Portrait of America Based on the Latest U.S. Census.* New York: Times Books.

Donzelot, J. (1979). *The policing of families.* New York: Pantheon.

Group for the Advancement of Psychiatry (1968). Cultural factors in adolescence. In *Normal Adolescence: Its Dynamics and Impact.* New York: Group for the Advancement of Psychiatry.

Holt, J. (1974). *Escape from childhood.* New York: Ballantine.

Keniston, K. (1976). Psychological development and historical change. In A. Skolnick (Ed.), *Rethinking childhood: Perspectives on development and society.* Boston: Little, Brown: 200–201.

Levine, C. (1991). AIDS and changing concepts of family. In D. Nelkin, D. P. Willis, and S. V. Parris (Eds.) *A Disease of Society: Cultural and Institutional Responses to AIDS.* Cambridge: Cambridge University Press.

Locke, J. (1963). *The second treatise of government.* Cambridge: University Press. (First published 1690).

Purdy, L. (1992). *In their best interest?* Ithaca, NY: Cornell University Press.

Roberts, S. (1995). *Who we are: A portrait of America based on the latest U.S. census.* New York: Times Books

Sumner, L. W. (1987). *The moral foundations of rights.* Oxford: The Clarendon Press.

PART I

Background Essays

1   The Adolescent Alone: Who and How?*

Audrey Smith Rogers and Susan Newcomer

Defining Adolescence

The "adolescent alone" is a subset of the category *adolescent,* for which a medical specialty – adolescent medicine – has developed over this century (Hall 1904; Hollingshead 1949; Coleman 1961). To consider whether the number of adolescents alone is growing, we need to: first, examine the generic medical literature on adolescents; second, craft a clear definition of the term; and third, consider that "adolescence" is a stage more than an age. This group is not exactly coterminous with "teenagers," those aged thirteen to nineteen, nor with "high school youth," ages thirteen to eighteen, nor with "minors" (who may be younger than age eighteen for some things, such as military service, or twenty-one for others, such as legal drinking), nor with "dependent child," in the IRS term, which includes some students over the age of twenty-one years.

According to those who study it, adolescence is specified as the period between childhood and adult status. It is a process that begins much earlier than age ten, and can end well after age twenty. The process of physical maturation begins early, has measurable markers by about the age of nine years, and is completed by about age seventeen (Brooks–Gunn and Petersen 1984). Puberty, the time during which most physiological changes occur, is contemporaneous with early adolescence, and occurs approximately between ages eleven and fifteen (Sommer 1978). These boundaries are elastic, and may change as the social definition of childhood and adolescence changes. Average age at menarche, a measurable marker for female pubescence, has dropped from about 14.5 years a hundred years ago to 12.5 years in the United States today. There are also racial and ethnic differences in mean and modal ages of onset and completion of puberty (Harlan, Harlan, and Grillo 1980).

The age ranges used in the literature also vary, partly as a function of the data available, partly as a function of the needs the data serve. For example, the National Commission on Children (1991) deals with issues of people up through eighteen years of age; while the American Medical Association (AMA), in its 1992 summary of Public Health Service youth goals for health in the year 2000, groups adolescents with young adults aged fifteen to twenty-four. A 1991 publication from the

*The opinions of the authors do not reflect the official policy of the United States Public Health Service.

U.S. Department of Education defines its target group as age fourteen to twenty-four. The definitive Office of Technology Assessment publication *Adolescent Health* (1991) uses ages ten to nineteen. These age range discrepancies frequently prevent meaningful comparisons and thus complicate the picture of the health problems of adolescents as a distinct age group.

Perhaps the most commonly used age range for "adolescent" is ten to nineteen. This range covers two five-year groupings used in the reporting of much data. Setting aside the numbers of potential immigrants in the age range who might be added to the pool, using data available in this age range makes possible the projection of needs for the next decade for such things as the number of high school classrooms or Nike shoes. It also permits an assessment of how the characteristics of that population will change in the coming years.

Although defining and categorizing people aged ten to nineteen years as "adolescents" is convenient, the breadth of the age range fails to solve the problems that result from grouping youth who are undergoing dramatic psychosociophysical changes at substantially different rates. The health and support needs of an eleven-year-old in the sixth grade who still looks like a child are not similar to those of an eighteen-year-old high school graduate who just got an apprenticeship in a skilled trade. The health needs of the seventeen-year-old high school honor student choosing a college and the nineteen-year-old parent of three toddlers are separated by much more than a mere two years. And behaviors appropriate to the married nineteen-year-old are generally thought to be unacceptable for the unmarried fifteen-year-old. Sales of one of our most lethal drugs, tobacco, are legal to eighteen- and nineteen-year-olds, while sales of another, alcohol, are not. Perhaps one of the most powerful rites of passage in the United States, getting a driver's license, happens in most states at sixteen years, placing a large proportion of sixteen- to nineteen-year-olds at extra health risk.

Nonetheless, there are strong arguments for defining "adolescents" as individuals aged ten to nineteen years. There are subcategories within that age range, with appropriate justification, such as "early adolescent," aged ten to fifteen, or school-aged adolescent, ten through eighteen years. Another categorization could be that of puberty to age fourteen as early adolescent, fifteen to seventeen as middle adolescent, and eighteen years through the early twenties as late adolescent.

The Numbers and Faces of Adolescents

As noted, because all of the children who will be adolescents in the year 2000 are already alive, reasonable projections about their numbers and proportions can be made. It is estimated that by 2000, 31 percent of adolescents will claim racial or ethnic identities other than white, up from 27 percent in 1989 (United States Department of Commerce, Bureau of the Census 1991). The fastest growing racial or ethnic minority group will be "Latino," an umbrella term representing culturally diverse groups.

In 1989, there were 16,950,000 youth between ten and fourteen years in the United States and 18,212,000 who were five to nine years old, so the numbers of teenagers has increased slightly over the last ten years. Of the fifteen- to nineteen-year-olds counted in 1989, about 10 million were under eighteen years of age. Information on the living arrangements of youth between ten and seventeen years in 1988 indicates that 1.1 percent of the young people in those ages were not living with an adult in that year. This translates to approximately 82,960 youth between ten and fourteen years and 233,552 youth between ten and seventeen years based on numbers in the National Health Interview Survey. This does not include institutionalized youth, who are estimated at about 700,000 (National Center for Health Statistics 1988). Although the numbers do include young people in boarding schools, the survey may have missed a certain proportion of young people who were runaways or throwaways.

Adolescents Alone

Counting runaways and throwaways presents a dilemma. Although the National Research Council recently issued a report emphasizing high-risk *settings,* not high-risk youth or behaviors (Commission on Behavioral and Social Sciences and Education 1993), others believe that certain youth are at higher risk. Dryfoos (1990) estimates that 7 million youngsters – one in four – have only a limited potential for becoming productive adults because they are at high risk for encountering serious problems at home, at school, or in their communities.

Obtaining accurate information on the numbers of youth who are runaways or throwaways is exceptionally difficult for several reasons. First, many of the factors determining their runaway or throwaway status cluster or co-vary in a manner that makes the reported numbers likely to be duplicative. One advocacy group may survey homeless youth; another group counts teens without health care; still another group records adolescents who have been arrested and spent time in a detention site. Not infrequently, these different numbers describe the same youth.

The second complication results from lack of consensus on working definitions of terms. Which youth should be considered runaways or throwaways? Certainly those whom most would consider conventionally homeless – adolescents on the streets or in shelters for extended periods – would be included. But how does one categorize youth who have experienced runaway or at-risk, out-of-home episodes in the past year? The episodes may have occurred over shorter periods of time, and many of these experiences may have been trivial and may not have even come to parental attention. Some investigators have derived definitions of runaways that include adolescents up through age twenty who have spent less than one month with parents or guardians in the previous six months (and no time in the past thirty days) and who have no "stable domicile" or home setting (Portland Youth Center, personal communication 1994). Even so, the size of the homeless youth population appears to undergo seasonal variation, with numbers decreasing in the fall (when school starts), increasing during the winter and spring months, and peaking in the summer. There are also issues of *stock* – the sum of those who have, do, or might meet the working definitions of "homeless" and "runaway/throwaway" – and *flow* – how many are in the system right now.

It is impossible to estimate with any precision the number of youth who are, in effect, heads of household. These must include teen mothers living on welfare with their baby or babies, teens who are attempting to manage a disintegrating family in situations where the dysfunction is public record (e.g., a drug-abusing parent) or is more private (alcoholism or prescription drug addiction in upper-middle-class parents). Furthermore, society has few systems in place to care for adolescents from shattered families. These young people are often entered into the public systems because their lives have already taken a downward trajectory. Society's solution in foster care too commonly translates into a holding pen from which teens "age out" at eighteen years or earlier into a world for which they remain ill-prepared emotionally, educationally, or economically. Since all but three states consider eighteen years the legal age of majority (English 1990), these youth represent a special category of adolescents alone.

The Adolescent Alone: AIDS as a Case Study

A specific issue that illustrates the problems adolescents alone confront is that of treatment for Human Immunodeficiency Virus (HIV) and Acquired Immunodeficiency Syndrome (AIDS). Like every other issue raised by HIV infection – individual rights, public safety, regulatory policies, the nature of research, and the role of the individual and community – concern about the adolescent alone in an era of HIV will force debate on what constitutes fitting and suitable policies for prevention, case finding, and treatment.

There is a broad consensus that a much larger number of HIV-infected adolescents exists than the numbers of reported AIDS cases in this age group would indicate (Lindegren 1994; Hein 1987; Vermund et al. 1989; D'Angelo et al. 1991a). Measurement of these numbers with any precision is impossible, but estimates of seroprevalence in certain urban areas range from 0.1 percent to 8 to 21 percent, depending on the city and the group characteristics of the adolescents studied (Burke et al. 1990; D'Angelo et al. 1991b; St. Louis et al. 1991; Stricof et al. 1991; Lemp et al. 1994). These estimates have been corroborated from other data (United States Congress, Office of Technology Assessment 1991; Lindegren et al. 1994; Rosenberg, Biggar, and Goedert 1994) and indicate that adolescents will represent a substantial proportion of cases of HIV infection in the United States over the next decade.

The capacity to respond to the unique needs of HIV-infected adolescents rests on an accurate assessment of the size of the affected population, their regional distribution, and their sociodemographic characteristics, transmission patterns, and living situations. Such a systematic measurement of the HIV epidemic in American youth has not occurred for a variety of reasons.

Within the health care system, there are three major routes of transmission, with each representing a distinct wave of the HIV epidemic in adolescents: vertical, blood, sexual (Rogers et al. 1996). The vertical transmission group refers to teens infected through maternal transmission before or during birth who have survived into adolescence. These youth typically have been identified through their own earlier illness or the illness or death of one or both parents. More than 90 percent of these early teens are still within their family of origin, although more than half are no longer with a parent. Their health care is mostly covered by public funds. There is a potential for many of these young teens to repeat parental or familial patterns of personal or social behavior from which not even well-intentioned relatives can save them. The synergistic burdens of HIV infection and orphanhood, particularly during the stresses of adolescent development, will at the very least generate the *perception* of being alone. Many, growing up without parental support, in shredded communities with dysfunctional institutions, will indeed be alone.

The blood transmission category includes teens who have been infected through blood transfusions or through the reception of blood products, most notably for the treatment of complications resulting from hemophilia. Eighty-six percent of these youth are living with one or both parents, a substantial proportion have private insurance, and there is little hard drug use among them. These teens are distributed across the United States, represent all social strata, and their family support systems are typical of the average American teen. Because of their hemophilia, they have been engaged in medical care since infancy and many are linked to organizational support as well.

The remaining category includes all sexual transmission: males having sex with other males or males or females having heterosexual relations with HIV-positive partners of known and unknown specific risk, or with partners unaware of risk or status. Surprisingly, injecting drug use accounted for only a small percentage of all primary transmissions; either this is not a major HIV transmission route in teens, or youth infected in this manner are not accessing health care.

Successfully accessing health care is a critical link in most epidemiologic surveillance networks, because routine case detection occurs within health care systems. However, achieving this task of entering the health care system represents no small effort for adolescents in general, for they must negotiate unique legal, financial, and institutional barriers that are unlike those for any other group (Kinsman and Slap 1992; Newacheck, McManus, and Gebhardt 1992; Society for Adolescent Medicine 1992). The challenges for HIV-positive youth are more daunting (English 1991; Arnold 1992). Not all HIV-infected adolescents are aware of their risk and, consequently, have not sought the counseling and testing that would have determined their serostatus. Not all HIV screening programs for teens are positioned to ensure linkage to health care, nor are all HIV-positive adolescents economically able to benefit when such links exist. Without specifically focused efforts, it is unlikely that the numbers of HIV-infected teens who would benefit from secondary prevention programs and direct health care will be known with any precision.

Complicating the profile of sexually infected HIV positive youth is information indicating that in 2.3 percent of all case reports, the primary exposure was nonconsensual sex resulting from abuse, rape, or incest; 6 percent of all case reports involved some other nonconsensual sexual component. Domestic sexual abuse, conflict over sexual orientation or sexual activity, pregnancy, and drug or alcohol abuse are important determinants of eventual homelessness in youth (Robertson 1991).

Of the sexually infected HIV-positive youth, whose mean age was 20.1 years, 44 percent were with their family of origin, and one-third of these were with one or both parents. Consequently, the majority (56%) was not living with parents for reasons that could have varied from parental death, apathy, antagonism, or abuse to parental powerlessness in managing adolescent acting-out. Many of these youth were without health insurance (public or private), although they regularly received clinical care. This group also exhibited the highest level of hard drug use history. In younger teens, those with a history of drug use were less likely to be living with parents and more likely to be with other family than were teens with no history of hard drug use. In older teens, a drug-using history was more associated with living in facilities (shelters, detention centers, etc.).

As a group, HIV-positive youth who were infected sexually present a more complicated set of personal and situational characteristics. These characteristics appear to influence whether antiretroviral therapy is prescribed when national guidelines specify it is indicated (El-Sadr and Oleske 1994). This transmission group has lower levels of antiretroviral treatment and prophylaxis at the same level of immunologic decline as youth who are vertically or blood-product-infected. In a statistical model, gender, race, and living situation were not significant factors in predicting antiretroviral treatment, although the level of immunologic decline, presence of HIV-related symptoms, private health insurance, younger ages, and no history of hard drug use were. Since the survey data of Rogers et al. (1996) represent youth who have successfully negotiated the care system, what does this lower level of treatment mean? Are there valid medical reasons for withholding treatment; that is, is there something about the spectrum of disease in these youth that changes treatment decisions? Is clinical judgment tempered by admitted, suspected, or measured noncompliance with the medical regimen? What is it about drug use history that affects treatment? Does drug use history explain living situation? Why should ability to pay with private insurance be more important than public insurance? These questions cannot be answered in the prevalence data contained in the Rogers et al. database, but they represent critical unknowns in addressing this numerically increasing, medically complex, and behaviorally challenging generation of young people.

Summary

Attention to the full spectrum of adolescent issues is overdue and will be successfully focused only when the nature and scope of the issues are accurately defined.

A necessary first step is consensus around the definition of terms and age groupings so that meaningful comparisons can be drawn. HIV infection in adolescents will drive responses to many of the more troublesome situations that society has managed to ignore for so long, including both legal and financial access to care and adequately funded social support networks to bolster or replace failing systems in shredded communities. Whether the response is grounded in wisdom, generosity, and compassion or is a continuation of the mood currently displayed against youth in the political and legal justice system is the ultimate question America must answer.

References

American Medical Association (1992). *Healthy youth 2000: National health promotion and disease prevention objectives for adolescents.* Chicago: American Medical Association.

Arnold, P. (1992). Betwixt and between: Adolescents and HIV. In N. D. Hunter and W. B. Rubenstein (Eds.), *AIDS agenda: Emerging issues in civil rights.* New York: New Press.

Brooks-Gunn, J., and A. Petersen. (1984). Problems in studying and defining pubertal events. *Journal of Youth and Adolescence, 13*(3), 181–196.

Burke, D. S., et al. (1990). Human immunodeficiency virus infections in teenagers: Seroprevalence among applicants for U.S. military service. *Journal of the American Medical Association, 263,* 2074–2077.

Coleman, J. (1961). *The adolescent society.* New York: Free Press.

Commission on Behavioral and Social Sciences and Education, National Research Council (1993). *Losing generations: Adolescents in high-risk settings.* Washington, D C: National Academy Press.

D'Angelo, L. J., et al. (1991a). A longitudinal study of HIV infection in urban adolescents (abs). Paper presented at 31st Intersciences Conference on Antimicrobial Agents and Chemotherapy, Chicago (October 1).

D'Angelo, L. J., et al. (1991b). Human immunodeficiency virus infection in urban adolescents: Can we predict who is at risk? *Pediatrics, 88,* 982–986.

Dryfoos, J. G. (1990). *Adolescents at risk: Prevalence and prevention.* New York: Oxford University Press.

El-Sadr, W., and J. M. Oleske (chairs) (1994). Evaluation and management of early HIV infection. *Clinical Practice Guideline Number 7.* U.S. Department of Health and Human Services: Public Health Service (Agency for Health Care Policy and Research Publication No. 94–0572).

English, A. (1990). Treating adolescents: Legal and ethical considerations. *Medical Clinics of North America:* 1097.

English, A. (1991). Runaway and street youth at risk for HIV infection: Legal and ethical issues in access to care. *Journal of Adolescent Health 12,* 504–510.

Hall, G. S. H. (1904). *Adolescence: Its psychology and its relation to physiology, anthropology, sociology, sex, crime, religion and education.* New York: Appleton.

Harlan, W. R., E. Harlan, and G. Grillo. (1980). Secondary sex characteristics of girls 12 to 17 years of age: The U.S. health examination survey. *Journal of Pediatrics, 96*(6), 1074–1078.

Hein, K. (1987). AIDS in adolescents: A rationale for concern. *New York State Journal of Medicine, 87,* 290–295.

Hollingshead, A. B. (1949). *Elmtown's youth: The impact of social class on adolescents.* New York: Wiley.

Kinsman, S. B., and G. B. Slap (1992). Barriers to adolescent prenatal care. *Journal of Adolescent Health, 13,* 146–154.

Lemp, G. F., et al. (1994). Seroprevalence of HIV and risk behaviors among young homosexual and bisexual men: The San Francisco/Berkeley young men's survey. *Journal of the American Medical Association, 272*(6), 449–454.

Lindegren, M. L. (1994). Provisional data, personal communication. Surveillance Branch, Division HIV/AIDS, National Center for Infectious Diseases, National Center for Disease Control and Prevention.

Lindergren, M. L., et al. (1994). Epidemiology of Human Immunodeficiency Virus Infection in Adolescents. *Pediatric Infectious Diseases Journal, 13,* 525–535.

National Center for Health Statistics (1991). Family structure and children's health, 1988. *Vital Health Statistics, 10* (178).

National Commission on Children (1991). *Beyond rhetoric: A new American agenda for children and families.* Washington, DC: U.S. Government Printing Office.

Newacheck, P. W., M. A. McManus, and J. Gebhardt (1992). Health insurance coverage of adolescents: A current profile and assessment of trends. *Pediatrics, 90*(4), 589–596.

Robertson, M. J. (1991). Homeless youth: An overview of recent literature. In J. H. Kiyder-Coe, J. M. Molnar, and L.M. Salamon (Eds.), *Homeless children and youth: A new American dilemma.* New Brunswick, New Jersey: Transaction Publishers.

Rogers, A. S., et al. (1996). A profile of human immunodeficiency virus-infected adolescents receiving health care services at selected sites in the United States. *Journal of Adolescent Health, 19,* 401–408.

Rosenberg, P. S., R. J. Biggar, and J. J. Goedert (1994). Declining age at HIV infection in the United States. Letter. *New England Journal of Medicine, 330*(11), 789.

St. Louis, M., et al. (1991). Human immunodeficiency virus in disadvantaged adolescents: Findings from the U.S. job corps. *Journal of the American Medical Association, 266,* 2387–2391.

Society for Adolescent Medicine (1992). Position paper: Access to health care for adolescents. *Journal of Adolescent Health, 13,* 162–170.

Sommer, B. B. (1978). *Puberty and Adolescence.* New York: Oxford University Press.

Stricof, R. L., et al. (1991). HIV seroprevalence in a facility for runaway and homeless adolescents. *American Journal of Public Health, 81*(s), 50–53.

U.S. Congress, Office of Technology Assessment (1991). *Adolescent health, volume 1: Summary and policy options (OTA-H-468).* Washington DC: U.S. Government Printing Office.

U.S. Congress, Office of Technology Assessment (1991). *Adolescent health, volume II: Background and the effectiveness of selected prevention and treatment services (OTA-H-466).* Washington, DC: U.S. Government Printing Office (November).

U.S. Department of Commerce, Bureau of the Census (1991). *Statistical abstract of the United States.* Washington, DC: U.S. Government Printing Office.

U.S. Department of Education (1991). *Youth Indicators 1991: Trends in the Well-Being of American Youth.* Washington, DC: U.S. Government Printing Office.

Vermund, S. H., et al. (1989). Acquired immunodeficiency syndrome among adolescents: Case surveillance profiles in New York City and the rest of the United States. *American Journal of Diseases of Children, 143,* 1220–1225.

2   Adolescent Development: Implications for the Adolescent Alone

Nancy Leffert and Anne C. Petersen

Introduction

Adolescence is both a time of change and a time of challenge. It is a time of considerable change because during adolescence young people complete their physical growth and acquire the social and cognitive skills needed for adult roles and responsibilities (Petersen 1988). It is a time of challenge because during the second decade of life the social contexts that are important to adolescents also change. The combination of individual and social contextual change provides adolescents many developmental opportunities to choose either risky health behaviors or healthy ones (Crockett and Petersen 1993).

A growing body of research has pointed to the potential influence of communities or other contexts on adolescent development (Blyth and Leffert 1995). Some settings have a positive effect on youth and others have negative effects. The National Research Council (Commission on Behavioral and Social Sciences and Education 1993) emphasized that high-risk settings have a deleterious impact on adolescent development. Although research supports this contention, it is also important to recognize that adolescents are not a homogeneous population; individual adolescents may surmount great deprivation through inner sources of strength and external support. Certain groups of young people, however, are at greater risk. For example, Dryfoos (1990) estimates that as many as one in four young people are at high risk; these young people have limited potential to become productive adults because of serious problems at home, at school, or in their communities.

Among the varied populations at risk, particularly vulnerable young people are adolescents who are growing up functionally alone. These adolescents grow to adulthood without the supports of caring families, schools, teachers, and health care professionals (Benson 1990). Adolescents who are alone have no one to guide them in making decisions about which behaviors to avoid and which to adopt. Their risk is greater than the risks facing those adolescents who have supports as they learn to make decisions and begin to function more and more independently of parental or nonparental adult guidance and/or supervision.

Although difficult to measure in exact numbers, approximately 200,000 to 300,000 adolescents are permanent street residents. Many more are periodically

31

homeless (U.S. Dept. of Health and Human Services 1986). In previous decades, adolescents were alone primarily as a result of intense family conflict, which resulted in the adolescent "running away" (Adams and Munro 1979). Today, youth are alone because their families are homeless (Benker, Boone, and Dehavenon 1990), the caretaking parent has died, they have been neglected or abandoned (Adams, Gullotta, and Clancy 1985), or because of intense and/or unresolved family conflict resulting in the adolescent either leaving home voluntarily or being thrown out. They might live in a household with adults but have no consistent and supportive guidance from them.

Many adolescents who are homeless due to family conflict cite as reasons physical and sexual abuse and parent–child conflict over the adolescent's sexual identity (Clatts 1989; Hersch 1989; Clatts and Atillasoy 1993). Today many homeless adolescents have been orphaned by the AIDS epidemic. The adolescent's caretaking parent (usually the mother) has died of AIDS, leaving no suitable alternative guardian (Levine and Stein 1994; Michaels and Levine 1992). This chapter will provide an overview of normal adolescent development, including puberty, cognitive development, psychosocial development, and the contextual changes that affect the adolescent. We will suggest some implications that normal development may have on the adolescent alone, keeping in mind that much further research is needed on this heterogenous population. Much of the research to date has focused on risky behaviors, rather than on the impact of being alone on overall development.

Development During Adolescence

Adolescence is part of the life course and, as such, it is affected by development during childhood and it is shaped by subsequent expectations of adulthood (Lerner 1987; Petersen 1987). Scholars (Elliott and Feldman 1990) have distinguished three distinct subphases within the adolescent decade (ages ten to twenty years): early adolescence (ten to fourteen years), middle adolescence (fifteen to seventeen years), and late adolescence (eighteen to twenty years). The three phases of adolescence have great individual variation in duration and timing, but each phase has distinct characteristics.

Early adolescence is generally considered to be the time of transition from childhood into adolescence; the hallmark of this period is pubertal development. Middle adolescence is characterized by the dominance of peer orientation and all the stereotypical characteristics that are associated with adolescence (e.g., choice of music, attire) (Crockett and Petersen 1993). Late adolescence marks the transition to adult life; the adolescent moves toward adult roles during this period. Because of tremendous individual variability, these age boundaries and characterizations are useful only as general guidelines. The adolescent alone may be thrust into the roles of the late adolescent by being faced with adult-like responsibilities, such as finding food and shelter and taking care of younger siblings or ill parents, but their actual physical, cognitive, and psychosocial maturity may not be commensurate with these demands.

Adolescence is characterized primarily by change and variability. Several developmental principles are important in determining or predicting the impact of development. First, the timing of onset and offset of developmental change, especially whether the change is in synch with or out of synch with the adolescents' peers, is critical. (Early and late puberty is discussed shortly.) Second, the nature and direction of the developmental trajectory is also important. For example, Offer and Offer (1975) identified different patterns of psychological development in boys, with some continuous, others periodic, and still others tumultuous in growth. Third, behavioral transitions can also shape many aspects of subsequent behavior. For example, the adolescent's first experience with sexual intercourse is a nonreversible behavior that gives the adolescent new status and is likely to affect many aspects of interpersonal and especially romantic relationships (Petersen and Kuipers 1996). Finally, developmental transitions are periods in life with significant social and/or biological changes that affect subsequent developmental and role relationships. For example, in early adolescence the biological changes of puberty and social changes of making a transition to secondary school significantly affect psychological and social development.

The adolescent decade is extremely challenging for some young people. Research has demonstrated that experiencing many changes, especially if they occur at about the same time, can produce negative outcomes (Simmons et al. 1987; Petersen et al. 1991). Being alone could increase the likelihood that these changes are misinterpreted by the adolescent, causing increased stress. In addition, the experience of being alone may in itself add to the extent of change experienced by adolescents.

Pubertal Development

The biological changes that occur during adolescence are dramatic and relatively rapid (Eichorn 1975; Petersen and Taylor 1980). The physical changes of puberty do not, however, produce maturation in other areas. Cognitive and psychosocial development may be on entirely different timetables. This is particularly important because adults often treat adolescents who look "mature" as though they are adults.

The physical changes of puberty are driven by hormonal change. During this period the adolescent experiences genital development, breast development (in girls), pubic and axillary hair development, facial hair and voice deepening (in boys), skin changes, and rapid changes in both height and weight (Tanner 1962).

Although all normal adolescents experience pubertal change, the timing and tempo of these changes is highly variable (Tanner 1972; Eichorn 1975). For example, girls begin puberty as early as eight years of age and as late as thirteen years of age. Boys generally begin puberty about one and one-half to two years later than girls, usually between ages nine and one-half and thirteen and one-half. The duration of puberty reflects its tempo, or the speed of change, and ranges from one and a half to six years, with an average of four years.

The differences in both timing and tempo mean that young people enter puberty at different times and consequently may have relatively different experiences in terms of their preparation (Crockett and Petersen 1993) and the extent to which their puberty precedes, is synchronous with, or follows other changes. Research has shown that pubertal timing influences individual responses to pubertal change as well as other aspects of adolescent development (Ruble and Brooks-Gunn 1982).

Pubertal change affects body image and self-esteem (Petersen and Leffert 1995a). Increased maturation is generally viewed more positively by boys than by girls (Dorn, Crockett, and Petersen 1988). Girls may view the changes in their bodies negatively; they tend to perceive increases in weight and changes in fat deposits (Frisch 1983) as in conflict with the cultural preferences that emphasize the long-limbed, slender body – a shape more like that of the prepubertal girl than the mature female (Faust 1983; Petersen and Leffert 1995a).

Research has demonstrated that early-maturing girls tend to be particularly at risk because their development is off-time with that of their peers. For example, Simmons and Blyth (1987) found that early pubertal development is associated with more negative psychological outcomes in girls and higher self-esteem in boys. The higher self-esteem in early-maturing boys is thought to be related to earlier muscle development that brings social benefits such as strength and ability in sports. In contrast, early-maturing girls may believe they are overweight and thus may engage in excessive dieting or develop eating disorders (Attie, Brooks-Gunn, and Petersen 1990).

Cognitive Development

The capacity for abstract reasoning increases during adolescence (Keating and Clark 1980), which has implications for other aspects of development, including the promotion of health care. In the adolescent alone, the normal developmental patterns of cognitive development may be altered. The ability to use formal logic and to think hypothetically increases during early adolescence (Inhelder and Piaget 1958). Formal logic allows the adolescent to go beyond the concrete to use verbal hypotheses and logical deductions (Petersen and Crockett 1986). Adolescents begin to imagine hypothetical situations and are increasingly conscious of future consequences of current actions (Greene 1986). However, if they are not enrolled in school, adolescents who are alone are not in an environment that stimulates abstract thinking; thus, their cognitive development may be compromised.

The cognitive capacities of adolescents are more sophisticated than those observed in younger children. The ability to make decisions also increases during adolescence (Weithorn and Campbell 1982). It is important to note that this improved ability does not consistently meet the challenges that are found in stressful and novel situations (Linn 1983; Petersen and Leffert 1995b). Although all adolescents will be faced with difficult decisions at one time or another, the adolescent alone is probably more likely to be confronted with them more frequently.

Both experience and emotion play a role in the decision-making process. Generally, adolescents are more likely than adults to be in situations in which they lack experience, which may tax their newly emergent cognitive abilities and decision-making skills (Crockett and Petersen 1993). Like adults, adolescents' increased cognitive abilities tend to break down when they are faced with situations that involve "hot" or emotionally laden cognitions (Hamburg 1986; Petersen and Hamburg 1986). Adolescents are more likely to be less sophisticated than they are capable of being in less arousing or familiar situations (Crockett and Petersen 1993). In these types of situations, adolescents may respond impulsively, without consideration of the consequences of their actions or alternative decision choices (Furby and Beyth-Marom 1990).

Typically, adolescents' responses are due to lack of experience with emotionally laden issues (Petersen and Leffert 1995a). Many of the experiences that adolescents confront may be "age-graded" (i.e., young people experience something at the same time/grade, such as a school transition from the elementary school to junior high or middle school). However, emotions are not age-graded. Lack of experience may increase the emotional impact of an experience. For example, adolescents have higher automobile accident rates because they have not yet learned how to control a car when they hit a patch of ice, and they frequently panic (Petersen and Kuipers 1996). Similarly, adolescents may be confused by the intensity of their feelings when they begin having sexual relationships. Although an adult might have the same emotional reactions, the adult may be better able to understand what is happening because of prior experience.

It is likely that the adolescent alone is confronted with more emotionally laden situations and difficult decisions than the adolescent who has the support of parents and/or other adults. In addition, the adolescent alone may have fewer age/graded experiences because he or she lacks a peer group of the same age/grade. The adolescent alone may have peers, but they may be younger or older rather than age-mates, and their experiences may differ broadly.

Decision-making ability increases over the course of the adolescent decade. With this increase, the awareness of risks and the ability to think about the future also increases. The increase in these skills occurs throughout the middle or junior high and high school years (Lewis 1981). Some researchers (Weithorn and Campbell 1982) report that by fourteen years of age, or mid-adolescence, decision-making and reasoning ability is as good as that seen in adulthood and involves the same flaws (Kuhn, Amsel, and O'Loughlin 1988).

Furby and Beyth-Marom (1990) suggest that adolescent decision making may differ from that of adults because the adolescent may have different options available or may consider different options. Adolescents might ignore certain options or not have the social skills needed to avoid taking risks. Further, adolescents may not be aware of or may have faulty beliefs about different consequences or risks associated with a decision. Adolescents may also reject what they consider to be adult values that would lead them to make more adult-like decisions (Fischoff and Quadresl 1991).

Despite growing decision-making capacity, adolescents are often thought to be impulsive and irrational. Consequently some statutes and policies limit their ability to make decisions or choices that are independent of parent or guardian approval. For example, these viewpoints have affected some states' policies regarding abortion decisions (Jacobs 1991).

Adler (1994) suggests that adolescents make rational decisions and choices just like adults, and that only when observers do not understand the intention of their decisions do their decisions *appear* irrational. Adler suggests a psychosocial model that incorporates the influence of perceived risk and benefits on motivation, which then become part of the decision-making process. In general, adolescents and adults are both *optimistically biased*; that is, they tend to believe that the outcomes of their behavior will be positive. Research has demonstrated that adolescents are no more optimistically biased than adults (Quadrel et al. 1993), nor do they underestimate risk any more than adults. Both adolescents and adults rely on psychological processes that lead them to see themselves as facing less risk than someone else (Fishoff and Quadrel 1991). However, adolescents' understanding of the facts or their expectations may be different, or even faulty, compared to that of adults. Again, the adolescent alone may have his or her decision-making capabilities taxed by a highly stressful environment.

Psychosocial Development

Significant changes in psychosocial development also occur during adolescence, but the normal pattern may be severely restricted in the adolescent alone. Because of adolescents' increased cognitive ability, they are able to think abstractly about themselves, make comparisons with others, and draw conclusions about their future prospects. At the same time, they feel pressure to conform to the norms of adult society. These influences affect their developing sense of self (Crockett and Petersen 1993).

Although aspects of self-image show different patterns of change in adolescence (Abramowitz, Petersen, and Schulenberg 1984), overall self-esteem increases during adolescence. In addition, longitudinal studies have shown increasing capacity for autonomy over adolescence (Steinberg and Silverberg 1986). These positive trends are in direct contrast with other data showing increased rates of problem behavior (Elliott 1993). It is important to note that not all adolescents engage in problem behaviors, such as delinquency or substance use, which partially accounts for the different observed trends (Petersen and Leffert 1995a). Rates of internalizing problems also increase, especially among girls (Achenbach et al. 1991; Petersen et al. 1991).

Contextual Change

Adolescents typically experience developmental changes in every important social context, including family, school, and the peer group. As adolescents' abilities increase in many areas, their ability to develop relationships also expands and matures (Leffert and Petersen 1995). This change can be seen in the changes occurring in their relationships with their parents and peers. These social contexts do not exist in isolation, but rather are embedded in the local community and the broader society (Hurrelmann 1989; Crockett and Petersen 1993). For the adolescent alone, the context may not change as much, and yet might be much more demanding than the adolescent's capacity to respond.

Parent–Child Relationships. The traditional view of parent–child relationships during adolescence is often characterized as stormy and conflictual. Psychoanalytic formulations (Freud 1958; Blos 1970) have characterized parent–adolescent conflict as a necessary part of the development of autonomy and the process of individuation, giving the adolescent the necessary "push" to carry on an independent life in adulthood. In most cases the process of individuation does not lead to detachment from parents (Crockett and Petersen 1993). Quite the contrary, closeness to parents continues (Youniss and Smollar 1985), as does the adolescent's respect for his or her parents and the tendency of adolescents to feel that they can rely on their parents (Offer, Ostrov, and Howard 1981; Crockett and Petersen 1993). Adolescents do report, however, decreased closeness to parents over the adolescent decade (Petersen et al. 1993). These patterns have been disrupted for the adolescent alone, either because of intense family conflict or because of the loss of a caretaking parent.

The normal course of parent–adolescent relationships during adolescence, however, is not conflict-free. Conflict increases during early adolescence, an increase that has been shown to be related to pubertal development (Steinberg 1981; Hill et al. 1985). Research has also shown that conflict reaches a plateau during mid-adolescence and declines by the time the adolescent leaves the family home (Montemayor 1983). Research on the types of conflicts most often occurring in homes with an adolescent center around mundane issues (e.g., clothing, chores) (Laursen and Collins 1994). Conflicts are considered severe in only 15 percent of families, and generally severe conflicts are related to prior psychopathology (Rutter et al. 1976; Montemayor 1983).

Another important aspect of change in parent–child relationships is the gradual shift to autonomous functioning over the course of adolescence. This comes about by a change in the regulation of activities and responsibilities from earlier parental control, to a time of coregulation, to self-regulation in early adulthood (Maccoby 1984). This involves a decrease in parental supervision; the adolescent's typical day involves many hours spent away from the family of origin in school and extracurricular activities (Crockett and Petersen 1993). This decrease in supervision can go well if the adolescent is prepared both cognitively and emotionally to deal with the increased access to risky behaviors (e.g., alcohol, sexuality). This is also an area of potential challenge for less competent youth, who may use this lack of supervision to socialize with deviant peers and subsequently engage in high-risk behaviors (Patterson et al. 1984). Poor parenting may have especially deleterious effects on some adolescents because of negative effects on behavior and because these adolescents miss the opportunity to learn about effective interpersonal relationships from their parents (Dornbusch, Ritter, and Liederman 1987; Steinberg 1990).

By definition, adolescents alone lack supportive relationships with parents and do not generally experience changes in those relationships. For the adolescent who is not alone but whose family is homeless, the parents are likely to be under incredible stress. This family environment could either be a source of strength for the adolescent or could be quite dysfunctional.

Peer Relationships. The structure of peer relationships also changes over the adolescent decade for those adolescents in school. During early adolescence, peer groups are generally comprised of neighbors, classmates, and other individuals that adolescents see on a daily basis (Brown 1990; Epstein 1989). As adolescents mature, they tend to select their peers directly and associate with those who have the same interests (e.g., same intensity of academic interest, similar extracurricular interests) (Epstein 1989; Savin-Williams and Berndt 1990).

Larger crowds are also common, particularly in early and mid adolescence (Crockett and Petersen 1993). These crowds are typically groups or cliques that associate with each other and tend to facilitate cross-sex interaction in a nonintimate setting (Dunphy 1963). Crowds are also thought to help adolescents organize the larger social structure, such as the middle school or junior or senior high school setting (Brown 1989; Crockett and Petersen 1993). Crowds may also play an important role in identity development, since adolescent groups may subscribe to particular values or norms of behavior (Crockett and Petersen 1993).

Adolescents tend to spend more time with their peers, particularly those of the same sex, than they did in childhood (Csikszentmihalyi and Larson 1974; Blyth, Hill, and Thiel 1982). Over the course of adolescence, closer relationships with peers of the opposite sex, including romantic relationships, develop (Brown 1990).

Because adolescents spend so much of their available time with peers it is generally thought that they are potentially more influenced by them. Recent research evidence suggests that peer groups influence adolescents' appearance and preferences that are associated with the wider adolescent culture. Contrary to a popularly held belief, however, peer groups do not dramatically change young people's values, which are based more on family upbringing (e.g., religion, life goals) (Lerner et al. 1975).

However, peer influence depends on the intensity of peer pressure and the individual adolescent's susceptibility to it. Conformity to peers tends to peak in early adolescence, between the ages of eleven and thirteen, and then begins to drop off sharply (Costanzo and Shaw 1966). Peer pressure for high-risk behaviors can increase over adolescence (Brown, Clasen, and Eicher 1986; Petersen and Leffert 1995a). In addition, some young people are at higher risk for negative peer influence, particularly young people from disrupted families and early-maturing girls (Magnusson 1987).

Although we often think of peer influence as negative, peer influences tend to be more prosocial or neutral rather than antisocial (Brown et al. 1986; Berndt 1979). However, adolescents may need adult guidance in order to select peer groups that can have these more positive effects, such as environmental commitment, academic-achievement orientation, or the adoption of health-enhancing behaviors (Perry, Kelder, and Komro 1993). Conversely, adolescents must learn to deal with negative peer pressure by developing the necessary social skills in order to make appropriate decisions about their own behavior (Botvin and Tortu 1988; Caplan and Weissberg 1989). Training in social skills development may be especially effective for young adolescents and other groups particularly susceptible to peer pressure (Crockett and Petersen 1993). The adolescent alone may very well have peer relationships in the form of other adolescents who are alone, but these may have a negative influence in terms of increased exposure to drug use and unprotected sex. On the other hand, it is possible that older peers who are alone may provide some measure of comfort and friendship to the younger adolescent who is alone.

Schools. For adolescents in school, the transition from elementary to middle school or junior high school is another important contextual change. These patterns differ for the adolescent alone who is not enrolled in school. Although schooling has become increasingly important in the United States to ensure future success, schools are not meeting the academic or developmental needs of many adolescents (Crockett and Petersen 1993). The failure of schools to meet developmental needs can be seen in the effects of school settings on adolescents' behavior (Petersen 1998). Beyond elementary school, schools tend to be larger, more complex, and farther from home. In such settings, young adolescents tend to feel more anonymous, have less opportunity to engage in autonomous behavior (Eccles and Midgley 1989), and may even feel unsafe outside the classroom (Petersen 1998). As the school setting changes little beyond early adolescence, middle adolescents generally have either developed enough experience to cope with large, impersonal high schools or they have dropped out.

The classroom experience contrasts sharply with the adolescent's developmental readiness, particularly for girls. In the junior high school setting, young adolescents have fewer choices, participate less in decision making (Feldlaufer et al. 1988), and are not involved in cooperative small groups. Instead, their classes are structured around the whole class (Rounds and Osaki 1982). They are also evaluated more frequently and more formally (Gullickson 1985), and their relationships with teachers are observed to be less positive (Hawkins and Berndt 1985).

Social Context Effects. Recently researchers have begun to examine the effects on development of variations in social contexts. Elliott (1993) concluded, for example, that lower-income and middle-income youth do not differ in the age of initiation of problem behaviors, nor in the extent of their experimentation. Socioeconomic differences appear primarily in their persistence and therefore the developmental trajectories of such behaviors. Middle-income adolescents tend to desist after a period of experimentation; lower-income adolescents continue these behaviors, adopting a problem behavior lifestyle. Elliott speculates that these differences are due to the existence of life opportunities for middle-income adolescents, whereas lower-income adolescents see little opportunity for their futures and therefore engage in high-risk behaviors (e.g., violence, substance abuse, and unprotected sex). The pattern for the adolescent alone fits more with that of low-income adolescents, in that these adolescents have few, if any, life opportunities.

Blyth and Leffert (1995) found that vulnerable youth (defined as those youth with fewer personal assets) benefit from living in healthier communities. In addition, and consistent with the findings of Elliott (1993), adolescents in the least healthy communities generally had more problem behaviors, which began at younger ages. Blyth and Leffert (1995) observed that high-risk behaviors tended also to start earlier in the least healthy communities.

Other research suggests that income level and opportunities available to adolescents influence mental health, as well as physical health. Adolescents in a resource-rich community, where resources were defined by material and social resources, reported lower rates of depression than adolescents in a resource-poor community (Petersen et al. 1991).

At a more basic level, extremely deprived environments have been shown to limit development at an early age. Beginning with the research of Spitz (1965), scholars have found that children need a minimum level of stimulation and human interaction to develop normally. Conditions of poverty and deprivation are likely to have adverse effects on adolescent development and behavior (Klerman 1993).

Stress and Resilience in Adolescence

Observers and scholars of adolescent development continue to view the adolescent decade as involving significant risk. Several studies have demonstrated that not all adolescents experience significant psychological turmoil and that the majority of adolescents traverse the period in a much calmer fashion than had been previously assumed (Offer 1969; Grinker and Werble 1974; Offer and Offer 1975; Rutter et al. 1976). Not until recently, however, have researchers begun to examine resilience in the face of stress and challenge (Garmezy and Rutter 1983; Garmezy 1984; Rutter 1983, 1987). The following section will review some of the risk and protective factors that may influence adolescent development.

Risk Factors

Risk factors that influence adolescent development may include family stress, social or school stress, or individual vulnerabilities carried over from childhood.

For example, family changes are often considered to be stressful life events at any point in the life course. The family has changed significantly in recent decades; divorce rates have increased, increasing the likelihood that adolescents will grow up with either a single parent or a "reconstituted" family, including a stepparent and perhaps stepsiblings. In addition, women have entered the labor force in large numbers, especially when their children become adolescents (Hess 1995).

Individual vulnerabilities may particularly influence adolescent development. Adolescents may enter the period already vulnerable as a result of chronic illness, disability, prior psychopathology, or family dysfunction. There are many examples in the literature of the particular vulnerabilities that may put adolescents at further risk for negative outcomes (Petersen and Ebata 1987; Ebata 1990; Petersen and Leffert 1995a). For example, adolescents who have difficulty coping with stress or adversity may turn to health-compromising behaviors (e.g., smoking or alcohol use) as a means of dealing with or muting the anxiety they feel as a result of weaknesses in coping skills (Compas 1993). At some point, the adolescent alone has experienced a family change of some kind. This may be connected to prior psychopathology and intense family dysfunction.

Protective Factors

The challenges and potential stress of development during adolescence may be buffered by factors exogenous to the individual, such as family and peer support. In addition, the individual may have coping skills that serve to protect him or her from stressors. For example, peers can provide supportive and positive influences during the course of adolescence (Brown et al. 1986; Hill and Holmbeck 1986). Particularly by later adolescence, peers especially provide a means of social support. There is also evidence that good peer relationships can buffer negative parental or other influences (Klepp, Halper, and Perry 1986; Sarigiani 1990). The adolescent alone may have the wherewithal to mobilize some measure of social support.

Coping

Individuals may vary in their responses to the same changes. Some adolescents may cope more effectively than others with the changes they experience during adolescence. Over the past decade, a body of research examining the coping responses of adolescents has emerged (Compas 1987a, 1987b, 1993). For example, Compas and colleagues (Compas, Orosan, and Grant 1993) suggest a model of the role of stress and coping in the development of depression and other psychopathology during adolescence. The biological changes of puberty combined with interpersonal stressful events may result in a depressed mood. The way that an individual copes with this experience of depressed mood may explain the development of depression. Specifically, Compas et al. (1993) posit that emotion-focused coping increases during adolescence. Emotion-focused coping style is used particularly by females, whereas males tend to use distraction. The emotion-focused style of coping may result in problems of depression when it is combined with the stressful changes of puberty and life events.

The Adolescent Alone: Impact on Normal Development

Homeless adolescents, one of the subcategories of adolescents alone, have numerous physical and mental health problems, including alcohol and drug abuse (Robertson 1991). More research has been done on homeless youth than on adolescents alone, possibly because these youth are in such extreme circumstances. Inadequate nutrition and poor hygiene in current living conditions compromise their physical development. It is also likely that the homeless adolescent has experienced a good deal of adversity during the family's process of becoming homeless or the adolescent's process of leaving home.

For whatever the reason he or she is homeless, the adolescent is not likely to have the adult support necessary for positive development (Benson 1990). In addition, it is probable that the separation from the parent, if such was the case, was at least stressful, if not traumatic. The homeless adolescent is likely to have some peer support in the form of other homeless youth, but these peer relationships are likely to be mostly negative. Because they may not be enrolled in school or may attend erratically, homeless youth may not be in an environment that stimulates planning, decision making, or abstract thinking; thus their cognitive development may also be compromised.

Although all adolescents are faced with making decisions about participating in risky behaviors, homeless adolescents are more likely to engage in health-risking behaviors. This is likely to be the result of peer influence as well as the street economy, which is characterized by drugs and violence (see Chapter 8).

These behaviors are consistent with research observations that problem behaviors tend to cluster together as a problem behavior lifestyle (Elliott 1993) or syndrome (Jessor 1991). Two explanations have been advanced to account for this: (1) young people who participate in problem behaviors have a tendency toward deviancy (Donovan and Jessor 1985); and (2) problem behaviors may be causally linked (e.g., an individual may steal in order to support the use of illicit drugs). Elliott (1993) suggests that both factors contribute to the covariation of problem behaviors or the development of problematic lifestyles. By virtue of their living arrangement, homeless adolescents are living in poverty, without external supports. They are likely to engage in prostitution, with sex as the currency for which they attain food, shelter, and drugs. They are therefore repeatedly exposed to sexually transmitted diseases, HIV, and unplanned pregnancies. They may steal or engage in other deviant or anti-social activities to provide for their needs.

The Adolescent Alone: Treatment Considerations

Normal adolescent development has a number of implications for decision making regarding adolescents alone. The very nature of adolescence as a period of tremendous change suggests that, in general, young people experience increasing capacity over the course of adolescence. However, the traumatic and stressful nature of being alone, for whatever reason, may compromise normal development or alter its timetable.

In general, early adolescents (ten to fourteen years) are more like children. Middle adolescents (fifteen to seventeen years) begin to have adult capacity, especially in cognition, but their behavior may oscillate between childlike and adult behavior. Late adolescents (eighteen to twenty years) are not different from adults in terms of average understanding and cognitive capacity (Petersen and Leffert 1995b). Despite the research demonstrating that by age fourteen adolescent decision making is as good as that of the adult (Weithorn and Campbell 1982), the middle adolescents may be functioning at a lower level at least some of the time, or in some situations, when faced with a stressful or novel situation. Therefore, the most conservative choice would be to assume that they should be treated as children (Petersen and Leffert 1995b). Those who would criticize this stance as too rigid would point to the need to assess individuals on the basis of the specific decision to be made, the importance of supporting emergent autonomy, and the lack of an alternate adult decision maker.

It is conceivable that health care providers or other providers of service to adolescents who are alone may erroneously assume that they are more mature, both emotionally and behaviorally (by virtue of living on the street and being faced with the pressures of finding his or her next meal and other "adult-like" responsibilities) than the adolescent growing up with the supports of family, teachers, and positive peer influence. Quite the contrary, some adolescents under extreme stress, whether because of an acute state such as poor health or because of a chronic condition such as being alone, are unlikely to be able to reason effectively about health risks, or the benefits of health care or health promotion (Petersen and Leffert 1995b). Others, especially those with a chronic condition, may be very experienced at determining their own self-interest.

Health care providers can help increase the adolescent's capacities by providing a supportive environment. This may decrease the adolescent's anxiety about the added stress of the health care situation. The homeless adolescent's pseudo-maturity, which manifests itself as a "street-wise" demeanor, should not be confused with true understanding and judgment. Given the transient nature of these young people's lives, treatment may be best provided in a drop-in setting. For the seriously ill or health-compromised adolescent, inpatient treatment may be required even when the disease process itself could be medically managed on an outpatient basis. This would allow the completion of a course of therapy, continuity of the health care relationship (which in itself provides much-needed support to the adolescent), and adequate follow-up.

Providers should evaluate adolescents alone in the context of a developmental perspective, which guides but does not preordain an individual's capacity to make well-reasoned medical decisions.

References

Abramowitz, R. H., A. C. Petersen, and J. E. Schulenberg (1984). Changes in self-image during early adolescence. In D. Offer, E. Ostrov, and K. Howard (Eds.), *Patterns of adolescent self-image,* San Francisco: Jossey-Bass: 19–28.

Achenbach, T. M., et al. (1991). National survey of problems and competencies among fourteen-1 to sixteen-year-olds. *Monographs of the Society for Research in Child Development, 56.*

Adams, G. R., T. Gullotta, and M. Clancy (1985). Homeless adolescents: A descriptive study of similarities and differences between runaways and throways. *Adolescence, 20,* 715–724.

Adams, G. R., and G. Munro (1979). Portrait of North American runaways: A critical review. *Journal of Youth and Adolescence, 8,* 359–373.

Adler, N. (1994). Adolescent sexual behavior looks irrational – but looks are deceiving. Washington, DC: Federation of Behavioral, Psychological, and Cognitive Sciences.

Attie, I. J., Brooks-Gunn, and A. C. Petersen (1990). A developmental perspective on eating disorders and eating problems. In, M. Lewis and S. M. Miller (Eds.), *Handbook of Developmental Psychopathology.* New York: Plenum: 409–420.

Benker, K., M. Boone, and A. Dehavenon (1990). The tyranny of indifference: A study of hunger, homelessness, poor health, and family dismemberment in 1,325 New York City households with children 1989–1990. New York: The Action Research Project on Hunger, Homelessness, and Family Health.

Benson, P. L. (1990). *The troubled journey.* Minneapolis, MN: Search Institute.

Berndt, T. J. (1979). Developmental changes in conformity to peers and parents. *Developmental Psychology, 15,* 608–616.

Blos, P. (1970). *The adolescent passage.* New York: International Universities Press.

Blyth, D. A., J. P. Hill, and K. S. Thiel. (1982). Early adolescents' significant others: Grade and gender differences in perceived relationships with familial and nonfamilial adults and young people. *Journal of Youth and Adolescence, 11,* 425–450.

Blyth, D. A., and N. Leffert (1995). Communities as contexts for adolescent development: An empirical analysis. *Journal of Adolescent Research* 10(1): 64–87.

Botvin, G. J., and S. Tortu (1988). Preventing adolescent substance abuse through life skills training. In R. Price et al. (Eds.), *A Casebook For Practitioners.* Washington, DC: American Psychological Association: 98–110.

Brown, B. B. (1989). The role of peer groups in adolescent adjustment to secondary school. In T. J. Berndt and G. W. Ladd (Eds), *Peer Relationships In Child Development.* New York: Wiley: 118–216.

Brown, B. B. (1990). Peer groups and peer cultures. In S. S. Feldman and G. R. Elliott, (Eds.), *At the Threshold: The Developing Adolescent,* Cambridge, MA: Harvard University Press: 171–196.

Brown, B. B., D. Clasen, and S. Eicher (1986). Perception of peer pressure, peer conformity, dispositions, and self-reported behavior among adolescents. *Developmental Psychology, 22,* 521–530.

Brown, B. B., M. J. Lohr, and E. L. McClenahan (1986). Early adolescents' perceptions of peer pressure. *Journal of Early Adolescence, 6,* 139–154.

Caplan, M. Z., and R. P. Weissberg (1989). Promoting social competence in early adolescence: Developmental considerations. In B. H. Schneider et al. (Eds.), *Social Competence In Developmental Perspective.* Boston,: Kluwer, 371–385.

Clatts, M. C. (1989). Substance abuse and AIDS prevention strategies for homeless youth: An ethnographic perspective. Paper presented at the Third International Gay and Lesbian Health Conference, San Francisco.

Clatts, M. C., and A. Atillasoy (1993). A demographic and behavioral profile of homeless youth in New York City: Implications for AIDS outreach and prevention. Paper presented at the Annual Meetings of the Society for Applied Anthropology, San Antonio, TX (March).

Commission on Behavioral and Social Sciences and Education, National Research Council (1993). *Losing generations: Adolescents in high-risk settings.* Washington, DC: National Academy Press.

Compas, B. E. (1987a). Coping with stress during childhood and adolescence. *Psychological Bulletin, 101,* (3), 393–403.

Compas, B. E. (1987b). Stress and life events during childhood and adolescence. *Clinical Psychology Review, 7,* 275–302.

Compas, B. E. (1993). Promoting positive mental health during adolescence. In S. G. Millstein, et al. (Eds.), *Promoting The Health Of Adolescents: New Directions For The Twenty-first Century.* New York: Oxford University Press: 159–179.

Compas, B. E., P. G. Orosan, and K. E. Grant (1993). Adolescent stress and coping: Implications for psychopathology during adolescence. *Journal of Adolescence, 16,* 331–349.

Costanzo, P. R., and M. E. Shaw (1966). Conformity as a function of age level. *Child Development, 37,* 967–975.

Crockett, L. J., and A. C. Petersen (1993). Adolescent development: Health risks and opportunities for health promotion. In S. G. Millstein, et al. (Eds.), *Promoting the health of adolescents: New directions for the twenty-first century.* New York: Oxford University Press: 13–37.

Csikszentmihalyi, M., and R. Larson (1974). *Being adolescent.* New York: Basic Books.

Donovan, J., and R. Jessor (1985). Structure of problem behavior in adolescence and young adulthood. *Journal of Consulting and Clinical Psychology, 53,* 890–904.

Dorn, L. D., 1. J. Crockett, and A. C. Petersen (1988). The relations of pubertal status to intrapersonal changes in young adolescents. *Journal of Early Adolescence, 8,* 405–419.

Dornbusch, S., P. Ritter, and P. Liederman (1987). The relation of parenting style to adolescent school performance. *Child Development, 58,* 1244–1257.

Dryfoos, J. G. (1990). *Adolescents at risk: Prevalence and prevention.* New York: Oxford University Press.

Dunphy, D. (1963). The social structure of urban adolescent peer groups. *Sociometry, 26,* 230–246.

Ebata, A. T., A. C. Petersen, and J. J. Conger (1990). The development of psychopathology in adolescence. In J. E. Rolf, et al. (Eds.), *Risk and protective factors in the development of psychopathology.* New York: Cambridge University Press: 308–333.

Eccles, J. S., and C. Midgley (1989). Stage/environment fit: Developmentally appropriate classrooms for early adolescents. In, R.E. Ames and C. Ames (Eds.), *Research on motivation in education* (Vol. 3) New York: Academic Press.

Eichorn, D. H. (1975). Asynchronization in adolescent development. In J.E. Dragastin and G.H. Elder (Eds.), *Adolescence in the life cycle: Psychological change and social context.* Washington, DC: Hemisphere: 81–96.

Elliott, D. S. (1993). Health enhancing and health compromising lifestyles. In S.G. Millstein et al. (Eds.), *Promoting the health of adolescents: New directions for the twenty-first century,* New York: Oxford University Press: 119–145.

Elliott, G. R., and S.S. Feldman (1990). Capturing the adolescent experience. In S.S. Feldman and G.R. Elliott (eds.), *At the threshold: The developing adolescent.* Cambridge, MA: Harvard University Press: 1–14.

Epstein, J. L. (1989). The selection of friends: Changes across the grades and in different school environments. In T.J. Berndt and G.W. Ladd (Eds.), *Peer relationships in child development.* New York: Wiley: 158–187.

Faust, M. S. (1983). Alternative constructions of adolescent growth. In J. Brooks-Gunn and A. (Eds.), *Girls at puberty: Biological and psychosocial perspectives.* New York: Plenum: 105–125.

Feldlaufer, H., C. Midgley, and J. S. Eccles (1988). Student, teacher, and observer perceptions of the classroom environment before and after the transition to junior high school.*Journal of Early Adolescence, 8,* 133–156.

Fischoff, B., and M. J. Quadresl (1991). Adolescent alcohol decisions. *Alcohol, Health, and Research World, 15,* 43–51.

Freud, A. (1958). Adolescence. *Psychoanalytic Study of The Child, 13,* 255–278.

Frisch, R. (1983). Fatness, puberty, and fertility: The effects of nutrition and physical training on menarche and ovulation. In J. Brooks-Gunn and A.C. Petersen (eds.) *Girls at puberty: Biological and psychosocial perspectives.* New York: Plenum: 29–49.

Furby, L., and R. Beyth-Marom (1990). *Risk-taking in adolescence: A decision-making perspective.* Washington, DC: Carnegie Council on Adolescent Development, Carnegie Corporation of New York.

Garmezy, N. (1984). Stress-resistant children: The search for protective factors. In J. E. Stevenson (Eds.), *Recent research in developmental psychology,* Oxford: Pergamon Press: 213–233.

Garmezy, N., and M. Rutter, eds. (1983). *Stress, coping, and development in children.* New York: McGraw-Hill.

Greene, A. L. (1986). Future time-perspective in adolescence: The present of things future revisited. *Journal of Youth and Adolescence, 15,* 99–113.

Grinker, R. R., and B. Werble (1974). Mentally healthy young men (homoclites): Fourteen years later. *Archives of General Psychiatry, 30,* 701–704.

Gullickson, A. R. (1985). Student evaluation techniques and their relationship to grade and curriculum. *Journal of Educational Research, 79,* 96–100.

Hamburg, B. (1986). Subsets of adolescent mothers: Developmental, biomedical, and psychosocial issues. In B. Lancaster and B.A. Hamburg. (Eds.), *School-age pregnancy and parenthood: Biosocial dimensions.* New York: Aldine de Gruyter, 115–145.

Hawkins, J., and T. J. Berndt (1985). Adjustment following the transition to junior high school. Paper presented at the biennial meetings of the Society for Research on Child Development, Toronto, Canada (April).

Hersch, P. (1989). *Exploratory ethnographic study of runaway and homeless adolescents in New York and San Francisco.* Rockville, MD: National Institute of Drug Abuse.

Hess, L. E. (1995). Changing family patterns in Western Europe: Opportunity and risk factors for adolescent development. In M. Rutter and D. J. Smith (Eds.), *Psychosocial disorders in young people: Time trends and their causes,* New York: Wiley, 104–193.

Hill, J., and G. Holmbeck (1986). Attachment and autonomy during adolescence. In G. Whitehurst, (Eds.), *Annals of Child Development.* Greenwich, CT: JAI Press.

Hill, J., et al. (1985). Menarcheal status and parent–child relations in families of seventh-grade girls. *Journal of Youth and Adolescence, 14,* 301–316.

Hurrelmann, K. (1989). Adolescents as productive processors of reality: Methodological perspectives. In K. Hurrelmann and U. Engel (eds.), *The social world of adolescents: International perspectives.* Berlin: Walter de Gruyter, 107–118.

Inhelder, B., and J. Piaget (1958). *The growth of logical thinking from childhood to adolescence.* New York, NY: Basic Books

Jacobs, J. E. (1991). Decision-making and risky behavior. Symposium presentation at the biennial meetings of the Society for Research on Child Development, Seattle, WA.

Jessor, R. (1991). Risk behavior in adolescence: A psychosocial framework for understanding and action. *Journal of Adolescent Health, 12,* 597–605.

Keating, D. P., and L. V. Clark. (1980). Development of physical and social reasoning in adolescence. *Developmental Psychology, 16,* 23–30.

Klepp, K. I., A. Halper, and C. L. Perry (1986). The efficacy of peer leaders in drug abuse prevention. *Journal of School Health, 56,* 407–411.

Klerman, L. V. (1993). The influence of economic factors on health-related behaviors in adolescents. In S. G. Millstein et al., (Eds.), *Promoting the health of adolescents: New directions for the twenty-first century.* New York: Oxford University Press, 38–57.

Kuhn, D., E. Amsel, and M. O'Loughlin (1988). *The development of scientific thinking skills.* San Diego: Academic Press.

Laursen, B., and W. A. Collins (1994). Interpersonal conflict during adolescence. *Psychological Bulletin, 155,* 197–209.

Leffert, N., and A. C. Petersen (1995). Patterns of development during adolescence. In M. Rutter and D. J. Smith (eds.), *Psychosocial disorders in young people: Time trends and their causes.* New York: John Wiley and Sons, 67–103.

Lerner, R. M. (1987). A life-span perspective for early adolescence. In R. M. Lerner and T. T Foch (Eds.), *Biological-psychosocial interactions in early adolescence.* Hillsdale, NJ: Erlbaum, 9–34.

Lerner, R. M., et al. (1975). Actual and perceived attitudes of late adolescents and their parents: The phenomenon of the generation gap. *Journal of Genetic Psychology, 126,* 195–207.

Levine, C., and G. L. Stein (1994). *Orphans of the HIV epidemic: Unmet needs in six U.S. cities.* New York: The Orphan Project.

Lewis, C. (1981). How adolescents approach decisions: Changes over grades seven to twelve and policy implications. *Child Development, 52,* 538–544.

Linn, M. (1983). Content, context and process in reasoning during adolescence: Selecting a model. *Journal of Early Adolescence, 3,* 63–82.

Maccoby, E. E. (1984). Middle childhood in the context of the family. In W. A. Collins (Ed.), *Development During Middle Childhood: The Years From Six To Twelve.* Washington, DC: National Academy of Sciences Press, 184–239.

Magnusson, D. (1987). *Individual development in an interactional perspective (Vol. 1. Paths Through Life).* Hillsdale, NJ: Erlbaum.

Michaels, D. and C. Levine. (1992). Estimates of the number of motherless youth orphaned by AIDS in the United States. *Journal of the American Medical Association, 268,* (24), 3456–3461.

Montemayor, R. (1983). Parents and adolescents in conflict: All families some of the time and some families most of the time. *Journal of Early Adolescence, 3,* 83–103.

Offer, D. (1969). *The psychological world of the teenager: A study of normal adolescent boys.* New York: Basic Books.

Offer, D., and J. B. Offer (1975). Three developmental routes through normal male adolescence. In D. Offer and J. B. Offer (Eds.), *From teenage to manhood: A psychological study.* D. New York, NY: Basic Books, 171–192.

Offer, D., E. Ostrov, and K. I. Howard (1981). *The adolescent: A psychological self-portrait.* New York: Basic Books.

Patterson, G. R., and M. Stouthamer-Loeber (1984). The correlation of family management practices and delinquency. *Child Development, 55,* 1299–1307.

Perry, C. L., S. H. Kelder, and K. A. Komro (1993). The social world of adolescents: Family, peers, schools, and community. In S. G. Millstein et al, (Eds.), *Promoting the health of adolescents: New directions for the twenty-first century.* New York: Oxford University Press: 73–96.

Petersen, A. C. (1987). The nature of biological-psychosocial interactions: The sample case of early adolescence. In R. M. Lerner and T. T. Foch (Eds.), *Biological-psychosocial interactions in early adolescence.* Hillsdale, NJ: Erlbaum: 35–61.

Petersen, A. C. (1988). Adolescent development. *Annual Review of Psychology, 39,* 583–607.

Petersen, A. C. (1998). Adolescence. In E. Blechman and K. Brownell (Eds.) *Behavioral medicine and women: A comprehensive handbook.* New York: Guilford Publications, 45–50.

Petersen, A. C., et al. (1991). Subcultural variation in developmental processes: The development of depressed affect. Poster presented at the International Society for the Study of Behavioral Development, Minneapolis, MN (July).

Petersen, A. C., and L. Crockett. (1986). Pubertal development and its relation to cognitive and psychosocial development in adolescent girls: Implications for parenting. In J. B. Lancaster and B. A. Hamburg (Eds.), *School-age pregnancy and parenthood: Biosocial dimensions.* New York: Aldine de Gruyter, 147–175.

Petersen, A. C., and A. T. Ebata (1987). Developmental transitions and adolescent problem behavior: Implications for prevention and intervention. In K. Hurrelmann, et al. (Ed.), *Social intervention: Potential and constraints.* New York: Walter de Gruyter, 167–184.

Petersen, A. C., and B. Hamburg (1986). Adolescence: A developmental approach to problems and psychopathology. *Behavior Therapy, 17,* 480–499.

Petersen, A. C., and K. S. Kuipers (1996). Understanding adolescence: Adolescent development and implications for the adolescent as a patient. Invited keynote lecture, Moyers Symposium on "Creating the Compliant Patient." Ann Arbor, MI: University of Michigan (March).

Petersen, A. C., and N. Leffert (1995a). What is special about adolescence? In M. Rutter (Ed.), *Psychosocial disturbances of young people: Challenges for prevention.* London: Cambridge University Press, 3–36.

Petersen, A. C., and N. Leffert (1995b). Developmental issues influencing guidelines for adolescent health research: A review. *Journal of Adolescent Health, 17,* 298–305.

Petersen, A. C., et al. (1993). The role of community and intrapersonal coping resources in the development of depressed affect and depression in adolescence. In *Depression in childhood and adolescence: Developmental issues.* A symposium presentation at the biennial meetings of the Society for Research in Child Development, New Orleans, LA (March).

Petersen, A. C., P. A. Sarigiani, and R. E. Kennedy (1991). Adolescent depression: Why more girls? *Journal of Youth and adolescence, 20,* 247–271.

Petersen, A. C., and B. Taylor (1980). The biological approach to adolescence: Biological change and psychological adaptation. In J. Adelson (Ed.), *Handbook of adolescent psychology.* New York: Wiley, 117–155.

Quadrel, M. J., B. Fischhoff, and W. Davis (1993). Adolescent (in)vulnerability. *American Psychologist, 48* (2), 102–116.

Robertson, M. J. (1991). Homeless youth: An overview of recent literature. In J. H. Kryder-Coe et al. (Eds.), *Homeless Children And Youth: A New American Dilemma.* New Brunswick, New Jersey: Transaction Publishers.

Rounds, T. S., and S. Y. Osaki (1982). The social organization of classrooms: An analysis of sixth- and seventh-grade activity structures. Report EPSSP-82-5. San Francisco, CA: Far West Laboratory.

Ruble, D. N., and J. Brooks-Gunn (1982). The experience of menarche. *Child Development, 53,* 1557–1566.

Rutter, M. (1983). Stress, coping, and development: Some issues and some questions. In N. Garmezy and M. Rutter (Eds.) *Stress, coping, and development in children.* New York: McGraw-Hill.

Rutter, M. (1987). The role of cognition in child development and disorder. *British Journal of Medical Psychology, 60,* 1–16.

Rutter, M., et al. (1976). Adolescent turmoil: Fact or fiction. *Journal of Child Psychology and Psychiatry, 17,* 35–56.

Sarigiani, P. (1990). A longitudinal study of relationship adjustment of young adults from divorced and nondivorced families. Unpublished doctoral dissertation, Pennsylvania State University, University Park, PA.

Savin-Williams, R. C., and T. J. Berndt (1990). Friendship and peer relations. In S. S. Feldman and G. R. Elliott (Eds.) *At the Threshold: The Developing Adolescent.* Cambridge, MA: Harvard University Press: 277–307.

Simmons, R. G., and D. A. Blyth (1987). *Moving into adolescence: The impact of pubertal change and school context.* Hawthorne, NY: Aldine de Gruyter.

Simmons, R. G., et al. (1987). The impact of cumulative change in early adolescence. *Child Development, 58,* 1220–1234.

Spitz, R. A. (1965). *The first year of life: A psychoanalytic study of normal and deviant development of object relations.* New York: International Universities Press.

Steinberg, L. (1981). Transformation in family relations at puberty. *Developmental Psychology, 17,* 833–838.

Steinberg, L. (1990). Autonomy, conflict and harmony in the family relationship. In S. S. Feldman and G. R. Elliott (Eds.), *At the Threshold: The Developing Adolescent.* Cambridge, MA: Harvard University Press, 255–276.

Steinberg, L., and S. Silverberg (1986). The vicissitudes of autonomy in early adolescence. *Child Development, 57,*841–851.

Tanner, J. M. (1962). *Growth at adolescence.* Springfield, IL: Thomas.

Tanner, J. M. (1972). Sequence, tempo, and individual variation in growth and development of boys and girls aged twelve to sixteen. In J. Kagan and R. Coles (Eds.), *Twelve To Sixteen: Early Adolescence.* New York: Norton, 1–24.

U.S. Department of Health and Human Services (1986). *Fiscal year 1985: Study of run-aways and youth.* Washington, DC. U.S. Government Printing Office.

Weithorn, L. A., and S. B. Campbell (1982). The competency of children and adolescents to make informed treatment decisions. *Child Development, 53,* 1589–1598.

Youniss, J., and J. Smollar (1985). *Adolescents' relations with mothers, fathers, and friends.* Chicago: University of Chicago Press.

3 The Health of American Adolescents: Current Issues and Service Gaps

Neal D. Hoffman

Background

Youth aged ten to twenty-four years make up one-fifth of the approximately 255 million persons in the United States. Of these approximately 54 million young persons, 69 percent are non-Hispanic white, 14 percent are African American, 12 percent are Hispanic or Latino, 4 percent are Asian or Pacific Islander, and 1 percent are Native American. Slightly more than half (51%) are male (U.S. Department of Commerce, Bureau of the Census 1994). Currently, children under age eighteen account for 40 percent of the 37 million Americans living below the poverty level, and approximately 5 million (12 percent) young adults, ages eighteen to twenty-four years, are also impoverished (U.S. Department of Commerce, Bureau of the Census 1994). Of equal importance in the grim picture of health of youth in this country, almost 15 percent of adolescents aged twelve to seventeen years old interviewed through the National Health Interview Study (NHIS) had no form of health insurance. Moreover, this figure doubled for comparably aged youth living under the poverty level. And, in contrast to the commonly held notion that adolescence is a time of good health, data extracted from the National Health Interview Study indicate that only half of all twelve- to seventeen-year-olds reported excellent health, and almost 10 percent reported fair to poor health, higher than any of the other studied children's groups (Coiro, Zill, and Bloom 1994).

Like many social institutions, health care systems often do not serve the interests and needs of youth. The NHIS reported that almost 15 percent of the twelve- to seventeen-year-olds were reported as having no regular source for routine medical care, and more than 20 percent were reported as having no particular provider for sick care (Coiro et al. 1994). Despite the fact that more than three-fourths of yearly deaths among American youth, aged ten to twenty-four years, are due to preventable causes such as motor vehicle accidents and other unintentional injuries, homicides, suicides, and the Acquired Immune Deficiency Syndrome (AIDS) (Kochanek and Hudson 1994), acute care, rather than preventive care, is often the focus of health care for youth. The National Ambulatory Medical Care Survey, conducted by the Centers for Disease Control and Prevention (CDC) on a sample of office-based physicians, found that preventive health screening procedures, includ-

50

ing Papanicolaou (Pap) smears, breast examinations, cholesterol measurements and vision exams, were each performed in less than 5 percent of visits by youth, and no counseling advice was provided during two-thirds of all visits by youth. In fact, issues of sexually transmitted diseases were discussed at less than 1 percent of visits by youth (Igra and Millstein 1993).

One confounding factor is the frequently brief nature of health care visits by youth. Data on office visits by youth with a U.S. health care provider indicate that nearly half the visits last less than ten minutes, and 30 percent last ten to fifteen minutes (Nelson 1991). Thus, youth often do not enter the health care system long enough for providers to communicate messages adequately about risk-reduction and health maintenance requirements, let alone to implement preventive health care strategies.

For this reason, many youth who enter the health care system at the time of a serious medical diagnosis will have had little experience with the health care system and will have inadequate understanding of how decisions about health care should be approached. This poses an especially difficult challenge to youth (and the health care providers caring for them) who do not have a supportive adult whom they trust to guide them in this process.

With these background statistics in mind, this chapter will discuss the most significant causes of morbidity and mortality for youth in the United States today, in order to understand the types of health decisions with which youth might be confronted. It will focus on certain subpopulations of youth, such as youth in foster care, youth in detention, homeless youth and immigrant youth, in an attempt to illuminate types of health issues that youth often face on their own.

Common Illnesses

Data on morbidity and mortality in the United States are collected and disseminated by several governmental and nongovernmental agencies on a periodic basis. The picture of health status presented has many limitations. Many surveys, such as NHIS, utilize household interviews, thus missing many youth who are institutionalized or living transiently. Moreover, the source of the health-related information is likely a parent, not the adolescent, and may offer an inaccurate account of the youth's health problems. Similarly, the CDC's Youth Risk Behavior Surveillance System (YRBSS) provides important information on several risk behaviors that often have adverse health effects for youth; however, this survey is limited to high school students in grades nine to twelve and has no capacity to provide data on out-of-school youth. A final shortcoming of these health data is the varying age intervals used for presentation of statistics; (e.g., ten to eighteen years, thirteen to twenty-one years, and less than seventeen years).

Valid and reliable data on subgroups must be obtained from smaller surveys. These, however, often reflect a limited population whose characteristics may not be generalizable. This makes comparisons to other age groups or other youth more difficult.

Trauma

Unintentional Injuries

Injury reduction has been extremely successful in this country over the last two decades. The age-adjusted accident-related death rates for adolescents and young adults declined by 21 percent between 1979 and 1988 (CDC 1993a). This continues to be one of the many important health objectives outlined by the Public Health Service for the year 2000 (Public Health Service 1991). Nevertheless, the NHIS estimated that in 1993 there were twenty-six and twenty-seven episodes of persons injured per 100 person-years for persons aged five to seventeen years and eighteen to twenty-four years, respectively, the highest of all the age-defined populations. Moreover, there were 121 and 237 restricted-activity days associated with episodes of persons injured per 100 person-years for these respective age groups, and twenty-four school-loss days associated with acute injuries per 100 person-years for five- to seventeen-year-olds (Benson and Marano 1994). Most significantly, accidents and adverse effects from such causes as firearms, drugs, medication overdose and asphyxiation (not associated with homicide or suicide) continue to be the leading cause of death for these age groups (Benson and Marano 1994). Particularly for youth aged fifteen to twenty-four years, motor vehicle accidents account for 75 percent of these unintentional injuries, with a rate of 28 per 100,000, the highest among all the age-defined populations. Approximately half these deaths for this age group involve drivers who are intoxicated with alcohol (although two other people groups, aged twenty-five to forty-four and those over age sixty-five, account for the majority of the cases overall) (CDC 1993b). In addition, 30 percent of fifteen- to twenty-year-olds and 50 percent of twenty-one- to twenty-four-year-olds who are killed in motor-vehicle accidents as pedestrians are intoxicated (CDC 1994a). These data reflect the effect of alcohol on attention, perception, vision, judgment, and motor control.

As an example of risk-taking behaviors with untoward health outcomes, 20 percent of high school students nationally reported rarely or never using safety belts when riding in a motor vehicle. These data emerge from the CDC's YRBSS, which surveys high school students in ninth- through twelfth-grades nationwide (Kann et al. 1995). This is worrisome, because surveys of injured motor vehicle occupants show that persons not wearing safety belts had more serious injuries, involving permanent disability and death (Nelson et al. 1993).

For young persons who survive motor vehicle accidents, injuries might involve abrasions, lacerations, and simple bone fractures that can be largely attended to in an emergency room setting. More significant injuries may involve hospitalization for intravenous antibiotics (for deeper infections), for surgical correction of more complex fractures, for skin grafting, and for other organ-related injuries. More than half of all acute spinal cord injuries are related to motor vehicle accidents (Kraus 1985). Spinal cord injuries involving paralysis often result in significant continued morbidity and even mortality, related to skin breakdown, pulmonary infections, and bladder and kidney dysfunction.

Falls and athletic activities, specifically diving and gymnastics, account for the remainder of the 10,000 to 20,000 cases yearly of acute spinal cord injuries (SCIs), and predominantly involve males aged fifteen to twenty-five years (Kraus 1985). Case reports of SCIs suggest that the majority occur in natural bodies of water, and the remainder in swimming pools. Diving-related SCIs are the best described of these injuries given the intense medical interventions required: the majority result in injuries between cervical levels four and six, affecting muscles that control breathing, as well as those that control function of the trunk and extremities (CDC 1988).

Finally, 25 percent of all serious burn injuries are work-related. This aspect of unintentional injury is particularly germane to adolescents and young adults, since restaurant-related burns represent the major source of burns, and restaurants, especially fast-food restaurants, represent a major source of part-time and full-time employment for young persons in both urban and suburban areas. Indeed, approximately 10 percent of all work-related thermal burns occur among persons aged sixteen to nineteen years (CDC 1993c).

Intentional Injuries (Nonsuicide-Related)

Homicide is the second leading cause of death among fifteen-to twenty-four-year-olds, with a rate of 22 per 100,000. However, for African-American males in this age group, homicide leaps into first place, with a rate of 154 per 100,000 (Kochanek and Hudson 1994). Equally alarming is that, in contrast to the progress made with unintentional injuries, there was a 7 percent increase in homicide rates for this age group between 1979 and 1988 (CDC 1993a).

The overwhelming majority of homicide deaths for this age group involve firearms, and it is estimated that by the year 2003 firearm-related deaths may become the leading cause of injury-related death, surpassing motor vehicle accidents (CDC 1994b). For all age groups, having a gun in a household is associated with a threefold increase in the risk of homicide at home (Kellerman et al. 1993). Approximately one-fourth of high school students reported having carried a gun, a knife, or a club within thirty days of participating in the YRBSS, a third of these specifically reporting gun possession. More than 40 percent reported being in a physical fight within the previous twelve months, and 10 percent sustained injuries serious enough to be treated by a doctor or a nurse (Kann et al. 1995).

A disturbing national trend has been the increase in youth gang membership. Although a discussion about the factors related to this phenomenon – such as adolescent developmental issues, social alienation, poverty, and drug trafficking – is outside the scope of this chapter, this phenomenon has particular relevance to the health of youth because the majority of homicide deaths in urban centers are gang-related. Moreover, the majority of victims of gang violence are young persons. An analysis of the epidemic of gang violence in Los Angeles showed that 43 percent of homicides were gang-related in 1994. Nearly 95 percent of these involved firearms, and 25 percent occurred during drive-by shootings. The peak, or modal, age of the victims was eighteen years; 35 percent of the victims were between ages fifteen and nineteen years. Also notable was the fact that one-third of the victims were not even gang members (Hutson et al. 1995).

Mental Health

The most salient mental health issues for adolescents and young adults are depression, suicide, and eating disorders. This chapter will not discuss schizophrenia, conduct disorders, or psychosomatic illnesses, since they represent less prevalent or less significant morbidity.

Depression and Suicide

Estimates of the prevalence of depression among adolescents and young adults range from 1 percent to 50 percent (Hodgman 1990). Different population samples and different case definitions account for this wide range. A recent survey of inner-city adolescents with no significant concurrent comorbidities being treated at a general health clinic found an overall 30 percent lifetime prevalence for depression, with 13 percent meeting criteria for a current major depressive disorder (Bartlett et al. 1991). Depression may also be more prevalent in populations with other associated morbidities, such as substance use, eating disorders, and chronic illnesses. Effective treatments, outpatient or inpatient, include psychotherapy, anti-depressant medications, and, in severe cases, electroconvulsive therapy.

Suicide is the third-leading cause of death for adolescents and young adults, at a rate of 15 per 100,000 (Kochanek and Hudson 1994). Especially disturbing is the continued upward trend in the suicide-related death rate for young persons, the rate having nearly doubled in the last fifteen years (CDC 1993a). The YRBSS found that during the twelve months preceding the survey, nearly 25 percent of high school students had seriously considered attempting suicide, 20 percent had actually constructed a plan, and 9 percent had attempted suicide one or more times, only a third of these coming to medical attention. The percentage of young women who had attempted suicide was 2.5 times the percentage of young men (Kann and Warren 1995), but males were six times more likely to actually commit suicide. Choice of method for suicide attempts explains these disparate rates. Firearms account for 70 percent of the male suicide deaths and for 55 percent of the female suicide deaths (Kochanek and Hudson 1994). Thus, male adolescents more often choose a method that more likely has a fatal outcome. As with homicide deaths, having a gun at home is associated with a fivefold risk for a suicide death (Kellerman et al. 1993).

Gay and lesbian youth account for almost 30 percent of all completed adolescent suicides (Gibson 1989). Many gay and lesbian youth experience verbal harassment and physical violence, ultimately lessening self-esteem and leading to depression and substance use as an attempt to relieve the sense of isolation and condemnation. In some cases, overt rejection from families leads to homelessness (Remafedi 1990). One study of gay and bisexual adolescent males found that 30 percent had made a suicide attempt; indeed, half of these had made multiple attempts. Attempters, compared to nonattempters, reported a higher incidence of sexual abuse and substance abuse (Remafedi 1991).

Eating Disorders

Eating disorders are varied in nature and degree, but share in common disturbances in body concept and abnormal eating patterns. Anorexia nervosa and bulimia nervosa are two common syndromes – specific criteria are outlined in the *Diagnostic and Statistical Manual of Mental Disorders,* Fourth Edition. Prevalence of these conditions have been estimated at 0.5 percent and 1 to 3 percent of adolescent and young adult women, respectively. Previously thought to be exclusive to middle and upper socioeconomic classes, eating disorders have been documented within all classes and ethnic groups. More recent attention has been given to males, who account for approximately 5 percent of cases (Fisher 1992). Medical complications include malnutrition, dehydration, and electrolyte disorders, all of which affect multiple organ systems such as the heart, kidneys, liver, the endocrine system, teeth, and bones (Golden 1992).

The YRBSS has found that almost half of female high school students and one-fourth of male high school students nationwide felt that they were overweight. More significantly, 60 percent of female students and 24 percent of male students were attempting some form of weight loss (Kann and Warren 1995). Thus, although the prevalence of actual eating disorders is low, a large portion of adolescents have weight concerns and worrisome eating behaviors. The use of diet pills and laxatives among adolescents is also high, though not well documented. Both can cause severe problems such as dehydration, electrolyte abnormalities, and potentially acute cardiac dysfunction.

Reflecting another disturbance in body concept, the YRBSS reported use of anabolic steroids to accelerate and augment body mass development by 1 percent of female high school students and by 3 percent of male high school students, not just athletes (Kann and Warren 1995). The Monitoring the Future Study (MTFS), which has surveyed eighth-, tenth- and twelfth-graders nationwide since 1975, has confirmed these findings, and noted a 3 percent decrease in the perceived harmfulness of steroids in surveys of twelfth graders between 1992 and 1994 (Johnston et al. 1994). Strength-training exercises, injection drug use, and multiple drug use have all been shown to predict anabolic steroid use among adolescents (DuRant, Escobedo, and Heath 1995). Use of steroids carries serious medical consequences such as hepatic and immune dysfunction, neuropsychiatric changes, as well as heart failure (Su et al. 1993). Needle sharing for the purposes of injections obviously carries the risk of infection with Hepatitis B and C and the Human Immunodeficiency Virus (HIV).

Substance Use

Tobacco and Alcohol

Knowledge about the harm of tobacco use has increased in the last few years, as has social disapproval regarding tobacco use. The rates of use for the general population have significantly declined. Nevertheless, 30 percent of students nationwide reported smoking cigarettes at least once within the thirty days preceding the YRBSS, and 24 percent reported daily cigarette use. There were no significant gender differences, although the percentage of white students who smoked daily was three times and one and a half times that of African-American and Hispanic students, respectively. Although the cardiovascular, pulmonary, and neoplastic effects of tobacco use are not seen during the adolescent and young adult years, these are significant causes of morbidity and mortality for the adult population. Approximately 90 percent of all American adults who have ever smoked daily tried their first cigarette prior to age twenty (USDHHS 1994). Recent nationwide prevention efforts are addressing the vulnerability of youth to media advertising and promotional messages (CDC 1995a).

There are upward trends in both customary drinking and in binge or episodic alcohol drinking among high school youth nationwide. The YRBSS found that 30 percent of students had had five or more drinks on at least one occasion within the last thirty days, and the MTFS found that 15 percent of eighth-graders, 24 percent of tenth-graders and 28 percent of twelfth-graders had five or more drinks within the last fourteen days.

Illicit Substances

Marijuana. The YRBSS found that, overall, 33 percent of high school youth had ever used marijuana, whereas 18 percent had smoked at least once in the preceding month. The MTFS has also noted that these figures reflect increases in use between 1991 and 1994. In the preceding twelve months, eighth-graders had doubled their marijuana use, tenth-graders had increased their use by two-thirds and twelfth-graders by two-fifths. The perception that smoking marijuana occasionally was harmful decreased by 7.5 percent.

Cocaine. Cocaine use among high school youth varies from 1 percent prevalence for use in the preceding thirty days to 3 percent prevalence for use in the preceding year, showing insignificant changes from previous years (Johnston et al. 1994; Kann and Warren 1995). Although overall disapproval of cocaine use remains close to 90 percent for high school students, eighth- and tenth-graders showed small but statistically significant decreases in how harmful they perceived cocaine use to be and in their disapproval of use (Johnston et al. 1994). The MTFS investigators have been quick to point out that declines in perceived risk precede declines in perceived peer norms and, ultimately, foretell rises in actual use.

Heroin, Hallucinogens, Sedatives, and Inhalants. The lifetime prevalence of heroin use through injection routes was 1.4 percent in the YRBSS. The MTFS reported a thirty-day prevalence of less than 0.5 percent, but found that three times that number had used other opiates not prescribed by a physician. Hallucinogens (such as LSD and Ecstacy) and stimulants (such as crystal methamphetamines or Ice) show lifetime prevalences of 11 percent and 15 percent, respectively, and thirty-day prevalences of 3 percent and 4 percent, respectively, both with gradual upward trends in the last few years (Johnston et al. 1994). Sedatives (such as barbiturates and methaqualone) and inhalants (such as amyl and butyl nitrites, glue, and other nonillicit inhalants) show lifetime prevalences of 7 percent and 18 percent, respectively, and thirty-day prevalences of 3 percent and 2 percent, respectively, also with recent gradual upward trends (Johnston et al. 1994). Notably, the lifetime prevalence for inhalants was highest among eighth graders, of the three grades surveyed, suggesting that a pattern of using substances to get high can start in early adolescence (Johnston et al. 1994).

In addition to the adverse health outcomes incurred through unintentional injuries and violence, substance use, through both injection and noninjection routes, is associated with other behaviors that are linked to additional adverse outcomes. For example, alcohol, marijuana, and crack cocaine may impair judgment and ability to safely negotiate sexual activity, thus putting youth at risk for exposure to sexually transmitted diseases (STDs). Adolescents and young adults who smoke crack cocaine may often exchange sex for drugs (Futterman et al. 1993). Several studies of crack users have shown an increased risk for infection with HIV, syphilis, gonorrhea, and herpes simplex virus, as these sexual contacts more likely involve unprotected vaginal and anal intercourse with multiple partners (Edlin et al. 1994).

Sharing unclean needles for either intravenous or subcutaneous heroin or cocaine use may cause bacterial skin infections and heart valve infections, often requiring regimens of oral and intravenous antibiotics for up to six weeks. Contaminants in injected heroin can cause damage to the lungs and kidneys. Youth also risks exposure to HIV, Hepatitis B and C, and syphilis, if their drug-using partners are infected. In addition, alcohol, cocaine, and heroin can cause direct injury to many organ systems, such as the heart and brain. Also, by affecting intention and intellect, substance use may interfere with school performance and interpersonal relationships (Brown and Coupey 1993).

Because treatments for substance abuse have limited effectiveness, prevention efforts are critical (although major controversies persist over the choice and timing of interventions) (O'Malley, Johnston, and Bachman 1995). Viewing substance abuse as a chronic disease, experts are increasingly utilizing harm-reduction models, which focus on decreasing the use of contaminated needles or syringes and changing the route of use. The goal is to minimize the adverse effects of substance use while assisting users in understanding ancillary issues that facilitate substance use (Des Jerlais et al. 1995). Harm reduction appears to work best for opiate use and least for crack cocaine. Pharmacologic applications include methadone treatment and short-term use of antidepressants and sedatives. Short-term detoxification programs and longer-term residential treatment programs have only recently begun to extend their services to adolescents and young adults (Brown and Coupey 1993).

Sexual Activity And Outcomes

Developing an understanding of oneself as a sexual person is an important developmental task of adolescence that requires incorporating fantasies, attractions, and behaviors. With limited access to information and resources, adolescents often lack the skills to negotiate this process safely. Those adolescents who do engage in sexual intercourse are, therefore, at high risk for such negative health outcomes as STDs and pregnancy.

Sexual Behaviors

The most recent YRBSS has shown that, overall, 53 percent of high school students have experienced sexual intercourse (38 percent of the ninth-graders, increasing to 68 percent of the twelfth-graders). There was virtually no gender difference, except for ninth-graders, where 44 percent of the males versus 32 percent of the females were sexually experienced. One-fourth of the ninth-graders and half of the twelfth-graders had had sexual intercourse within the preceding three months. More importantly, in terms of risk for STDs and pregnancy, less than 50 percent of the female students who were currently sexually active reported that their male partner used condoms during the last sexual intercourse, and only a little more than 20 percent reported using oral contraceptive pills (OCPs). Less than 60 percent of the male students who were currently sexually active reported condom use at last sexual intercourse, and only 14 percent reported that their female partners used OCPs (Kann et al. 1995). One-fourth of the sexually experienced female patients receiving care at a general adolescent health program acknowledged having had anal intercourse in addition to vaginal intercourse, but only 11 percent of those having anal intercourse reported always using condoms and 74 percent never used condoms. Nearly half practiced oral intercourse (Jaffe et al. 1988). In one study comparing HIV-positive and HIV-negative adolescents, seropositive females were more likely to have engaged in anal and oral intercourse (Hein et al. 1995).

Homosexuality. Estimates of homosexual activity among youth are rarely attempted and are often unreliable because of the sensitive, often stigmatizing nature of homosexual activity within various cultures; as a result, studies more likely underestimate prevalence. One study of sexual orientation among secondary school youth in Minnesota found that 88 percent described themselves as predominantly heterosexual and 1 percent described themselves as bisexual or predominantly homosexual. Significantly, 11 percent felt unsure about their sexual orientation. In contrast to behavior, nearly 5 percent reported having homosexual attractions and 3 percent reported having homosexual fantasies (Remafedi et al. 1992). The National Survey of Adolescents in 1988 and 1991 found that 1 to 2 percent of young men reported ever masturbating with or having oral or anal intercourse with another male, and 1 percent reported ever having receptive anogenital intercourse (Ku, Sonenstein, and Pleck 1993).

Of the forty-one gay men less than twenty-two years entering the Multicenter AIDS Cohort Study (MACS) between 1988 and 1992 who reported anal receptive intercourse in the prior six months, only 30 percent reported using condoms all of the time (Silvestre et al. 1993). Indeed, unprotected male-to-male sexual contact continues to be the leading primary exposure for HIV-infected young men (CDC 1995b). Lesbian, gay, and bisexual youth, compared to heterosexual youth, often have less of a social network through which to explore their sexual feelings, and, therefore, may be more likely to participate in high-risk sexual activity. Those not yet identifying with a larger gay community may not be aware of safe sex information provided by the adult gay community (Paroski 1987).

Opposite-sex experiences are also common for lesbian and gay youth, and, if unprotected, add further to the risk for HIV, STDs, and pregnancy. These experiences are often part of self-discovery, but also serve to conceal their homosexuality from themselves and from their peers, family, and larger community (Paroski 1987). More than half a cohort of sixty gay and bisexual males had engaged in vaginal intercourse (Rotheram-Borus et al. 1992). Seventy-five percent of the cohort of lesbian and bisexual female youth in New York City reported having had penile–vaginal intercourse, with a median number of four lifetime partners. Moreover, penile–vaginal sex was initiated one year before initiation of oral sex with females (Hunter, Rosario, and Rotheram-Borus 1993).

Sexual Abuse. Sexual abuse is estimated to occur in one-fourth of girls and one-tenth of boys before the age of sixteen (Jenny 1990). Sexual victimization may not only put a youth at immediate risk for STD infection but also for future risk by affecting their psychosocial development with regard to sexual self-esteem, self-concept, and overall adaptive functioning. Ultimately, abuse may affect their ability to negotiate consensual sexual experience safely. A cohort of pregnant, sexually victimized female youth, compared with a nonabused control, initiated sexual activity one year earlier, were less likely to use contraception at first intercourse, and were more likely to have used drugs or alcohol during their first intercourse (Boyer and Fine 1992). One study comparing HIV-positive and HIV-negative youth found that the HIV-positive youth were more likely to have been sexually abused

(Hein et al. 1995). More than half of females and about a quarter of males in a cohort of HIV-positive youth in New York City reported a history of sexual abuse as minors (Futterman et al. 1993).

Sexually Transmitted Diseases

STDs share a common mode of transmission – namely, unprotected sexual inter-course with an infected person – and, therefore, serve as an indicator of risk for other STDs. There is also increasing evidence that certain STDs, especially those causing genital ulcers, facilitate HIV infection (Wasserheit 1992). This is espe-cially a problem for sexually experienced youth for whom the rates of certain STDs, including gonorrhea, chlamydia, and pelvic inflammatory disease (PID), are highest compared to other age groups (Bell and Hein 1984; Aral et al. 1988; Cates 1991; Hillis et al. 1993; Richert et al. 1993).

Young adolescent females may be at higher risk for infection with gonorrhea and chlamydia, and possibly HIV, because of the presence of endocervical columnar cells on the immature vaginal cervix, which have not yet receded during the normative course of puberty and are more susceptible to infection. Also, younger women may be more susceptible to PID during the first two years after the onset of menarche as a result of thinner, and therefore, more permeable, cervical mucus, which results from inadequate progesterone levels due to frequent anovulatory menstrual cycles (Bell and Hein 1984). One study estimated an incidence of one to eight for fifteen-year-olds, compared to one to eighty for twenty-four-year-olds (Westrom 1980).

Bacterial infections, such as gonorrhea, chlamydia, and chancroid, can be treated with short-duration oral antibiotic regimens. All stages of syphilis require long-act-ing injected antibiotics; advanced stages often require consecutive injections or even daily intravenous doses. Hospitalization for at least seven days is recom-mended for all adolescent women with PID to ensure completion of therapy, in an attempt to limit future complications, such as infertility and ectopic pregnancy (CDC 1993d).

Genital infection with human papillomavirus (HPV) is the most prevalent STD in women under twenty-five years of age (deVilliers 1987). Varying strains of HPV can cause genital warts and dysplastic, or potentially precancerous, changes on the cervix (Lungu et al. 1992). Yearly visual inspection of the vulva, vaginal mucosa, and cervix and a yearly cervical Pap smear is recommended for all women after age nineteen and all adolescent women who have had sexual intercourse. If cervical cytology is abnormal, colposcopy is needed to improve visualization and to guide biopsies.

Approximately 9 percent of all cases of Hepatitis B infection in the United States occur in people aged fifteen to nineteen years (CDC 1989). Due to the high risk for chronic infection, for which no cure exists, the American Academy of Pediatrics currently recommends Hepatitis B vaccination for all adolescents, with a series of three injections over a six-month period.

Two other forms of viral hepatitis are of concern for adolescents. Hepatitis A, a severe but limited illness, is mainly contracted by an oral-fecal route, which includes unprotected oral–anal intercourse with an infected partner and consumption of infected food or water. Hepatitis C, a chronic infection like Hepatitis B, has a peak incidence among fifteen- to forty-four-year olds. Although parenteral exposure through needle-sharing for injection drug use and transfusion of blood products is the major risk for Hepatitis C infection, sexual transmission is also possible (Osmond et al. 1993). A vaccine is now available for persons at risk for Hepatitis A, but no vaccine exists for Hepatitis C (Westblom et al. 1994).

Acquired Immune Deficiency Syndrome (AIDS) is the sixth leading cause of death for persons aged fifteen to twenty-four years, with a rate of 1.6 per 100,000 (Kochanek and Hudson 1994). Young women are disproportionately affected, compared to older women. And, young persons of color are represented among the nation's AIDS cases two to three times their representation in the general adolescent population (CDC 1995b). Data on numbers of youth infected with HIV is not known, because only half of the states in the U.S. require HIV, as opposed to AIDS, case reporting. Seroprevalence studies have provided some helpful data to estimate the larger HIV epidemic among youth. The U.S. Job Corps, a federally funded training program for disadvantaged youth aged sixteen to twenty-one years, noted a seroprevalence of 3 per 1,000 youth tested on entry into the Job Corps (St. Louis et al. 1991). The National Cancer Institute in the United States used *back-calculation* methods linking data on the incidence of AIDS to the incidence of HIV infection and noted that one in four persons newly infected with HIV between 1987 and 1991 in the United States was under twenty-two years of age (Rosenberg et al. 1992).

The course of HIV infection among youth is presumed to be similar to that seen in most adults, in which approximately 50 percent of persons will develop AIDS ten years from the time of initial infection (Rutherford et al. 1990). Although making up a small proportion of HIV-infected adolescents, long-term survivors of congenital infection are now entering adolescence, with varying clinical patterns (Grubman et al. 1995). Studies of HIV-positive youth in care indicate that approximately half show some degree of immunodysfunction at the time of diagnosis (Futterman et al. 1993), suggesting that many HIV-infected youth are losing out on the benefits of early intervention for HIV.

New hope for adequately controlling, although not yet curing, HIV infection has arisen, because of newly available medications and improved understanding of how the virus causes disease. New consensus guidelines exist on the most appropriate time to initiate antiretroviral therapy and in which combinations (Carpenter et al. 1996). Although all currently available antiretroviral medications are approved for use in adolescents, these medications require daily use, and often consist of ten or more pills, presenting great challenges to good adherence. Medications used for primary and secondary prevention of opportunistic infections (OI), such as pneumocystis carinii pneumonia (PCP) and disseminated mycobacterium avium intracellularae (dMAC), have significantly decreased both morbidity and mortality for persons with advanced HIV infection, but also present challenges for the young patient.

Pregnancy

Birth rates for young women aged fifteen to nineteen years have increased gradually over the last ten years, with a rate of 62 births per 1000 women in 1991, compared to 115 per 1000 for women aged twenty to twenty-four and twenty-five to twenty-nine years. The abortion ratio, defined as the number of abortions per 1000 abortions and live births, was 403 for fifteen- to nineteen-year-olds, compared to 328 and 224 for women aged twenty to twenty-four and twenty-five to twenty-nine years, respectively. The birth rates and abortion ratios for African-American adolescents have consistently been twice that of white adolescents, although these figures do not control for socioeconomic variables. Births in which the father was between fifteen and nineteen years occurred at a rate of 25 per 1000 men, compared to 88 per 1000 men aged twenty to twenty-four years and 115 per 1000 men aged twenty-five to twenty-nine years (National Center for Health Statistics 1993). In addition to limited access to family planning services and reproductive health information, some have also suggested, as a cause for these high rates of pregnancy, young women's aspirations toward a higher social status within poorer urban and rural communities where young women already have limited social and economic opportunities (Klerman 1993).

Adolescent and young adult women often sustain significant obstetric problems, such as poor weight gain, hypertension and puerperal complications. Deaths due to complications of pregnancy, childbirth, and delivery occur at a rate of 0.6 per 100,000 for women aged fifteen to twenty-four years, ranking eighth for the age group and surpassing other age groups (Kochanek and Hudson 1994). These poor outcomes are no longer thought to be intrinsic to younger women, since several studies have recently shown that they relate to late prenatal care, poor nutrition, and poor preparation for and support during delivery (Stevens-Simon and White 1991; Klerman 1993). Longer-term health outcomes may be predicted by the reality that pregnancy and parenting often hinder young women from completing their education, thus limiting their access to gainful employment and even forcing them to depend on public assistance (Blum 1991).

Choices for contraceptive methods include both barrier methods (e.g., condoms), spermicides (e.g., foam and sponges) and synthetic hormones to prevent ovulation (e.g., combined estrogen-progesterone pills), and Depoprovera and Norplant. Depoprovera is injected intramuscularly every twelve weeks, whereas Norplant capsules are placed subcutaneously for an anticipated period of up to five years and must be removed by a trained health care provider (*The Medical Letter* 1995).

Malignancies

Malignancies rank fourth as a cause of death for persons aged fifteen to twenty-four years, accounting for 5 percent of the total deaths. Leukemias and other hematologic and lymphatic malignancies account for approximately 44 percent of the total. Nevertheless, the overall rate has decreased over the last decade, from 6 per 100,000 in 1979 to 5 per 100,000 in 1992 (Kochanek and Hudson 1994). The cancers with the leading incidence (rate per 100,000) for fifteen- to nineteen-year-olds are Hodgkin's Disease (3.8), leukemia (2.1), and brain and other central nervous system tumors (2.0). The incidence of testicular cancer for males in the age group is 2.6; the incidence of ovarian cancer for females is 2.3. Rates for breast, cervical, and uterine malignancies in this age group are less than 0.3 (Ries et al. 1994).

Treatment protocols for leukemia are very rigorous, involving several phases of chemotherapy, involving both oral and intravenous medications and lasting as long as one to two years. Cranial radiation may be necessary for some patients with or at risk for central nervous system involvement. Allogeneic bone marrow transplantation is now more readily available, although with toxic effects and high mortality, and is reserved for poor responders (Pui 1995).

Surgical resection remains a mainstay of treatment for most brain tumors. Radiation and chemotherapy are also important components of treatment (Pollack 1994). In addition to its role as an adjuvant therapy, radiation therapy has assumed a more prominent role both as a primary therapy in surgically unresectable tumors and as a palliative therapy for malignancies of the central nervous system and other organs (Lichter and Lawrence 1995).

Important advances have also been made in the treatment of gynecologic malignancies, especially for young women. Use of less radical surgery has helped to avoid loss of reproductive function. And, improvements in chemotherapeutic regimens has allowed for minimization of radiation therapy that might cause ovarian failure (Hicks, Jenkins, and Parham 1995).

Use of indwelling catheters for administration of intravenous medications is common, but carry the risks of serious, often life-threatening, bacterial, and fungal infections (Pizzo et al. 1991a; 1991b). With all malignancies, but more commonly with the leukemias and with brain tumors, possible late sequelae include decrease in heart function, hormonal deficiencies (e.g., diabetes mellitus), and even second malignancies (Pollack 1994; Pui 1995).

Tuberculosis

Public health efforts emphasizing early diagnosis and treatment of tuberculosis infection and directly observed therapy for challenging treatment regimens finally bore fruitful results in 1993 with a decline in new cases from the previous year (CDC 1994c). However, for youth aged fifteen to nineteen years, the rate of TB infection in New York City increased from 12 per 100,000 to 14 per 100,000, and nearly doubled for youth aged ten to fourteen years (from 5 per 100,000 to 9 per 100,000) (New York City Department of Health 1992, 1994). Several reasons may account for this phenomenon, including improper screening practices, exposure to infected adults as well as homelessness. Moreover, adolescence is known to be a time of increased likelihood of reactivating TB infection, presumably due to hormonal changes (Hoffman, Kelly, and Futterman 1996).

Patients with TB infection without active disease are given preventive therapy with one or more drugs, for six to twelve months, depending on the possibility of exposure to multi-drug-resistant TB and on their immune status (CDC 1992). Patients with active disease require six to nine months of treatment, according to immune status, and initiate four or more drugs until drug sensitivity patterns of the organism are known. Some patients must complete the entire course with multiple drugs (CDC 1993e).

Directly observed therapy (DOT) programs are more readily available and provide a means to supervise, as well as educate and motivate, the adolescent during the long treatment (Hoffman, Kelly, and Futterman 1996).

Chronic Illnesses

The effect of chronic illness on adolescents and young adults has grown as medical advances have brought about significant decreases in the mortality during childhood. In fact, the average expenditures for health services for children with chronic conditions are two to three times those for the average child (Neff and Anderson 1995). Moreover, a new focus is the provision of transitional services for these adolescents as they enter adulthood and move to adult health care systems (Blum et al. 1993). Three chronic conditions (not including HIV Infection) are included among the top ten leading causes of death for fifteen- to twenty-four-year-olds: diseases of the heart, with a rate of 2.7 per 100,000; congenital anomalies, 1.2 per 100,000; and chronic obstructive pulmonary diseases, 0.5 per 100,000. Deaths due to diabetes mellitus occurred at a rate of 0.4 per 100,000 (Kochanek and Hudson 1994).

Overall, defining chronic conditions as those of greater than three months' duration, the prevalence of chronic conditions among a non-institutionalized sample of adolescents aged ten to seventeen years was 32 percent. One-third of these had multiple conditions. Overall, 16 percent of adolescents with chronic conditions reported some limitation in their ability to attend school and in the types of in-school and extracurricular activities in which they could participate. The most prevalent conditions, in decreasing order, were asthma, chronic severe headaches, heart disease, arthritis, seizure disorders, diabetes mellitus, and sickle cell disease. All of these conditions caused a loss of one-half to five school days yearly (Newacheck, McManus, and Fox 1991).

Chronic diseases affect quality of life and often interfere with growth and pubertal development, especially in the case of sickle cell disease (Platt et al. 1984).

Chronic diseases often are associated with a greater prevalence of behavioral problems, such as anxiety, depression, social withdrawal, and peer conflict (Newacheck et al. 1991).

Sickle Cell Anemia. Adolescents with sickle cell disease, for example, suffer with acute and chronic pain due to bone marrow ischemia (decreased blood flow) and necrosis. Acute painful episodes are generally referred to as *sickle cell crises.* In one longitudinal study looking at nearly 4,000 children and adults with sickle cell disease, 40 percent of the ten- to nineteen-year-olds reported one painful episode a year, 20 percent reported one to three episodes a year, and 6 percent had three to six episodes a year. Furthermore, although pain rate did not correlate with mortality for patients aged ten to nineteen years, patients over twenty years with three or more painful episodes yearly had twice the mortality of those who had less than three (Platt et al. 1991). Treatment for pain consists of fluid hydration and nonsteroidal and narcotic analgesics (administered orally or parenterally), and, often, blood transfusions. New innovations in pain control, such as patient-controlled analgesia, minimize fluctuations in analgesic effect. Another benefit is eliminating the often underestimated anxiety incurred while awaiting the next dose of pain medication. Hydroxyurea, an oral medication, has been shown to ameliorate the course of sickle cell disease, such as decreasing the number of painful episodes and limiting other complications, especially in patients with three or more painful episodes a year (Charache et al. 1995). Future prospects for therapy for this hereditary disease include allogeneic bone marrow transplants and direct gene transfer (Walters et al. 1996).

Hemophilia. Hemophilia is a bleeding disorder inherited via the X-chromosome, the incidence of severe disease being 1 in 10,000 males (Conway and Hilgartner 1994). The disease is characterized by a deficiency in Coagulation Factors VIII or IX. This leads to a propensity for painful, often destructive, bleeding into joints and bleeding into soft tissues. Ninety percent of patients are identified by the age of one (Conway and Hilgartner 1994). Treatments to mitigate bleeding complications include infusion of Factor concentrates and recombinant preparations, as well as an intranasally administered synthetic hormone called desmopressin, or DDAVP, for milder forms of the disease (Lusher and Warrier 1991). Prior to 1985, many patients with hemophilia were infected with HIV through contaminated Factor concentrates. Currently, patients with hemophilia account for 43 percent of AIDS cases diagnosed among thirteen- to nineteen-year-olds, although only 4 percent of AIDS cases diagnosed among twenty- to twenty-four-year-olds (CDC 1995b).

Cystic Fibrosis. Cystic fibrosis is the most common life-shortening disease among white persons in the United States; it is inherited in an autosomal recessive pattern. With a median life expectancy of twenty-eight years, the disease is characterized by the production of abnormally thick mucus, which causes obstruction and ultimate destruction of ducts and glands in various organs, such as the lungs, the liver, and the pancreas. Patients are at risk for severe pneumonias, which account for the majority of deaths in this disease. Advances in the use of rotating antibiotic regimens and the use of pancreatic enzyme replacement have significantly improved the lives of these patients. An important outcome of these advances is that reproductive health decisions are a reality for young women with cystic fibrosis. One study of women with cystic fibrosis, with a median age of twenty-two years, found that one-third were taking oral contraceptive pills and half indicated that they were interested in becoming pregnant sometime in the future. One-fifth had actually tried to conceive, with a conception rate of 67 percent (Sawyer, Phelan, and Bowes 1995). Recent advances in the understanding of genetic defects will hopefully impact greatly on the morbidity and mortality from this disease (Ramsey and Boat 1994).

End-Stage Renal Disease. End-stage renal disease (ESRD) currently results in 0.2 deaths per 100,000 yearly (Kochanek and Hudson 1994). Because of significant advances in transplant technology and increased public awareness of the need for organ donors, more than a fourth of all children and adolescents with ESRD now move directly to renal transplantation, bypassing the process of dialysis (Tejani et al. 1995a). Since 1987, the North American Pediatric Renal Transplant Cooperative Study (NAPRTCS) has followed 3,438 pediatric transplant recipients up to age seventeen years (at enrollment) in the United States and Canada. The report of the first five years' experience showed a dramatic rise in the two-year survival of the kidney transplant itself, from approximately 60 percent to 80 percent. Data have shown that, although the annual rate of rejection does not differ significantly across the age groups, the recipients younger than six years have significantly poorer outcomes from the rejection episodes with an increased risk of failure (Tejani et al. 1995). The average number of transplant rejections, however, tended to be greater for adolescents thirteen years and older. We propose that the adolescents may have had greater difficulty with adherence to the regimens of immunosuppressive medications that are used to prevent the body's immune system from rejecting the transplant (Tejani et al. 1995b). The medications, often consisting of several pills daily, cause side effects such as fever, rash, low blood pressure, and headaches. An unintended, although anticipated, effect is the recipient's new vulnerability to life-threatening infections, for which preventive medications regimens are prescribed.

Diabetes Mellitus. Diabetes mellitus is a group of disorders characterized either by a deficiency of insulin or a lack of effectiveness of existing insulin. Due to abnormal carbohydrate and fat metabolism, these disorders have both short-term consequences, such as extreme fluctuations in blood sugar levels and potentially fatal levels of acid in the blood, and long-term consequences, such as kidney, eye and heart disease, and problems with nerve sensation and wound healing. In addition to careful dietary restrictions, medication regimens to manage diabetes mellitus pose great challenges to affected adolescents. Noninsulin-dependent diabetes responds to oral hyperglycemic pills, which are intended to stimulate the production of insulin, whereas insulin-dependent diabetes requires at least twice-daily insulin injections with blood or urine sampling to monitor the immediate effect of the medication. The results of a longitudinal study conducted by the Diabetes Control and Complications Trial Research Group, in which thirteen- to eighteen-year-olds represented approximately 15 percent of the population studied, found that a more intensive regimen of three or more daily insulin rejections, compared to the conventional therapy, significantly reduced the risk, as well as the progression, of end-organ complications (DCCT 1993).

Disabilities. Youth with chronic mental and physical disabilities also have an increased dependence on both the health care and social-service systems. Data about disabilities gathered through the Survey of Income and Program Participation (SIPP) looked specifically at functional limitations among noninstitutionalized youth. Approximately 5 percent of the fifteen- to seventeen-year-olds interviewed were limited in their ability to do school work and 3 percent had some form of autism, cerebral palsy, or mental retardation (CDC 1995c). Within the previously mentioned sample of adolescents aged ten to seventeen years, the following specific conditions were noted: musculoskeletal impairments, 3 percent; deafness or some hearing loss, blindness or some visual impairment, and speech defects, 1.5 percent each; and cerebral palsy, 0.2 percent. These adolescents had an average yearly loss of 4.4 school days and spent an average of 3.4 days in bed due to the respective chronic condition (Newacheck, McManus, and Fox 1991).

Special Populations

Foster Care

More than half a million American youth are in foster care. Acknowledging multiple reasons for placement, about 50 percent are placed for reasons of parental neglect, 30 percent for parental incapacity, 25 percent each for physical abuse and abandonment, 15 percent for disruptive behavior on the part of the child, and 6 percent for sexual abuse (Chernoff et al. 1994). Between 1981 and 1996, AIDS alone has orphaned 18,000 children, 7,000 adolescents aged thirteen to seventeen years and 3,000 young adults aged eighteen to twenty-one years. By the end of 2001, those numbers are expected to have doubled (Michaels and Levine 1996).

The majority of studies on the health of youth in foster care either focus on young children or do not separate adolescents from young children. Also, most studies examine health issues only at the time of entry into foster care and not longitudinally. The few surveys of adolescents in the foster care system that exist provide some helpful information, nevertheless, highlighting the prevalence of chronic illnesses, mental health problems, and adverse outcomes of unprotected sexual activity. One study of youth entering kinship foster care in Baltimore found that less than 40 percent of the adolescents, aged twelve to nineteen years, were adequately immunized, and only 1 percent had received adequate health supervision (defined as at least two-thirds of the recommended visits during the previous three years). Less than half had received adequate dental care, and one-fifth had dental caries or other dental problems requiring urgent treatment. Chronic problems were also noted, including asthma in almost 10 percent, and obesity in 20 percent of the youth (Dubowitz et al. 1992).

Looking at mental health issues, one study of adolescents entering foster care, also in Baltimore, found that three-quarters of the adolescents required urgent mental health referrals (Chernoff et al. 1994). An analysis of Medicaid-reimbursed health care services in California found that the utilization rate for outpatient mental health services by adolescents in foster care was twenty-eight times that of the adolescents who were also eligible for these services but not in foster care (Halfon, Berkowitz, and Linnea 1992).

Among a group of adolescents in Columbus, Ohio, who had been placed in foster care because of abuse and neglect, medical providers found at the time of preentry assessments that 6 percent of the females had cervicitis from gonorrhea or chlamydia, or vaginitis from trichomonas. As an indication of exposure to HPV, abnormal Pap smears were found for 7 percent of the females and 1 percent had genital warts. Seven percent were pregnant (Flaherty and Weiss 1990). In the study of adolescents entering Baltimore's foster care system, one quarter required gynecologic or family planning services (Chernoff et al. 1994). Although no data currently exist on HIV seroprevalence among youth in foster care, other markers of risk have been documented. As a result, many states, such as New York, have initiated mandatory HIV risk assessment for children and adolescents at entry to foster care, with appropriate referral for HIV counseling and testing.

Homeless Youth

As many as one and half million adolescents are living on and off the streets in this country. Many are runaways, having left home without parental consent; others have been forced out of their homes by parental rejection (throwaways), as in the case of gay and lesbian youth. Others have become homeless when they were orphaned or when their families lost their homes as a result of poverty (Luna and Rotheram-Borus 1992). Surveys have shown a significant prevalence of mental illnesses, with nearly half reporting psychiatric care and substance use (Yates et al. 1988; Deisher and Rogers 1991; Kruks 1991).

Often forced to survive on the streets by engaging in survival sex, exchanging sex for food, clothing, shelter and protection, homeless youth are at increased risk for various STDs (Deisher and Rogers 1991; Kruks 1991), as well as for pregnancy (Yordan and Yordan 1995). One study of homeless and runaway youth at a shelter in New York City found an HIV seroprevalence of 5 per 1000. HIV seropositivity was associated with injection drug use, prostitution, same-sex activity among males and previous STDs (Stricof et al. 1991). Homeless youth are also at increased risk for infection with tuberculosis due to increased exposure both on the streets and in shelters and single-room occupancy hotels (Brudney and Dobkin 1991). Other morbidities include frostbite and hypothermia from exposure to cold, physical trauma, and sexual assault (Yates et al. 1988; Deisher and Rogers 1991).

Youth In Detention

According to the Children in Custody Census, approximately 58,000 juveniles are in U.S. public facilities, for an overall rate of 221 juveniles in custody per 100,000 juveniles (Moone 1993a). Approximately 36,000 juveniles are in privately run facilities such as halfway houses and training centers; half of these youths are thirteen to fifteen years old (Moone 1993b). Annually, another 300,000 youth who are tried in juvenile court for crimes that would result in criminal prosecution if committed by an adult may be held in secure detention facilities prior to adjudication, for an average of fifteen days (Butts 1994).

Mental health issues are also highly prevalent within this subpopulation. Reports from detention facilities around the country indicate that more than half the youth experience depression, one-fifth are actually suicidal or self-violent, one-third exhibit disruptive behaviors, and one-fifth have thought disorders (Snyder and Sickmund 1995).

Youth in detention may be at increased risk for certain infectious diseases. Although no information exists on the specific incidence of tuberculosis among incarcerated youth, adult studies have shown an increased risk for pulmonary tuberculosis, with one year of jail time doubling the odds (Bellin et al. 1993). More suggestive of risk for exposure is the fact that more than half of detained youth are housed in detention centers operating above capacity, and often in undersized rooms (Snyder and Sickmund 1995).

High-risk sexual and substance use behaviors are prevalent among incarcerated youth. Although not necessarily greater than data available on cohorts of noninstitutionalized adolescents, these data still serve as an indication of risk for HIV and other STDs. One study of all detained youth in Virginia found that one-quarter reported never using condoms during sexual activity. One-fifth actually had a current STD, and 22 percent reported a past history of an STD (Canterbury et al. 1995). Also, results of blinded HIV seroprevalence studies in the U.S. between 1990–1992 found a median prevalence of 2 per 1000 among youth less than nineteen years of age in detention centers, similar to the seroprevalence rate among the Job Corps cohort; some facilities reported HIV seroprevalence rates greater than 10 per 1000 (Sweeney et al. 1993). According to administrators of U.S. detention facilities, 15 percent of youth in detention were victims of rape and 15 percent participated in commercial sex exchange (Snyder and Sickmund 1995). One-third of juveniles entering detention centers for less than forty-eight hours tested positive for at least one illicit drug, and a quarter of these tested positive for more than one drug. Approximately 25 percent tested positive for marijuana, 7 percent tested positive for cocaine, and 2 percent tested positive for heroin (Snyder and Sickmund 1995).

Immigrant Youth

Several studies on health issues for immigrant youth exist in the literature but remain limited to issues around infectious disease and risk behaviors. Most studies focus only on Latina women. Furthermore, these studies usually fail to differentiate among countries of origin, characterizing immigrants as a homogeneous group, and, as a possible result, often yield contradictory findings, such as in the area of pregnancy and childbearing.

One such study of Latino high school students in California found that 50 percent of Latino immigrants were sexually experienced, compared to 38 percent of native-born Latinos and 15 percent of native non-Hispanic whites. Only 20 percent of the Latino immigrants reported always using a method of birth control, compared to one-third of native-born Latinos and native non-Hispanic whites (Brindis et al. 1995). Another study that examined the issue of acculturation and sexual behavior controlled for ethnic background by looking only at a group of pregnant women of Mexican-origin followed at one obstetrics clinic. For recently immigrated women aged twelve to eighteen years the mean age of first intercourse was 16.2 years, versus 15.3 for already acculturated women. Notably, three times as many recently immigrated women were married at the time of conception, compared to already acculturated women. Those who had newly immigrated had proportionately fewer premarital births than those whose families had been in the United States for three generations (Reynoso et al. 1993).

One study compared birth rates for Latina women aged fourteen to twenty-one years across different ethnic groups. Whereas young women of Mexican origin had similar birth rates to Puerto Rican women (both greater than that for whites, but less than for African-Americans), the majority of births to women of Mexican origin were in the context of marriage, and the majority of births to Puerto Rican women were not (Darabi and Ortiz 1987).

In terms of health outcomes for pregnancies, the study of young pregnant women of Mexican origin also found that, despite having a later initiation of prenatal care, recently immigrated women had the same number of prenatal visits as acculturated women and no greater incidence of pregnancy-related complications. Three times as many recently immigrated women had cesarean sections, although they were significantly less likely to have infants born with distress. Notably, neither group had any low-birth-weight infants (Reynoso et al. 1993).

In contrast to the recent overall gains in controlling the tuberculosis epidemic in this country, persons newly immigrated to the United States are at greatest risk of infection. Between 1986 and 1994, the annual incidence of tuberculosis among foreign-born persons, most of whom are newly immigrated, increased by 55 percent

(CDC 1995d). One study of school-based tuberculosis screening found that 85 percent of those high school students with tuberculosis were foreign-born (Barry et al. 1990). As such, immigrant youth still figure prominently in the most recent recommendations for tuberculosis screening, which have been drastically pared down to only those at high risk (AAP 1994).

Conclusion

Significant morbidity and mortality for youth are attributable to identifiable and preventable events, violence and risk-taking being perhaps the most important factors contributing to disease and death. In addition, chronic illness is an increasing health issue for youth as a result of progress in both medical treatment and health care delivery. Limited information on health issues for subpopulations of youth, such as youth in foster care, youth living on the streets, youth in detention, and newly immigrated youth indicate they are risk for the same illnesses as other youth, often to a greater degree. All youth confront difficult decisions related to their health care, and need support and guidance from concerned providers and guardians. Youth alone or youth who depend on emotionally chaotic or disabled adult guardians need more support.

The ability for many youth to receive appropriate care and treatment is severely impaired by poverty and social discrimination, which interfere with their access to adequate health care services. Moreover, although some risk taking is expected during the period of adolescence, serving as an integral part of learning to be an adult, risk taking that surrounds day-to-day survival on the streets to secure shelter and food, or even to satisfy a drug addiction, is a reflection of society's abandonment of a vulnerable portion of the population.

Youth should be elevated to a more respected stratum of society and provided with safer environments in which to grow and develop. With more consistent opportunities to receive information and gain skills, youth will be better empowered to make the necessary decisions to minimize or prevent illness, as well as to limit adverse consequences of various risk-taking behaviors inherent to this stage of development.

References

American Academy of Pediatrics, Committee on Infectious Diseases (1994). Screening for tuberculosis in infants and children. *Pediatrics, 93,* 131–134.

Aral, S. O., et al. (1988). Gonorrhea rates: What denominator is most appropriate? *American Journal of Public Health, 78,* 702–703.

Barry, M. A., et al. (1990). Tuberculosis infection in urban adolescents: Results of a school-based testing program. *American Journal of Public Health, 80,* 439–441.

Bartlett, J. A., et al. (1991). Depression in inner city adolescents attending an adolescent medicine clinic. *Journal of Adolescent Health* 12: 316–318.

Bell, T. A., and K. Hein (1984). Adolescents and sexually transmitted diseases. In K. K. Holmes et al. (Eds.), *Sexually Transmitted Diseases.* New York: McGraw-Hill, 73–84.

Bellin, E. Y., D. D. Fletcher, and S. M. Safyer (1993). Association of tuberculosis infection with increased time or admission to the New York City jail system. *Journal of the American Medical Association, 269,* 2228–2231.

Benson, V., and M. A. Marano (1994). Current estimates from the National Health Interview Survey, 1993. National Center for Health Statistics. *Vital and Health Statistics, 10,* (190).

Blum, R. (1991). Global trends in adolescent health. *Journal of the American Medical Association, 265,* 2711–2719.

Blum, R., et al. (1993). Transition from child-centered to adult health-care systems for adolescents with chronic conditions. A position paper of the Society for Adolescent Medicine. *Journal of Adolescent Health, 14,* 570–576.

Boyer, D., and D. Fine (1992). Sexual abuse as a factor in adolescent pregnancy and child maltreatment. *Family Planning Perspectives, 24,* 4–11,19.

Brindis, C., et al. (1995). The associations between immigrant status and risk-behavior patterns in Latino adolescents. *Journal of Adolescent Health, 17,* 99–105.

Brown, R. T., and S. M. Coupey (1993). Illicit drugs of abuse. In *Adolescent Medicine: State of the Art Reviews.* Philadelphia: Hanley and Belfus, Inc., 4: 321–340.

Brudney, K., and J. Dobkin (1991). Resurgent tuberculosis in New York City. *American Review of Respiratory Disease, 144,* 745–749.

Butts, J. (1994). Offenders in juvenile court, 1992. Office of Juvenile Justice and Delinquency Prevention. Washington, DC: U.S. Department of Justice, October.

Canterbury, R. J., et al. (1995). Prevalence of HIV-related risk behaviors and STDs among incarcerated adolescents. *Journal of Adolescent Health, 17,* 173–177.

Carpenter, C. C. J., et al. (1993). Antiretroviral therapy for HIV infection in 1996. Recommendations of an international panel. *Journal of the American Medical Association, 276,* 146–154.

Cates Jr., W. (1991). Teenagers and sexual risk taking: The best of times and the worst of times. *Journal of Adolescent Health, 12,* 84–94.

Centers for Disease Control and Prevention. 1988. Diving-associated spinal cord injuries during drought conditions–Wisconsin, 1988. *Morbidity and Mortality Weekly Report, 37,* 453–454.

Centers for Disease Control and Prevention (1989). Hepatitis surveillance report, *52,* 32.

Centers for Disease Control and Prevention (1992). Management of persons exposed to multidrug-resistant tuberculosis. *Morbidity and Mortality Weekly Report, 41* (RR-11), 1–8.

Centers for Disease Control and Prevention (1993a). Mortality trends and leading causes of death among adolescents and young adults–U.S., 1979–1988. *Morbidity and Mortality Weekly Report, 42,* 459–462.

Centers for Disease Control and Prevention (1993b). Reduction in alcohol-related traffic fatalities–U.S. 1990–1992. *Morbidity and Mortality Weekly Report, 42,* 905–909.

Centers for Disease Control and Prevention (1993c). Occupational burns among restaurant workers–Colorado and Minnesota. *Morbidity and Mortality Weekly Report, 42,* 713–716.

Centers for Disease Control and Prevention (1993d). STD treatment guidelines. *Morbidity and Mortality Weekly Report, 42,* 1–102.

Centers for Disease Control and Prevention (1993e). Initial therapy for tuberculosis in the era of multi-drug resistance. Recommendations of the Advisory Council for the elimination of tuberculosis. *Morbidity and Mortality Weekly Report, 42,* (RR-7), 1–8.

Centers for Disease Control and Prevention (1994a). Motor-vehicle-related deaths involving intoxicated pedestrians–US, 1982–1992. *Morbidity and Mortality Weekly Report, 43,* 249–253.

Centers for Disease Control and Prevention (1994b). Deaths resulting from firearm- and motor-vehicle-related injuries–US, 1968–1991. *Morbidity and Mortality Weekly Report, 43,* 37–42.

Centers for Disease Control and Prevention (1994c). Expanded tuberculosis surveillance and tuberculosis morbidity–United States, 1993. *Morbidity and Mortality Weekly Report, 43,* 361–366.

Centers for Disease Control and Prevention (1995a). Trends in smoking initiation among adolescents and young adults–US, 1980–1989. *Morbidity and Mortality Weekly Report, 44,* 521–525.

Centers for Disease Control and Prevention (1995b). HIV/AIDS surveillance report. *Morbidity and Mortality Weekly Report, 7,* 1–34.

Centers for Disease Control and Prevention (1995c). Disabilities among children aged less than 17 years–US, 1991–1992. *Morbidity and Moratality Weekly Report, 44,* 609–613.

Centers for Disease Control and Prevention (1995d). Tuberculosis among foreign-born persons who had recently arrived in the US–Hawaii, 1992–1993, and Los Angeles County, 1993. *Morbidity and Mortality Weekly Report, 44,* 703–707.

Charache, S., et al. (1995). Effect of hydroxyurea on the frequency of painful crises in sickle cell anemia. *New England Journal of Medicine, 332,* 1317–1322.

Chernoff, R., et al. (1994). Assessing the health status of children entering foster care. *Pediatrics, 93,* 504–601.

Coiro, M. J., N. Zill, and B. Bloom (1994). Health of our nation's children. National Center for Health Statistics. *Vital and Health Statistics, 10*(191).

Conway, J. H., and M. W. Hilgartner (1994). Initial presentations of pediatric hemophiliacs. *Archives of Pediatric and Adolescent Medicine, 148,* 589–594.

Darabi, K. F., and V. Ortiz (1987). Childbearing among young Latino women in the United States. *American Journal of Public Health, 77,* 25–28.

Deisher, R. W., and W. M. Rogers (1991). The medical care of street youth. *Journal of Adolescent Health, 12,* 500–503.

Des Jarlais, D. C., et al. (1995). Maintaining low HIV seroprevalence in populations of injecting drug users. *Journal of the American Medical Association, 274,* 1226–1231.

DeVilliers, E. M., D. Wagner, and A. Schneider (1987). Human papillomavirus infections in women with and without abnormal cervical cytology. *Lancet, 2,* 703–706.

Diabetes Control and Complications Trial Research Group (1993). The effect of intensive treatment of diabetes on the development and progression of long-term complications in insulin-dependent diabetes mellitus. *New England Journal of Medicine, 329,* 977–986.

DSM–IV (1994). Washington D. C. American Psychiatric Association.

Dubowitz, H., et al. (1992). The physical health of children in kinship care. *American Journal of Diseases of Children, 146,* 603–610.

DuRant, R. H., L. G. Escobedo, and G. W. Health (1995). Anabolic-steroid use, strength training, and multiple drug use among adolescents in the United States. *Pediatrics, 96,* 23–28.

Edlin, B. R., et al. (1994). Intersecting epidemics-crack cocaine use and HIV infection among inner city young adults. *New England Journal of Medicine, 331,* 1422–1427.

Fisher, M. (1992). Medical complications of anorexia and bulimia nervosa. In *Adolescent Medicine: State of the Art Reviews (Vol. 3)* Philadelphia: Hanley and Belfus, Inc., 487–502.

Flaherty, E. G., and H. Weiss (1990). Medical evaluation of abused and neglected children. *American Journal of Diseases of Children, 144,* 330–334.

Futterman, D., et al. (1993). HIV-infected adolescents: The first 50 patients in a New York City program. *Pediatrics, 91,* 730–735.

Gibson, P. (1989). Report of the Secretary's task force on youth suicide, Volume 3: Prevention and interventions in youth suicide. Washington, DC: USDHHS.

Golden, N. H. (1992). Osteopenia in adolescents with anorexia nervosa. *Children's Hospital Quarterly, 4,* 143–148.

Grubman, S., et al. (1995). Older children and adolescents living with perinatally acquired human immunodeficiency virus infection. *Pediatrics, 95,* 657–663.

Halfon, N., G. Berkowitz, and Klee Linnea (1992). Mental health service by children in foster care in California. *Pediatrics, 89,* 1238–1244.

Hein, K., et al. (1995). Comparison of HIV+ and HIV– adolescents: Risk factors and psychosocial determinants. *Pediatrics, 95,* 96–104.

Hicks, M. L., S.A. Jenkins, and G. P. Parham (1995). Quality-of-life advancements in the treatment of adolescent and pediatric patients with gynecologic malignancies. *Adolescent and Pediatric Gynecology, 8,* 121–124.

Hillis, S., et al. (1993). Risk factors for recurrent chlamydia trachomatis. Paper presented at the IX International Conference on AIDS, Berlin, Germany. Abstract PO-D02-3446.

Hodgman, C. H. (1990). Adolescent suicide and depression. In *Adolescent Medicine: State of the Art Reviews.* Philadelphia: Hanley and Belfus, Inc.: 1:81–95.

Hoffman, N. D., C. Kelly, and D. Futterman (1996). TB Infection in HIV-positive Adolescents: A NYC Cohort. *Pediatrics, 97,* 198–203.

Hunter, J., M. Rosario, and M. J. Rotheram-Borus (1993). Sexual and substance abuse acts that place adolescent lesbians at risk for HIV. Paper presented at the IX International Conference on AIDS, Berlin, Germany. Abstract PO-D02-3432.

Huston, H. R., et al. (1995). The epidemic of gang-related homicides in Los Angeles County from 1979 through 1994. *Journal of the American Medical Association, 274,* 11031–11036.

Igra, V., and S. G. Millstein (1993). Current status and approaches to improving preventive services for adolescents. *Journal of the American Medical Association, 269,* 1408–1412.

Jaffe, L. R., et al. (1988). Anal intercourse and knowledge of AIDS among minority-group female adolescents. *Journal of Pediatrics, 112,* 1005–1007.

Jenny C. (1990). Child sexual abuse and STD. In K. K. Holmes et al. (Eds.), *Sexually Transmitted Diseases* (2nd ed.). New York: McGraw-Hill, Inc., 895–902.

Johnston, L. D., et al. (1994). The Monitoring the Future Study, 1994. Ann Arbor: University of Michigan.

Kann, L., C. W. Warren, and W. A. Harris (1995). Youth risk behavior surveillance–US, 1993. *Morbidity and Mortality Weekly Report, 44* (No. SS-1): 1–56.

Kellerman, A. L., et al. (1993). Gun ownership as a risk factor for homicide in the home. *New England Journal of Medicine, 329,* 1084–1091.

Klerman, L. V. (1993). Adolescent pregnancy and parenting: Controversies of the past and lessons for the future. *Journal of Adolescent Health, 13,* 553–561.

Kochanek, K. D., and B. L. Hudson (1994). Advance report of final mortality statistics, 1992. *Monthly Vital Statistics Report, 43,*(6 suppl). Hyattsville, MD: National Center for Health Statistics.

Kraus, J. F. (1985). Epidemiologic aspects of acute spinal cord injury: A review of incidence, prevalence, causes, and outcome. In D. P. Becker and J.T. Povlishock. (Eds.), *Central Nervous System Status Report-1985.* Bethesda, MD: National Institute of Neurological and Communicative Disorders and Stroke: 313–321.

Kruks, G. (1991). Gay and lesbian homeless/street youth: Special issues and concerns. *Journal of Adolescent Health, 12,* 515–518.

Ku, L., F. L. Sonenstein, and J. H. Pleck (1993). Young men's risk behaviors for HIV infection and sexually transmitted diseases, 1988 through 1991. *American Journal of Public Health, 83,* 1609–1615.

Lichter, A. S., and T. S. Lawrence (1995). Recent advances in radiation oncology. *New England Journal of Medicine, 332,* 371–379.

Luna, G. C., and M. J. Rotheram-Borus (1992). Street youth and the AIDS pandemic. *AIDS Education and Prevention,* Supplement: 1–13.

Lungu, O., et al. (1992). Relationship of human papillomavirus type to grade of cervical intraepithelial neoplasia. *Journal of the American Medical Association, 267,* 2493–2496.

Lusher, J. M., and I. Warrier (1991). Hemophilia. *Pediatrics in Review, 12,* 275–281.

The Medical Letter. (1995). Choice of contraceptives. New York: The Medical Letter, Inc. 37: 9–12.

Michaels, D., and C. Levine (1996). Estimated numbers of children and adolescents orphaned by maternal HIV/AIDS deaths in New York State. *Families in Crisis: Report of the Working Committee on HIV, Children, and Families,* June: 7–16.

Moone, J. 1993a. Children in custody 1991: Private facilities. Office of Juvenile Justice and Delinquency Prevention. Washington, DC: U.S. Department of Justice. Fact sheet #2.

Moone, J. 1993b. Children in custody 1991: Public juvenile facilities. Office of Juvenile Justice and Delinquency Prevention. Washington, DC: U.S. Department of Justice. Fact sheet #5.

National Center for Health Statistics. 1993. Advance report of final natality statistics, 1991. *Monthly Vital Statistics Report, 42,*(3suppl.), Hyattsville, Maryland.

Neff, J. M., and G. Anderson (1995). Protecting children with chronic illness in a competitive marketplace. *Journal of the American Medical Association, 274,* 1866–1869.

Nelson, C. (1991). Office visits by adolescents. Advance Data from Vital and Health Statistics, #196. Washington, DC: USDHHS.

Nelson, D. E., et al. (1993). Cost savings associated with increased safety belt use in Iowa, 1987–1988. *Accident Analysis and Prevention, 25,* 521–528.

Newacheck, P. W., M. A. McManus, and H. B. Fox (1991). Prevalence and impact of chronic illness among adolescents. *American Journal of Diseases of Children, 145,* 1367–1373.

New York City Department of Health (1992). Tuberculosis in New York City, 1991: Information summary.

New York City Department of Health (1994) Tuberculosis in New York City, 1993: Information summary.

O'Malley, P. M., L. D. Johnston, and J. G. Bachman (1995). Adolescent substance use. Epidemiology and implications for public policy. *Pediatric Clinics of North America, 42,* 1–20.

Osmond, D. F., et al. (1993). Risk factors for Hepatitis C virus seropositivity in heterosexual couples. *Journal of the American Medical Association, 269,* 361–365.

Paroski, P. A. (1987). Health care delivery and the concerns of gay and lesbian adolescents. *Journal of Adolescent Health Care, 8,* 188–192.

Pizzo, P. A., et al. (1991a). The child with cancer and infection. I. Empiric therapy for fever and neutropenia, and preventive strategies. *Journal of Pediatrics, 119,* 679–694.

Pizzo, P. A., et al. (1991b). The child with cancer and infection. II. Nonbacterial infections. *Journal of Pediatrics, 119,* 845–856.

Platt, O. S., et al. (1991). Pain in sickle cell disease: Rates and risk factors. *New England Journal of Medicine, 324,* 11–16.

Platt, O. S., W. Rosenstock, and M. A. Espeland (1984). Influence of sickle hemoglobinopathies on growth and development. *New England Journal of Medicine, 311,* 7–12.

Pollack, I. F. (1994). Brain tumors in children. *New England Journal of Medicine, 331,* 1500–1507.

Public Health Service (1991). Healthy people 2000: National health promotion and disease prevention objectives–full report, with commentary. Washington, DC: U.S. Department of Health and Human Services. DHHS publication no. (PHS) 91–50212.

Pui, C. H. (1995). Childhood leukemias. *New England Journal of Medicine, 32,* 1618–1630.

Ramsey, B. W., and T. F. Boat (1994). Outcome measures for clinical trials in cystic fibrosis. *Journal of Pediatrics, 124,* 177–192.

Remafedi, G., et al. (1992). Demography of sexual orientation in adolescents. *Pediatrics, 89,* 714–721.

Remafedi, G. (1990). Fundamental issues in the care of homosexual youth. *Medical Clinics of North America, 74,* 1169–1179.

Remafedi, G., J. A. Farrow, and R. W. Deisher (1991). Risk factors for attempted suicide in gay and bisexual youth. *Pediatrics, 87,* 869–875.

Reynoso, T. C., M. E. Felice, and G. P. Shragg (1993). Does American acculturation affect outcome of Mexican-American teenage pregnancy? *Journal of Adolescent Health, 12,* 257–261.

Richert, C. A., et al. (1993). A method of identifying persons at high risk for STDs: Opportunity for targeting intervention. *American Journal of Public Health, 83,* 520–524.

Ries, L.A.G., et al., eds. (1994). *SEER cancer statistics review, 1973–1991: Tables and graphs, National Cancer Institute.* NIH Pub. No. 94–2789. Bethesda, Maryland.

Rosenberg, P. S., M. H. Gail, and R. J. Carroll (1992). Estimating HIV prevalence and projecting AIDS incidence in the U.S.: A model that accounts for therapy and changes in the surveillance definition of AIDS. *Statistics in Medicine, 11,* 1633–1655.

Rotheram-Borus, M. J., et al. (1992). Lifetime sexual behaviors among predominantly minority male runaways and gay/bisexual adolescents in New York City. *AIDS Education and Prevention,* supplement: 34–42.

Rutherford, G. W., et al. (1990). Course of HIV-1 infection in a cohort of homosexual and bisexual men: An 11-year follow-up study. *British Medical Journal, 301,* 1183–1188.

St. Louis, M. E., et al. (1991). HIV infection in disadvantaged adolescents; findings from the U.S. Job Corps. *Journal of the American Medical Association, 266,* 2387–2391.

Sawyer, S. M., P. D. Phelan, and G. Bowes (1995). Reproductive health in young women with cystic fibrosis: Knowledge, behavior and attitudes. *Journal of Adolescent Health, 17,* 46–50.

Silvestre, A. J., et al. (1993). Changes in HIV rates and sexual behavior among homosexual men, 1984 to 1988/92. *American Journal of Public Health, 83,* 578–580.

Snyder, H. N., and M. Sickmund (1995). Juvenile offenders and victims: A national report. Office of Juvenile Justice and Delinquency Prevention. National Center for Juvenile Justice. August.

Stevens-Simon, C., and M. M. White (1991). Adolescent pregnancy. *Pediatric Annals, 20,* 322–331.

Stricof, R. L., et al. (1991). HIV seroprevalence in a facility for runaway and homeless adolescents. *American Journal of Public Health, 81,* 50–53.

Su, T-P., et al. (1993). Neuropsychiatric effects of anabolic steroids in male normal volunteers. *Journal of the American Medical Association, 269,* 2760–2764.

Sweeney, P. A., et al. (1993). Adolescents at risk for HIV-1 infection: Results from seroprevalence surveys in clinic settings in the United States, 1990–1992. Paper presented at IX International Conference on AIDS, Berlin, Germany. Abstract WS-C13-6, June.

Tejani, A., et al. (1995a). Steady improvement in renal allograft survival among North American children: A five-year appraisal by the North American Pediatric Renal Transplant Cooperative Study. *Kidney International, 48,* 551–553.

Tejani, A., et al. (1995b). Analysis of rejection outcomes and implications–A report of the North American Pediatric Renal Transplant Cooperative Study. *Transplantation, 59,* 500–504.

U.S. Department of Commerce, Bureau of the Census (1994). Statistical Abstract of the United States, 1994 (114th ed.). Washington, DC: U.S. Government Printing Office.

U.S. Department of Health and Human Services (1994). Preventing tobacco use among young people: A report of the Surgeon General. Atlanta: U.S. Department of Health and Human Services, Public Health Service, Centers for Disease Control and Prevention, National Center for Chronic Disease Prevention and Health Promotion, Office on Smoking and Health.

Walters, M. C., et al. (1996). Bone marrow transplantation for sickle cell disease. *New England Journal of Medicine, 335,* 369–376.

Wasserheit, J. N. (1992). Epidemiological synergy: Interrelationships between HIV infection and other sexually transmitted diseases. *Sexually Transmitted Diseases, 19,* 61–77.

Westblom, T. U., et al. (1994). Safety and immunogenicity of an inactivated Hepatitis A vaccine: Effect of dose and vaccination schedule. *Journal of Infectious Diseases, 169,* 996–1001.

Westrom, L. (1980). Epidemiology: Incidence, prevalence and trends of acute pelvic inflammatory disease and its consequences in industrialized countries. *American Journal of Obstetrics and Gynecology, 138,* 880–892.

Yates, G. L., et al. (1988). A risk profile comparison of runaway and non-runaway youth. *American Journal of Public Health, 78,* 820–821.

Yordan, E. E., and R. A. Yordan (1995). Problems associated with homelessness and young pregnant teenagers. *Adolescent and Pediatric Gynecology, 8,* 135–139.

4   Health Care for the Adolescent Alone: A Legal Landscape*

Abigail English

Introduction

The health care of adolescents raises myriad legal issues. When those adolescents are literally or functionally *alone,* the number and complexity of the legal issues increases. Adolescents who are alone include not only those who are runaway or homeless, but also many who have been abandoned or rejected by their parents, others who are in foster care or in the custody of the state but without any real surrogate parent, and still others who might live with their families but receive no meaningful support from them.

Adolescents are neither little children nor full adults and, therefore, occupy a somewhat ambiguous legal status, which may be even more ambiguous if they are "alone." In addition, the health care needs of adolescents often require that they have access to services on an independent or confidential basis, presenting challenges both for health care providers and for the public and private systems that finance their care. As a group, adolescents are uninsured and under-insured at higher rates than other age groups, which places them at risk for more limited access to necessary health services. Moreover, specific groups – or special populations – of adolescents are, compared to adolescents generally, at increased risk for serious health problems and limited access to health services. Adolescents alone are one of those special populations, although the specific issues for individual adolescents or subpopulations within that group may vary.

The legal issues associated with the health of adolescents, including adolescents alone, and their use of health care include questions pertaining to consent for services, confidentiality of care, and the financing of services they receive. Key questions in these areas include:

- Who is authorized to give consent, and whose consent is required?
- Who has the right to control the release of confidential information, including medical records, and who has the right to receive such information?

* Portions of this chapter were prepared with support from the ABA Center on Children and the Law, under a contract with the Office of Adolescent Health in the federal Maternal and Child Health Bureau. Used here with permission. Additional support was provided by the Carnegie Corporation of New York. The views expressed herein are those of the author and not of the funding entities.

- Who is financially responsible for payment, and is there a source of insurance coverage, public funding, or free care available that the adolescent can access?

Addressing these issues in a way that meets adolescents' need for services while taking account of their specific characteristics and legal status is a significant challenge for health care professionals, other service providers, program administrators, health insurance companies, managed care plans, advocates, and policy makers.

Health Status of Adolescents

A widespread impression exists that adolescents are generally healthy and therefore do not need extensive health services: beyond a periodic sports physical for school, it is believed, they do not need to go to the doctor frequently. Not only is this prevailing myth at odds with the preventive care guidelines for adolescents recommended by all of the professional organizations and multidisciplinary expert groups that have addressed the issue (e.g., American Medical Association [AMA] 1992; Green 1994; American Academy of Pediatrics [AAP] 1995), it is belied by current facts about the actual health status of adolescents (Dryfoos 1990; Office of Technology Assessment [OTA] 1991a, 1991b, 1991c; Centers for Disease Control and Prevention [CDC] 1995a; AMA 1996; Ozer et al. 1998). Although many adolescents are healthy, many are also at risk for serious health problems as a result of the situations and environments in which they live, as well as their own behaviors. In addition, a smaller number of adolescents – approximately 9.3 percent of fifteen- to seventeen-year-olds, for example – have a serious chronic illness or disabling condition (CDC 1995b). Common chronic illness and disabling conditions for adolescents include leukemia, asthma, cystic fibrosis, traumatic brain injury, cerebral palsy, diabetes, hearing or visual impairment, and sickle cell disease (OTA 1991a: I-90). The leading cause of disability for adolescents is mental illness (Gans, et al. 1991), and millions of adolescents suffer from emotional and behavioral disorders (Institute of Medicine 1989).

Adolescent health can be defined expansively or narrowly, focusing on specific physical and mental illnesses and disabilities or looking more broadly at the range of issues in adolescents' lives that jeopardize their health. In its extensive report on adolescent health, the Office of Technology Assessment (OTA) adopted the latter approach, including in its catalog of adolescent health problems not only chronic physical illness and disability, nutrition and fitness problems, dental and oral health problems, HIV/AIDS and other sexually transmitted diseases (STDs), pregnancy, mental health problems, and alcohol, tobacco, and illicit drug abuse, but also family problems, school problems, lack of recreational opportunities, parenting, delinquency, and homelessness (OTA 1991a: I-8 to I-16). Thus, although risk-taking behavior is a major cause of health problems among adolescents, situational or environmental factors are also extremely important in placing many adolescents' health at risk. For the adolescent alone, these factors are often of overriding significance.

The leading causes of death for adolescents include drinking and driving, unintentional injury, homicide, and suicide (Simons 1991; Ozer et al. 1998). Adolescents frequently witness or experience violence: homicide is the second-leading cause of death for adolescents. More than 3,500 adolescents were murdered in 1993 (Ozer et al. 1998). An estimated 400,000 adolescent boys and girls attempt suicide every year (American School Health Association 1989).

Approximately 1 million adolescents – one in ten fifteen- to nineteen-year-old females – become pregnant each year (Alan Guttmacher Institute [AGI] 1994), more than 80 percent unintentionally (Brown and Eisenberg 1995). About one-third of these girls have abortions and one-half have babies (AGI 1994). The remainder miscarry. Three million adolescents contract a sexually transmitted disease each year (CDC 1993). HIV infection among adolescents is spreading rapidly, and many of the young adults with AIDS – approximately 20 percent of the AIDS cases – were likely infected with HIV as adolescents (Rosenberg, Biggar, and Goedert 1994; CDC 1996).

Special Populations of Adolescents

The foregoing statistics make clear that while adolescents as a group generally may be considered healthy, a large number of them have or are at risk for significant health problems. In addition, certain groups of adolescents experience a higher incidence of particular health problems. For example, a higher proportion of children and adolescents in state custody – foster children and incarcerated youth – have both serious physical and mental problems at a much higher rate than the general population in their age group (Hochstadt et al. 1987; Schor 1989; Halfon and Klee 1991; Thompson 1993). Also, for example, young and minority gay and bisexual men, as well as young and minority heterosexual women in the Southeast where there is a high prevalence of HIV, appear to be at significantly increased risk for HIV infection (Homberg 1996). Adolescents who are alone, particularly homeless and runaway youth (Ensign and Santelli 1998), often experience these health problems at higher rates than other young people. Conversely, young people who experience these health problems sometimes find themselves "alone" as a consequence. For example, both the pregnant young woman who cannot involve her parents and the gay teen who fears he is HIV positive but has been rejected by his family are, in some sense, alone because of their health issues.

Special populations include those with a chronic physical or mental illness or disability, adolescents who are infected with HIV, severely injured adolescents, impoverished adolescents, members of racial or ethnic minority groups, gay and lesbian teens, homeless and runaway youth, those in foster care or juvenile correctional facilities, immigrant and migrant adolescents, and pregnant or parenting teens. Many of these young people are, at least at times, adolescents alone. Not only are many of these groups at increased risk for specific health problems, they may also be at greater risk of limited access to necessary health services as a result of their lack of insurance coverage or other medical, social, legal, or financial factors (English 1994).

Service Needs and Delivery Systems

Adolescents need a broad array of health care and related services to address their diverse medical and psychosocial health problems. Many health care professionals and service providers who work with adolescents think that their health-related needs can often best be addressed by services that extend beyond the traditional medical model, including comprehensive preventive services, as well as a variety of supportive and facilitative services such as transportation, anticipatory guidance or counseling, and care coordination. This may be particularly true for the adolescent alone who receives minimal, if any, family support.

Several professional organizations and public agencies recently have issued guidelines for the delivery of preventive services to adolescents (AMA 1992; Green 1994; AAP 1995). There is substantial consistency among these guidelines with respect to the appropriate content of preventive services for adolescents: notably, all three recommend annual comprehensive health exams for teenagers. Although none of these guidelines has the force of law, the federal Medicaid statute does require states, in developing their periodicity schedule for the comprehensive health assessments required as part of the Early and Periodic Screening, Diagnosis, and Treatment (EPSDT) program, to consult with professional organizations involved in child health (42 U.S.C. § 1396d(r)(1)–(4)). In addition to comprehensive preventive services, adolescents need a full range of diagnostic and treatment services for both acute and chronic problems.

Often the needed services can best be delivered by health care providers with appropriate training and experience in the care of adolescents, whether those professionals be primary care providers or specialists. Moreover, certain sites and delivery models have been particularly effective in reaching the adolescent population, taking account of the special access problems that affect this age group. The innovative delivery systems that have been developed to improve access for adolescents include school-based and school-linked health clinics, comprehensive teen clinics, adolescent clinics within outpatient departments of children's hospitals and academic institutions, and teen services within community clinics or public health departments (Bearinger and McAnarney 1988; Klein et al. 1992; McKinney and Peak 1995; Schlitt et al. 1995).

Many adolescents – including some with access to other sites such as an HMO through their family's insurance coverage – choose to use these adolescent-focused services (Brindis et al. 1995). However, a majority continue to receive their care through more traditional sites such as private physician's offices, public and private hospital outpatient departments, family planning programs, public health clinics, and community health centers. Some, but not all, of these sites have worked to make their services more accessible to adolescents, even adolescents alone; but encounters with the health care system remain fraught with potential obstacles for young people without familial and social supports.

Legal Status of Adolescents

The legal status of most adolescents differs from that of both adults and younger children. In almost every state, the age of majority is eighteen (English et al. 1995), at which point an adolescent becomes legally an adult for most purposes. Although many adolescents are legally minors, they do not share all of the "disabilities of minority" that characterize younger children. Historically, the law gave parents extensive authority over their minor children until those children reached the age of majority or became legally emancipated (*Meyer* v. *Nebraska* 1923; *Pierce* v. *Society of Sisters* 1925; *Prince* v. *Massachusetts* 1944). This authority is reflected in the common law, in state statutes, and in constitutional doctrine. Nevertheless, state and federal statutes and court decisions have permitted adolescents, before the age of eighteen, to make a variety of decisions usually reserved to adults. For example, in most states a minor who bears a child may decide to relinquish the child for adoption (Donovan 1992; AGI 1995) and, as will be discussed, in all states minors are permitted at varying ages to make some medical decisions for themselves (English et al. 1995).

Most adolescents live with at least one parent. They are legally subject to parental custody and control unless they are legally emancipated or their parents' authority has been limited by a court (Davis et al. 1997). The traditional criteria for legal emancipation are marriage, service in the armed forces, or living separate and apart from parents while managing one's own financial affairs (Katz 1973).

While few adolescents are legally emancipated, many are living in circumstances which affect their legal status as well as their access to health care. For example, hundreds of thousands of adolescents are living in state custody under the jurisdiction of the child welfare or juvenile justice authorities – more than 100,000 in foster care (William T. Grant Foundation 1988) and nearly three-quarters of a million in public or private juvenile justice facilities (OTA 1991a). As such, the authority to make decisions, including medical decisions, about important aspects of their lives either shifts entirely to state custodians and the juvenile courts – both of which are reluctant to make difficult health care decisions – or is shared between their parents and the state (Gittler, Quigley-Rick, and Saks 1990). Homeless and runaway youth may gain the right to make medical decisions (Paradise and Horowitz 1994), but usually have no right to arrange shelter for themselves without their parents' permission unless state law grants them some limited authority to do so (e.g., California Family Code § 6922; Paradise and Horowitz 1994). Immigrant youth whose health status and living circumstances are otherwise indistinguishable from many of their adolescent peers often find their access to essential services, including health care, circumscribed by their immigration status (NHeLP 1996). Teen parents who are still minors might have full parental authority with respect to their own young children, while their ability to act for themselves – in seeking health care, applying for welfare, or enrolling in school – still depends on the cooperation of their parents (Donovan 1993; AGI 1995).

The law presumes, as a general matter, that parents act in the best interests of their children (*Parham* v. *J.R.* (1979). Most parents do, but an unfortunate number of parents do not. This may occur for a variety of reasons: some parents are too pre-occupied with their own interests; others are too burdened by work-related responsibilities or by their own illness; still others are abusive or dysfunctional, sometimes as a result of mental illness or drug or alcohol problems (Carnegie Council 1995). For whatever reason, some parents are unwilling or unable to provide the necessary care and support that their adolescent children need. For those adolescents whose parents are not providing adequate support, legal dependence on their parents may serve as a barrier to appropriate services in general and health care in particular.

In the more extreme cases of parental or adolescent misbehavior, official state intervention may occur and adolescents may come under the jurisdiction of the juvenile courts – either as dependents who have been abused, neglected, or abandoned by their parents or as delinquents who have committed an offense that would be considered a crime for an adult (Davis et al. 1997). Often these youth are removed from their parents' custody and are placed in foster care under child welfare agency jurisdiction or in correctional facilities under juvenile justice agency jurisdiction. Once there, they are among the adolescents whose access to necessary health care can be the most problematic (Burrell 1993). For these young people, as for others, some of the legal barriers relate to issues of consent or confidentiality, while others arise from difficulties associated with the financing of their care. Most adolescents in foster care are eligible for Medicaid (English and Freundlich 1997); however, solely because of their custodial status, many, if not most, adolescents in the juvenile justice system are not (Burrell 1993).

Consent for Health Care

The consent of the patient or a legally authorized representative is required for medical care provided to patients of any age. In the absence of legally authorized consent, a physician or other health care professional may be liable for battery (unconsented touching) or for negligence. In some cases, consent must be explicit, while in others it may implied from the circumstances. In addition, informed consent must be obtained in many situations in order to satisfy both ethical and legal requirements (Appelbaum et al. 1987).

In the case of minors, the basic common law rule is that the consent of one or both parents is required to authorize medical care (Rosovsky 1990). There are, however, numerous alternatives and exceptions to this requirement. Although specifics of these rules vary from state to state, certain basic principles generally apply (Holder 1985; Morrissey et al. 1986; English 1990; Gittler 1990; Rosovsky

1990). Adoptive parents have the same rights as the biologic parents of a child to give consent; and stepparents who formally adopt a child would also have these privileges. In addition, certain adult caretakers of minors may have partial or complete authority to make medical decisions for the children in their physical or legal custody. For example, legal guardians usually are authorized to give consent for most or all medical care; foster parents are usually allowed by law to consent for a limited range of health care services, such as routine or ordinary care; and other adults with brief or long-term custody of a child may sometimes consent to care if they are authorized in writing to do so by a parent.

For children in the custody of the state, the authority to make medical decisions for them is usually shared by their parents and either the juvenile court or a child welfare or juvenile justice agency assigned that authority by a court or by statute. Moreover, in emergencies, a minor child almost always may be treated without the prior consent of a parent because consent is implied, although parents would usually have to be informed after the emergency care was provided (Rosovsky 1990). In some states, minors are authorized to give their own consent for care in emergencies (Paradise and Horowitz 1994; English et al. 1995).

As a practical matter, occasions arise in which health care providers accept consent from adult relatives or caretakers of children who may or may not, technically, have the legal authority to provide it. This practice often helps to facilitate the provision of care in situations when insistence on legal technicalities would create almost insurmountable barriers. At least when the care being provided is not controversial in nature and does not present high risks, this practice appears to create few legal consequences.

Consent of Minors

The basic rules of consent that apply to younger children have been modified in many ways with respect to adolescents who are minors. Courts have delineated some parameters based on common law and constitutional principles for minors' consent to medical care. Certain federal statutes provide support for minor consent, and every state has enacted statutes which authorize minors to give their own consent for medical care under certain circumstances (Paradise and Horowitz 1994; AGI 1995; English et al. 1995).

Beginning in 1976, the U.S. Supreme Court decided a series of cases addressing the question of whether a pregnant minor has the right to obtain an abortion without parental involvement and whether a state may constitutionally require parental consent or notification when minors seek abortions (Planned Parenthood of Central Missouri v. Danforth 1976; *Bellotti* v. *Baird* 1979; *Hodgson* v. *Minnesota* 1990). A key element of these cases is the recognition that adolescents who are mature enough to give their own consent must, at least with respect to abortion, be permitted to do so without the necessity for involving their parents (*Bellott* v. *Baird* 1979). This is consistent with the mature minor doctrine, discussed later, that has been recognized in decisions by federal and state courts based on the common law (e.g., *Cardwell* v. *Bechtol* 1987).

Statutory support for minors to give their own consent appears both in federal and state statutes. Certain federal laws – such as the Title X Family Planning Program statute and regulations (42 U.S.C. §§ 300 et seq.; 42 C.F.R. Part 59) and the federal confidentiality requirements for drug and alcohol programs (42 C.F.R. Part 2) – explicitly or implicitly recognize that under state law minors are permitted to give their own consent for specific services. State statutes in every state, sometimes referred to as *minor consent statutes* or *medical emancipation statutes,* authorize minors to give their own consent based on their status or on the specific services they are seeking (Paradise and Horowitz 1994; English et al. 1995). The state minor consent statutes include some provisions that allow minors to consent based on their status and others that allow them to consent based on the services they are seeking.

The different categories of minors who are authorized to consent to their medical care in one or more states based on their status are (English et al 1995):

- Emancipated minors
- Married minors
- Minors in the armed forces
- Mature minors
- Minors living apart from their parents
- Minors over a certain age
- High school graduates
- Pregnant minors
- Minor parents

The various services for which minors are authorized to give their own consent in one or more states are (English et al. 1995):

- Emergency care
- Pregnancy related care
- Contraceptive services
- Abortion
- Diagnosis or treatment of venereal or sexually transmitted diseases
- Diagnosis or treatment of reportable, infectious, contagious, or communicable diseases
- HIV/AIDS testing or treatment
- Treatment or counseling for drug or alcohol problems
- Collection of medical evidence or treatment for sexual assault
- Inpatient mental health services
- Outpatient mental health services

Clearly, both the status and the service categories encompass many situations affecting adolescents who are alone.

Not only do the status and service categories vary from state to state, but other provisions of the minor consent statutes vary as well. For example, in some states the minor consent provisions also include specific confidentiality or disclosure provisions, or specification that parents have no financial liability for services to which a minor consents (Paradise and Horowitz 1994). In some states authorization for minors to give their own consent is time limited, such as for the first few visits of outpatient mental health counseling (e.g., Ohio Revised Code § 5122.04). And, in many states, the right to consent to specific services is limited by age, such as to minors over the age of twelve, fifteen, or sixteen (e.g., California Family Code § 6926; Minnesota Statutes § 253B.03(6)(d)). Statutes may also require that minors meet certain other criteria, such as the ability to give informed consent (e.g., New York Public Health §§ 2780(5); 2781), or demonstration that they are at risk for a particular harm (e.g., California Family Code § 6924).

The Mature Minor Doctrine and Informed Consent

Key elements in the evolution of the legal framework within which minors may give their own consent for health care are the related concepts of the mature minor and informed consent. Over the past several decades, courts have recognized that some minors have the capacity to give – or to withhold – informed consent for medical care and have issued decisions authorizing them to do so (*Bellotti* v. *Baird* 1979; *Cardwell* v. *Bechtol* 1987; In Interest of E.G. 1987). These decisions have been grounded both in the common law and in the constitutional right of privacy. As the concept has developed through these court decisions, and by statute in a small number of states, the mature minor doctrine would generally authorize a minor to give consent for medical care in the following circumstances (Morrissey et al. 1986):

- The minor is an older adolescent (e.g., older than fourteen or fifteen years)
- The minor is capable of giving an informed consent
- The care is for the benefit of the minor
- The care does not present a high level of risk
- The care is within the range of established medical opinion

Although only a few states have formally enacted statutes codifying the mature minor doctrine (English et al. 1995), there appear to be no reported cases in the past several decades in which physicians have been held liable, solely on the basis of a failure to obtain parental consent, for providing nonnegligent care to a mature minor who has given informed consent, where the care was not controversial and was solely for the benefit of the minor (Holder 1985).

The mature minor doctrine is, of course, premised upon the notion that at least some minors have the cognitive capacity to give informed consent. Although not universally accepted, and although relevant research is not extensive, this concept has received a significant degree of support in the research literature as well as in court decisions (Gittler et al. 1990). From a legal perspective, the basic criteria for determining whether a patient, including a minor, is capable of giving an informed consent are that the patient must be able to understand the risks and benefits of the proposed treatment or procedure and of any alternatives to it and must be able to make a voluntary choice among the alternatives (Morrissey et al. 1986).

Confidentiality and Disclosure

Maintaining the confidentiality of information about adolescents' health care serves important purposes (Hofmann 1980; Soler, Shotton, and Bell 1993). First, adolescents may be more willing to disclose sensitive information if they can do so on a confidential basis, thus providing health care practitioners with a more accurate health history. Second, adolescents may be encouraged to seek care for issues that place not only their own health but the public health at risk. Third, protecting confidential information may shield adolescents from the humiliation or discrimination that might result from disclosure. Fourth, honoring adolescents' need for protection of their privacy supports their developmental need for increased autonomy. A considerable degree of protection for the confidentiality of adolescents' health care does exist in the law, but there is an accompanying recognition that in certain circumstances disclosure is required for protection of the life or safety of adolescents themselves or of others.

The confidentiality obligation has numerous sources in law and policy, including federal and state constitutions, federal statutes and regulations (such as those pertaining to Medicaid, Title X family planning programs, federal drug and alcohol programs, Title V maternal and child health programs, or community and migrant health centers), and state statutes and regulations (such as medical confidentiality statutes, medical records statutes, privilege statutes, professional licensing statutes, or funding statutes). Other sources include court decisions and professional ethical standards (Soler et al. 1993; Bussiere et al. 1997).

Confidentiality protections are rarely, if ever, absolute, for adolescents or for adults. Health care practitioners, therefore, are faced with challenging legal questions in determining what may be disclosed, what may not be disclosed, and what must be disclosed. In general, confidential information may not be disclosed without the permission of the patient or an authorized representative. A considerable degree of confusion prevails concerning the following questions:

- When does the law permit a minor to authorize disclosure of confidential information?
- When does the law require the authorization of a minor for disclosure of confidential information?
- When does the law permit a parent to have access to confidential information about health care for which a minor has given his or her own consent?
- When is the parent permitted to receive confidential information about care for which a minor has not provided consent, but consent has been provided by the parent or some other adult authority?

In some cases, state statutes that authorize minors to consent to their own care also entrust them with the right to make decisions concerning disclosure of information about that care (Paradise and Horowitz 1994). This is not always the case, however, and there are a number of circumstances in which disclosure over the objection of the minor may be required or permitted by the law. Examples include when a specific statute requires or allows disclosure to parents (English et al.

1995), a mandatory reporting statute requires the reporting of sexual or physical abuse (Soler et al. 1993), or the minor poses a severe danger to himself or herself or others (Holder 1985).

Adolescent Health Research

Biomedical and social science research related to adolescent health and the health care of adolescents serves important purposes in furthering understanding of adolescent health problems and the service delivery needs of this age group (Santelli et al. 1995). This increased knowledge is essential for policy and program development and for advocacy to secure adequate resources for adolescent-focused programs. In addition, for adolescents with specific diseases, participation in clinical trials may provide an important avenue of access to treatment. Nevertheless, researchers seeking to conduct adolescent health-related studies or to include adolescents in their clinical trials have encountered legal barriers. Most significant among the barriers is the actual or perceived need to obtain consent from the parents of the adolescent participants in the research. Many institutional review boards considering proposed research protocols that involve adolescents as subjects of the research are reluctant to approve them unless parental consent is to be obtained (Mammel and Kaplan 1995), even though federal research regulations include a basis for allowing mature minors to participate in research in a number of circumstances without parental permission (45 C.F.R. Part 46).

In 1994, the Society for Adolescent Medicine undertook a project to develop guidelines for adolescent health research. Extensive consultation among a multidisciplinary group of experts on adolescent health and research issues resulted in the publication of a comprehensive set of guidelines (Society for Adolescent Medicine 1995). The guidelines offer an interpretation of how the federal research regulations should be applied with respect to research studies involving adolescents as subjects. One of the key issues addressed in the guidelines is when adolescents who are legally minors should be allowed to participate in research studies without requiring parental permission. Two background papers that accompany the guidelines address the legal and ethical issues, respectively (English 1995; Levine 1995). The key recommendations of the guidelines provide for waiver of parental permission under designated circumstances. The protections recommended to accompany such a waiver are increased as the degree of risk is heightened (Society for Adolescent Medicine 1995).

Although in certain respects these recommendations represent an expansive interpretation of the federal research regulations, the basis for them is clearly included in the regulations themselves. The regulations require, for most human subjects research, that informed consent be obtained from the subject of the research (45 C.F.R. § 46.116). In the case of "children," the regulations require both the permission of parents and the children's assent (45 C.F.R. §§ 46.404, 46.405(c), 46.406(d), 46.407(b)(iii)). Notably, the regulations' definition of *chil-*

dren is not co-extensive with the legal definition of *minor,* but rather, incorporates by reference the state law provisions that authorize some minors to give their own consent for medical care (45 C.F.R. § 46.402(a)). Thus, for adolescents who do not fall within the regulations' definition of children, parental permission would not be required at all. Moreover, the regulations also contain a specific provision that allows for the waiver of parental permission when it is "not a reasonable requirement," as long as alternative protections are included (45 C.F.R. § 46.408).

Financing of Health Care and Related Services

The ability of adolescents to receive essential care depends not only on the absence of barriers related to consent or confidentiality but also, even more importantly, on the availability of a source of financing for the care, either through insurance coverage or through categorical funding programs. Whatever the source of financing, the explosive growth in managed care is having a significant effect on the financing and delivery of adolescent health services (English et al. 1998; Society for Adolescent Medicine 1998).

Insurance Status of Adolescents

Many adolescents lack insurance entirely or are underinsured, covered by plans that fail to offer the full range of benefits that adolescents need (Newacheck and McManus 1990; Newacheck 1992). Insured adolescents include both those with private insurance and those with Medicaid or other public insurance – including coverage under the new State Children's Health Insurance Program (CHIP), enacted by Congress in 1997. The advent of CHIP, which allows states to expand Medicaid or establish separate programs, offers the potential to significantly reduce the number of uninsured adolescents.

Young people with Medicaid coverage – including those whom states have added to the Medicaid rolls through their CHIP programs – are eligible for Medicaid's mandatory Early and Periodic Screening, Diagnosis, and Treatment (EPSDT) benefit (42 U.S.C. § 1396d(r)(5)), one of the most comprehensive sets of benefits available to children or adolescents in any public or private insurance plan. As will be discussed, EPSDT requires that any Medicaid individual under age twenty-one receives comprehensive health assessments according to a schedule determined by each state in consultation with professional organizations concerned with child health, such as the American Academy of Pediatrics (AAP). In addition, these children and adolescents must be able to receive any medically necessary diagnostic or treatment service as long as it is included as a mandatory or optional service in the federal Medicaid law. EPSDT also includes supportive services such as outreach, scheduling, transportation, and case management.

However, most adolescents are not eligible for Medicaid. Moreover, many adolescents who are alone have difficulty qualifying for Medicaid, either because they cannot supply the necessary family financial information or cannot meet the eligibility criteria.

Insured adolescents who have private insurance rather than Medicaid coverage are much more likely to be underinsured. Depending on the scope of benefits in the specific policy that covers them, or plan in which they are enrolled, the private insurance may or may not meet their needs. Moreover, many adolescents who are alone cannot access their families' private insurance, so they are effectively uninusured.

Adolescents have been uninsured at high rates, with older adolescents more likely to lack health insurance. In recent years the situation has been worsening. In 1993, for example, the percentage of uninsured adolescents ranged from 14.4 percent for the ten- to fourteen-year-old age group, and 19.3 percent for the fifteen- to eighteen-year-old age group, to 25.2 percent for the nineteen- to twenty-one-year-old age group (Hughes 1996). This represented an increase in the percentage of uninsured adolescents in every age group compared with 1988 data (Hughes 1996). Poor adolescents fare even worse than adolescents generally: in 1989, one in three poor adolescents was without coverage, compared with one in seven among adolescents overall (Newacheck et al. 1992). However, the new CHIP program has the potential to change this situation.

Adolescents who are uninsured or underinsured may go without necessary health care and related services. Alternatively, they may seek care in one of the many settings in which it is financed from other public or private sources. This infrastructure of sites where adolescents can obtain health care without having to rely on insurance payments has been a significant component of the service delivery system for adolescents, but is currently at serious financial risk.

Managed Care

In both the private and public insurance arenas, the shift has been rapid to managed care as the dominant methodology for financing health care services for all age groups, including adolescents (Freund and Lewit 1993; Rowland et al. 1995). In addition, other service systems, such as child welfare and juvenile justice, are also moving rapidly to explore and adopt managed care models for financing and delivering services (Winterfeld 1995).

Numerous models of managed health care exist, which vary in terms of both their financing and reimbursement mechanisms and the service delivery structure that they support. However, prepaid or capitated (in contrast to fee-for-service) models are becoming increasingly common, as are network models (in contrast to staff model HMOs). Whatever the model, most managed care organizations restrict patients' choice of providers and control patients' use of services and access to specialists through mechanisms such as prior authorization requirements and financial incentives (GAO 1992).

The shift to managed care has important implications for adolescent health care for a variety of reasons (English et al. 1998; Society for Adolescent Medicine

1998). Providers and sites with training and experience in serving the adolescent population are not yet well integrated into managed care networks and financing systems (Darnell et al. 1995). Few managed care plans have targeted or adapted their services to this age group (Schwalberg and Hill 1995). Yet the financial viability and even the continued existence of many of the specialized delivery systems that have been particularly effective in serving adolescents in general, and adolescents alone in particular, are being placed at risk by the shift to managed care. One welcome development is that in a few states some initial efforts are underway to structure relationships between managed care plans and school-based health clinics (SBCs) (Brellochs et al. 1996). Although SBCs serve a small minority of the adolescent population, if these efforts are successful they may provide a model that can be used by other "safety net" providers, many of whom are critically important in the service delivery network for adolescents who are alone.

Private Insurance

Most adolescents who have health insurance are covered as dependents under a private insurance plan covering their families (Hughes 1996). If employer-based plans continue to eliminate or reduce dependent coverage (Newacheck, Hughes, and Cisternas 1995), the proportion of adolescents with private insurance may continue to decrease, but the legal issues related to private health insurance coverage for adolescents will remain significant for a large percentage of the adolescent population. Key issues include the scope of covered benefits in many private plans, standards for determining medical necessity, and the ability of adolescents to access insurance coverage for confidential services.

Many private insurance plans do not include a benefit package that is broad enough to cover the full range of services adolescents need. Important services that might be underinsured in private plans include certain preventive services such as "well-adolescent" visits, mental health benefits, rehabilitative therapies, and interdisciplinary team services for complex problems such as eating disorders (Newacheck and McManus 1990; Newacheck 1992). There are currently no legal requirements for private insurance plans to cover this full range of benefits. Even the state HMO laws that mandate a basic set of benefits do not require coverage of the full range of services adolescents need (Aspen 1996).

Adolescents may experience difficulty in accessing even those services that are covered under their private insurance plan. First, access may be restricted by the application of limited standards of medical necessity. For example, many private plans only cover services if they are necessary to treat an illness or injury, thus placing certain services for chronic conditions beyond reach (Newacheck et al. 1994). This is in contrast to Medicaid, which uses the more expansive medical necessity standard of the EPSDT program that encompasses physical, mental, and developmental concerns. Second, many adolescents need services on a confidential basis, but if their parents' participation is required to file an insurance claim or if statements identifying services rendered are sent home to families, adolescents are unable to receive both insurance coverage and confidential treatment (AMA 1993).

Medicaid

Medicaid has several critically important advantages over private health insurance plans as a source of financing for health care services that adolescents need. It also has some important disadvantages.

Chief among the advantages of Medicaid is the breadth of the benefit package. Early and Periodic Screening, Diagnosis and Treatment (EPSDT) is a mandatory benefit for Medicaid-eligible individuals up to age twenty-one (42 U.S.C. §§ 1396d(a)(4)(B); 1396d(r)). The EPSDT benefit includes not only a requirement for comprehensive health assessments on a periodic state-determined schedule, but also a mandate that, for children, states must cover all mandatory and optional Medicaid benefits (42 U.S.C. § 1396d(r)). Some of the benefits that are least well covered in private insurance plans – such as rehabilitative therapies – are, therefore, mandatory for adolescents eligible for EPSDT. Moreover, the medical necessity standard that must be used in determining whether an adolescent is entitled to a particular service is broader than that used in many private insurance plans. Specifically, the EPSDT statute requires coverage of any Medicaid service that is medically necessary to treat an identified physical or mental problem, which would include, for example, "diagnostic, screening, preventive, and rehabilitative services, including any medical or remedial services . . . for the maximum reduction of physical or mental disability and restoration of an individual to the best possible functional level (42 U.S.C. § 1396d(r))."

In spite of the advantages of Medicaid coverage for those adolescents who have it, not even all poor adolescents currently qualify for Medicaid. Thus, pursuant to federal mandates, Medicaid only partially addresses the problem of increasing coverage for uninsured adolescents living below the federal poverty level; and coverage of low-income teens with family incomes above the federal poverty level is left almost entirely to state option. Prior to the enactment of the CHIP program, federal law only required that states phase in coverage of poor adolescents one year at a time until, by 2002, all poor adolescents up to age 19 would be covered. Only about half the states had chosen to move more quickly than the federal mandate required. The CHIP program provided an incentive for states to move more quickly in expanding Medicaid coverage for poor adolescents, but even CHIP did not require them to do so.

Moreover, there are important groups of adolescents for whom provision has not been made under current Medicaid law. For example, adolescents in juvenile correctional facilities are not eligible for Medicaid because of the exclusion of certain institutionalized individuals in the Medicaid statute (Burrell 1993), although they have a very limited right to basic medical care under the U.S. Constitution. Also, homeless or runaway adolescents have difficulty enrolling even in states that have accelerated coverage of poor adolescents, because they cannot provide necessary family financial information (Paradise and Horowitz 1994).

In addition, despite the broad scope of EPSDT benefits, EPSDT screening rates for adolescents is lower than for other age groups – only 17 percent nationally for 1993 – suggesting that adolescents are not receiving comprehensive health assessments at the required intervals (HCFA 1994). Medicaid billing by school-based health clinics and other adolescent-focused providers, while increasing, still remains limited to a small number of providers (Schwalberg and Hill 1995). And participation in the Medicaid program by pediatric providers continues to be limited, despite specific requirements designed to increase it (42 U.S.C. §§ 1396a(a)(30)(A); 1396r-7), so that even those adolescents who are eligible and enrolled are not always able to find an appropriate provider willing to accept Medicaid. In spite of these problems, Medicaid remains a key source of financing for adolescent health services.

The New Children's Health Insurance Program (CHIP)

In 1997 Congress enacted, as part of the Balanced Budget Act of 1997, a new federal program: the State Children's Health Insurance Program (CHIP) (Balanced Budget Act 1997). CHIP makes available to states about $48 billion in federal funds over a ten-year period to expand health insurance for uninsured low-income children and adolescents. States with approved plans are entitled to receive an allotment of federal funds that they may use, together with state matching funds, either to expand Medicaid, create a separate state program, or both. States have broad flexibility in designing their programs. States may cover adolescents living in families with incomes under 200 percent of the federal poverty level (FPL) (or higher in some circumstances) and are authorized to provide a broad benefit package. A significant feature of CHIP is that states receive federal funds at a more favorable matching rate than they do for their regular Medicaid programs (NHeLP et al. 1997).

In addition to states' ability to cover adolescents up to 200 percent FPL and to provide broad benefits, CHIP includes two elements of importance for adolescents. First, states may accelerate their coverage of poor adolescents up to age nineteen in their Medicaid programs and receive the enhanced CHIP matching rate for doing so: many states have availed themselves of this option. Second, states may choose to spend up to 10 percent of their federal CHIP funds on outreach or on direct provision of services. These 10 percent funds could be spent on health care provider sites that have traditionally served homeless youth or other adolescents who are alone. Many of these sites have depended in the past on federal and state categorical funding programs. Full implementation of CHIP could dramatically reduce the number of uninsured adolescents overall, although its implications for adolescents who are alone will depend on the manner in which states choose to spend their CHIP funds (English 1998).

Federal and State Categorical Funding Programs

The funding available through federal and state categorical programs to support health services for adolescents has been critically important in establishing and maintaining the infrastructure of service delivery for this population. Even some of those adolescents who have insurance coverage utilize services from these alternative sites because they lack assurance of being able to obtain confidential services when an insurance claim requires parental involvement (AMA 1993; Brindis et al. 1995).

The federal programs that have provided funding, directly or indirectly, for health care services received by adolescents include, among others (OTA 1991c):

- Community health centers
- Migrant health centers
- Health care for the homeless
- Maternal and child health block grant
- Ryan White Pediatric AIDS demonstrations
- Family planning
- National Institutes of Child Health and Human Development
- Children's mental health services
- Substance abuse prevention demonstrations for high-risk youth
- Adolescent family life programs
- Special education grants to the states (Individuals with Disabilities in Education Act [IDEA] Part B)

A similarly broad array of programs exist at the state level. Few of these programs fund health care and related services to adolescents exclusively, much less services to adolescents who are alone, and many of them have experienced actual reductions in funding or a slowing in their funding's rate of growth.

Thus, several different phenomena are simultaneously threatening the stability of financing for adolescent health care: the increase in the percentage of adolescents who are insured, although this may be mitigated with the advent of the CHIP program; the explosive growth in managed care enrollment in both the private and public sectors; the increasing pressure on state health and welfare budgets that might result from welfare reform; and the erosion of funding for categorical services that teens use.

Conclusion

Adolescents experience numerous barriers that impede their access to health care. The complexity of the process and the severity of the impediments often increase when adolescents are alone. Many of the barriers are specifically legal in nature and others have legal underpinnings. In view of the serious health issues that affect this age group, and the importance of health care and health related services in addressing these issues, removal of the legal barriers is an essential component of any strategy to improve adolescent health. For adolescents alone, this is unlikely to occur without concerted advocacy by a broad range of individuals who care about them.

References

Alan Guttmacher Institute (AGI) (1994). *Sex and America's teenagers.* Washington, DC: Alan Guttmacher Institute.

Alan Guttmacher Institute (AGI) (1995). Lawmakers grapple with parents' role in teen access to reproductive health care. *Issues in Brief, 1* (November), 3–4.

American Academy of Pediatrics (AAP) (1995). Committee on Practice and Ambulatory Medicine. Recommendations for pediatric preventive health care. *Pediatrics, 96,* 373–374.

American Medical Association (AMA) (1992). *Guidelines for adolescent preventive services.* Chicago: American Medical Association.

American Medical Association (AMA) (1996). *Healthy youth 2000: A mid-decade review.* Chicago: American Medical Association.

American Medical Association Council on Scientific Affairs (1993). Confidential health services for adolescents. *Journal of the American Medical Association, 269,* 1420–1424.

American School Health Association, Association for the Advancement of Health Education, and Society for Public Health Education, Inc. (1989). *The national adolescent student health survey: A report on the health of America's youth.* Oakland, CA: Third Party Publishing.

Appelbaum, P. S., C. W. Lidz, and A. Meisel (1987). *Informed consent: Legal theory and clinical practice.* New York: Oxford University Press.

Aspen Systems Corporation (1996). *Health maintenance organizations: State law compliance guide.* Gaithersburg, MD: Aspen Publishers, Inc.

Bearinger, L. H., and E. R. McAnarney (1988). Integrated community health delivery systems for youth: Study group report. *Journal of Adolescent Health Care, 9,* 36S–40S.

Bellotti v. Baird (1979). 443 U.S. 622.

Brellochs, C., et al. (1996). School-based primary care in a managed care environment: Options and issues. *Adolescent Medicine: State of the Art Reviews, 7,* 197–206.

Brindis, C., et al. (1995). The impact of health insurance status on adolescents' utilization of school-based clinic services: Implications for health care reform. *Journal of Adolescent Health Care, 16,* 18–25.

Brown, S. S., and L. Eisenberg, eds. (1995). *The best intentions: Unintended pregnancy and the well-being of children and families.* Washington, DC: Institute of Medicine.

Burrell, S. (1993). Financing. In L. S. Thompson and J. A. Farrow (Eds.), *Hard time, healing hands.* Arlington, VA: National Center for Education in Maternal and Child Health.

Bussiere, A., A. English, and C. Teare (1997). *Sharing information: A guide to federal laws on confidentiality and disclosure of information for child welfare agencies.* Washington, DC: American Bar Association.

Cardwell v. Bechtol (1987) (Tenn.). 724 S.W. 2d 739.

Carnegie Council on Adolescent Development (1995). *Great transitions: Preparing adolescents for a new century.* Washington, DC.

Centers for Disease Control and Prevention (CDC) (1996). *HIV/AIDS Surveillance Report* 7(2).

Centers for Disease Control and Prevention (CDC) (1995a). Youth risk behavior surveillance – United States, 1993. *Morbidity and Mortality Weekly Report CDC Surveillance Summaries, 44*(1), 1–56 (March 24).

Centers for Disease Control and Prevention (CDC) (1995b). Disabilities among children aged ≤ 17 years – United States, 1991–1992. *Morbidity and Mortality Weekly Report, 44*(33), 609–613 (August 25).

Centers for Disease Control and Prevention (CDC), Division of STD/HIV Prevention (1993). *Annual Report 1992.* Atlanta: Centers for Disease Control and Prevention.

Costello, E. J. (1989). Developments in child psychiatric epidemiology. *Journal of American Academy of Child and Adolescent Psychiatry, 28,* 836–841.

Darnell, J., et al. (1995). *How has managed care affected the urban minority poor and essential community providers?* Washington, DC: George Washington University Center for Health Policy Research.

Davis S. M., E. S. Scott, W. Wadlington, and C. H. Whitbread (1997). *Children in the legal system: Cases and materials.* (2d ed). Westbury, NY: The Foundation Press, Inc.

Donovan, P. (1992). *Our daughter's decisions: The conflict in state law on abortion and other issues.* Washington, DC: Alan Guttmacher Institute.

Dryfoos, J. G. (1990). *Adolescents at Risk: Prevalence and Prevention.* New York: Oxford University Press.

English, A. (1990). Treating adolescents: Legal and ethical considerations. *Medical Clinics of North America – Adolescent Medicine, 74,* 1097–1112.

English, A. (1994). Adolescents and health care reform: Protecting special populations. In C. E. Irwin (Ed.), *Health care reform: Opportunities for improving adolescent health.* Arlington, VA: National Center for Education in Maternal and Child Health.

English, A. (1995). Guidelines for adolescent health research: Legal perspectives. *Journal of Adolescent Health, 17,* 277–286.

English, A. (1998). The new children's health insurance program: Early implementation and special populations. *Clearinghouse Review.* In Press.

English, A., and M. D. Freundlich (1997). Medicaid: A key to health care for foster children and adopted children with special needs. *Clearinghouse Review, 31,* 109–131.

English A., C. Kapphahn, J. Perkins, C.W. Wibbelsman (1998). Meeting the health care needs of adolescents in managed care: A background paper. *Journal of Adolescent Health, 22,* 278–292.

English, A., M. Matthews, K. Extavour, C. Palamountain, and J. Yang (1995). *State minor consent statutes: A summary.* Cincinnati, OH: Center for Continuing Education in Adolescent Health.

Ensign J., and J. Santelli (1998). Health status and service use. Comparison of adolescents at a school-based health clinics with homeless adolescents. *Archives of Pediatrics and Adolescent Medicine, 152,* 20–24.

Freund, D. A., and E. L. Lewit (1993). Managed care for children and pregnant women: Promises and pitfalls. *The Future of Children, 3,* 92–122.

Gans, J. E., M. A. McManus, and P. W. Newacheck (1991). Adolescent health care: Use, costs, and problems of access. *American Medical Association Profiles of Adolescent Health Series (Vol.2).* Chicago, IL: American Medical Association.

Gittler, J., M. Quigley-Rick, and M. J. Saks (1990). *Adolescent Health Care Decision Making: The Law and Public Policy.* Washington, DC: Carnegie Council on Adolescent Development.

Green, M., ed. (1994). *Bright futures: Guidelines for health supervision of infants, children, and adolescents.* Washington, DC: National Center for Education in Maternal and Child Health.

Halfon, N., and L. Klee (1991). Health and development services for children with multiple needs: The child in foster care. *Yale Law and Policy Review, 9,* 71–95.

Health Care Financing Administration (HCFA) (1994). *EPSDT Program Indicators: Fiscal Year 1993.* Washington, DC (November 22).

Hochstadt, N., et al. (1987). The medical and psychosocial needs of children entering foster care. *Child Abuse and Neglect, 11,* 53.

Hodgson v. Minnesota (1990). 497 U.S. 417.

Hofmann, A. D. (1980). A rational policy toward consent and confidentiality. *Journal of Adolescent Health Care, 1*(1), 9–17 (September).

Holder, A. R. (1985). *Legal issues in pediatric and adolescent medicine* (2nd ed.). New Haven, CT: Yale University Press.

Homberg, S. D. (1996). The Estimated Prevalence and Incidence of HIV in 96 Large U.S. Metropolitan Areas. *American Journal of Public Health, 86*(5), 642–654 (May).

Hughes, D. (1996). *Unpublished Tabulations from the Current Population Survey.* San Francisco: University of California at San Francisco.

In the Interest of E.G. (1987) (III. App.). 515 N.E.2d 287.

Institute of Medicine (1989). Research on children and adolescents with mental, behavioral, and developmental disorders. Washington, DC: National Academy Press.

Katz, S. N., et al. (1973). Emancipating our children – Coming of legal age in America. *Family Law Quarterly, 7(3),* 211–241.

Klein, J. D., et al. (1992). *Comprehensive adolescent health services in the United States 1990.* Chapel Hill, NC: University of North Carolina.

Levine, R. J. (1995). Adolescents as research subjects without permission of their parents or guardians: Ethical considerations. *Journal of Adolescent Health, 17,* 287–297.

Mammel, K. A., and D. W. Kaplan (1995). Research consent by adolescent minors and institutional review boards. *Journal of Adolescent Health, 17,* 323–330.

McKinney, D. H., and G. L. Peak (1995). *Update 1994: School-based and school-linked health care centers.* Washington, DC: Advocates for Youth.

Meyer v. Nebraska (1923). 262 U.S. 390.

Morrissey, J. M., A. D. Hofmann, and J. C. Thrope. (1986). *Consent and confidentiality in the health care of children and adolescents: A legal guide.* New York: Free Press.

National Health Law Program (NHeLP), National Center for Youth Law, National Senior Citizens Law Center (1996). *An analysis of the new welfare law and its effect on medicaid recipients.* Los Angeles: National Health Law Program (August).

National Health Law Program (NHeLP), National Center for Youth Law, National Senior Citizens Law Center (1997). *Reshaping the health safety net for America's poor: An analysis of the Balanced Budget Act of 1997.* Los Angeles: National Health Law Program.

Newacheck, P. W. (1992). Characteristics of children with low and high usage of physician services. *Medical Care, 30,* 30–42.

Newacheck, P. W., D. Hughes, and M. Cisternas (1995). Children and health insurance: An overview of recent trends. *Health Affairs, 14,* 244–254.

Newacheck, P. W., et al. (1994). Children with chronic illness and medicaid managed care. *Pediatrics, 93*(3), 497–500 (March).

Newacheck, P. W., M. A. McManus (1990). Health care expenditure patterns for adolescents. *Journal of Adolescent Health Care, 11,* 133–140.

Newacheck, P. W., M. A. McManus, and J. Gephart (1992). Health insurance coverage of adolescents: A current profile and analysis of trends. *Pediatrics, 90*(4), 589–596 (October).

Ozer, E. M., C. D. Brindis, S. G. Millstein, D. K. Knopf, and C. E. Irwin, Jr. (1998). *America's adolescents: Are they healthy?* San Francisco: National Adolescent Health Information Center, University of California, San Francisco.

Paradise, E., and R. M. Horowitz (1994). *Runaway and homeless youth: A survey of state law.* Washington, DC: American Bar Association Center on Children and the Law.

Parham v. J.R. (1979). 442 U.S. 584.

Pierce v. Society of Sisters (1925). 268 U.S. 510.

Planned Parenthood of Central Missouri v. Danforth (1976). 428 U.S. 52.

Prince v. Massachusetts (1944). 321 U.S. 158.

Rosenberg, P. S., R. J. Biggar, and J. J. Goedert (1994). Declining age at HIV infection in the United States. *New England Journal of Medicine, 330*(11), 789–790 (March 17).

Rosovsky, F. A. (1990). *Consent to treatment: A practical guide 255* (2nd ed.). Boston: Little Brown & Co.

Rowland, D., et al. (1995). *Medicaid and managed care: Lessons from the literature – A report of the Kaiser Commission on the future of Medicaid.* Washington, DC: The Henry J. Kaiser Family Foundation.

Santelli, J. S., et al. (1995). Guidelines for adolescent health research: A position paper of the society for adolescent medicine. *Journal of Adolescent Health, 17,* 270–276.

Schlitt, J. J., et al. (1995). State initiatives for support of school-based health centers: A national survey. *Journal of Adolescent Health, 17,* 68–76.

Schor, E. L. (1989). Foster Care. *Pediatrics in Review, 10,* 209–216.

Schwalberg, R., and I. Hill (1995). *Coordinating adolescent health centers and managed care: State experiences and lessons learned.* Washington, DC: Health Systems Research.

Simons, J., B. Finlay, and A. Yang (1991). *The adolescent and young adult fact book.* Washington, DC: Children's Defense Fund.

Society for Adolescent Medicine (1995). Guidelines for adolescent health research. *Journal of Adolescent Health, 17*(5), 264–269.

Society for Adolescent Medicine (1998). Meeting the health care needs of adolescents in managed care: A position paper of the society for adolescent medicine. *Journal of Adolescent Health, 22,* 271–277.

Soler, M. I., A. C. Shotton, and J. R. Bell (1993). *Glass walls: Confidentiality provisions and interagency collaborations.* San Francisco: Youth Law Center.

Thompson, L. S. (1993). Health Status and Health Care Issues. In L. S. Thompson and J. A. Farrow (Ed.), *Hard time, healing hands.* Arlington, VA: National Center for Education in Maternal and Child Health.

U.S. Congress Office of Technology Assessment (OTA) (1991a). *Adolescent health – Volume I: Summary and policy options.* Washington, DC: U.S. Government Printing Office.

U.S. Congress Office of Technology Assessment (OTA) (1991b). *Adolescent health – Volume II: Background and the effectiveness of selected prevention and treatment services.* Washington, DC: U.S. Government Printing Office.

U.S. Congress Office of Technology Assessment (OTA) (1991c). *Adolescent health – Volume III: Crosscutting issues in the delivery of health and related services.* Washington, DC: U.S. Government Printing Office.

U.S. General Accounting Office (GAO) (1992). *Factors to consider in managed care programs* (Statement of Janet L. Shikles, Director of Human Resources Division). Washington, DC: U.S. Government Printing Office (June 29).

William T. Grant Foundation Commission on Work, Family and Citizenship (1988). *The forgotten half: Pathways to success for America's youth and young families.* New York: W.T. Grant Foundation.

Winterfeld, A. P. (1995). Managed care, privatization, and their impact on the child welfare system. *Protecting Children, 11,* 3–6.

Statutes and Regulations

Balanced Budget Act of 1997, Public Law No. 105–33, §§ 4901–4923, 42 U.S.C. §§ 1397aa–1397jj.

California Family Code § 6922.

California Family Code § 6924.

California Family Code § 6926.

California Family Code § 6924.

California Family Code § 6926.

Minnesota Statutes § 253B.03(6)(d).

Ohio Revised Code § 5122.04.

New York Public Health Code § 2780(5).

New York Public Health Code § 2781.

42 Code of Federal Regulations (C.F.R.) Part 2.

42 C.F.R. Part 59.

42 United States Code (U.S.C.) §§ 300 et seq.

42 U.S.C. §§ 1396a(a)(30)(A).

42 U.S.C. § 1396a(I)(1)(D).
42 U.S.C. § 1396d(a)(4)(B)
42 U.S.C. § 1396d(r).
42 U.S.C. § 1396d(r)(1)-(4).
42 U.S.C. § 1396d(r)(5).
42 U.S.C. § 1396r-7.
45 C.F.R. Part 46.
45 C.F.R. § 46.402(a).
45 C.F.R. § 46.404,
45 C.F.R. 46.405(c).
45 C.F.R. 46.406(d).
45 C.F.R. 46.407(b)(iii).
45 C.F.R. § 46.408.
45 C.F.R. § 46.116.
45 C.F.R. §§ 46.404, 46.405(c), 46.406(d), 46.407(b)(iii).

5 Valid Consent to Treatment and the Unsupervised Adolescent

Jeffrey Blustein and Jonathan D. Moreno

In this chapter we are concerned with the conditions under which an unsupervised adolescent can give ethically valid consent to medical treatment. We will not be concerned with the legal and financial obstacles that prevent those adolescents who are capable of making their own treatment decisions from doing so. There are many such obstacles, and sometimes they are insuperable. Rather, our focus is on the implications of the bioethical consensus for adolescent consent in general, and more particularly, for the unsupervised adolescent. We want to know how the lack of parental or adult supervision affects the psychological development of young people, and what conclusions can be drawn about adolescent decisional capacity. Even if the adolescent's capacity is questionable, there may be other reasons for extending to the youth the authority to make treatment decisions.

A Minor's Capacity to Consent: Emergence of a Moral Self

Most developmental psychologists agree that in the normal child the ability to conceptualize the cause of illness achieves a milestone around the ages of twelve to fourteen. At this point, many are able to understand that there are interactions between external events and internal structures and functions; what was before comprehensible only as the effect of an independent "germ" is now conceivable as the net result of an interactive process. This new understanding of the causation of illness is related to the development, around this age, of several capacities that make up what Piaget called the formal operations stage of cognitive development. As characterized by Grisso and Vierling (1978), "this stage includes the development of an increased cognitive capacity to bring certain operations to bear on abstract concepts in problem-solving situations." Also at this age, children develop the ability to "perform inductive and deductive operations or hypothetical reasoning at a level of abstraction that would be represented by many consent situations involving treatment alternatives and risks." Indeed, by mid-adolescence, many researchers report, reasoning ability is as good as that seen in adulthood and involves the same flaws (Kuhn, Amsel, and O'Laughlin 1988).

Strictly intellectual obstacles to adolescent capacity to consent appear to be less troublesome than emotional and other psychological factors, especially with regard

100

to the vaunted, if not always well understood, bioethical principle of autonomy. In the following discussion *autonomy* refers to "self-government," and *self-determination* refers to the individual's practical ability to implement autonomy. Thus a teenager may be autonomous but not self-determining, because laws or customs may restrict the exercise of autonomy to those who have reached a certain chronological age. Although this is not a common distinction in the bioethics literature, which tends to use the terms *autonomy* and *self-determination* interchangeably, we believe our usage better reflects the practical situation of adolescents.

According to the way we understand autonomy, an autonomous individual is, at a minimum, one who has a "self" to govern. The government of a self, like that of a state, requires a more or less stable entity, one that is recognizable by the "governor" as the "same thing," even though it might undergo change in some nonessential characteristics. Whatever metaphysical account one might give of the nature of personal identity – a subject we shall not attempt to address here – we take it to be uncontroversial that, unless there are some enduring characteristics, there is no self to be governed.

Common notions of moral responsibility also seem to depend on the idea that holding someone responsible for his or her actions requires at a minimum a relatively stable person. The mentally ill and very young adolescents are usually disqualified from responsibility, unless there are exceptional conditions – for example, if a crime is heinous and shocking enough.

The question of whether adolescents in general are capable of making autonomous decisions is closely tied to the question of whether, and at what point, adolescents have enduring personal characteristics that are relevant to moral self-government. That is, there is no doubt that the normal adolescent is capable of recognizing selfhood: a teenager has long since achieved the ability to say "I" with meaning. However, it is not nearly so clear that or when the normal adolescent develops a *moral* self, so that he or she can say with meaning, "I value this or that," so that a particular decision is *authentic,* an expression of who I am in a moral sense, of what kind of person I am, or what is really important to me.

It comes as no surprise that the adolescent's moral self is often incompletely formed, because one of the developmental goals of adolescence is precisely the evolution of a moral self. One often hears the teenage years described in the language of experimentation and exploration, of discovering who one is, and so forth. This results in a substantial problem for the contemporary bioethical consensus on consent, which typically operates under one of three conditions:

1. A person has a moral self, and therefore A's decisions should be respected.
2. A person once had a moral self, and therefore A's relevant and reasonably specific decisions should still be respected.
3. A person never had a moral self, and therefore what will be done is what A would have wanted had A been able to recognize his or her own best interests.

A variant of the second point that seems at first glance similar to the adolescent situation is this:

A person has a moral self, but A's capacity to decide based on that moral self is diminished. Therefore, until A regains full capacity, decisions will be made either according to what is known about what A would have wanted, or according to what is in A's best interests (what is surmised about what A would have wanted were A reasonable).

But the adolescent's situation is not one of diminished capacity; rather, it is one of *emerging* capacity. The moral self is evolving, not diminishing. Emergence and evolution occur in fits and starts, not in an even and consistent progression. Two steps forward can be followed by one or more steps back. One feature of this process is the tendency to overidentify with the perceived values of others, such as peers or strong adult figures (rarely parents!), in an effort to "try on" those values to see how they feel. Thus, before the age of fourteen or fifteen, for example, an adolescent's ability to make a voluntary decision is limited by hypersensitivity to influential others.

According to contemporary medical ethics, ethically valid consent to medical treatment requires more than the possession of capacities for communication and understanding of information, reasoning, and deliberation. The ability to comprehend and weigh the risks and benefits of medical alternatives is only one aspect of the consent process. According to the standard view, especially concerning major or life-sustaining treatment, these decisions are necessarily moral ones in the sense that they have to do with the patient's goals for life, and what one considers preferable in light of one's conception of the "good life." The presence, absence, or degree of development of the moral self is therefore an important factor in determining whether an individual can give ethically valid consent to treatment. This element of valid consent may not be required in the law, but it is implicit in the philosophical idea of "appreciating," as well as understanding, the relevant treatment alternatives.

Standards of Competence

Two rival conceptions of competence in the bioethics literature can be identified: an all-or-none or *absolute* conception, and a shifting, or relative, standard. According to the absolute conception, one either is or is not competent to decide about one's medical treatment. According to the relative conception, one may be competent to make one treatment decision but not another. The absolute conception has tended to be favored in the law, but has been subjected to vigorous criticism on philosophical and psychological grounds. On this view, competence is global and admits of no exceptions. But it is clear that different decision-making situations call upon different skills, and so bioethicists have come to favor a "task-specific" conception, and they attempt to emphasize this interpretation by parsing competence as *decisional capacity*. Regarding adolescents, the relative view suggests that, as the teenager's moral development advances, decisional capacity will extend to a greater number and variety of decisional tasks. The implication is that one can gradually attribute more and more decisional capacity to adolescents.

Gaylin (1982) combined this sort of relative view of competence with a risk–benefit approach to decision making for children. He argued that when the risks of treatment are low and the benefits are high, the child should have to meet a higher threshold of capacity when declining treatment than when agreeing to treatment. Likewise, the child should have to meet a higher threshold when agreeing to a high-risk, low-benefit treatment than when declining such treatment. In other words, decisions that seem suspicious on their face, considering the patently more favorable risk–benefit ratio of another option, would have to meet a higher standard of decision-making capacity and be subjected to greater scrutiny than others. Determinations of capacity are made by employing what is called a *sliding scale.*

Although the decisional capacity of adolescents and patients in other categories, such as the mentally ill, might ethically be scrutinized somewhat more carefully than that of the apparently competent adult patient, a sliding scale is also utilized clinically with adults. Typically, when dealing with seemingly competent adults, no in-depth assessment of capacity is initiated or required, and even when the expected consequences to adults of accepting their decisions are adverse, we tend to give patients the benefit of the doubt, in accordance with the high value our society places on personal autonomy. Among so-called normal adults, therefore, decisions to assess competence for decisional capacity must be triggered for some good reason. This assessment might reveal an underlying clinical depression, the influence of a major pharmacologic regimen, or some other capacity-diminishing condition.

Presumptions of Capacity and the Sliding-Scale

We do not, as a rule, raise questions about the capacity of adults to make their own treatment decisions. There are at least two ways to try to justify this practice. First, we can invoke the notion of a moral presumption: adults, as we often say, should be presumed to have the capacity to decide for themselves about treatment. Second, we can invoke the sliding scale: in most cases, the anticipated consequences of accepting the patient's decision are not so adverse for the patient as to warrant an individualized assessment of capacity. That is, in the usual run of things, treatment decisions are not problematic from the standpoint of their risk–benefit ratios, and so there is no particular reason to initiate an examination of capacity. Because of this, most adults can be presumed to have the capacity to give their own informed consent, but it is important to note that in this account, it is the sliding scale, not some independent notion of a presumption of decisional capacity, that is doing the moral work.

Much the same can be said about normal adolescents who, by about the age fourteen or fifteen, have achieved the cognitive capacity of the average adult. Here, too, it might be said either that there should be a presumption of capacity in these adolescents, or that presumption of capacity is a derivative notion and that what is really doing the moral work is the sliding scale. Of course, there will be differences between normal adults and normal adolescents in this age range. What counts as a risk or harm for adolescents may not be so for adults, and in judging whether a risk–benefit ratio is favorable or unfavorable, this must be taken into account. But for both groups of patients, the sliding scale tells us when and whether an individualized assessment of capacity is required.

There is a way, internal to this account, of drawing a distinction between judging capacity in adults and judging it in adolescents, and this is the approach we favor. The sliding scale represents an attempt to balance two principles in determining whether a patient will decide about his or her own treatment – the principle of respect for patient autonomy and the principle of beneficence. We can reintroduce the notion of a presumption of capacity among adults if we stipulate that in this group of patients – and not in the elderly or in children and adolescents – the former principle has significantly greater moral weight than the latter. Thus, it will remain the case that among adults, a contrary decision in the face of a patently favorable risk/benefit ratio should be grounds for an individualized assessment of capacity. But because the principle of respect for patient autonomy has significantly greater moral weight among adults, we do not initiate an assessment of capacity unless the risk–benefit ratio is *extremely* favorable. (A parallel point can be made about the case where an adult agrees to a treatment with an unfavorable risk–benefit ratio.) In other words, the threshold for the risk–benefit ratio that should trigger an assessment of capacity is higher for adults than for adolescents. The reason for the distinction is that the developing moral selfhood of the normal teenager renders the authenticity of his or her judgments more suspect than that of the normal adult. A teenager's oppositional stance, while perhaps not defective in a purely cognitive sense, is probably not based on a well-established set of values that constitute a stable and recognizable moral self.

Consent as Event and as Process

It is commonplace of autonomy-based ethics that one not only should respect an individual's autonomy but, where reasonable, should also promote it. Arguably there are special obligations in this regard with respect to adolescent patients, because they are on the "cusp" of achieving this status, and every generation of adults has an interest in seeing that teenagers achieve their autonomy and become cognitively integrated and reflective adults. Adolescents, too, have a special interest in autonomy-promoting practices, since this period is uniquely characterized by the relatively rapid evolution of personal autonomy, and a "successful" adolescence will normally be one in which personal autonomy has been realized.

Unfortunately, most of the "consent" practices that take place in our health care institutions fail to promote, let alone respect, patient autonomy.

Two models of informed consent highlight different possibilities for adolescents in this regard. According to one model, informed consent is a singular *event* in which the patient has the opportunity to learn about a proposed treatment and its alternatives. The event is embodied and punctuated in the signing of an informed consent form. According to another model, informed consent is a *process* of conversation and education that takes place between a health care professional and a patient. The original consent form may be supervened by subsequent versions that reflect the evolving perspective of the patient.

Adolescents seem especially well-positioned to benefit from the far more intensive process model of informed consent. Developmental maturity can be promoted and reflected at successive moments in the process. Especially in treatments that require weeks or even months for complete administration, such as some cancer treatments, or for interventions that are elective and can be anticipated well in advance, the opportunity to engage in repeated sessions can make a great deal of difference to a teenager with emerging capacity. An adolescent patient who is not capable of consent to treatment at the beginning of a consent process, and perhaps in the early stages of treatment, may well achieve capacity at some time during the consent process or treatment, a capacity that health care professionals have an obligation both to nurture and, once achieved, to respect.

Unsupervised Adolescents: Developmental Considerations

Whatever generalizations we may be able to formulate about the decisional capacity of more or less *normal* adolescents at a certain stage of their development, there is good reason to believe that they will have to be modified in significant ways when dealing with special populations such as runaways, homeless, and street kids. Indeed, the category of *unsupervised adolescent* is itself a heterogeneous one, and empirical generalizations about the moral and psychological development of these youngsters will have to take into account the diverse histories and life circumstances of the various subgroups of adolescents within this broad category. Specifically, we need to attend to at least these two factors: the age of onset of the lack of supervision and the character of the parental relationship. How the lack of parental or adult supervision affects adolescent development, it is reasonable to suppose, depends on which phase of adolescent development the young person is going through at the time of onset, and on the developmental tasks the adolescent is expected to master at that stage.

Further, adolescents who are unsupervised have various family histories. Some unsupervised adolescents have taken care of parents dying of AIDS and essentially become surrogate parents for younger siblings after the parents die; some adolescents live on the streets, or in one homeless shelter after another, because they have run away from abusive parents. Some adolescents are homosexuals who have been kicked out of their homes by disapproving parents; some spend years in a series of foster homes. In each case, the adolescent is deprived of the benefits of an intimate and loving relationship with adults, and in each case the specific psychological and emotional impact of the lack of psychological parents has to be examined. What we need is a detailed typography of the different categories of adolescents who lack ongoing parental or adult supervision and a fine-grained empirical analysis of the impact of this lack of supervision on adolescent developmental capacity. Only then will we be able to proceed with confidence to address the ethical concerns that arise for adolescent health care professionals.

Nothing like comprehensive and systematic research has been done on the developmental characteristics of unsupervised adolescents. Nevertheless, we believe that the existing literature on child development can give us some insight into the psychological difficulties that may be experienced by these youngsters, and that reasonable inferences about unsupervised adolescents can be drawn from the developmental literature.

The clear consensus that emerges from a review of this literature is that children's psychological development is profoundly influenced by the kind of care they receive. There is also significant consensus within society at large on a number of childrearing goals, and research has identified characteristics of the most adequate kinds of environment and care for children. These include the following: consistency, predictability or stability of parental behavior over time; stimulation from things and people; responsiveness to the child's behavior; reasonable limit-setting, with limits firmly but gently enforced; positive encouragement of the child's independent strivings; and affection. When all or some of these caregiving qualities are absent or expressed only sporadically – and this is what the expression *unsupervised* is actually shorthand for – various psychological deficits can be expected to result. How far-reaching and long-lasting these deficits will be depends on various factors, including the vulnerability of the adolescent and the particular conflicts and tensions within the parent–child relationship.

We will briefly consider deficits in the following five areas and their effects on the capacity to give an ethically valid informed consent: (a) self-esteem, (b) control of drives and impulses, (c) temporal perspective, (d) cognitive abilities, and (e) development of trust.

Effects on Self-esteem

In order to develop healthy self-esteem, a child needs to feel loved, valued, and wanted by at least one person who can be loved in return. The child can then become convinced of personal value and confident of the ability to fulfill life goals. A child who feels unwanted – whose sense of personal worth is not nurtured and supported by caring adults – is plagued by failure and self-doubt, apathy, and cynicism in later childhood and adult life. This is shown in various ways: by an inability to begin or complete projects, diminished concern for the well-being of one's own body or appearance, and a tendency toward self-destructive activities. Severe depression is also a concomitant of low self-esteem.

Even if an older adolescent is able to grasp, intellectually, the consequences of choices and actions, these factors are clearly detrimental to the development of decisional capacity, if this is thought of as involving appreciation as well as understanding of consequences. This has particular relevance for unsupervised youth, many of whom have been neglected, abandoned, or abused by their parents from a young age.

Effects on Control of Drives and Impulses

Along with love, a child needs limits. These help to control behavior and to cope with impulses. In time, these external limits become internalized, and the child develops adequate internal coping mechanisms. Without firm and consistent adult control, however, the child does not develop the capacity to postpone gratification and to cope with internal stresses and external frustration. The child becomes narcissistic and excessively dependent on others for the satisfaction of needs. The adolescent impulsively engages in adult-like behaviors (e.g., drinking, drug use, sexual relations) in an attempt to mask deep-seated feelings of anxiety and inadequacy.

Limit-setting also has a particular developmental role in adolescence. A certain degree of impulsive behavior occurs from time to time in most adolescents as a way of testing the limits of adult authority. But adolescents need and often want externally imposed limits, and many become frightened when they feel that limits have not been defined. Without parents or parent surrogates to impose controls – and this is the case with unsupervised adolescents – the normal confusions of adolescence are intensified, and this casts serious doubt on the adolescent's capacity for giving informed consent.

Effects on Temporal Perspective

Closely related to the ability to control impulses and drives is a sense of the future as continuous with the present. Present-oriented thinking is, again, a normal developmental characteristic of children and adolescents, but normally during adolescence there is an increased consciousness of and concern for future roles and experiences. The lack of stable and predictable relations with parents or parent substitutes, however, impedes the development of future-time perspective. In the chaotic conditions in which most street kids, runaways, and other unsupervised adolescents live, there are few external supports to help the adolescent organize experiences in an orderly temporal sequence. In contrast to adolescents who come from functioning families, temporal perspective tends to remain more focused on the present, on immediate wants and needs, rather than on long-term consequences.

In the perilous environments in which runaways and street kids live, it is often difficult to plan far ahead, and the press of immediate needs takes precedence over concern for the future. But, in addition, the lack of continuous parental or adult supervision may adversely affect the development of a capacity critical to autonomous decision making – the capacity to give due consideration to potential future outcomes of current decisions.

Effects on Cognitive Abilities

The exact chronologic age at which certain cognitive abilities are attained depends on factors such as individual differences in physiologic functioning, experience, and environmental stimulation. Lack of appropriate stimulation from people and things may result in serious language deficits, which are associated with deficiencies in the ability to conceptualize. In addition, even if an individual attains a higher level of cognitive functioning, stress can have a profound influence on his ability to use these higher-order cognitive skills in solving problems. The general physical and emotional regression seen in hospitalized children, for example, is often accompanied by a cognitive regression, regardless of their usual functional ability.

Further empirical research is needed to determine how lack of parental or adult supervision interferes with cognitive development and how the stressful conditions in which unsupervised adolescents live affect their ability to use such cognitive skills as they possess. Significant adverse effects in both areas are likely.

Effects on Development of Trust

The first stage of psychosocial development, according to Erikson (1963), is the development of basic trust and the overcoming of mistrust. Basic trust is the foundation of success in future relationships and endeavors. For trust to develop, the child needs to experience a mutually satisfying relationship based on familiarity, regularity, and predictability. If this is missing, if the child experiences unalleviated physical discomfort or is uncertain about whether basic needs will be met, new experiences will be faced with apprehension or mistrust. This mistrust will carry over into later childhood and adulthood and poison relationships with others outside the family.

Many of the unsupervised adolescents we describe have not been raised in environments that are regularly and predictably responsive to their needs, and so have not been able to develop a sense of confidence in the good will of others. Moreover, life on the streets is dangerous and precarious, in itself a reason for mistrust and apprehension.

This lack of trust, developmentally grounded and socially reinforced, has important implications for the informed consent process, because the informed consent process can only accomplish its purpose within a framework of trust between the one is who is being informed (here the unsupervised adolescent) and the one doing the informing (the health care professional). If this trust is lacking, the adolescent either will refuse to listen to what is being said or, feeling that there is no choice, will reluctantly go along with what is being recommended.

The Strengths of Unsupervised Adolescents

Although many unsupervised adolescents develop serious behavioral and psychological difficulties as a result of their exposure to the adversities and stresses that often attend life without parental or other adult supervision, this is not invariably the case. Even with the most dreadful experiences of living on the streets, experiences that would be deeply traumatic to many young people, a significant number of unsupervised adolescents escape serious sequelae. The quality that enables individuals who are exposed to multiple risk factors to function effectively and to buffer the effects of stressful life experiences, is called *resilience*.

There is a large and growing body of clinical and developmental literature on resilience that helps us to understand why some children are able to cope successfully with significant ongoing stress and adversity (Cohler 1982; Luther and Zigler 1991; Rutter 1993). The factors that contribute to the capacity of the resilient child to cope with stress have been grouped into three main categories: the personal attributes of the child, the nature of the relationship with parents or parent substitutes, and the availability of supportive persons and networks beyond the family. Although unsupervised adolescents typically come from families that lack many of the characteristics that contribute to resilience – such as unconditional acceptance by their parents and firm but nonpunitive parental discipline – they may nevertheless possess qualities of temperament and social skills that enable them to triumph over the challenges and stresses of daily life. At the same time, we must be careful not to equate behavioral with psychological competence, for adolescents who are labeled resilient may be as prone to internal distress, such as anxiety and depression, as their less resilient counterparts.

We do not want to deny that credit is due to those unsupervised adolescents who manage to survive adversity and who are skilled at using their social world to meet their needs. However, resilience is a complex phenomenon that does not correlate in any simple and direct way with the capacity to give an ethically valid informed consent. Resilience and the possession of successful coping skills may indicate a certain kind of psychological maturity, but decisional capacity might still be impaired because of the absence of a consistent, nurturing adult in the adolescent's life.

Conclusion

Although the teenagers we have been discussing may be less likely than others in their age group to possess the psychological prerequisites for competence in health care decision making (on the assumption that the psychological profile of such youth is accepted by the relevant professional community), we do not believe that this justifies a comparatively reduced effort to gain their consent, because the obligation to raise their level of capacity, and thus their self-determination, would remain. Ingenious measures may be required; one group of investigators has designed consent forms with the participation of street youth (Larkin Street Youth Center 1990).

Further, we do not want to leave the impression that adolescent decisional *capacity* is the only factor to consider in determining whether adolescents ought to have decisional *authority* about their medical care. Allowing adolescents to consent to

medical care on their own, even when there is reason to suspect that they lack sufficient decisional capacity due to arrested psychological development, may sometimes be justified on consequentialist grounds. A significant number of
unsupervised adolescents come from dysfunctional families. They are living on
their own because they believe, rightly or wrongly, that their parents have not been
concerned, understanding, and supportive, or because their parents have physically
or sexually abused them. A requirement of parental consent, or even parental notification, may thus be harmful to these youngsters, and may also drive them away
from seeking needed medical care.

A major challenge confronting adolescent health care professionals is determining how to gain and maintain the trust of adolescents who, for deep-seated psychological reasons, may have a pervasive distrust of others. Simply put, without trust
in the provider, the provider's efforts to serve the adolescent's medical needs will
be frustrated. This is one reason why involving parents in the care of unsupervised
adolescents – even if this were feasible – is so problematic. At the same time, if our
account of the psychological development of these youngsters is correct, many of
these adolescents lack the ego structures that are usually indicative of emotional
maturation by the mid- and late-teen years. How this should be factored into decisions about the care of adolescents with no parent or other involved adult in their
lives is a question of critical moral and professional importance.

References

Cohler, B. (1982). Adversity, resilience, and the study of lives. In E. James, A. and B. Cohler
    (Eds.) *The invulnerable child.* New York: Guilford Press.
Erikson, E. (1963). *Childhood and society* (2nd ed.). New York: W. W. Norton and Co.,
    247–251.
Gaylin, W. (1982). Competence: No longer all or none. In W. Gaylin and R. Macklin (Eds.)
    Who speaks for the child. New York: Plenum Press.
Grisso, T., and L. Vierling (1978). Minors' consent to treatment: A developmental perspec-
    tive. *Professional Psychology, 9,* 412–427.
Kuhn, D., E. Amsel, and M. O'Laughlin (1988). *The development of scientific thinking
    skills.* San Diego: Academic Press.
Larkin Street Youth Center (1990). *HIV and homeless youth: Meeting the challenge.* San
    Francisco: Larkin Street Youth Center.
Luther, S., and E. Zigler (1991). Vulnerability and competence: A review of research on
    resilience in childhood. *American Journal of Orthopsychiatry, 61,* 6–22.
Rutter, M. (1993). Resilience: Some conceptual considerations. *Journal of Adolescent
    Health, 14,* 626–631.

6 The Impact of Growing Up Orphaned on Decision-Making Capacity

Francine Cournos

The impact of being orphaned on adolescent decision-making capacity may, unfortunately, be a topic of growing interest as an increasing number of adolescents are left parentless by the HIV epidemic. This chapter draws upon both my childhood experience as an orphan and my work as a psychiatrist with adult patients. I examine the psychiatric literature on the subject, and, as a case example, I discuss the effect of my own losses on my reasoning about an episode of medical illness during my adolescence.

Of course, any one person's story about growing up orphaned is unique; indeed, there must be as many different reactions to it as there are orphans (Furman 1974). On the other hand, perhaps only first-person accounts can fully capture its intense impact.

Growing Up Orphaned

These are the bare facts of my childhood. I was three years old when my father died after a two-week illness caused by brain cancer. I had a brother two years older than me, and my mother was two months pregnant with my younger sister. My father had been the sole wage earner, and had left little money. My mother's parents moved in with her to help out with finances and child care. Two years later, when I was five, my grandfather died suddenly when he hemorrhaged from a stomach ulcer. Shortly after that, my mother developed breast cancer, which soon metastasized. She lived until I was eleven, undergoing multiple surgeries and other disfiguring treatments. During her terminal years, I watched the world disintegrate around me as my mother became increasingly more ill and our neighborhood – the South Bronx – became a violent ghetto. For two years following my mother's death, we continued to live with our grandmother, who, now approaching senility, took care of us until she no longer could. Then my brother went to live in a group home, and my younger sister and I were placed together in foster care. I was thirteen, my brother was fifteen, my sister was nine.

Placement in foster care was a devastating experience. I felt close to my mother's three healthy married siblings, who did not volunteer to take us in, and the feeling of rejection was profound. In addition, at thirteen, I balked at the task of starting over again with a new set of parents, and this became another source of distress.

111

One year into my placement in foster care, at the age of fourteen, I underwent surgery to remove a needle from the bottom of my foot after I accidentally stepped on it while I was barefoot. This seemingly minor matter took two procedures, general anesthesia, hours of a surgeon's operating time, and three weeks of recuperation on crutches. Would I have had the cognitive and emotional skills to make the medical decisions involved for myself?

Decision-Making Capacity: Adults and Adolescents

In general, when we think about decision-making capacity for a specific group of people, we compare them to a general population of adults. For the most part adults are allowed to make their own health care decisions without having passed strict tests of capacity (Cournos 1993). In fact, most treatment occurs with patient assent rather than informed consent (Lidz et al. 1984).

Despite the lack of attention to capacity in routine medical practice, the topic has evoked considerable debate among both academic psychiatrists and lawyers. There is no single definition of capacity, although any definition contains within it an attempt to balance individual autonomy on the one hand and the protection of the patient's needs and the public's safety on the other (Cournos et al. 1993). Appelbaum, a prominent writer in this field, has emphasized four widely accepted tests of capacity: (1) communicating choices; (2) understanding relevant information; (3) appreciating the situation and its consequences; and (4) using information rationally (Appelbaum and Grisso 1988). However, in practice, often only the first two of these standards are used.

The literature on the ability of adult patients to engage in an informed consent process shows that a substantial number of them manifest serious deficits (Cournos 1993). For example, Cassileth and colleagues studied 200 cancer patients who signed consent forms for chemotherapy, radiation therapy, or surgery. When recall was tested one day later, only 60 percent of patients understood the nature and purpose of the procedure, and only 55 percent correctly listed even one major risk or complication (Cassileth et al. 1980). Other similar studies of short-term recall among medical and surgical patients reveal that patients forget 28 percent to 71 percent of what they are told shortly after receiving verbal explanations (Wallace 1986). Because consent to treatment will generally involve agreement by the treating physician, and, where present, by the family, this check on the reasonableness of the patient's decision is assumed to protect the patient from harm (President's Commission for the Study of Ethical Problems in Medicine and Biomedical and Behavioral Research 1982).

More rigorous standards of capacity have been applied to patients who refuse hospitalization or treatment than to those who accept it (Cournos 1993). This practice takes into account the greater harm that may follow from the failure to receive necessary medical care.

How do the decision-making capacities of adolescents compare to those of adults? There is some literature on this topic, much of it focusing on teenage girls who face decisions about contraception and the choice to continue or terminate a pregnancy. Adolescent medical decision making has also been examined among children with cancer or other chronic diseases.

There is a consensus that adolescents of fourteen years and older appear to have adult or near-adult reasoning abilities, and are, from that perspective, competent to consent to medical decisions (Weithorn and Campbell 1982; Shields and Johnson 1992; Leikin 1993). Most authors refer to Piaget's concept of formal operational thinking (Weithorn and Campbell 1982; Gordon 1990; Leikin 1993). Formal operational thinking includes the ability to generate or envision alternatives, and to reason about chance and probability. This stage is reached by most adolescents between twelve and fourteen years old (Grisso and Vierling 1978; Fish-Murray, Koby, and van der Kolk 1987; Shields and Johnson 1992), although even younger children can meaningfully participate in their own medical decisions (Weithorn and Campbell 1982). Age, of course, is not the only factor, and even many adults do not possess fully developed skills in these areas (Gordon 1990).

Adolescent cognitive functioning, even when it becomes as sophisticated as that of adults, must also be seen from other developmental perspectives. Concerns that have been raised about the ability of adolescents to make their own health care decisions include their tendency to conform (Grisso and Vierling 1978; Langer and Warhelt 1992; Shields and Johnson 1992); a greater willingness to take risks and indulge impulses (Trad 1993); lack of life experience (Gordon 1990); difficulty keeping in mind a future perspective rather than the here and now (Gordon 1990; Langer and Warhelt 1992; Trad 1993); and the tendency to perceive choices as externally determined (Lewis 1980).

As with adults, refusal of treatment may be more problematic than its acceptance. Some adolescents may engage in *unwillful dissent* – feeling obliged to say no for its own sake (Grisso and Vierling 1978), or they may demonstrate an inability to accept help from adults (Gordon 1990). Taking refusal at face value would be a disservice under these circumstances.

The Psychological Impact of Being Orphaned

Whatever conclusions may apply to the capacity of average adolescents, the trauma of being orphaned might cause disturbances beyond those experienced by teenagers living in more fortunate circumstances. At the same time, orphaned adolescents may demonstrate the ability to carry out adult tasks that more sheltered children have not yet developed.

By the time my mother died when I was eleven, I knew how to defend myself against physical threats in my neighborhood, I could shop for food, repair clothes on a sewing machine, accomplish all my schoolwork without any adult prompts, and take care of my seven-year-old sister. Between eleven and thirteen, when I lived with my grandmother, who was unable to read and spoke no English, I became accustomed to negotiating my own health care. My grandmother required five minutes to laboriously write her signature on a form, and the only thing she understood of its contents was what I elected to tell her. In high school, I was an honors student, and worked twenty hours a week to pay for my own clothes and other personal items.

While in foster care, I acted, in effect, like a miniature adult. But inside, underneath the bravado and the cool competence, was a very needy child who suffered from depression, distrust of adults, an inability to make any new intimate connections, and a tremendous loss of sense of structure.

How does one understand such examples of precocious functioning accompanied by a disturbed inner life, and what is the impact on decision-making capacity?

The Psychiatric Literature About Parental Loss

There is a modest amount of psychoanalytic writing about parental loss, which contains many important insights about children's emotional reactions to death. Miller (1971) provides an overview of literature by psychoanalysts between 1897 and 1969. Whereas healthy adult mourning involves the gradual and painful detachment from the inner representation of the person who has died, the majority of analytic writers conclude that children have a need to continue their emotional investments in their deceased parents. They may do this by identifying with the dead parent, even with the parent's illness, and by idealizing and glorifying the parent. Children can simultaneously acknowledge the fact of a parent's death, yet emotionally remain connected to the fantasy of the parent's return, or to reunion with the parent in death. Children experience a parent's death as both dangerous and damaging, and their self-esteem suffers. Because of the anger toward their parents, present in all children, they feel guilty, finding it hard to believe that the death was the result of anything but their own malevolence. Children may have to pass through adolescence before healthy adult mourning is possible.

For the most part, writings by analysts and psychodynamically oriented therapists focus on children in treatment where one parent has died and the remaining parent and family are available to assist the child (Barnes 1964; Wolfenstein 1966; Miller 1971; Greenberg 1975). In addition, most reports concern children in treatment, who have therefore already been identified as having difficulty, which in some instances began prior to the parent's illness or death (Laufer 1966; Wolfenstein 1966; Miller 1971; Furman 1974; Greenberg 1975). A community sample might reveal a different pattern. Although often not stated, it is probably safe to assume that many articles in the analytic literature concern children from a white, middle-class background.

Adolescents orphaned by the HIV epidemic will likely differ from these children in a number of ways. The majority are African-American or Latino. They do not have a surviving parent. And they may have experienced many other traumas prior to becoming orphaned. For our purposes, it is perhaps of even greater relevance that analytic insights can be derived during psychotherapy and psychoanalysis by allowing ideas that are otherwise unconscious to become conscious. Knowledge of typical childhood reactions to parental death may be helpful to care givers in dealing sensitively with adolescent orphans, but outside a treatment setting, these reactions are unlikely to be easily observed.

Bowlby (1988), in his book *A Secure Base,* pulls together earlier analytic writings, the general psychiatric literature, and developmental psychology to offer a flexible model of how we might think of children in adverse circumstances. He sees development as a lifelong process. Favorable early attachment experiences may promote resilience in the face of later adversity. This could apply to some of the adolescents who are orphaned by HIV. On the other hand, at any age, children from adverse backgrounds may find positive experiences that can alter their development in favorable ways.

Bowlby summarizes six large studies of adult women with incapacitating depression. There is a powerful association between this condition and death of a mother in childhood. The association is stronger among poor girls than among the middle class, primarily because the poor are far less likely to receive adequate care following the mother's death. This, in turn, is associated with the likelihood of a negative self-image and poor adult life choices. Recent literature examining psychopathology in children following parental death also demonstrates that dysthymia and depression are common (Van Eerdewegh, Clayton, and Van Eerdewegh 1985; Cheifetz, Stavrakakis, and Lester 1989; Weller et al. 1991).

The Trauma Response

A developing literature builds on our current knowledge of psychodynamic theories and biological psychiatry, but adds a new dimension: the influence of traumatic experiences that overwhelm psychological and biological coping mechanisms (Van der Kolk 1987). Work in this area has resulted in the description of a relatively new diagnostic entity: post-traumatic stress disorder (PTSD).

As currently defined in DSM-IV (1994), PTSD requires exposure to a traumatic event that involved actual or threatened death or serious injury to oneself or others. The person's response involved intense fear, helplessness, or horror (in children sometimes expressed by disorganized or agitated behavior). The syndrome is defined by a variety of characteristic symptoms, including recurrent and intrusive recollections or dreams; acting or feeling as if the traumatic event were recurring; intense psychological distress when exposed to cues that are reminiscent of some aspect of the traumatic event; persistent avoidance of stimuli associated with the trauma; numbing of general responsiveness; and persistent symptoms of increased arousal, such as difficulty sleeping, outbursts of anger, trouble concentrating, excessive vigilance, and exaggerated startle response. Onset of this syndrome may be delayed, but to meet diagnostic criteria, its duration must be at least one month. Clinically significant distress or impairment in functioning is present.

Van der Kolk, in his book *Psychological Trauma* (1987), summarizes the growing literature on this topic, and offers his own perspective. Regardless of the population studied, the human response to severe trauma is remarkably consistent. The traumatic response might come to dominate mental life long after the original exposure, and might cause profound personality changes.

Some psychoanalytic writers (e.g., Kardiner 1941), address this type of trauma, emphasizing the affected person's obligation to reenact the event as if it were a contemporary experience, instead of remembering it as something in the past. However, most psychoanalytic writings focus on ordinary developmental events, such as the birth of a sibling, or common sources of childhood distress, such as divorce. The degree of psychological trauma caused by these events is related, in large measure, to how they are linked to disturbing unconscious fantasies. The diagnosis of PTSD, however, requires exposure to an actual severe external threat.

The goal of almost any psychological treatment of trauma is making the transition from its unrecognized unconscious impact to a successful contemporary perspective on it, although confronting trauma, if it cannot be worked through and integrated, could have an adverse impact.

Children are believed to be especially vulnerable to the effects of trauma, which may have a devastating effect on trust and can cause collapse of earlier developmental accomplishments. There is a loss of faith that there is order and continuity in life, and loss of the certainty of a safe place in which to retreat. Bowlby emphasizes that a secure home base remains indispensable in adolescence for optimal functioning, including the ability to explore and to experience pleasure.

Traumatized children make powerful attempts to avoid associated feelings of helplessness and meaninglessness. Early traumatic experience may adversely affect the development of an internal locus of control – the belief that one can exert significant influence over one's fate. Girls who have been traumatized may manifest depression, self-destructive behavior, phobic avoidance, and somatization, whereas boys may be more prone to aggressive behavior.

In addition to these psychological events, it is postulated, based on animal studies, that long-term neurobiological changes may occur as well, and may be responsible for some of the persistent physiological disturbances associated with PTSD.

There is disagreement in the psychiatric literature about whether the loss of a parent in childhood is, per se, a psychic trauma (Eth and Pynoos 1984). The degree of disturbance will depend on many variables, including the nature of the parent's death. Much discussion of trauma stresses that it is often caused by sudden, unpredictable, and violent events. Children who live with a chronically ill parent who dies in a hospital may be significantly less traumatized than those who, for example, witness a parent die in a car accident or by murder (Eth and Pynoos 1984).

Other influences on a child's adjustment following parental death include the child's prior relationships to the parents, the child's preexisting character structure and psychopathology, and the arrangements for care that follow the death (Furman 1974; Van der Kolk 1987). For these reasons, children orphaned by the HIV epidemic may have variable adjustments. We already know that many of these children come from families with multiple problems (Draimin 1993), and therefore optimal outcomes may be uncommon.

Reflections

When, as an adult, I explore my responses to my parents' deaths, I find that many of the ideas of analytic writers accurately describe important aspects of my own reactions, although this self-knowledge was inaccessible to me as a child.

The actual deaths of my parents were not as disturbing, however, as my family's sudden decision to place me in foster care, which I experienced as a total loss of continuity and a shocking betrayal. It was then that I developed what, on a purely descriptive level, is best described by the literature on PTSD. In particular, I find it easy to identify with the descriptions of the fear, the psychic numbing, the vivid reliving of the experiences as if they were actually happening again, the guilt about survival, and the shame and its association with a feeling of permanent damage.

Because my situation involved a *series* of events, I find no clear starting point for my troubles. Nor is there any permanent resolution. Each stage of life reawakens old memories that need to be worked through still another time. When I lived in foster care, I was assigned to a social worker who pressed me to acknowledge my anger, confront my denial, display pictures of my mother, and so on. I couldn't follow any of these suggestions. There are many things that cannot be immediately approached in the aftermath of severe loss, and rebuilding one's life is a very slow process.

Some years back, I selected a quote from James Agee's famous book *A Death in the Family* (1955) to describe what it was like to have built a successful adult life – career, marriage, family – on the shaky foundation of my childhood experience. Agee wrote:

> Everything was good and better than he could have hoped for, better than he ever deserved; only whatever it was, and however good it was, it wasn't what you had once been, and had lost, and could never have again, and once in a while, once in a long time, you remembered, and knew how far you were away, and it hit you hard enough, that little while it lasted, to break your heart.

The impact of being orphaned endures, and any associated impairments in decision-making capacity will not necessarily resolve when an adolescent reaches adulthood.

What effect did these experiences and my responses to them have on my reasoning about the medical care I received for my foot injury when I was fourteen? I still remember the surgeon's name and appearance. I immediately developed a tremendous crush on him, which, I believe, was part of my endless search to find substitute parents. So, emotionally, I might have been susceptible to going along with whatever he suggested. On the other hand, I didn't trust him. I secretly worried that he planned to amputate my entire leg. I remembered hearing a story that if you step on a needle, it could travel to your heart, so I figured that I might have to lose my leg for him to save my life. I didn't have much of a sense of why I thought this way, even though one obvious link might have been to my mother's loss of a breast in her own futile attempt to save her life. I could have sought reassurance, but I felt my suspicions were a little crazy, and besides, adults were dishonest and unlikely to reveal the truth anyway. This confused thinking would hardly seem to form the basis for making an informed consent decision.

On the other hand, at another level, I fully understood that this was a surgeon to whom I had no intimate connection, working in an established health care setting, who wanted to remove a needle from the bottom of my foot. And in the more rational part of my mind I assumed that this was all that was happening. This part of me probably was capable of giving informed consent.

I'm not sure how different my thinking was from that of many adults who might be overly impressed with a doctor's authority or overly distrustful due to early life experiences. Perhaps it is a matter of degree. I believe that had I been interviewed as part of an informed consent process, I would have presented only my rational thoughts, and I would have met any reasonable person's criteria for capacity. We depend on the ability of people to separate their irrational beliefs from their ability to think and behave rationally when confronted with danger or important life decisions. Perhaps children who grow up under severe circumstances and survive them in a functional way are among the masters of this split.

The dilemma of the adolescent alone may have less to do with the ability to understand a medical procedure and make a reasoned decision about it than with the problem of needs that haven't been met. An adolescent has the wish that a trustworthy adult will be available to help at a time of crisis. Despite a rather troubled relationship with my foster mother, it was a comfort to know that she was with me in the hospital emergency room, and was looking out for me. I was hardly prepared to think through the logistical issues: How would I get to and from the hospital? How would my care be paid for? Who would the doctor talk to if something went wrong while I was under anesthesia? How would I get help while recuperating at home? I believe most adults would feel uncomfortable without firm answers to these questions; but most adolescents would feel abandoned, alone, even desperate.

Adolescents who are alone have a terrible dilemma. They have a developmental need to break away from their parents, but their parents have beaten them to the punch. They need continued adult involvement, but it feels like the wrong time to begin again. This may result in an exaggeration of the normal adolescent posture of simultaneously wanting and refusing help.

I think most troubled adolescents want to be pursued, even if they claim otherwise. A process model of informed consent, or the use of a medical rather than a judicial bypass to approve treatment, each offer the possibility that an adolescent can have a meaningful dialogue with a clinician about an important medical decision.

Adolescents without parents rely on substitutes to play important roles in their lives. And when they reject what adults have to offer, it is not to be taken at face value. For example, despite being an excellent high school student, I seriously considered not attending college. I desperately wanted to work, make my own money, and bring my period of dependency to an end. But I had a guidance counselor, a fatherly man, who took an interest in me. We didn't meet often, but whenever we did he would insist that I belonged in college, and I had the impression that he didn't plan to take no for an answer. He finally persuaded me. To this day, he has a special place in my heart.

If adolescents consent to treatment that clinicians believe to be in the adolescents' best interest, it may not be fair to hold them to a higher standard of capacity than the one currently used with adults. But adolescents who are alone probably need, and often secretly want, a level of involvement from the treating medical staff that is greater than that required by most adult patients. Determining what that involvement should be and how to provide it is the challenge.

References

Agee, J. A. (1955). *A death in the family.* New York: Putnam.

Appelbaum, P. S., and T. Grisso (1988). Assessing patients' capacities to consent to treatment. *New England Journal of Medicine, 319,* 1635–1638.

Barnes, M. J. (1964). Reactions to the death of a mother. *The psychoanalytic study of the child, 19,* 334–357. New York: International Universities Press.

Bowlby, J. A. (1988). *A secure base.* New York: Basic Books.

Cassileth, B. R., et al. (1980). Informed consent: Why are its goals imperfectly realized? *New England Journal of Medicine, 302,* 896–900.

Cheifetz, P. N., G. Stavrakakis, and E. P. Lester (1989). Studies on the affective state in bereaved children. *Canadian Journal of Psychiatry, 34,* 688–692.

Cournos, F. (1993). Do psychiatric patients need greater protection than medical patients when they consent to treatment? *Psychiatric Quarterly, 64,* 319–329.

Cournos, F., et al. (1993). Report of the task force on consent to voluntary hospitalization. *Bulletin of the Academy of Psychiatry and the Law, 21,* 293–307.

Draimin, B. (1993). Adolescents in families with AIDS: Growing up with loss. In C. Levine (Ed.), *A death in the family: Orphans of the HIV epidemic.* New York: United Hospital Fund.

DSM-IV (1994). Washington, DC: American Psychiatric Association.

Eth, S., and R. S. Pynoos (1984). *Post-traumatic stress disorder in children.* Washington, DC: American Psychiatric Press, Inc.

Fish-Murray, C. C., E. V. Koby, and B. A. van der Kolk (1987). Evolving ideas: The effect of abuse on children's thought. In B. A. van der Kolk (Ed.) *Psychological Trauma.* Washington, DC: American Psychiatric Press, Inc.

Furman, E. (1974). *A child's parent dies.* New Haven, CT: Yale University Press.

Gordon, D. E. (1990). Formal operational thinking: The role of cognitive-developmental processes in adolescent decision-making about pregnancy and contraception. *American Journal of Orthopsychiatry, 60,* 346–356.

Greenberg, L. I. (1975). Therapeutic grief work with children. *Social Casework, 56,* 396–403.

Grisso, T., and L. Vierling (1978). Minors' consent to treatment: A developmental perspective. *Professional Psychology, 9,* 412–427.

Kardiner, A. (1941). *The traumatic neuroses of war.* New York: Harper and Brothers.

Langer, L. M., and G. J. Warheit (1992). The pre-adult health decision-making model: Linking decision-making directedness/orientation to adolescent health-related attitudes and behaviors. *Adolescence, 27,* 919–948.

Laufer, M. (1966). Object loss and mourning during adolescence. *The Psychoanalytic Study of the Child, 21,* 269–293. New York: International Universities Press.

Leikin, S. (1993). The role of adolescents in decisions concerning their cancer therapy. *Cancer Supplement, 71,* 3342–3346.

Lewis, C. C. (1980). A comparison of minors' and adults' pregnancy decisions. *American Journal of Orthopsychiatry, 50,* 446–453.

Lidz, C. W., et al. (1984). *Informed consent.* New York: The Guilford Press.

Miller, J. B. M. (1971). Children's reactions to the death of a parent: A review of the psychoanalytic literature. *Journal of the American Psychoanalytic Association, 19,* 697–719.

President's Commission for the Study of Ethical Problems in Medicine and Biomedical and Behavioral Research (1982). *Making health care decisions.* Washington, DC: U.S. Government Printing Office.

Shields J. M., and A. Johnson (1992). Collision between law and ethics: Consent for treatment with adolescents. *Bulletin of the American Academy of Psychiatry and Law, 20,* 309–323.

Trad, P. V. (1993). The ability of adolescents to predict future outcomes, part 1: Assessing predictive abilities. *Adolescence, 28,* 533–555.

Van Eerdewegh, M. M., P. J. Clayton, and P. Van Eerdewegh (1985). The bereaved child: Variables influencing early psychopathology. *British Journal of Psychiatry, 147,* 188–194.

Van der Kolk, B. A. (1987). *Psychological trauma.* Washington, DC: American Psychiatric Press, Inc.

Wallace, L. N. (1986). Informed consent to elective surgery: The "therapeutic" value?' *Social Science in Medicine, 22,* 29–33.

Weithorn, L. A., and S. B. Campbell (1982). The competency of children and adolescents to make informed treatment decisions. *Child Development, 53,* 1589–1598.

Weller, R. A., et al. (1991). Depression in recently bereaved prepubertal children. *American Journal of Psychiatry, 148,* 1536–1540.

Wolfenstein, M. (1966). How is mourning possible? *The Psychoanalytic Study of the Child, 21,* 93–123. New York: International Universities Press.

7 Experiences of Coming Out Among Gay and Lesbian Youth: Adolescents Alone?

Andrew M. Boxer, Judith A. Cook,
and Gilbert Herdt

Introduction

This chapter concerns a pioneering group of youth who identify themselves as lesbian or gay. They challenge one hundred years of social oppression, secrecy, and silence on the rights of those who desire the same sex (see Murray 1984 and 1996). These teens are a new cultural phenomenon: a generation who self-identify as lesbian and gay, the first in human history. However, the youth were assisted by prior political and social changes, which resulted in a new and more powerful community of adults who were willing to brave discrimination and violence, harassment and isolation by committing themselves to the construction of a new culture (Herdt and Boxer 1993).

We suggest that gay and lesbian culture is a powerful critique of moral ideals and justice in our society. Gay and lesbian teenagers have taught us this; they have forced us to recognize that their desire and struggle to come out is a new form of moral career. They are exercising a moral "choice," the liberty to come out and live as self-identified gays and lesbians (Herdt and Boxer 1996). American culture continues, in spite of much progress in social equality, to define the nature of sexual and gender development in terms of the old heterosexual versus homosexual duality. For many Americans, this dualism is equated naively with a moral dualism of *good* and *bad,* the homosexual, of course, being all "bad." The shift in the social and psychological landscape of the past twenty years has changed the categories of personhood, from the secret closet homosexual to the publicly self-declared lesbian and gay (Herdt and Boxer 1992a), but it has not eliminated the moral dualism. Teenagers continue to learn and be exposed to negative stereotypes of homosexuality.

Since the 1960s the growth and development of both gay and lesbian culture and individuals' identities as gay male or lesbian has proved an especially dynamic coevolution in American society (Herdt and Boxer 1992a). More than a generation ago, the issues raised by the presence of gays and lesbians were dismissed by the diagnosis of homosexuality, including the stigma of disease discourse in psychiatry. The historical categories – *homosexual* and *gay* in particular – must be taken into account in understanding the formation of gay culture. We have argued elsewhere (Herdt and Boxer 1992a) for the existence of a gay cultural system (as contrasted with a "homosexual" one), with a distinct identity and distinct institutions and social supports in particular times and places (see Murray 1984 and 1996).

Studies conducted over the last three decades indicate that adolescents are engaging in a wider range of sexual behaviors at earlier ages (Boxer, Levinson, and Petersen 1990). These changes in adolescent sexual behavior have lowered the mean age of adolescents' first sexual experience, including youths' first homosexual as well as heterosexual activity (Gagnon 1989a; Troiden 1989; D'Augelli 1996). The cultural categories of gay and lesbian adolescents are a newly emerging generation of youth. They should be distinguished from other adolescents who may experience same-sex desires or engage in same-sex behavior but who do not (or at least do not yet) identify themselves as gay or lesbian.[1]

The experience of this group of gay and lesbian youth and their ongoing identity development is the subject of our study. Often they have nowhere to turn in exploring and expressing the dimensions of their identity because they feel hindered from approaching adults (including parents), friends, and teachers, whom they fear will dismiss or disapprove of their feelings. The life course approach, which considers both change over time as well as its cultural meanings, can help to elucidate the current experiences of lesbian and gay youth in a unique historical context (Boxer and Cohler 1989; Herdt 1992). These changes and their meanings to the youth themselves, their families, peers, schools, and the larger society raise issues relevant to the concept of the *adolescent alone.*

Review of the Literature

Theories of Sexuality

Despite many changes, including the sexual revolution of the 1960s and increasing recognition and awareness of gay rights (including such issues as domestic partner benefits; and the recent U.S. Supreme Court decision upholding the right of states granting gays and lesbians equal protection under the constitution [see *Romer, Governor of Colorado et. al.,* v. *Evans* 1996]), society remains uncomfortable with claiming the erotic, particularly the homoerotic, as a part of human nature. Science, of course, reflects the interests, concerns, and values of society; and nowhere is this more apparent than in the developmental study of sexuality, particularly adolescent sexuality. These interests and values are reflected in the concerns of conservative politicians and the fears of public health officials who have either attempted to prevent or not supported the study of teen sexuality. These opinion leaders have argued that asking youth about their sexual desires and behaviors leads them to engage in such behaviors. The result limits or prohibits research on adolescent sexual behavior, which has seriously hindered our understanding of the needs of gay and lesbian youth seeking support and guidance as they come to terms with their emerging sexual identities.

Prevailing theories of sexuality, not surprisingly, also reflect the societal belief that heterosexuality is privileged – that is, natural and biologically driven – and that homosexuality is abnormal and unnaturally activated. Heterosexual sexual identity among teenagers is largely taken for granted, particularly among the two major institutions having the strongest impact on youth: schools and families (see Sears 1992; Eisen and Hall 1996). The social organization of schools and the socializing influences of families prepare youth for heterosexual activities and outcomes. This poses one of the first and primary developmental milestones for gay and lesbian youth – shedding the presumptive heterosexual identity and constructing a gay or lesbian one. This process of constructing a gay or lesbian identity has certain features and sequelae that create "aloneness" among youth who come out to themselves and others.

Scientific theories of adolescence mirror these cultural assumptions. Erik Erikson (1959) viewed homosexuality in terms of problems of gender confusion. Harry Stack Sullivan (1958) proposed that homosexuality could be a phase of "chumship" on the road to heterosexual outcomes. Thus, transient homosexual contact between heterosexually active adolescent males was typically not defined as homosexuality (Gagnon and Simon 1973). Transient homosexual contact, Kinsey argued, was most frequent before age fifteen and more likely to be experienced by boys than by girls (Kinsey, Pomeroy, and Martin 1948; Kinsey et al. 1953). These theories were challenged by the large numbers of males who failed to move out of this so-called *chumship* phase.

On the other hand, *true* homosexuality was viewed as a problem of disordered or reversed gender or, to use an old term, *gender inversion* (Stoller and Herdt 1985; Herdt 1989). Homosexuality was attributed to various causes, including sexual abuse and seduction (typically from an older perpetrator to a younger "victim"); social learning through the associative pairing of sexual gratification within a same-sex dyad (Tripp 1975); and restriction or lack of opportunities for heterosexual outlets (see Kinsey et al. 1948; Stoller and Herdt 1985). These causal theories reflect a heterosexual bias. Such theories inhibit our ability to understand adolescents who self-identify as gay or lesbian and assert their identities voluntarily, free from duress, often after having opportunities to compare their feelings about opposite and same-sex sexual experiences.

Identity Development of Gay Youth: Adolescents Alone?

In the past, sexual identity was thought to emerge from one's gender identity – the individual's sense of maleness or femaleness. More recently, however, theorists have equated sexual identity with sexual orientation or one's preferred sexual behaviors and one's feelings about them. But here the AIDS epidemic has been instructive. Anthropological and epidemiological studies of the behavior of persons at risk for or infected with HIV have identified a group of persons engaging in same-sex behavior but maintaining a heterosexual identity. A further distinction has been drawn between those who limit their self-definition as *homosexual* to their sexual activities and those who view themselves as *gay* by embracing gay culture and sensibility (reviewed in Herdt 1992; Whitney 1989; Herdt and Boxer 1991; Parker, Herdt, and Carballo 1991). Indeed, studies of homosexuality and gay culture have begun to delineate the lack of congruence of homosexual erotic desires, homosexual sexual behavior, and gay/lesbian self-identification, acculturation, or sense of belonging (Foucault 1980; Greenberg 1988; Herdt 1992; Murray 1996).

Gay and lesbian teens' efforts to develop a gay/lesbian identity support the voluntary and self-initiated nature of the coming-out process among these youth. First, they are challenging the culture's expectation that they are heterosexual. Second, they are asserting their membership in a group that is culturally devalued and stigmatized. The likelihood is great that their initial attempts to assert their gay/lesbian identities will meet with rejection from parents, other family, friends, peers, and teachers. Moreover, they are coming out into gay communities that are struggling with the impact of the HIV/AIDS epidemic, which has isolated these communities and inhibited their attempts to reach out, in turn, to gay youth.

In this volume, the concept of *adolescents alone* is used to refer to youth who do not have an involved parent or who lacked functional supervision and care because of parental desire for noninvolvement or hostility toward the child. For gay and lesbian adolescents, the very nature of their developing sexual identity carries with it isolating influences that can affect their transitions and make them vulnerable to the status of being alone. Heterosexism in the larger society can increase this isolation, as can attendant fears of rejection from friends, peers, and teachers. Parents may express their own homophobia and rejection, as well as mourning as they come to terms with different types of role-loss, such as loss of the roles of grandparent and in-law. Many parents initially experience a sense of disappointment, failure, and guilt, feeling somehow responsible for causing their child's homosexuality (reviewed in Boxer, Cook, and Herdt 1991). Teachers and peers may offer little support for assuming such an identity, since educational and peer activities are organized around heterosexual norms and values. Because health care decisions are typically made with the family, friends, and other physicians, these youth face the need for caring guidance around issues of safer sex and risk-reduction practices, along with psychoeducational approaches to understanding their own developing sexuality. Mental health care needs may also exist among a group of gay and lesbian youths experiencing potential stress, isolation, and role redefinition, especially when dealing with other life problems.

To a certain extent, the category of adolescent alone might better be understood not as a feature of the youth per se, but of the relationship between the child and the service system. The youth's aloneness does not become salient unless service providers are called upon to bridge an acknowledged gap in support and legal decision-making responsibility. Although a range of parental reactions are possible upon learning that a teenager is gay, it is reasonable to expect that some cases would bring the service or support provider into conflict with the teen's parents or guardians. The youths' desire for secrecy might also entail conflicting goals. Some parents might be absent, unknown, or unavailable due to incarceration or institutionalization, placing the provider in a morally ambiguous role. In the current analysis, the youth's attendance at the Horizons support group signaled their selection of the gay culture as their socializing agent in helping them to redefine their identities, as next described.

The Study Site

The Chicago study (Herdt and Boxer 1993) examined developmental and cultural dimensions of identity development as they were occurring among 202 self-identified gay and lesbian adolescents (ages fourteen to twenty-one) who were attending a youth support group at an urban gay/lesbian social service agency. Until relatively recently, much of what we know about adolescent homosexuality has been based on retrospective data collected from adults (Boxer and Cohler 1989). Few studies have gathered data from youth regarding the emergence and development of their sexual desires and identities.

The larger project was an interdisciplinary psychosocial and anthropological study of youth attending the Horizons Youth Group. The social space of the Youth Group situated the teens between their mainstream heterosexual parents and associates, on the one hand, and the gay and lesbian community, including adult advisors, role models, and friends, on the other. The group introduced the teens to a cultural system of normative gay and lesbian beliefs, concepts, and goals in the shared discourse of local newspapers, churches, sports activities, shopping areas, and the Youth Group itself (Herdt 1989 and 1992). This cultural community provided an alternative socialization structure to that of the youth's mainstream heterosexual homes and schools.

This generation of youth is a unique and pioneering one, entering adolescence during the AIDS epidemic. They are coming of age in a world in which, throughout their lifetimes, there has always been a visible gay and lesbian cultural community, although not always within their personal horizons. Thus, our study focused on addressing the lack of knowledge about sexual identity, already discussed, and began *remapping* the developmental trajectories of gay and lesbian youth.

At the same time, our knowledge leads us to expect that youth coming out as gay teenagers today are vulnerable in a number of ways. They are at risk for HIV infection if they engage in certain types of unprotected sex (Herdt and Boxer 1992b). Especially for the young women, their youth and inexperience may make them vulnerable to coercive or abusive sexual experiences, either heterosexual or homosexual. Their lack of role models and social supports may lower morale and contribute to feelings of stress or discouragement leading to sadness or depression. They may have health and mental health needs related to the coming out process.

Methods

The methods of investigation included data collected through both individual, face-to-face interviews with each teen, and ethnographic research employing standard anthropological field methods (see Gerstel et al. 1989; Herdt 1992). Data summarized herein were drawn from the interview study (ethnographic and quantitative findings from the larger research project have appeared in Gerstel, Feraios, and Herdt 1989; Boxer, Cook, and Herdt 1991; Herdt 1992; Herdt and Boxer 1993; for background see also Boxer and Cohler 1989; Herdt 1989).

Sample

The nonclinical sample was drawn from the youth group over a two-year period. Membership in the group was limited by age, from fourteen to twenty-one. Those who reached their twenty-first birthday were no longer eligible for group participation. The criterion for being interviewed in our project was that each potential respondent had to have attended the group for a minimum of three sessions. Most of the youth lived at home and attended school.

Two hundred and two youth completed individual, face-to-face, semi-structured interviews with a trained interviewer, as well as a battery of paper-and-pencil assessments. The in-depth protocols took approximately three hours to complete, and all interviews were conducted at the social service agency. Each youth was asked about a series of life-domains, including school, work, family, mental health, sexual identity, and past history. The refusal rate among the youth was quite low (5 percent). The adolescents in this study were a heterogeneous group who came from all parts of the greater Chicago area. The sample included 147 males and 55 females. This unbalanced gender ratio reflected the actual composition of the group. The mean age of the sample was 18.3 years (SD = 1.45, range = 14 to 21 years, females = 17.96 years, males = 18.41 years). Thirty percent of the sample were African-American, 40 percent were Caucasian, 12 percent were Hispanic, 3 percent were Asian-American, and the remaining 15 percent were of mixed ethnic backgrounds. Thirty-eight percent of the youth lived with both parents, 25 percent lived in single parent households, and the remainder lived either on their own or in various types of blended families (seven of the youth were living in shelters at the time of their interviews). The religious backgrounds of the youth were 45 percent Protestant, 37 percent Catholic, 9 percent from mixed religious backgrounds, 4 percent atheist/agnostic, 2 percent Jewish, and 4 percent with no reported religious affiliation. Their family backgrounds were evenly divided between working- and middle-class backgrounds. Almost three-quarters of these youth (72 percent) were attending school, and close to two-thirds (63 percent) were employed, either part- or full-time.

Findings

First Sexual Fantasies, Desires, and Behavior

The mean age of self-identification among this culturally diverse sample was 16.7 years for males and 16.0 for females. Data from our study indicated that sexual development must be viewed as an ongoing process rather than as a series of stages or phases. The developmental subjectivity of sexual desire begins with language development and symbolic acquisition. Three levels of symbolic action are relevant to this discussion: fantasies, the development of object representations, and behavioral expression of desires in social relations. The youth in this study were able to reflect upon each of these three levels by discussing the ages at which they first became aware of their homoerotic attractions, sexual fantasies, and their first homoerotic sexual experiences.

In examining the emergence of the adolescents' same-sex attractions we found that most youth reported a sequence from an awareness of their same-sex desires, to sexual fantasies, to some type of same-sex experience. Generally this began around age nine and one-half to ten for both males and females (see also McClintock and Herdt 1996). An eighteen-year-old female of mixed ethnic background (black and Caucasian) described her first attraction:

> It was a girlfriend I knew from school. The sex part has always come second to wanting to be with the person. I'd always want to be around her. I'd always find some way to touch her.

Others became aware of their attractions through daily interactions with persons older than themselves (e.g., high school teens or teachers), who sometimes were targets of idolization. Several of the youth described attractions to movie stars, singers, or men or women in various communications media, (e.g., books, films). When asked how they felt at the time about their first homosexual attractions/fantasies, the youth's responses were diverse and ranged widely for both genders. Some youth reacted with fear to their emerging awareness of homosexual attraction, as one of our white male respondents explained:

> I just started having a feeling . . . I was more interested in men. It scared the hell out of me. I kind of forced myself to be interested in girls at the time. It felt very bad. I guess at the time it freaked me out. I thought, "I can't be like that, no, I can't be."

Most of these youth reported discernible same-sex erotic attractions and fantasies prior to their first same-sex sexual experiences. The mean ages at first same-sex fantasies were highly similar for both genders: 11.2 years (SD = 3.5) for males and 11.9 years (SD = 2.9) for females. Not surprisingly, while the ages were similar across genders, the content of these fantasies appeared to differ. Typically, fantasies that males reported were often more explicitly sexual than those of females. Females might have been more reluctant to express explicitly sexual fantasies due to differential gender socialization regarding the social acceptability of female sexuality; on the other hand, males may have been more likely to respond with explicit sexual fantasies for the same reasons.

Multivariate analyses of our data indicated that males first acted on their homo-erotic desires at significantly earlier ages than did the females. The first homosexual experience occurred at an average age of thirteen for males and fifteen for females. Three-quarters of the youth initiated their first same-sex sexual experience with a peer or friend (i.e., someone who was within three years of their own age).

Females in this sample reported significantly later ages at first same-sex sexual experiences than was the case for males. These lesbian youth also reported different interpersonal contexts for their first same-sex experience than did males. Males were more likely to initiate sexual behavior in sexual context; for girls, friendship or a dating/romantic context were the most frequent settings. On the other hand, the females in this sample reported significantly more positive ratings of their first same-sex sexual experiences than did males.

The data presented here demonstrate that the time difference between genders regarding average age of first same-sex sexual experience, as reported in other studies (see Troiden 1989; D'Augelli 1996), continues to persist. These findings also mirror the findings of studies of heterosexual youth, which demonstrate that boys begin heterosexual sexual activity at earlier average ages than girls (Gagnon and Simon 1973; Gagnon 1989a; Boxer et al. 1990). Differing explanations of why males act on their sexual desires earlier than females have included hormonal explanations (e.g., Feder 1984) as well as divergent sexual socialization (Gagnon and Simon 1973; Gagnon 1989a and 1989b). Sexual expression in general has been typically more acceptable for men in our society than for women (Gagnon and Simon 1973). It is likely that a combination of factors may influence males' earlier and females' later behavioral expression.

More than two-thirds of the sample's first same-sex experience occurred with a peer or friend. However, abusive or coercive situations characterized a small but notable minority. Sixteen percent of the youth reported coercive or abusive experiences, and this was more likely among females than among males.

A significant proportion of our young gay and lesbian respondents (55 percent consisting of thirty-seven females and seventy-four males) reported having engaged in some kind of opposite-sex erotic activity. Sixty-seven percent of all females and 50 percent of all males reported such activity. When asked the ages at which they first engaged in opposite-sex activity, males reported an average age of 13.7 years (SD = 3.6) and females an average age of 13.6 years (SD = 3.6). Thus, while a majority of these youth have had the opportunity to engage in opposite sex interactions, they chose to identify themselves as gay or lesbian.

The youths' descriptions of their feelings and experiences regarding first same-sex and opposite-sex sexual activity suggest that comparing these experiences helped clarify their feelings about their sexual identities (Cook, Boxer and Herdt 1989; Boxer and Herdt 1996).[2] As one male (who first engaged in opposite-sex, then same-sex experience) explained about his first same-sex experience: "I liked it, it felt natural to me. I had (had) sex with a woman before, and this felt better to me, more natural."

A female respondent (in the homosexual/heterosexual pathway category) reported comparing her own feelings with the demands of societal norms and feeling: "[I felt] confused as to whether I should be with a guy because society said so, or if I should be with Brigit [her female lover]."

The large majority of these youth did not manifest confusion about their sexual orientation, but rather came to the youth group with confusion about how to express and manage it. Sexual identity for these youth – as gay or lesbian – had much more to it than sexual behavior. Love and sex were important – critical aspects of self-development – but not the only ones.

Coming Out[3]

In individual interviews the youths were asked about the ways in which coming out had affected areas of their life including self-esteem, friends, future plans, and family relationships. For a majority of young men and half of the women, coming out had a positive impact on their self-esteem. These positive effects on self-esteem are not surprising, given that many youth reported feeling better about themselves through the self-disclosure process. A common scenario described this process as being first an admission to the self, prior to discussing it with others. This process was manifested in the youth's first visits to the Horizons Youth Group where, for many, entering the building and group for the first time was an anxiety-provoking yet self-defining, experience. Cultural preconceptions of gays and lesbians informed this anxiety, as evidenced in the ethnographic data (see Herdt 1992).

These young men and women also clearly felt the need to suppress the expression of their sexual identity in the family, at school and in the workplace. This posed problems of identity management simultaneous to those of identity development. Despite these counteracting pressures, a large majority of the youth were able to function reasonably well in school, at work, and in their families.

We asked each of the youths in the interviews to tell us what *coming out* meant to them and whether they had come out according to their own definition. Eighty percent of the youth said they had *come out* as they defined it. Most of our sample discussed their concepts of coming out in terms of a self-dialogue, involving self-recognition and acceptance of homosexuality; while others added the proviso that coming out meant informing others. Here, the others often were personal friends or family. A nineteen-year-old Italian-American male said:

> I have two definitions. One is coming out to yourself, realizing yourself – your own personal preferences, your emotional, sexual, social . . . . Coming out to other people is letting other people know, not standing on rooftops waving cardboard signs, but telling your family, your closer friends.

An eighteen-year-old black female said coming out is "no longer feeling the burden of homosexuality. Accepting yourself finally." An eighteen-year-old Hispanic female said, "I know it's a very frightening experience. It's like you're not afraid of your sexuality or of what people will think of you."

A sixteen-year-old white male, who said he had not yet come out, told us:

> Openly admitting it and freely showing it by my lifestyle and the things in my home. Yet, I am not out. I like living in the closet, especially in the suburbs, for social reasons.

Family Reactions

A higher proportion of females than males reported that their mothers and fathers were aware of their sexual orientation. Among the female respondents, 63 percent of the mothers and 37 percent of the fathers were reported to be aware of their daughter's lesbian status. Among males, 54 percent of the mothers and 28 percent of the fathers were aware that their offspring was gay. Some youth reported that their parents knew about and were aware of their sexual orientation, although the youth had not discussed it with that parent. For example, a fifteen-year-old female told us that her mother had read her diary, which revealed her love for a female classmate and her feelings about being a lesbian. When asked if she had ever talked with her mother about this, or if her mother had ever brought it up, she said:

> No, it's never been mentioned. It would be too scary to tell your mom. I think I can tell her when I move out to go to college . . . I overheard my Mom tell my Dad that she thought I was a lesbian because of what she read in the diary.

Other youth in our study directly disclosed their sexual orientation to their mothers and fathers. This was the more common mode of parents learning about their children's sexual orientation. For example, an eighteen-year-old female said:

> Yes, I told her. I was so frustrated from hiding that I just told her, so it wasn't that hard. But at that point I didn't care anymore. She thinks it's totally wrong and that I'm making a big mistake.

Statistical analyses (multivariate regression and probit analyses employing a number of control variables such as minority status, age, living situation, and employment status) were used to examine the associations between self-disclosure (both direct and indirect disclosure) of sexual orientation to parents and measures of parent–child relationships (Boxer et al. 1991). In general, self-disclosure to parents was not associated with disruptions in parent–child bonds. Youth were most likely to disclose to mothers, although there were no associations between mothers and the quality of or changes in these relationships among those who disclosed. Interestingly, disclosure to fathers was associated with more positive parental relationships, as well as changes in these relationships. It is likely that adolescents who disclosed their identities to parents were those with more positive preexisting relationships to begin with. However, the direction of change was not predicted by disclosure or parental awareness. The young women were more likely to report changes in relations with fathers than were the males, and these changes were more likely to be negative.

On the other hand, even parents who reacted negatively to the disclosure of homosexuality were judged by these offspring to not have let it disrupt their relationships. A high-school-age male told us that his mother found out (indirectly) that he was gay:

> She told me she was aware that I was leading an alternative lifestyle and she was concerned about me getting AIDS. I just about died. I felt like I was a big disappointment to my parents. But the joke's on me. Nothing changed between us. I thought there would be a lot of those long, dragged out conversations about being gay, but everything remained the same.

Similarly, one nineteen-year-old male told us, "My mother doesn't treat me as an issue. She regards me as her son who is gay and not her *gay son*."

It should be noted, however, that seven youth reported being forcibly excluded from their homes after their parents' discovery of their homosexuality. These estranged youth were living in shelters at the time of their interviews. Obviously, this was not the modal response of the parents, but it posed a difficult and wrenching break for this small group of adolescents. Further research is needed to examine the characteristics and processes in families of gay and lesbian teens who are forced to leave home following disclosure or discovery of their gay identity.

School Experiences

The youth in our study were attending school in a variety of secondary and postsecondary educational settings such as public, private, and special education. Virtually all these settings, as described by the youth, did not provide support, guidance, or assistance regarding development of a positive gay identity.[4] The youth felt forced to withstand a variety of pressures to conform and to negotiate constraining school environments that negated their sexual identities. Many strategies were employed by the youth to conceal their sexual identities at school (for a review see Harbeck 1992). These include simple *passing*, or showing interest in having relationships with the opposite sex, to other types of concealment. For example, one young man described changing pronouns, so that the "he" became "she" when referring to a boyfriend. Other youth used avoidance or withdrawal from school activities as a way to hide what they described as their "true" selves. Some youth described magical thinking, in which they felt that avoiding gay people and associating with straight people would make their homosexual desires disappear.

In the individual interviews youth were asked whether and to what extent they felt that they had to hide their sexual identities at school and, in particular, from whom. Two-thirds of the youth told us that they felt they had to hide "partially" or "totally." Only one youth in the entire sample stated that he felt there was no one from whom he had to hide the fact that he was gay. Frequently, both males and females stated that they had to selectively hide their identity from both teachers and peers. However, not unique to gay and lesbian adolescents, the predominant concerns were focused on peers. One seventeen-year-old eleventh grade male told us:

> [At school] I'm hidden mostly – cause of the ways they'll treat you. Okay, there are lots of gangs . . . they find out you're [what they call] a faggot and they beat on you and stuff. If they ask me I say it's none of their business.

Another seventeen-year-old related:

> I was very much hidden [at school]. I was attracted to a few of my friends and tried very hard not to let it show. Mostly I'm afraid about classmates. I think most of my teachers were open minded, one told me about the gay pride parade.

Unfortunately, teachers were not typically viewed as a source of assistance or protection. An eighteen-year-old female said about her teachers:

> I think once you get older, you become more and more closed minded, you get set in your ways. People your own age are still growing with you so they're more open minded.

Another high-school-aged youth told us:

> I'm totally hidden. The environment is not conducive to come out as people take an idea that already existed as negative without questioning. High school is small intellectually. I'm looking forward to college to be more open.

An eighteen-year-old told us:

> I'm hidden from some but not from others. They never ask me questions like, "Are you?" I used to be real afraid that the word would get around, but now it's like, if you don't like it, are you going to do something about it? I'm out to a few girls that I know. But very close friends think I'm straight.

Mental Health and Future Time Perspective

We compared the youth in our study with groups of putatively heterosexual youth on a set of standardized measures of mental health. Although our sample is nonrepresentative in comparison to normative samples, overall these youth compare favorably with adolescents at large in terms of psychological resilience and distress (Boxer et al. 1993; D'Augelli and Hershberger 1993). Gay and lesbian youth did not manifest major differences from straight youth in anxiety, confusion, or insecurity, but they did tend to be more depressed, vigilant, and vulnerable than their heterosexual counterparts. Given the constraints that society places on gay and lesbian teenagers, this is not surprising. During the process of self-identification, some youth may experience feelings of sadness in giving up images of a heterosexual identity as a precursor to the construction of a gay identity. Similarly, some lesbian and gay youth, in response to their circumstances, may be more vigilant and suspicious of others than their heterosexual counterparts.

Moreover, 29 percent of the youth reported at least one suicide attempt. These data are similar to those reported in other studies of gay males (see Ryan and Futterman 1998). Here, lesbian youth were disproportionately represented, in that more than 50 percent of the sample of young women reported at least one suicide attempt, as contrasted with 20 percent of the males. Forty-five percent of those youth who had attempted suicide had made multiple attempts (Healy 1992). These proportions are noteworthy, and further research should assess the generalizability of these findings to other young lesbians.

We also asked youth about their expectations and images of their futures. Future narratives are the beliefs that individuals hold about the timing and content of events in the life course. Such narratives are thought to assume particular salience during periods of developmental transition because they shape goal-setting and planning activities as well as much of later outcomes. The youth were asked to describe all the events and experiences that they thought would occur in the future, as well as the age at which each event was most likely to occur. These data were analyzed and contrasted with a set of data from putatively heterosexual youth (Greene et al. 1992). The gay and lesbian youth anticipated significantly fewer events than did heterosexual adolescents. Heterosexual youth anticipated a more even distribution of events across the projected life course and extended themselves to more distant points in the future than did the gay and lesbian youth. Differences were also found in the type of future events described. Gay and lesbian youth described a higher percentage of achievement events (e.g., buying a house, starting a career, going to school). By contrast, heterosexual adolescents described a higher percentage of relational (e.g., marriage/committed relationship) and lifestyle (e.g., travel, participation in a social organization, a move to a new city or environment) events. No differences emerged in the percentage of existential events (greater knowledge, spirituality, etc.). Thus, gay adolescents had a more restricted future life course perspective in their expectations of relationships and in the ways they saw their future development. These findings are best understood in terms of the combined effects of two cultural influences: negative sanctions regarding the expression of gay and lesbian identity by the culture and the absence of positive norms of gay and lesbian adulthood. One of the major developmental tasks of gay and lesbian youth is the deconstruction of previously internalized heterosexual expectations and the construction of a new set of future expectations of the gay and lesbian life course.

Discussion

The narratives of the youth reveal the opposite of stereotypes that portray the murky past of the closeted, shameful, homosexual mythology. These youth generally regarded themselves as pioneers of a new generation whose special nature affords an insight into the timeless struggle to be human. Far from being mentally disturbed, sexually fixated, or antisocial, as studies in the past have portrayed such youth, we found them to be courageous, intelligent, and healthy adolescents grappling with the many challenges involved in coming out so early in the lifecourse. Most have needs for community and have found a supportive gay culture. And because they come out as adolescents and they are self-identifying as gay or lesbian, we have a new cultural phenomenon: a generation of gay and lesbian youth, the first ever in human history.

At the same time, there were many ways in which these youth were functionally alone. They were alone, for example, in their initial and often painful self-awareness of their homosexual identity, represented by what many spoke of as coming out to themselves. They also were alone within their peer groups, especially when friends and classmates rejected their emerging homosexuality and identity formation. They were alone in their families as their parents struggled to cope with the knowledge that their son or daughter was gay or lesbian, facing their own adult homophobia and disappointment over role loss. Finally, these youth were alone in their future perspective on expectable and desirable life events because few formalized outlets for gay socialization exist in a society that looks with suspicion on contact between older and younger gay cohorts.

The experiences of these youth show how the process of constructing a gay or lesbian identity as a teenager has certain features and sequelae that are relevant to the adolescent alone. Among youth whose parents have withdrawn their support and guidance, the current trend toward beginning sexual activity at earlier and earlier ages creates a series of needs related to health and mental health care. First, gay youth, like all other sexually active youth, need education and support regarding HIV risk reduction and safer sex practices, including avoidance of other STDs (Savin-Williams and Lenhart 1990; Hunter and Schaecher 1994; Ryan and Futterman 1998). Second, youth without guidance from healthy gay and lesbian role models are at risk for sexual abuse and coercion from both same-sex and opposite sex partners (Hunter 1992; D'Augelli 1993; Savin-Williams 1994; Hershberger and D'Augelli 1995). Third, the emotional stresses of coming out, coupled with rejection from family and peers, can create mental health needs for dealing with problems such as depression. The severity of this need is apparent in the suicide histories of the youth, especially the young women. In the absence of parents or other legal guardians, gay youth may need the support and guidance of a "chosen family," such as the Horizons Youth Group (Farrow et al. 1992; Mallon 1992).

Many of the youth in our Chicago study described a kind of *double bind* regarding their sexual identity. Parents and teachers stressed the virtues of truth and honesty; however, remaining true to themselves often resulted in disclosure to others, which could bring about difficult experiences including discrimination and harassment. This left many youth feeling a keen sense of vulnerability, requiring them to exercise a guarded and vigilant watchfulness in their interpersonal relationships. It also is important to remember that seven youths lived in shelters after being forced by relatives to leave home. This vulnerability to emotional and residential exclusion is one of the sequelae of coming out faced by the adolescent alone.

These youths also were constricted in their views of their own futures. Lack of cultural socialization into the expectable course of events for gay and lesbian individuals left them with little precedent around which to plan their lives. However, with the support of their gay and lesbian peers in the Horizons Youth Group, as well as lesbian and gay adult role models, their bolstered self-confidence and self-esteem enabled some of them to begin expanding their conceptions of their futures.

Like the survivors of older "homosexual" cohorts (Herdt and Boxer 1992), these youth are in varying degrees of accepting the desires and necessities of their individual lives. Moreover, the problems of minority youth differ from those of whites, where racism must also be handled. The religious turmoil of devout youth is another additional stressor for teens highly involved in their churches or synagogues. In general, however, compared to earlier cohorts, it is more probable than before that youth will eventually "come out" across the range of contexts in which they situate themselves: school, home, work, and friendships. Like heterosexual youth, when threatened they may defend themselves with denial or deceit. When supported and encouraged, they are at their best: full of energy, curiosity, and resilience.

When we ask the question of how and why the gay or lesbian adolescent is alone, our answers touch upon some strongly held and prevailing cultural norms. One is the deep ambivalence in our culture about the nature and acceptability of teenage sexuality. Another consists of fears about exposing youths, especially teenagers, to adult gay and lesbian role models. Yet another is the stigma borne by parents and other relatives of gay and lesbian youth. However, all these norms and values indicate that patterns of growth and change are never the same for any given group, generation, or historical cohort (Elder 1980). Development across the lifespan is not nearly as ordered or predictable as some had previously assumed (Kohlberg, Ricks, and Snarey 1984). It is precisely these sociocultural processes – the context of lives – that transforms the study of the life span or life cycle into the study of the life course. Without consideration of the cultural meanings implicit in making sense of such change we miss the transitions that help to create the adolescent alone.

Acknowledgment

The data presented in this chapter were part of a larger cultural and developmental investigation of a cohort of youth titled, "Sexual orientation and cultural competence in Chicago," funded by a grant from the Spencer Foundation awarded to The University of Chicago, Gilbert Herdt, Principal Investigator. Andrew Boxer served as co-investigator and project director. Additional investigators of the study were Floyd S. Irvin and Richard Herrell. Major findings and detailed methodology from this investigation are reported in the recently expanded volume by Herdt and Boxer (1993 and 1996).

Notes

1 Some youth as well as adults have employed the formerly pejorative word *queer,* using the term to include a range of sexualities, including but not limited to lesbian, gay, bisexual, and transgender identities. The use of the term is historically bound and is related to historical and cultural changes, including the political/advocacy AIDS movements Act-Up as well as Queer Nation. Central to the use of the

term *queer* is the idea of resistance to categorization and to reproductive ideologies of heterosexual dualisms. Simultaneously, primarily within the humanities, literary theory and criticism, have developed a new postmodern intellectual tradition, *queer theory*, (see DeLauretis 1991) influenced by the work of, among others, Michel Foucault (1980 and 1986; see also Greenberg 1988; Sedgewick 1990). At the time we conducted interviews of youth in our study, no youth called him or herself *queer*. Today, several years later, among a different birth cohort of youth in the same social service agency and support group as our study, many youth use the term *queer*.

2   In order to further understand their sexual subjectivities, and because of the divergent mean ages at which the young men and women had reported their first same-sex and opposite-sex sexual experiences, we classified the sexual developmental pathways of each youth according to which of a series of three sequences had occurred in these initial sexual encounters. That is, those who had a heteroerotic experience first and subsequently engaged in a same-sex experience; or homoerotic experience first and later an opposite-sex sexual experience (a third group had engaged only in homoerotic experiences). Larger proportions of boys were found in the same-sex /opposite-sex and same-sex only groups. The percentage of females was significantly higher in the opposite-sex/same-sex pathway group. That is, young women were much more likely to have had a first opposite-sex sexual experience prior to their first same-sex sexual experience. Multivariate analyses (Cook, Boxer, and Herdt 1989; see also Herdt and Boxer 1996) of these data have confirmed that the sex of the youth allowed us to predict the sequencing of first same-sex and opposite-sex experiences, regardless of the influence of other variables such as the youth's ethnicity, employment status, or age at the time of the interview.

3   *Coming out* has emerged to refer to many psychocultural processes and social events (Herdt 1992). Typically, coming out has referred to self-disclosure as homosexual or gay, or lesbian, to family, friends, or others who assumed the individual to be heterosexual. The emphasis has historically been on one attribute: being homosexual. Historically the meaning of the term has changed. For example, in the 1950s among the psychologist Evelyn Hooker's (1965) ethnographic studies, *coming out* often referred to a "sexual debut." In our study of youth we asked the teens to define the term for us.

4   Since we conducted our study the situation has changed somewhat with regard to support for gay and lesbian youth in the schools. There have been several city-wide in-service educational sessions for teachers and school counselors, sensitizing them to the needs and concerns of gay and lesbian youth. Additionally, there are now at least four teen support groups serving the greater Chicago area. There is also an organized group of gay/lesbian/bisexual teachers who are part of a national coalition.

References

Boxer, A., J. Cook, and G. Herdt (1991). Double jeopardy: Identity transitions and parent-child relations among gay and lesbian youth. In K. Pillemer and K. McCartney (Eds.), *Parent-child relations throughout life*. Hillsdale, NJ: Lawrence Erlbaum Publishers, 59–93.

Boxer, A. M., et al. (1993). Gay and lesbian youth. In P. Toland and B. J. Cohler (Eds.), *Handbook of clinical research and practice with adolescents*. New York: Wiley-Interscience 249–280.

Boxer, A. M., and B. J. Cohler (1989). The life course of gay and lesbian youth: An immodest proposal for the study of lives. *Journal of Homosexuality, 18,* 315–355.

Boxer, A. M., R. A. Levinson, and A. C. Petersen (1990). Adolescent sexuality. In J. Worrell and F. Danner (Eds.), *The adolescent as decision-maker.* New York: Academic Press.

Cook, J., A. M. Boxer, and G. Herdt (1989). First homosexual and heterosexual experiences reported by gay and lesbian youth in an urban community. Paper presented at the annual meetings of the American Sociological Association, San Francisco.

D'Augelli, A. (1993). Preventing mental health problems among lesbian and gay college students. *Journal of Primary Prevention, 13* (suppl. 4), 1–17.

D'Augelli, A. (1996). Lesbian, gay, and bisexual development during adolescence and young adulthood. In R. Cabaj and T. S. Stein (Eds.), *Textbook of homosexuality and mental health.* Washington, DC and London: American Psychiatric Press, 267–288.

D'Augelli, A., and S. L. Hershberger (1993). Lesbian, gay, and bisexual youth in community settings: Personal challenges and mental health problems. *American Journal of Community Psychology, 21,* 421–448.

DeLauretis, T. (1991). Queer theory: Lesbian and gay sexualities – an introduction. *Differences, 3* (2), iii–xviii.

Eisen, V., and I. Hall (1996). Introduction to special issue: Lesbian, gay, bisexual, and transgender people and education. *Harvard Educational Review, 66,* v–ix.

Elder, G. (1980). Adolescence in historical perspective. In J. Adelson (Ed.), *Handbook of adolescent psychology.* New York: Wiley: 3–46.

Erikson, E. (1959). Identity and the life cycle. *Psychological Issues, 1* (1), 50–100.

Farrow, J. A., et al. (1992). Health and health needs of homeless and runaway youth. A position paper of the Society for Adolescent Medicine. *Journal of Adolescent Health, 13,* 717–726.

Feder, H. H. (1984). Hormones and sexual behavior. *Annual Review of Psychology, 35,* 165–200.

Foucault, M. (1980). *The history of sexuality, Vol. 1* (Transl. R. Hurley). New York: Random House.

Foucault, M. (1986). *The use of pleasure* (Transl. R. Hurley). New York: Random House.

Gagnon, J. (1989a). Sexuality across the lifespan in the United States. In C. F. Turner et al. (Eds.), *AIDS: Sexual behavior and intravenous drug use.* Washington, DC: National Academy Press.

Gagnon, J. (1989b). Disease and desire. *Daedalus, 118,* 47–77.

Gagnon, J., and W. Simon. (1973). *The social sources of human sexuality.* Chicago: Aldine.

Gerstel, C., A. J. Feraios, and G. Herdt (1989). Widening circles: An ethnographic profile of a youth group. *Journal of Homosexuality, 17,* 75–92.

Greenberg, D. (1988). *The history of homosexuality.* Chicago: The University of Chicago Press.

Greene, A. L., et al. (1992). Future time perspectives among gay and lesbian youth. Paper presented at the Biennial Meetings of the Society for Adolescent Research, Washington, DC (March 20).

Harbeck, K. M., ed. (1992). *Coming out of the classroom closet: Gay and lesbian students, teachers and curricula.* New York: Harrington Park Press.

Healy, S. (1992). Suicidal behavior among gay and lesbian youth. Unpublished master's of arts thesis. Committee on Human Development, The University of Chicago.

Herdt, G. (1989). Gay and lesbian youth: Emergent identities and cultural scenes at home and abroad. *Journal of Homosexuality, 18,* 1–42.

Herdt, G. (1990). Developmental continuity as a dimension of sexual orientation across cultures. In D. McWhirter, J. Reinisch, and S. Sanders. (Eds.), *Homosexuality and heterosexuality: The Kinsey Scale and current research.* New York: Oxford University Press, 208–238.

Herdt, G. (1992). `Coming out' as a rite of passage: A Chicago study. In G. Herdt (Ed.), *Gay Culture In America.* Boston: Beacon Press, 29–67.

Herdt, G., and A. M. Boxer (1991). Ethnographic issues in the study of AIDS. *Journal of Sex Research, 28,* 171–189.

Herdt, G., and A. M. Boxer (1992a). Introduction: Culture, history and life course of gay men. In G. Herdt (Ed.), *Gay culture in America.* Boston: Beacon Press, 1–28.

Herdt, G., and A. M. Boxer (1992b). Sexual identity development and AIDS sexual risk. In T. Dyson (Ed.), *Anthropological demography and AIDS.* Liege, Belgium: International Union for the Scientific Study of Demography.

Herdt, G., and A. M. Boxer (1993); (2nd expanded ed. 1996). *Children of horizons: How gay and lesbian youth are leading a new way out of the closet.* Boston: Beacon Press.

Herdt, G., and R. J. Stoller (1990). *Intimate communications: Culture and the study of erotics.* New York: Columbia University Press.

Hershberger, S. L., and A. R. D'Augelli (1995). The consequences of victimization on the mental health and suicidality of lesbian, gay, and bisexual youth. *Developmental Psychology, 31,* 65–74.

Hooker, E. (1965). Male homosexuals and their worlds. In J. Marmor (Ed.), *Sexual inversion: The multiple roots of homosexuality.* New York: Basic Books, 83–107.

Hunter, J. (1992). Violence against lesbian and gay male youths. In G. M. Herek and K. T. Berrill (Eds.) *Hate crimes: Confronting violence against lesbians and gay men.* Newbury Park, CA: Sage Publications, 76–82.

Hunter, J., and R. Schaecher (1994). AIDS prevention for lesbian, gay, and bisexual youth. *Families in Society, 75* (Suppl 6), 346–354.

Kinsey, A. C., W. B. Pomeroy, and C. E. Martin (1948). *Sexual behavior in the human male.* Philadelphia: Saunders.

Kinsey, A. C., et al. (1953). *Sexual behavior in the human female.* Philadelphia: Saunders.

Kohlberg, L., D. Ricks, and J. Snarey (1984). Child development as a predictor of adaptation in adulthood. *Genetic Psychology Monographs, 110,* 91–173.

McClintock, M. K., and G. Herdt (1996). Rethinking puberty: The development of sexual attraction. *Current Directions in Psychological Science,* December: 178–183.

Mallon, G. (1992). Gay and no place to go: Assessing the needs of gay and lesbian adolescents in out-of-home care settings. *Child Welfare, 6,* 547–556.

Murray, S. O. (1984). *Social theory, homosexual realities.* New York: Gay Academic Union.

Murray, S. O. (1992). Components of gay community in San Francisco. In G. Herdt. (Ed.), *Gay culture in America.* Boston: Beacon Press, 107–146.

Murray, S. O. (1996). *American gay.* Chicago: The University of Chicago Press.

Parker, R., G. Herdt, and M. Carballo (1991). Sexual culture, HIV transmission and AIDS research. *Journal of Sex Research, 28,* 75–96.

Roy Romer, Governor of Colorado et al., petitioners v. *Richard G. Evans et al.,* 64 *U.S.L. W.* 4353. 1996. Docket 94–1039. Equal protection clause, holds invalid a provision of Colorado's constitution.

Ryan, C., and D. Futterman (1998). *Lesbian and gay youth: Care and counseling.* New York: Columbia University Press.

Savin-Williams, R., and R. E. Lenhart (1990). AIDS prevention among gay and lesbian youth: Psychosocial stress and health care intervention guidelines. In D. Ostrow (Ed.), *Behavioral aspects of AIDS,* ed. New York: Plenum Publishing, 75–99.

Savin-Williams, R. (1994). Verbal and physical abuse as stressors in the lives of lesbian, gay males, and bisexual youths: Associations with school problems, running away, substance abuse, prostitution and suicide. *Journal of Consulting and Clinical Psychology, 62,* 261–269.

Sears, J. T. (1992). Educators, homosexuality, and homosexual students: Are personal feelings related to professional beliefs? In K. M. Harbeck (Ed.), *Coming out of the classroom: Gay and lesbian students, teachers, and curricula.* New York: Harrington Park Press: 29–79.

Sedgewick, E. K. (1990). *Epistemology of the closet.* Berkeley: University of California Press.

Stoller, R. J., and G. Herdt (1985). Theories of the origins of homosexuality: A cross-cultural look. *Archives of General Psychiatry, 42,* 399–405.

Sullivan, H. S. (1958). *The interpersonal theory of psychiatry.* New York: W. W. Norton.

Tripp, C. (1975). *The homosexual matrix.* New York: McGraw-Hill.

Troiden, R. (1989). The formation of homosexual identities. *Journal of Homosexuality, 17,* 43–73.

Whitney, C. (1989). Living amid the ruins of the sexual revolution. *Christopher Street, 12*(9), 23–32.

8   Lives in the Balance: A Profile of Homeless Youth in New York City

Michael C. Clatts, Deborah J. Hillman,
Aylin Atillasoy, and W. Rees Davis

> For ten or eleven hours a day these children of ten and eleven years stoop over the chute and pick out the slate and other impurities from the coal as it moves past. The air is black with coal dust, and the roar of the crushers, screens, and rushing millrace of coal is deafening. Sometimes one of the children falls into the machinery and is terribly mangled, or slips into the chute and is smothered to death. Many children are killed in this way. Many others, after a time, contract coal-miner's asthma and consumption, which gradually undermines their health. (Hunter 1904: 24)

Introduction

Sweeping changes in the structure of American social and economic institutions have resulted in an influx of large numbers of homeless youth onto the streets of many urban areas (Pries and Silbert 1991:19), a pattern that parallels increased homelessness in the U.S. population in general (Hopper Susser, and Connors 1985; Rossi 1989; Benker, Boone, and Dehavenon 1990; Link et al. 1994). Some of these youth are transitionally homeless, having left home or foster care for a limited and relatively brief period of time. Although at high risk for violence and victimization on the streets, these youth do not necessarily become deeply entrenched in the street economy. A substantial and apparently growing number of these youth, however, enter street life and remain abjectly homeless for extended periods of time, living from day to day on the streets, sleeping in parks, subways, tunnels, and abandoned buildings, finding basic sustenance in the street economy. Evidence for these patterns of behavior is abundant in a number of demographic surveys conducted of runaway and homeless youth (Ringwalt, Greene, and Iachan 1994; Kipke et al. 1995), as well as in surveys of local and state agencies serving high-risk youth (Gunn 1988).

There is also a considerable body of pertinent literature on the involvement of youths in high-risk behaviors (Hein 1988; Kegeles, Adler, and Irwin 1988; Yates 1988; Rotheram-Borus and Koopman 1989). For example, although drug use in the general adolescent population appears to have peaked in the late 1970s, and to have

139

dropped precipitously in the late 1980s, there is ample evidence that drug and alcohol abuse continues to be widespread among some parts of the high-risk youth population (Deykin, Levy, and Wells 1986; Kufeldt and Nimmo 1987; Robertson 1989; Kipke et al. 1995).[1]

Although precise figures about the size of this population are problematic (Caton 1986; Robertson 1991), some studies indicate that as many as 2 million youth in the United States are homeless, and that as many as 200,000 youth live as permanent residents of the streets (U.S. Department of Health and Human Services 1986). It is noteworthy, however, that attempts to estimate the size of the population are fraught with substantial methodological limitations, not the least of which is the fact that the population is highly diverse, both locally and nationally.[2] Historically, the population was thought to be primarily composed of youth who had run away (Adams and Munro 1979). More recently, however, it has become clear that it now also includes substantial numbers of youth who are homeless because their families have become homeless (Benker et al. 1990), youth who have left foster care or group homes, and youth who are homeless due to neglect and abandonment (Adams, Gullotta, and Clancy 1985). Finally, it also includes large numbers of youth who may have some contact with family members but who, for whatever reason, do not think that they can return home (Pries and Silbert 1991). For many of the youth in this latter group, physical and sexual abuse are frequently cited factors, as is conflict related to the young person's sexual identity (Hersch 1988, 1989; Clatts 1989; Clatts and Atillasoy 1993).

Whatever the multiple causes of increased homelessness in this population, it is apparent that large numbers of youth have become part of the population living on and from the streets – a social and economic environment in which they are dependent upon the vagaries of the street economy. In this precarious and often violent world, these young people do what they can to stay afloat. Often this means exchanging sex for money, food, shelter, and drugs. Much like the children in the previous century who faced disease and early death resulting from working conditions in coal mines, the constellation of risk behaviors associated with youths' roles in the street economy results in exceptional vulnerability to a number of interrelated poor health outcomes. These include high rates of repeated exposure to sexually transmitted diseases (STDs), unplanned pregnancies, untreated tuberculosis, HIV infection, and rapid development of opportunistic infections associated with progressive immune dysfunction and AIDS (Institute of Medicine 1988; D'Angelo et al. 1991; Stricof et al. 1991; Futterman et al. 1993).

Despite the overwhelming evidence of the increasing incidence of homelessness among youth and its attendant poor health outcomes, relatively little is known about why youth enter street life, about how they survive on a day-to-day basis, and why some youth remain in street life while others do not.[3] Moreover, relatively little is known about these youths' contacts with public and private institutions that are charged with protecting their welfare, particularly in terms of health. The lack of information about these issues leaves a substantial and critical gap in our understanding of the kinds of prevention strategies and policies that are likely to be most effective among this diverse population, particularly in relation to reducing risk for HIV infection – arguably the most critical public health challenge of our time.

In an effort to begin to fill these gaps, this chapter has three primary goals. First, it provides an overview of recent evidence regarding the demographic and behavioral characteristics of the street youth population in one metropolitan area, New York City. Second, based on a series of parallel qualitative studies, it provides an ethnographic profile of life experiences of these youth, including experiences that precipitated entry into street life and those that characterize youths' subsequent life on the streets. Third, it considers the significance of these data for understanding the special needs of this segment of the youth population, particularly in relation to the development of effective public health strategies and policies.

A Demographic and Behavioral Profile of Street Youth in New York City

It has been estimated that there are at least 20,000 street youth in New York City (Shaffer and Caton 1984). Some of these youth live transiently in overcrowded welfare hotels or in various kinds of transitional living programs. The vast majority, however, have spent considerable amounts of time in which they were alone, living on the streets without adult assistance or supervision.[4] In an effort to better document the service-related needs of this population, the Youth at Risk Project was initiated in 1992 as part of a program funded by the Centers for Disease Control and Prevention (CDC) to evaluate street outreach programs targeted to homeless youth in New York City. A series of street-based survey interviews were conducted among 432 street youth in the central Manhattan area (Clatts and Davis 1993).[5]

Approximately 80 percent were male and 20 percent were female. Nearly 75 percent were between nineteen and twenty-three years of age. The vast majority identified themselves as ethnic minorities, with about 25 percent black and nearly 40 percent Latino. Roughly half were born in New York City, although more than 7 percent were born outside the United States. While most self-identified as heterosexual, nearly 50 percent identified as gay, lesbian, or bisexual.

More than half were abjectly homeless at the time of the interview, and nearly 80 percent had lived on the streets at least some amount of time in the past year. Roughly 60 percent of those who were homeless at the time of the interview had been homeless for more than one year. Only 33 percent received financial support from parents. Nearly 33 percent had some type of legal employment. Only about 25 percent received some kind of public assistance. Roughly a third obtained money from panhandling. More than 33 percent supported themselves through prostitution, and about 25 percent earned money through the sale and distribution of illegal drugs.

Many had used a wide variety of drugs in their lifetimes (Clatts and Davis 1994). Well over 33 percent have used crack, over half have used cocaine, and more than 33 percent have used heroin. Nearly 25 percent have used speedballs (mixed cocaine and heroin). More than 25 percent have used speed or ampheta- mines, and more than 33 percent have used LSD. More than 25 percent used mari- juana and alcohol on a daily basis and nearly 50 percent did so at least occasionally. In the last five years, 20 percent injected drugs at some point. Within the thirty days prior to the interview, more than 10 percent had used cocaine, crack, heroin, and LSD. It is noteworthy that less than a third of the entire sample had ever been in drug treatment. [6]

Youth also reported a wide range of high-risk sexual activity. More than 50 per- cent were sexually involved with more than one other person. More than 33 percent were involved in prostitution. More than 33 percent had a sexually transmitted dis- ease at some time in the past, and roughly 15 percent had a sexually transmitted disease within the past six months. More than 75 percent said that they knew some- one with HIV or AIDS. More than 50 percent reported they believed that it was "somewhat likely" or "very likely" that they would get AIDS. Approximately 4 per- cent disclosed that they already had HIV infection or AIDS, although earlier sero- prevalence studies of HIV infection among these youth indicate a much higher rate of infection.[7]

Multiple risks in this sample of youth are highly intercorrelated. For example, youth who had ever participated in prostitution were less likely to use condoms in vaginal, anal, and oral sex with main partners. Similarly, crack use was associated with greater sexual risk for vaginal sex with multiple partners as well as for anal sex with both main and multiple partners. Ever having injected drugs was statisti- cally associated with unprotected multiple partner sex, prostitution, unprotected sex, and homelessness.[8]

Involvement in multiple high-risk behaviors is by no means unique to street youth in New York City. In a comparative analysis of street youth in Los Angeles, New York, San Diego, and San Francisco, for example, Kipke (1995) found that a high percentage of street youth in all four cities reported the use of a wide range of illicit drugs, including cocaine, crack, heroin, and speedballs. Lifetime cocaine use among street youth was particularly high across all four cities (New York, 58 per- cent; Los Angeles, 54 percent; San Francisco, 69 percent; and San Diego, 49 per- cent), and is substantially higher than rates in the general adolescent populations in these cities. In a similar analysis of the same data set, Kennedy (1995) found high rates of sexual risk among street youth in New York (71 percent), Los Angeles (53 percent), and San Francisco (52 percent), rates that are well in excess of those evi- denced in the general adolescent population in these cities (Forst 1994). Examining three risk behaviors (sexual behavior, drug use, and involvement in the illegal street economy), for example, Kennedy (1995) found that all the youth in this three-city study had engaged in at least one high-risk behavior, that about 75 percent were involved in two categories of risk, and approximately half were involved in all three kinds of risk behavior.

An Ethnographic Profile of Street Youth in New York City

As alarming as these statistical data are, they do not in and of themselves reveal much about the early life experiences of these youth or about their experiences on the streets. Similarly, we know little about how youth themselves experience street life, particularly how they view their involvement in the street economy and the multiple dangers that confront them there. Finally, we know little about how early experiences of trauma and abuse influence street youth's subsequent capacity to make positive and sustained changes in behavior, including leaving the streets.

As part of a series of ethnographic studies of street youth that used a combined *life history* and *life event* methodological approach (McLaughlin and Sorenson 1985; Clatts 1990), an ethnographic profile of this population has been constructed.[9] Interview data were analyzed with reference to seven interconnected themes that are discussed later:

1. Youths' tendency to frame their experiences on the streets in terms of freedom and independence, proving themselves, and making it on their own
2. The considerable sense of loss and depression that characterizes their lives
3. The harshness and violence of everyday life on the streets
4. The daily struggle with hunger and exhaustion
5. The issue of "trust" and the difference between "friends" and "associates"
6. The effect of watching others close to them get sick and die from AIDS
7. The tremendous barriers that confront them in trying to leave the streets

The Notion of Freedom

Many youth described their lives on the streets as a chance to make it on their own, to experience freedom. Many described the move to the streets as a viable escape from intolerable home circumstances. A twenty-two-year-old Hispanic gay youth involved in prostitution said of the many times he had run away in his early teens:

> I just, you know, I had gotten a taste of the street, like what it was, it felt like freedom, like complete and total freedom, and I just didn't want to be home anymore.

A nineteen-year-old black youth described his move to the streets as a way to fulfill his quest for adulthood. After having exhausted the aid of relatives while "totally strung out" on cocaine and crack, he realized, "Well, I'm getting older, it's time that I get out on my own. I have to start looking after my own responsibilities as I get older."

Once on the streets, that environment soon became a way of life:

> I've slept on the subways. When it's hot, I have slept in parks . . . trucks and vans, you know . . . things like that. But, it's not like I could never, it's not like I had to do this, because my mother and my father, my brothers and sisters, they say, you don't have to do that. But I tell them, I'm not your responsibility. I'm old, I'm getting older. I have to learn how to look out for myself. And I figure if I be doing this, this is part of survival. If, even if I, like, don't have to do it, this is just an experience for me.

Other youth, though proud of their ability to survive on their own, spoke of the conflicts that led them to opt for "freedom." A nineteen-year-old black youth talked about the difficulties at home with his mother and his abusive stepfather, a "hard man" who drank a lot:

> [It] was based on domestic, you know, like household problems, you know, in the house. Arguments, a lot of quarrels, you know, a lot of altercations broke out. We'd argue over silly stuff, you know? It started getting rougher and rougher, and rougher, you know, so it was like a thing where you live in my house, you're gonna do what I want you to do, or get out. Staying at a place that you're not running it, is a pain you know, it goes deep, you know what I'm saying? The pain goes deep down and you want to leave, you know? So that's when you really get yourself together, sit down and think, you know? What do I got to do here, you know, to be on my own. Can I survive out there? Basically, so I put together, put together my own plan, master plan, and I went out on my own and did a lot of praying. Thank God I am still here today to talk about it.

After some time spent on the streets, the "independence" he values in himself had been severely tried. He explained:

> I'm at the bottom right now, I can't go no lower. I'm sleeping outside, in boxes. Barely sleep, can't go no lower, I'm not eating, hungry. Can't go no lower, see? We just pray. Try not to be sad and, you know, cry, and let the anger take over. Keep a sort of good mentality. Not try to rob. Have a lot of faith.

For a seventeen-year-old youth born in Jamaica, street life meant freedom from foster care. He mused:

> I have to be free, you know what I'm saying? I can't be living with this and living with that. I gotta, you know, I pray till this day to live on my own. I wanted to live on my own since . . . they said put you in a foster home. You know what I'm saying, it's just like it's easier for me, 'cause I can solve my own problems. I like that. See, I like a challenge. I like a challenge, you know, that's going to make me work to get what I want, you know what I'm saying. I like a challenge, I like to solve my problems.

The street economy is one of the only avenues of survival accessible to many street youth, and often becomes synonymous with being "on their own." A twenty-year-old black youth involved in prostitution for the past ten years, beginning in his New Jersey hometown, summarized his feelings about leaving home:

> I don't think I will ever regret [it]. Never. Because I can always go back if I wanted to, even now, but I don't think I would. I like being on my own. I mean, it's hard, but it's the price you have to pay.

Although his HIV-positive status has enabled him to get a subsidized room, he continues to "turn tricks" and spend most of his time on the streets. His goal in coming to New York was to find independence:

> To get out on my own. You know, see what it feels like to pay bills and stuff, and I do that now, so far what I planned for myself is coming for me. It's coming slowly but surely. I always said I wanted to live on my own with my own, you know even if it's nothing but a room, it's mine. And it's coming for me.

An eighteen-year-old bisexual youth from a large and affluent family in Texas complained that material things did not make up for the lack of attention in his home. Surviving in the New York street economy primarily through prostitution, he said, "I couldn't take the spoiled life. I wanted to see what it was like being like everyone else. Having to work and do things on your own. So that's why I left Texas and came to New York."

For many street youth, their surface bravado and pride in surviving on their own hides tremendous stores of pain – pain from their daily struggles on the streets and the many losses and abuses they have suffered, both before and after entering street life.

The Experience of Loss and Depression

A striking feature of the lives of street youth is the tremendous shadow of loss that looms over their lives. Many of them have survived multiple losses early in life, including parental divorce, death, and separation from family to live in group/foster homes. Along with the devastation of physical and sexual abuse, which is all too common in their lives, these losses often lead to chronic depression.

A nineteen-year-old gay youth described a series of losses and abuses that led him to the brink of suicide. Born in Harlem, he was "shifted around between family members" and spent some years with a physically abusive grandmother. At the age of eight, his father moved out and his mother's boyfriend began sexually abusing him. Three years later, when his mother was incarcerated for the second time, the Bureau of Child Welfare put him in a group home. A few months later his mother came to visit, and he ran away with her, "moving from place to place constantly" while she sold drugs to earn money. Eventually, the Bureau of Child Welfare intervened again, and he went to a group home outside the city. When he was fourteen, his mother died, possibly of suicide. As he recalled:

> I went to her funeral, and that was the roughest thing to have to deal with, too. I mean, oh man, it was just so hard to deal with. I mean, when I first found out she died, I thought I would never survive. I really thought I would never make it through. But I'm still here!

After his mother's death, he went to live with an abusive aunt. After one particularly severe beating, he ran away. For four days he lived on the streets, hungry and sleeping on a subway train. Finally, he sought help from a mission house and ended up in another group home. He ran away numerous times and gradually became more accustomed to street life. At fifteen, "life just got so much for [him]" that he "decided to turn to suicide." As he remembers it:

> I mean, my mother had died, and my aunt told me she hated my guts, and I didn't belong with the family, and at that time, my family was the only thing I had. And it just hurt me so much I couldn't deal with it, so I tried to jump off a roof. But I couldn't. I don't know why. I stood on the ledge for hours! But I just couldn't move. It's like, the wind wouldn't blow hard enough. That's all the wind had to do

was blow, all you needed was a strong wind. But the wind wouldn't blow hard enough, I'm telling you.

At eighteen, he started dating a man three years older and for the first time acknowledged (to himself and others) that he was gay. Despite frequent bouts of homelessness and cruel encounters with homophobia, he graduated from high school. "Don't know how!" he exclaimed.

> And, at this time, I used to just walk around. And, till I met this guy, I never really slept, I slept on trains. I really started to fall in love with him, too. I slept with him in Penn Station. It was really dirty there, but, you gotta sleep somewhere. And then he started to beat up on me. He was really abusive. He claimed he loved me, and yet he abused me. I never quite understood that.

To become self-sufficient so he could leave his abusive lover, he began to hustle sex in bars. Prostitution quickly became a "last resort" and he would resort to it "when things got bad again." He began to suffer from the degradation and futility of his circumstances and attempted to slit his wrists. He was aided by outreach programs and gradually "things started to go up . . . ever so slowly."

Other young people talked of suicidal depression following the death of a parent or caretaker. For example, an eighteen-year-old Hispanic youth said of his mother's death a few years earlier, "I took it hard. And once, I wanted to kill myself, `cause she died, and I wanted to be with her." For the nineteen-year-old black youth who as a toddler lost his parents and who as a teenager lost the grandparents who raised him, the prospect of his own death offered the possibility of relief from feelings of loss:

> I really wanted, to get rid of, get over life, you know get my life over with. Go through life, zip through my teens, zip through my twenties, zip through my thirties and forties, and pass away, and join my grandma and grandpa. `Cause I thought that life here was poison, that they take the good people off the earth, and leave all the bad people here.

The magnitude of loss in these young people's lives creates a stark backdrop against which they face the harshness and violence of life on the streets. Indeed, the realities of street life perpetuate experiences of loss and abuse and contribute to the sense of despair so common among street youth.

Daily Life on the Streets

Life on the streets is fraught with a host of difficulties and dangers, demanding both vigilance and ingenuity. Survival – whether meeting everyday needs or facing threats to one's life – is a constant source of stress among street youth. Even for those who receive help from street outreach programs, there is only a limited respite from the streets. Drop-in centers are not open twenty-four hours a day, and most programs are forced to ration services. For many street youth, the greatest struggle is simply staying alive. As one drug dealer who fears for his life explained:

> Because you know, especially if you're in the business that I'm in, you know, it's
> like, you sell drugs and you know, people could come up and shoot you in the back
> or, you know, try to get you arrested or something like that. `Cause everyday you
> got to constantly live with that fear.

Even for youth not involved in dealing drugs, the streets are a threatening environment. As a nineteen-year-old said, it may not be apparent to the daytime passerby, but "it's dangerous out there on Forty-second [Street]." His strategy for dealing with the streets at night is to stay awake and alert, walking around as much as possible. "Sometimes," he said, "I would go and hop a [subway] and purposely get arrested, just so I can sit in jail and have a place to stay."

Though the hazards of street life affect young people of both sexes, girls who survive on the streets face particular perils. One young black woman who entered the streets after repeated sexual victimization in a group home described the difficulties facing women on the streets:

> I'm telling you it's hard. There's a lot out there that will hurt you. I'm twenty-two
> and I been there. I done seen. There's nothing out there. Especially not for a
> female. A male could make it out there. But a female, she can't because people are
> always saying, 'I'll help you,' . . . and 'do this' and 'do that.' Some people just do it
> because they want something in return. I learned that too.
>
> The reason why I say males could make it out there better than females is
> because a man knows how to take care of his self. But say that [a girl's] mother
> threw them out at eleven years old . . . they won't know where to go and what to
> do. And then they still in that stage where they are friendly with everybody.
>
> All a man got to do is walk up to a female and say, "are you okay?" And all she
> got to do is cry and be kind of innocent and then he'll say, "Okay I'll help you."
> And then most females just go with that man. And then Lord knows what can happen to her. He could be a killer. He might be a nice person. Then again, he might
> not. You don't never know.
>
> But a man is better [off] because most of the time people don't bother them.
> They will be friends and they will be out there, they'll be out there with each other.
> Helping each other.

Obtaining the daily necessities of life – shelter from the elements, food, showers, clothing, a place to sleep – is conditioned by the streets. So, too, is the decision to steal, sell drugs, and/or engage in prostitution. As one youth explained:

> It's a survival thing. You panic, and you're thinking, 'What do I got to do to survive?' And you got your options right in front of you. I mean, I could steal, I could
> have sex, I could do this, I could do that. And then you think about it. And then,
> whichever one you feel most comfortable with, that's the one you go with.

Even when these activities are used to support a drug habit, they cannot be divorced from issues of survival. For many, drug use is intricately woven into the whole survival scheme, as a means of controlling hunger, of staying awake and alert, and of enduring that which seems unendurable. As one youth put it, "I can't conceive of doing robbing without, you know, being under the influence of alcohol, or something like that, you know? I mean, [it gives] some kind of alteration." And for some, the temporary act of "getting high" serves as refuge from despair and hopelessness. As one youth explained:

> And at this time it's all I have. So, I drink and smoke a little herb and feel a little better and then I don't feel as depressed. Therefore I won't go out and do something drastic and I'll regret it.

Chronic Exhaustion

Most street youth, due to lack of sleep, face the challenges of the streets in a state of chronic exhaustion. For many, finding a safe place to sleep is the most difficult task on the streets. "Not sleeping, not getting the right sleep, not sleeping where you want to sleep, how you want to sleep" is, in one youth's words, a constant problem. Activities in the street economy take place during both the day and the night. Youth sometimes view sleep as a loss of much needed revenue: "'Cause see, like when I sleep," one youth explained, "I miss a lot of business that way."

Outreach programs provide temporary respite from the streets in the form of a place to "crash," and many street youth nap in the safety of a drop-in center. Apart from this opportunity, youth conform to the elements. An eighteen-year-old male prostitute, living on the streets, explained:

> In the summertime it's cool. In the summertime you get a sheet, right, a jacket. Fall asleep in the park, you know? Or in a truck. Sometimes I have fell asleep on the same block where I whore, sitting on the steps. On a cold night, however, you've got to go out there and do the best you can. Got to make sacrifices. When it gets too cold, I just hop into a subway. That's all. Or I get drunk.

"Friends" and "Associates"

Social networks among street youth are often defined by interconnected factors such as gender, sexual identity, and access to drugs. These relationships are often tenuous, expedient, and very transient. Although street youth share the street scene with youth in similar straits, many explain that their relationships with other youth on the streets contribute to their overall sense of alienation and stress. One youth described his lack of supports in this way:

> When you're out here on the streets, and you're by yourself, you know, you got nobody in your corner, nobody sticking behind you, no type of support, you know what I'm saying? You know, it hurts. You feel by yourself.

Past experience lead youth to a general wariness about friendship. By referring to most of their street-based companions as *associates* rather than *friends,* street youth emphasize the pragmatic and conditional nature of these relationships. One youth put it quite simply: "I don't have friends. I have associates. People who I socialize with. You know, because there's people who say they want to be your friend and they turn around and stab you in the back."

Another young man, asked to describe his friendships on the streets, defined the situation clearly:

> It wasn't really friends. It was associates. They were with me whenever I had money or drugs on me. Besides that, they never wanted to know me if I didn't have the means to buy their friendships for about an hour or two hours a day. Yeah, 'cause they were just associates, not friends. Friends are people who care about you, who try to help you whichever way they can and not wait for anything in return. They just, like, want to spend time with you.

A nineteen-year-old Hispanic youth, homeless and hustling since the age of sixteen, explained the lack of "true" friendships on the streets as due to the fact that youth respond to the stresses of street life by "building up walls." They have become acclimated, in a way, to a life of pain and hardship and have learned to respond by lowering their expectations and keeping their feelings to themselves. He summed it up this way:

> Out here, you don't really have friends. You know, everybody out here is materialistic. People come from broken homes, they been hurt a lot and everybody . . . just want[s] to keep peace to themselves, like not depend on nobody, you know? So they don't want to care about nobody. Everyone is so self-centered. Everybody got so many problems in their head they be like "damn, please." They just don't want to hear it. You tell them something and they be like, "yeah" and "okay." Out here, you just got to keep that stuff in you and with you. And if you're depressed and everything, you just got to keep it to yourself.

Some street youth describe a high degree of jealousy and rivalry on the streets, which, among male hustlers, includes competition for "good tricks." A *good trick* is one who pays well, provides desirable drugs, and behaves in a kind fashion. A transsexual youth explained the "politics" of prostitution among transsexual youth in Port Authority. She said that some tricks don't know that the transsexuals are male, and if there are bad feelings between a transsexual and a female prostitute, the woman may tell a potential customer the truth about her rival.

Lives Touched by AIDS

The daily challenge to meet the demands of survival in the street environment makes it difficult for youth to protect themselves against HIV infection, particularly in the context of street prostitution. Although AIDS education is a primary focus of outreach efforts for street youth and youth are fairly knowledgeable about AIDS (Atillasoy and Clatts 1993; Clatts and Davis 1993), it is often a personal relationship with someone who has AIDS that forces them to confront it. Too often, street youth watch someone close to them live with, and die from, AIDS. A nineteen-year-old black youth described his experience:

> When I was in Philadelphia, I was aware of the AIDS virus, and I was aware of what it could do. But, it didn't really scare me, like it's scaring me now. Because I really, never really, sat down and actually spoke with somebody who had it and was about to die. I arrived in New York, and I spoke with an individual who had

the virus. He was going into the hospital for treatment. I discussed this disease and the things it could do. He told me it was no joke . . . and I believed him.

Another nineteen-year-old black youth recalled the pain of watching a friend die:

He was really close to me, and when he caught it, he died. Six months ago he passed away, of AIDS. The parents were telling everybody he had the flu, but he told me. When I went to visit him in the hospital he told me, like, he don't have the flu. He have AIDS. But he was telling me about it for me to be careful. And I'll tell you, thanks. You know? God. He died.

For someone who has felt impervious to the threat of AIDS, the news of a friend's illness can be deeply shocking. A nineteen-year-old bisexual youth described the sense of disbelief he and others felt when they learned, two years earlier, that a friend had AIDS:

We were thinking . . . you know, he don't look sick or nothing. He found out he had AIDS and he told all of us. And we were like, "What! You?! Come on man, you're joking." "Nah, man." And ever since that day, I started wearing condoms.

It is the combination of fear and sorrow, on losing a friend or relative to AIDS, that personalizes the issue and brings many street youth to think about their own vulnerability. When asked how he first became aware of his risk for AIDS, and of the need to protect himself, a nineteen-year-old black youth, engaged in survival sex, said quite succinctly, "Well, my friend died from AIDS. That terrified me, so I knew I have a chance of doing the same thing. So I was like, I have to protect myself or face the consequences."

Getting Off the Streets

Neither the process of protecting oneself on the streets, nor of leaving street life itself, is as simple as making the decision to do so. The economic, social, and emotional forces that keep youth on the streets include a lack of jobs and housing, and insufficient education and social support. Many youth come to the streets with mental health problems (Caton 1986). Once on the streets, moreover, many develop coping patterns that serve to reinforce the structural barriers they encounter in trying to change.

A nineteen-year-old African American youth described a typical day:

I get up in the morning. I run around looking for a job until about noontime. If I don't find nothing then I am over in the Port Authority trying to make a couple of dollars hustling, you know selling your body . . . from noon till after rush hour, and after that if I make some money, I go get something to eat, go to the movies, go to sleep. The next day, the same routine.

A nineteen-year-old Hispanic youth, involved in prostitution, contends that his drug use prevents him from getting off the streets. This youth explained that the only way out is to leave New York City altogether:

> But I'd have to go away! That would be my best thing, to go away to a long-term residential drug treatment program and get it together. The way I support myself, it's tough.

Street youth have particular needs regarding drug treatment that often are not addressed in traditional programs. For the large number of drug-involved street youth who are gay, lesbian, or bisexual, drug treatment is especially problematic since many providers are not sufficiently educated about issues related to sexuality in general and the relationship between sex and drugs among street youth in particular. Moreover, after some time on the streets, drug use becomes an integral part of many street youths' lives, often playing an adaptive role; conventional forms of treatment that hold abstinence as their goal are seldom realistic approaches if they fail to consider the void that drug use sought to fill in the first place (Alexander 1990; Clatts et al. 1993; Clatts and Davis 1995).

For youth who find other avenues closed to them, and who feel a lack of support, the street economy itself can be addictive. The situation for most street youth is a vicious circle. They need a place to live in order to look for, and hold, a job; they need a job in order to afford a room or apartment. A nineteen-year-old African American youth explained:

> A stable place to stay would be the best thing [for me]. If I had a stable place to stay, I could go in and out to work, you know, and it would be alright . . . I mean, if I had a place to stay, I could get my own food, and I could support myself. But, you know, not a shelter system.

Subsisting on $215 a month in public assistance and occasional earnings from prostitution, a twenty-two-year-old black youth said that the only people he knew who had been able to acquire housing were those whose illness with AIDS entitled them to subsidized housing. It occurred to him that if he contracted HIV it would solve his housing problem but decided that it was not worth the new set of problems he would face.

The multiple difficulties in the lives of street youth are compounded by the barriers they encounter in trying to obtain services. A twenty-three-year-old white youth described his feelings about being homeless, mentally ill, and addicted to drugs. This youth had spent his early childhood and adolescence moving from one foster home to another and had endured physical and sexual abuse at the hands of foster parents. He ran away from the foster care system at the age of seventeen and began living on the streets. There, he took up hustling, drug dealing, robbing, and stealing in order to survive. On his own, he sought admission to a program for mentally ill chemical abusers, but he was not accepted. He explained the futility of his efforts:

> And then they want to know why I got to hustle and sell crack and do all that bullshit, and meanwhile I'm always getting arrested. They want to know why. And then they want to know why it's our fault because we're out here. It's not our fault. Maybe it's our parents' fault sometimes. It's not always us. We didn't pick the choice to be out on the street. And now it's too late. Now I can't do nothing. Every time people walk past me they look at me like I'm some kind of slouch. That makes me look bad. I feel hurt . . . I feel left out.

Discussion

As reflected in their life stories, many of these youth come to the streets having already been exposed to profound emotional trauma, experiences that are exacerbated by the violence and exploitation that characterize everyday life on the streets (Clatts 1990; Clatts and Atillasoy 1993). However, the mainstream service delivery system is often ill-equipped to meet the needs of this particular population of youth. Drug treatment resources, for example, are very limited. Prevailing treatment modalities have little efficacy and may do more harm than good. They are not equipped to deal with the clinical issues these youth confront, and absence of attention to these issues often results in youth leaving services prematurely and increases their sense of failure. Similarly, gay and lesbian street youth have a wide range of special needs that are not met by mainstream services. Moreover, the mainstream service delivery system is ill-prepared to establish the kinds of service-oriented relationships that effective work with this particular population requires, a fact that has only served to further alienate these youth.

In response to the complex and largely unmet service needs, street outreach programs have begun to develop a wide range of services tailored to the specific needs of these youth. Outreach workers engage youth on the streets, providing crisis intervention, AIDS prevention information and materials, and assistance with food and shelter. Youth are encouraged to utilize drop-in center services that include both daily living needs (food, clothing, showers, etc.) as well as a wide array of counseling, educational, and health services. Both street-based services and those provided in the drop-in centers are designed so as to afford youth with as much flexibility as possible, focusing particularly on needs identified by the youth themselves and working at a pace that is also in large part determined by them.

Providing ready access to health care has become a central goal of these programs and an especially important part of their AIDS prevention strategy. A recent evaluation of AIDS outreach services targeted to these youth compared service delivery outcomes of street youth who had been contacted by street outreach programs and those who had been contacted by other kinds of street-based prevention services (e.g., needle exchange programs, religious groups, soup kitchens, etc.). Youth contacted by street outreach were found to be much more likely to have sought health care services, AIDS testing and counseling services, treatment for an STD, and treatment for substance abuse (Clatts and Davis 1995), clearly indicating the efficacy of street outreach as a bridge between youth on the streets and critical prevention services such as health care. And yet, with limited existing resources, these outreach programs are only able to reach about a third of the youth in need, leaving much of this population to fend for themselves in the vagaries of the streets economy. For these latter youth, illness, incarceration, suicide, and death from diseases such as AIDS are likely outcomes.

Summary and Conclusion

Numbering in the thousands, street youth suffer the cumulative "harm" of the loss of their childhood and of life on the streets. Faced with overwhelming feelings of self-doubt and self-blame, many turn to the ephemeral comfort of crack-cocaine and the numbing effects of alcohol and opiates. Lost in a downward spiral of self-destruction, many become dependent upon the street economy and increasingly vulnerable to the lack of power they exercise within this exploitative and violent system of exchange (Atillasoy and Clatts 1993). Some of these youth will survive and eventually find a way out of street life. Many others will be lost to violence and self-destruction.

The life stories of these youth indicate that disease outcomes, especially those associated with HIV/AIDS, are unlikely to be prevented by simplistic notions of these youth "pulling themselves up by their boot straps." Such an approach is based on the mistaken assumption that the problem is entirely, or primarily, a matter of altering youths' knowledge and psychological response to the health risks. The fact is that the vast majority of the homeless youth in New York City, and indeed, homeless youth throughout the world, are at risk not just because of inadequate knowledge, mistaken beliefs, or failures of intention, but as a result of systemic factors, in particular, social and economic inequities. Certainly the development of appropriate intervention messages, materials, and programs is an important public health goal. But we also need to confront the systemic conditions – poverty, lack of education, sexual abuse, homophobia, and limited employment opportunities – that propel these youth into high-risk situations and prevent them from leaving street life.

One youth, who described his living on the streets as "no money to eat," has found that by joining an outreach program he's able to "get by." He explained:

> I go there, and they help me a lot. And I think it's an extremely good program. It helps the youth today, and it keeps kids off the street [during the daytime]. You know, it gives them, like a future. And in actuality it helps them focus better on their future. 'Cause we all have a future. We don't know what it's going to be.

The hope is that the future of this young man, and of the thousands of youth on the streets like him, will offer more promise than that of just "getting by." However, neither the short-term survival and security needs (food, shelter, and a feeling of safety and of belonging) nor the long-term goals of education, health, and employment, will be met as long as these youth continue to be invisible to, and ignored by, those who control the resources needed to protect and nurture them. Nor will they be met if the goals of public health policy are subverted through mechanisms of social control – surveillance, blame, and punishment. The scope of this chapter does not permit an exhaustive examination of the many policy issues that are emerging in relation to this growing and fragile population. We have, however, attempted to take the first step that should attend any policy process – namely, listening to the voices of the youth themselves.

Acknowledgments

The data reported in this paper are derived from three studies: The Youth at Risk Project (grant #U62/CCU207192-01 from the Centers for Disease Control and Prevention) was conducted under a collaborative agreement between Metropolitan Assistance Corporation, National Development and Research Institutes, Inc., The Hetrick-Martin Institute, and The Community Health Project. The Street Teens At Risk Project was supported by the National Institute on Drug Abuse (grant #271-90-8402), under subcontract from the University of California at San Francisco, and was conducted in collaboration with Project Safespace. Finally, a study titled "HIV Risk and Survival Sex among Street Youth in NYC" was supported by grant #00214-16-RG from the American Foundation for AIDS Research. The authors would like to acknowledge the support of Richard Haymes, Frances Kunreuther, Helene Lauffer, John Santelli, Sherry Deren, Mary Washburn, and John Wright. Views expressed are the responsibility of the authors and do not necessarily represent the position of any of the aforementioned individuals or institutions. All correspondence should be sent to Dr. Michael C. Clatts, National Development Research Institutes, Inc., 2 World Trade Center, 16th Floor, New York, N.Y. 10048.

Notes

1 A number of data sets such as the Monitoring the Future survey, the National Household Survey, and the Drug Use Forecasting program provide evidence about drug use trends in the general adolescent population. For a number of complex methodological reasons, however, it is noteworthy that none of these systems is likely to include representative numbers of homeless and runaway youth.

2 The Department of Health and Human Services, for example, estimates that approximately one million U.S. youth are away from their homes in the course of a year, over 20 percent of whom are believed to be homeless (Health and Human Services 1983). Other studies, however, place the number at nearly 2 million (Davidson 1986). Part of the difficulty in establishing a number has been the fact that different sources have defined the population in different ways. For example, the Office of Juvenile Justice reported a national total of nearly one half million runaways in their facilities, but this figure did not include the nearly half a million children and youth who were residing in foster care.

3 Very little is known about the nature of the homeless and runaway youth population. In part at least, this lack of information is due to the fact that relatively few of these youth are included in the usual kinds of places in which research data are collected, such as high schools, after school programs, and mainstream youth organizations. Even the programs that serve this particular population (e.g., runaway shelters, hospital emergency rooms, drug treatment facilities, and juvenile detention facilities) are unlikely to include a representative sample of the population on the streets. By their very nature as institutional environments, such settings are not the best contexts in which to obtain representative demographic and behavioral samples. Many street youth are alienated from mainstream services, many do not utilize even specialized programs, and many are extremely distrustful of adults in these settings (Clatts, Davis, and Atillasoy 1995). Moreover, because critical services are often denied to youth who evidence involvement in illicit and/or illegal behaviors, these institutional contexts are also poor environments in which to obtain reliable self-report data. Youth mold their representation of themselves in order to enhance the likelihood that they will be deemed eligible and deserving of services. It is also noteworthy that many of these youth suffer from overwhelming feelings of guilt and shame associated with sexual victimization, and often block out aspects of their life experience that are painful or that they think will be sources of shame and recrimination. Thus, much

of the available empirical evidence about the street youth population is of limited utility, on grounds of both reliability and validity.

4 The estimate that there are 20,000 homeless youth in New York City has been circulating for several years, and there has been little attention to changes that have occurred in the population. Originally, the figure included many youth who were living in midtown welfare hotels, moving in and out of the midtown street economy. Most of these hotels are now closed, and fewer of these youth are mixing in with the street youth population on a regular basis. The Director of Program Planning for New York City's Department of Youth Services, in a recent assessment, felt that the 10,000 to 12,000 youth who have used services and shelters represent most of the 12,000 to 15,000 runaway and homeless youth in New York City (S. Mulgrav, personal communication, 1992). When considering the question of how many of these youth are involved in activities that may include risk of HIV exposure, DYS claimed that less than 10 percent had ever been involved in prostitution and that few have sold drugs (S. Mulgrav, personal communication, 1992). Whatever the actual size of the population, the claim that relatively few of these youth are involved in the sale of sex and drugs differs sharply from the perceptions of the service providers who work more directly with the youth themselves (H. Lauffer, personal communication, 1992). Indeed, there is substantial recent evidence that suggests that all of the "systems data" that has been used to characterize the street youth population in New York City suffers from a number of acute limitations, making such data of very limited utility, and perhaps even serving to obfuscate the scope of the population and the nature of the problems with which they are confronted (Clatts 1994).

5 Youth were contacted on the streets using a time-by-location, targeted sampling plan in which interviewers systematically canvassed five primary street locations at various times of the day and week (Clatts, Davis, and Atillasoy 1995). In keeping with the parameters of the street outreach services that the study was intended to evaluate, youth included in the sample were between the ages of twelve and twenty-three, were homeless and/or are known to be participants in the street economy. Homelessness was defined as having lived on the streets, in a squat, in a shelter, or in an abandoned building at any time in the past six months. The street economy was defined as including illegal activities like drug distribution and prostitution, as well as quasi-legal activities like panhandling. Parallel studies were conducted in both Los Angeles and San Francisco (Kipke et. al. 1995).

6 Similarly, in a parallel study conducted among street youth in Los Angeles, Kipke (1995: 517) also found exceptionally high rates of alcohol, marijuana, methamphetamine, crack, LSD, and heroin use.

7 For example, in a study conducted at Covenant House/NYC, a shelter for homeless youth in New York City, blood from 2,667 youth receiving routine treatment in the shelters' clinic was screened for HIV infection. Among those youth between fifteen and twenty years of age, the overall rate of infection was 5.3 percent (Stricof et al. 1991). Among the first 1,111 individuals in the study screened between October 1987 and August 1988, more than 7 percent (7.42 percent) of the males, and more than 5 percent (5.41 percent) of the females, tested positive for HIV infection. Among those youth who were at least twenty years of age, more than 10 percent (10.45 percent) were seropositive, indicating exposure to HIV infection during the teenage years. As alarming as these figures are, however, they probably substantially underrepresent the seropositivity in this population because Covenant House does not have consistent contact with some of the segments within the chronically homeless street youth population that are likely to be at highest risk. More recent studies bear this out. For example, in a 1989 study of 100 clients served by the Health Outreach to Teens program, 20 percent were found to have HIV infection (Affoumado 1991). Of particular concern is the fact that the Covenant House sample is unlikely to have included representative numbers of gay, lesbian and bisexual youth – youth whose involvement in risk behavior and contact with other high seroprevalence populations places them at particularly high risk (Affoumado 1991; Clatts et al. 1995). Concern about the generalizability of the existing data notwithstanding, it is clear enough from the available evidence that HIV infection has already made substantial in-roads into the street youth population. Similar findings are evidenced in other cities in which there are high numbers of homeless youth. A study in San Francisco, for example, found HIV rates as high as 8.2 percent (Schalwitz 1990)

8 Some have suggested that these kinds of intercorrelation are a function of common psychosocial antecedents (Botvin 1985; Hawkins and Weis 1985; Jessor and Jessor 1977). However, data from this study suggest that youths' economic dependency on the street economy is a much more significant determinant of poor health outcomes than are psychological antecedents.

9 The data presented here are based on ethnographic research among street youth in New York City that was conducted between February 1992 and August 1993. It draws on twenty-five open-ended interviews, approximately forty-five minutes in length, with youth at a multiservice social services agency for street youth in the Times Square area of Manhattan, as well as from seventeen Life History Interviews conducted among street youth found in the midtown area. The open-ended interviews followed a specific protocol developed by the granting agency (NIDA), while the life history interviews followed a life history approach in which youth were encouraged to tell their story in their own way, and to identify for themselves the events and experiences that were important in shaping their lives. Most of the interviews took place in the drop-in center of another multiservice street outreach program in Times Square, although some were also conducted in parks and fast-food restaurants in areas frequented by street youth. Participants in both studies were reimbursed for their time in the form of food coupons, or a small meal, and in some cases in the form of a small amount of money. In addition to interviews, ethnographic observation took place in three of the eight outreach programs in Manhattan, as well as in street settings in the East and West Village and Times Square.

References

Abel-Peterson, T. (1993). Outreach services to homeless adolescents. National Institute of Mental Health. Unpublished manuscript.

Adams, G. R., T. Gullotta, and M. Clancy (1985). Homeless adolescents: A descriptive study of similarities and differences between runaways and throwaways. *Adolescence, 20,* 715–724.

Adams, G. R., and G. Munro (1979). Portrait of the North American runaway: A critical review. *Journal of Youth and Adolescence, 8,* 359–373.

Affoumado, R. (1991). Personal communication. New York City: Deputy Director, Community Health Project.

Alexander, B. K. (1990). The empirical and theoretical bases for an adaptive model of addiction. *Journal of Drug Issues, 20*(1), 37–66.

Anderson, J., et al. (1996). HIV risk behavior, street outreach, and condom use in eight high risk populations. Forthcoming in *AIDS Education and Prevention.*

Atillasoy, A, and M. C. Clatts (1993). Survival sex among street youth in New York City: The consequence of time and place for AIDS outreach and prevention. Paper presented at Annual Meetings of the American Anthropological Association, Washington DC.

Benker, K., M. Boone, and A. Dehavenon (1990). The tyranny of indifference: A study of hunger, homelessness, poor health, and family dismemberment in 1,325 New York City households with children, 1989–1990. New York: The Action Research Project on Hunger, Homelessness and Family Health.

Botvin, G. (1985). *The life skills training program as a health promotion strategy: Theoretical issues and empirical findings.* New York: Hayworth Press.

Caton, C. (1986). The homeless experience in adolescent years. In E. Bassuk (Ed.), *The mental health needs of homeless persons.* San Francisco: Jossey-Bass Series, New Direction for Mental Health Services, Publication 30.

Clatts, M. C. (1989). Substance abuse and AIDS prevention strategies for homeless youth: An ethnographic perspective. Paper presented at Third International Gay and Lesbian Health Conference, San Francisco.

Clatts, M. C. (1990a). Ethnography and AIDS intervention in New York City: The use of life history as an ethnographic strategy in community-based AIDS prevention. *Studies of Intravenous Drug Users and Their Sexual Partners* 225–233.

Clatts, M. C. (1990b). Rage on Crack Street: An ethnographic journey. *The Family Therapy Networker, 11,* 37–41.

Clatts, M. C., and K. M. Mutchler (1989). AIDS and the dangerous other: Metaphors of sex and deviance in the representation of a disease. *Medical Anthropology, 10* 2(3), 105–114.

Clatts, M. C. (1994). Getting 'real' about HIV and homeless youth. *American Journal of Public Health, 83*(4), 1492–1494.

Clatts, M. C., and A. Atillasoy (1993). Where the day takes you: Homeless youth and the structure of the street economy. Paper presented at Annual Meetings of the Society for Applied Anthropology, San Antonio (March 12).

Clatts, M. C., and W. R. Davis (1993). A demographic and behavioral profile of homeless youth in New York City: Implications for AIDS outreach and prevention. Paper presented at Annual Meetings of the American Public Health Association, San Francisco.

Clatts, M. C., and W. R. Davis (1994). Correlates of risk behavior among high risk youth in New York City: Implications for AIDS prevention. Paper presented at Annual Meetings of the American Public Health Association, Washington DC.

Clatts, M. C., and W. R. Davis (1995). The public health impact of street outreach to homeless youth in New York City: Implications for AIDS education and prevention. Paper presented at the Second Annual Conference on Drug Abuse and AIDS, Flagstaff, AZ.

Clatts, M. C., W. R. Davis, and A. Atillasoy (1995). Hitting a moving target: The use of ethnographic methods in the evaluation of AIDS outreach programs for homeless youth in New York City. Paper presented at NIDA Technical Review on Use of Ethnographic Methods in AIDS and Drug Abuse Research, Bethesda, MD. Forthcoming in *National Institute of Drug Abuse Monograph.*

Clatts, M. C., E. Springer, and M. Washburn (1990). Outreach to homeless youth in New York City: Implications for planning and practice in social services. Paper presented at Annual Meetings of the American Public Health Association, New York.

Clatts, M. C., et al. (1994). The New York City Youth at Risk project: A community-based approach to AIDS prevention for homeless youth. Paper presented at the DSTD-HIV Conference, Washington, DC (August 24).

D'Angelo, L. J., et al. (1991). Human immunodeficiency virus infection in urban adolescents: Can we predict who is at risk? *Pediatrics, 88,* 982–986.

Davis, W. R., and M. C. Clatts (1994). HIV risk and other factors associated with high risk youth having an outreach contact in Manhattan. Paper presented at Annual Meetings of the American Public Health Association, Washington, DC.

Deykin, E. Y., J. C. Levy, and V. Wells (1986). Adolescent depression, alcohol, and drug abuse. *American Journal of Public Health, 76,* 178–182.

DiClemente, R., J. Zorn, and L. Temoshok (1986). Adolescents and AIDS: A survey of knowledge, attitude, and beliefs about AIDS in San Francisco. *American Journal of Public Health, 76*(12), 1443–1445.

Dunford, F., and T. Brennan (1976). A taxonomy of runaway youth. *Social Services Review, 50,* 457–470.

Forst, M. L. (1994). Sexual risk profiles of delinquent and homeless youth. *Journal of Community Health, 19,* 101–104.

Futterman, D., et al. (1993). Human immunodeficiency virus-infected adolescents: The first 50 patients in a New York City program. *Pediatrics, 91,* 730–735.

Gunn, B. (1988). Results of the study of street youths and runaways. New York: Office of the Mayor.

Hawkins, J., and J. Weis (1985). The social development model: An integrated approach to delinquency and prevention. *Journal of Primary Prevention, 6,* 73–97.

Haymes, R. (1994). Personal communication. Deputy director, community health project, New York.

Hein, K. (1988). AIDS in adolescence: A rationale for concern. *New York State Journal of Medicine, 87,* 290–295.

Hersch, P. (1988). Coming of age on city streets. *Psychology Today,* 28–37 (January).

Hersch, P. (1989). Exploratory ethnographic study of runaway and homeless adolescents in New York and San Francisco. Rockville, MD: National Institute of Drug Abuse.

Hopper, K., E. Susser, and S. Connors (1985). Economies of makeshift: Deindustrialization and homelessness in New York City. *Urban Anthropology, 14,* 183–236.

Institute of Medicine (1988). *Homelessness, health, and human needs.* Washington, DC: National Academy Press.

Institute of Medicine (1989). *Research on children and adolescents with mental, behavioral, and developmental disorders: Mobilizing a national initiative.* Washington, DC: National Academy Press.

Jessor, R., and S. L. Jessor (1977). *Problem behavior and psychological development: A longitudinal study of youth.* Academic Press: New York.

Kegeles, D. B., N. E. Adler, and C. E. Irwin. (1988). Sexually active adolescents and condoms: Changes over one year in knowledge, attitudes and use. *American Journal of Public Health, 78,* 460–461.

Kennedy, M. G., et al. (1994). Patterns and correlates of high-risk behavior among street youth. Paper presented at National Conference on Risk-Taking Behaviors Among Children and Adolescents, Vienna, VA.

Kennedy, M. G., et al. (1995). Do outreach workers refer street youth engaged in multiple risk to multiple services? Unpublished manuscript.

Kipke, M. D., et al. (1995). Street youth in Los Angeles: Profile of a group at high risk for human immunodeficiency virus infection. *Archives of Pediatric and Adolescent Medicine, 149*(5), 513–519.

Kipke, M. D., et al. (1995). Substance use and injection drug use behaviors among street youth in four U.S. cities. Unpublished manuscript.

Kufeldt, K. and M. Nimmo (1987). Youth on the street: Abuse and neglect in the eighties. *Child Abuse and Neglect, 11,* 531–543.

Lauffer, H. (1992). Personal communication. New York City: Director, Homeless and Immigrant Services/Victims Services.

Link, B., et al. (1994). Lifetime and five-year prevalence of homelessness in the United States. *American Journal of Public Health, 84*(2), 1907–1912.

McLaughlin, S., and A. B. Sorenson (1985). Life events and psychological well-being over the life course. In G. Elder, Jr. (Ed.), *Life course dynamics: Trajectories and transitions.* Ithaca, NY: Cornell University Press.

Mullgrav, S. (1992). Personal communication. New York.

National Network of Runaway and Youth Services, Inc. (1985). To Whom Do They Belong? Washington, DC.

Pries, S., and J. Silbert (1991). *On their own: Runaway and homeless youth and programs that serve them.* Washington, DC: Georgetown University Child Development Center.

Ringwalt, C. L., J. M. Greene, and R. Iachan (1994). Prevalence and characterisitics of youth in households with runaway and homeless experiences. Paper presented at Annual Meeting of the American Public Health Association, Washington, DC.

Robertson, M. J. (1989). Homeless youth: Patterns of alcohol use: A report to the National Institute on Alcohol Abuse and Alcoholism. Berkeley, CA: Alcohol Research Group.

Rossi, P. (1989). *Down and out in America.* Chicago: University of Chicago Press.

Rotherman-Borus, M., and C. Koopman (1989). Sexual risk behavior, AIDS knowledge, and beliefs about AIDS among heterosexual runaway and gay male adolescents. Paper presented at Fifth International Conference on AIDS, Montreal, Canada.

Schafer, D., and C. Caton (1984). Runaway and homeless youth in New York City. New York: Ittelson Foundation.

Schalwitz, J., et al. (1990). Prevalence of sexually transmitted diseases (STD) and HIV in a homeless youth medical clinic in San Francisco. Paper presented at the Sixth International Conference on AIDS, San Francisco (June 23).

Stricof, R., et al. (1991). HIV Seroprevalence in a facility for runaway and homeless adolescents. *American Journal of Public Health, 81* (supplement), 50–53.

U.S. Department of Health and Human Services for Runaway and Homeless Youth (1983). National Program Inspection. Washington, DC: Office of the Inspector General.

U.S. Department of Health and Human Services (1986). Fiscal year 1985: Study of runaways and youth. Washington, DC: U.S. Government Printing Office.

Yates, G., et al. (1988). A risk profile comparison of runaway and non-runaway youth. *American Journal of Public Health, 78*(37), 820–821.

9   Adolescents and Medical Decision Making: Observations of a Medical Anthropologist

Betty Wolder Levin

Introduction

The Project on Medical Decision Making for the Adolescent Alone, by its nature, has focused on the most problematic cases – difficult issues concerning medical decision making for adolescents with the least family support. As a medical anthropologist, I conducted a brief ethnographic study to provide information and analysis of a range of cases intended to illuminate the broader context of adolescents and medical care. In this chapter, I will describe the study and report observations in two areas, family involvement and the adolescent alone, and medical decision making and consent. Finally, I will briefly discuss implications of this anthropological perspective.

Description of the Study

The primary sites for this study were the adolescent inpatient unit and the HIV/AIDS program of a large voluntary teaching hospital in a northeastern city, serving an ethically and economically diverse inner-city population. I also observed care in a neonatal intensive care unit, focusing on decision making for infants born to adolescent mothers. In this unit, I followed the obstetrical care of two teens whose infants had congenital problems diagnosed prenatally.

In each location, I observed on-going care, attended staff rounds, and reviewed charts. I also interviewed physicians, nurses, social workers and other staff members, patients, and a few parents or parental surrogates. The research was conducted from Fall 1994 to Spring 1995. Because of the nature of the study, I was only able to observe directly a limited number of cases at each site. Research on current cases was supplemented by information provided by staff about cases they had encountered previously.

Because of the nature of the project, I sought the prototypic problematic cases of *adolescents alone* – patients between the ages of thirteen and eighteen, without kin, who faced ethically significant medical decisions. I was particularly interested in those youth who encountered difficulties because they were not mature enough to choose among options or were not legally empowered to give consent. During the course of my study, I could find *no* cases that fit all elements of this prototype. I personally encountered no cases in which the lack of a legal guardian led to a significant problem in reaching a decision about what medical care to provide or about the timing of treatment. Nor did I encounter any adolescents under eighteen who were not in contact with family members.

Clearly such cases occur, creating serious problems for the adolescents and their caretakers; some are reported elsewhere in this volume. However, at least in the settings where I did my research, such cases are rare. This was true not only because adolescents are rarely totally without family, but also because medical decision making seen as having significant ethical complexity was also rare. There were, however, many teens with nontraditional, unstable, or inadequate family situations, which led to a range of problems. To illustrate the complexity of situations for these adolescents, I will briefly describe a range of situations and, using pseudonyms, will describe and discuss a few cases in greater depth.

The Adolescent Alone and the Complexity of Family Life

Many adolescents cared for in the inpatient unit and in the HIV program had parents who were dead or absent, or who suffered from problems that prevented them from being able to function in parental roles.

I was struck by the number of adolescents whose parents had died. Some died as a result of complications of the same disease that led to their child's admission; this not only occurred for adolescents who were congenitally infected with HIV, but also for a girl whose mother died of complications related to sickle cell disease and another patient whose mother died from asthma. At least ten of the approximately sixty HIV-infected adolescents whose cases I heard discussed had parents who were HIV-infected; in the majority of these cases the adolescents were not perinatally infected; parents and teens had independently contracted the virus. (In addition to parents with HIV, many of the HIV-infected patients have at least one relative – such as siblings, cousins, aunts or uncles, children, partners, and partners' relatives – with HIV.) At least two other patients cared for on the inpatient floor during my period of observation were not HIV infected, but had mothers who had died from AIDS or whose HIV infection interfered with their ability to parent. Others had parents who had died or were dying from other diseases (e.g., lung cancer, stomach cancer, and a brain tumor).

A number of the adolescents had lost parents to violence or to long absences in jail. Some had permanent alternate living arrangements because of a parent's long prison sentence. For example, one fifteen-year-old with sickle cell disease and serious psychological problems saw his father kill his mother when he was six years old. Since his father was in prison, he was raised by his maternal aunts. In another case, formalization of an additional relative's ability to provide legal consent took place after the primary caretaker had been in jail when consent previously had been sought for a procedure.

Many adolescents had parents who suffered from drug addiction and/or psychiatric problems. Despite the fact that these parents were often absent, unstable, inconsistent and/or nonsupportive caretakers, they remained the primary, legally responsible caretakers in many instances. Sometimes, however, patients had been raised from infancy by their grandmothers or other relatives. Others had moved to the homes of other relatives later in childhood. Some adolescents were in foster care. However, all the patients I observed, including those in foster care, had relationships with parents and/or other older relatives. In some cases, patients still lived with their parents, although their parents were not their primary caretakers.

A few patients were removed from their parents' care after physical or sexual abuse. In three cases this occurred after a shift from another caretaker to the father. Two girls, from different families, were each sent to live with their fathers in the United States by their mothers who lived in developing countries and said they could no longer care for them. One girl was physically abused and the other was sexually abused by her father, each girl was subsequently placed in foster care. Another girl who was raised by her grandmother was sent to live with her father after her grandmother became ill. This girl was also sexually abused by her father, and was admitted to the adolescent unit because of suicidal ideation. In a fourth case, a girl, who had lived with both parents, had been placed under the supervision of the child welfare authorities after her father physically abused her.

In addition to losing their parents, a number of these patients later lost their substitute primary caretakers. For example, one older adolescent, whose mother was an addict, had been raised by his grandfather; his grandfather suffered from emphysema and congestive heart failure and had moved to the South, leaving him behind. Some suffered multiple losses; one fifteen-year-old with HIV was raised by her grandmother after her mother died of AIDS, but then had to move in with her aunt after her grandmother died from cancer.

Considering the number of parents who had died or were otherwise unavailable, I was surprised to find that *all* the minor adolescents I encountered in my study were involved with family. Although many of the adolescents under age eighteen did not live with their parents, almost all lived with family members, or, in at least one case, lived with *fictive kin,* individuals not biologically related but referred to by kin terms and thought of as family.

During the research period, only two teens under eighteen were admitted to the inpatient unit from nonkinship foster care placements. However, as I will describe later, even these teens in nonkinship foster care were involved with family. In most cases, the people they lived with were their legal guardians. However, in some cases, the people they lived with did not have the legal authority to make medical decisions for them. For some, another relative had that right; for others, the family had lost custody to child welfare authorities. Nevertheless, in the cases I observed, this never presented a problem in the timely provision of care.

Most teens who were not living with a biological parent lived with older female relatives. According to the generally recognized pattern, many had been raised by and lived with their grandmothers, often since early childhood. However, although I did not have systematic data, among the cases I heard about, I was surprised to find that in the instances in which adolescents were described as "living with other relatives," more were living with aunts than grandmothers. Most of the aunts were older adults; however, in one instance, an eighteen-year-old was described as living alone with her young aunt (in her early twenties) and cousins in her grandmother's house after the grandmother had died. Some teens were cared for by others beside older female relatives, such as a brother or a stepfather.

Most adolescents who lived away from their parents spent long periods of time in a single household. Others, however, had no stable home environment. For example, one sixteen-year-old girl with HIV (probably not congenitally infected) was removed from her mother's house; her mother used crack and was also infected with HIV. The girl was described by her doctor as shuttling between her brother's home, her mother's ex-boyfriend's house, and foster households.

Not only did many move away from their biological parents to surrogates, but some had moved from surrogates to biological parents after their surrogates' situations had changed. A few had been sent back to live with their mothers and one to her father after their grandmothers could no longer care for them. Some, after living on their own, had returned home because they were sick. In some cases, their mothers had overcome drug-related or other problems and were able to provide good support; in others, the drug-related, psychiatric, or other problems continued to prevent their mothers from adequately playing a parental role.

For example, when Tameka[1] was fifteen, she was admitted to the hospital. Her 33-year-old mother and 35-year-old father had divorced thirteen years earlier. Since then, she had had no contact with her father. For a while after the divorce, she and her mother both lived with her mother's mother. However, her mother became heavily involved with drugs and moved out. During her childhood, Tameka was primarily raised by her maternal grandmother. When she was twelve, Tameka had increasing conflicts with her grandmother over what her social worker described as "adolescent issues" and moved in with her maternal aunt, who became her legal guardian.

When she was thirteen, Tameka moved in with her mother, who was then in drug recovery; her mother regained legal custody. Tameka's doctor reported that her mother "never set boundaries for her. She acted more like a friend than a mother." Nevertheless, she and her mother sometimes had conflicts; Tameka often stayed overnight in the homes of other relatives or friends. In August, she moved back to her grandmother's house. In September, her grandmother reported her mother to the child welfare authorities for neglect and initiated efforts to obtain legal custody. When Tameka became ill with cancer in October and her grandmother brought her to the hospital, her mother still had legal custody but was unreachable. Risk management officials were consulted and recommended that abdominal surgery be performed because her doctors stated that the need was urgent and her grandmother had given consent. Her mother then became involved again; at the end of the first admission, she was discharged in her mother's care.

Although most teens lived with relatives of a more senior generation, some lived with only fairly young siblings, at least for a period of time. For example, sixteen-year-old Tammy was admitted after an acute asthma attack. She had lived with her sister, a young adult, for a few years after she was orphaned at age thirteen. She then moved to her aunt's house because she did not like her sister's new boyfriend. Sometimes adolescents moved back and forth between households. For example, shortly after being diagnosed with HIV, one girl left her mother's home to move in with her brother, then returned to her mother's home a few months later. In another family, both the mother and father died of HIV-related disease, leaving ten children. Eight of the children and two grandchildren lived together; the oldest was twenty-five. Family foster care was involved for the seventeen- and fifteen-year-old girls and fourteen-, thirteen-, and eleven-year-old boys in that family.

Often teens are involved with a network of relatives who may have the potential of playing parenting roles. However, the number of relatives and the frequency of contact is no necessary indication of the degree to which the adolescent has the support one would hope would be provided by parents. Seventeen-year-old Nelson, who had Hodgkin's lymphoma, lived with his mother and her female partner. His grandmother, four maternal aunts, and nineteen cousins, ranging in age from one to twenty, lived in other apartments in the same building. His father and his maternal uncle were no longer living in the area, but his paternal uncle and his four children also lived in the neighborhood. He was closely involved with all his relatives who lived nearby. His mother was an addict who had spent time in jail. While in prison, she contracted HIV; her female partner was also HIV-infected. His grandmother had always been very involved in the care of her grandchildren, including Nelson. His ten-year-old sister sometimes stayed in his mother's apartment, sometimes with his grandmother. Both his grandmother and his mother were with him when he received his cancer diagnosis.

Although Nelson was deeply involved with kin, since his mid-teens he had been largely independent and made important life decisions essentially on his own. He decided to leave school, had earned a General Education Diploma (GED), and had found a job program that enabled him to support himself and contribute to his family financially until he became sick. In addition to his involvement with family, he was also very involved with his friends, a group of young men in their twenties. Nevertheless, despite his extensive network, his social worker described him as lacking the support necessary to enable him to keep clinic appointments and take his medications regularly.

Although not living with biologically related relatives, some teens live with *fictive kin* – individuals whom they consider "family" even though they are not biologically related. Often such arrangements work very well. Not because of the fictive nature of the kinship relationship, but because of the characteristics of the individuals involved, one of the most problematic living arrangements I observed was that of Dushan, a thirteen-year-old boy who looked and acted as if he were about ten years old. When he was eight, Dushan's mother died of AIDS; his stepfather, Mr. Paul, promised to take care of him and became his legal guardian. Mr. Paul and Dushan lived with Mr. Paul's own stepfather, Mr. Lester, who was seventy-six years old and had severe emphysema.

When he was twelve, Dushan was admitted to the inpatient unit for herpes zoster. He was tested and found to be HIV-infected. He was probably infected through perinatal transmission. Review of records at a nearby public hospital revealed that five years before, a patient with the same unusual name and the same age had been with admitted with pneumonia, diagnosed as HIV-infected, and referred to a pediatric AIDS clinic for care. However, the child never attended the clinic and was listed by them as "lost to follow-up." Mr. Paul denied knowing that Dushan was HIV-infected.

Because Dushan had not received medical care following the prior diagnosis, the staff was concerned about his welfare. His teachers reported that Dushan did not seem to be receiving proper care at home – he often came to school without breakfast, wearing inappropriate clothes for the season. The staff learned that his stepfather was an addict, sometimes absent, and his step-stepgrandfather was limited in his ability to care for the boy, at least in part because of his own poor health. Dushan would now require a complex regimen of medications and regular medical follow-up. Foster care placement was considered. However, Dushan was very attached to both Mr. Paul and Mr. Lester, whom he called his "father" and "grandfather." He continually talked about and looked forward to returning to their apartment; when he was upset he would sob, "I want to go home." Later, when offered two tickets to the circus, he explained he really needed three because he wanted to bring *both* his father and grandfather.

When Dushan was ready for discharge, Mr. Paul and Mr. Lester both met with the social worker. Mr. Lester said he did not want to accept responsibility; Mr. Paul was hesitant, saying he couldn't tolerate seeing Dushan in pain. Moreover, the staff doubted the ability of either man to provide adequate and appropriate care. However, despite what one of his physicians called "the saddest family life in the whole world," the staff decided it was best to "try to patch things together . . . rather than pull him out of his home." They arranged to send Dushan home with eight hours a day of help from a home health aide, twelve hours a day on weekends. Even though his "family" was limited in their ability to provide care, with support he was able to stay "home." His teachers reported he was now well fed and well dressed. He took his medications and attended the adolescent HIV clinic regularly.

As far as I know, only two of the adolescents under eighteen whose care I observed were not living with "family." However, even these two adolescents who were in nonkinship foster care placements were in contact with family members. One had been placed in nonkinship foster care because of physical abuse. When she was admitted to the inpatient unit with abdominal pain, a description of a diagnostic procedure and request for consent was faxed to the child welfare authority; the head nurse expected approval without a problem. Shortly thereafter, the social worker received a call informing her that her father "happened to be at the foster care agency" (no one at the hospital knew why). Since he still had the authority to give consent, he arranged to come to the hospital later that day to sign the consent forms.

The other patient not living with family was the girl with sickle cell disease described later in Case Two, referred to by the pseudonym "Sabrina," who tried to refuse placement in a shelter. After the initial case study was completed, she was discharged to a large shelter. Soon after, Sabrina's mother suffered a stroke, a complication of her own sickle cell disease, and died. Following her mother's death, Sabrina became very depressed. Another resident of the shelter found her hanging out of a bathroom window, threatening to commit suicide. Sabrina was again admitted to the inpatient unit.

In the interim, Sabrina's aunt, who had been estranged from her psychotic sister (Sabrina's mother), became involved with Sabrina. The aunt said that she wanted to care for Sabrina. The staff enthusiastically supported the idea; they were very impressed and felt that she would be a kind and competent caretaker. Although she hardly knew her aunt and cousin, Sabrina was glad that she was going to be home with family and was eager to go with them. Even though she was medically cleared for discharge, and despite constant efforts by the social workers, it took more than a month to work with the bureaucracies to find a suitable apartment, obtain furniture, and make the other necessary arrangements. Finally, when she was discharged, Sabrina went home to live with her aunt and her sixteen-year-old cousin. When I started this commentary, I wrote, "Sabrina is happy and her social worker says she is doing very well. She is living with her aunt in kinship foster care – no longer an `adolescent alone.'" I saw this case as a wonderful example of the fact that even an adolescent alone at one point in time may not be alone at another. Although in some cases that happens, sadly for Sabrina, six months later, after a subsequent hospital admission, her aunt decided she could or would no longer care for her. The last time I saw Sabrina, she was again in the inpatient unit, medically cleared for discharge, awaiting placement. She was, again, a very sad "adolescent alone."

The two pregnant teens whose infants had problems diagnosed before birth and three other teens under eighteen whose children were in the NICU during the course of my observations were all very involved with their families, as were many of the mothers in their later teens and twenties. Even if they had previously lived elsewhere, all five of the mothers under eighteen whom I met during the course of this study planned to live with their mothers after discharge from the hospital. Unlike many of the adolescents who, despite contact with relatives, were in important respects "alone," all these young mothers had considerable support from their families.

For example, seventeen-year-old Jenny had moved out of her parents' home to live with her twenty-year-old boy friend, Raymond and Raymond's mother about eight months before the birth. She had been "going with" Raymond for three years. Jenny's mother liked Raymond and accepted the move; her stepfather did not approve. Jenny had thought about having a baby, but planned to finish high school first. Shortly after the move, she missed a second period, performed a home pregnancy test and found out she was pregnant. Even though she had left home, she described her mother as her "best friend."

Since Raymond was working, Jenny said her mother came with her for her first prenatal visit at a local public clinic. Her mother, who had always gone with her for all her previous doctor's visits, accompanied her in the examining room. Her mother was with her when routine blood tests and an ultrasound revealed a gastroschisis (a serious congenital malformation in which the abdomen is open and the intestines are outside the body). The next day, both her mother and Raymond returned with her to talk with the doctors and genetic counselors. As will be discussed later in the section on decision making, Jenny, Raymond, and her mother and stepfather all talked about whether to continue the pregnancy and about the care of the baby.

In this hospital, women were allowed to have a number of family members with them during labor but only one person was allowed to be with them for the birth. When Jenny was in labor, Raymond, her mother, her stepfather, and her eighteen-year-old brother were all in and out of the labor room all day and into the evening; Raymond remained with her through the night. Because the birth was not expected for some time, in the morning, Raymond went to work at his job in a barber shop and her mother came to stay with her. Shortly thereafter, she gave birth to Matthew. When I asked if she was sorry that Raymond was not there, she said no, she had wanted her mother to be the one to be with her for the birth anyway.

During Matthew's first surgery, while Jenny was still in the recovery room, and later that evening, when Jenny visited Matthew in the NICU for the first time, Raymond and many members of her extended family were with her. Although Raymond continued to visit each day in the mid-morning before going to work, and many family members came at night, when Jenny was discharged three days after the birth in the middle of the day, only her teenage brother was with her. A week and a half later, when Matthew had surgery for the second stage of the repair, Raymond, Jenny's mother, and other members of the family had all returned to their normal routines. Jenny, nervous about the procedure, sat alone in the family room outside the surgical suite.

Later, Jenny said she was not getting along with Raymond's mother and had decided to move back home. She, Raymond, and Matthew would share a bedroom; when renovations were completed, they planned to move into an apartment downstairs in her mother's house.

Perhaps there were fewer adolescents under eighteen who were without family in the sites where I did research (compared to other settings where adolescents receive care) for at least four reasons.

1. The adolescents were seriously ill or were giving birth and having a child with a serious problem. When an adolescent is sick enough to be admitted to a hos-

pital inpatient unit, or when a young woman delivers an infant, especially one admitted to an NICU, they may be more likely to seek or draw the involvement of family members than when involved with more routine medical care.

2. Many of the patients cared for in the adolescent inpatient unit were chronically ill with sickle cell disease, asthma, cancer, or HIV. Chronically ill adolescents, both because of developmental delays and also because of their families' concern, may be more involved with family. Some of the chronically ill adolescents were already involved in specialty clinics of this medical center. The social workers and staff from these programs may have successfully encouraged family involvement.

3. Adolescents with family may have been more likely to have been ambulatory care patients at this medical center, which has well-known and well-respected pediatric and adolescent general and specialty clinics, including a well-established teen pregnancy program. Adolescents with family members to advocate for them or to help them choose a source of care may have been more likely to obtain care at this center rather than at another hospital. In contrast, adolescents who are in foster care are routinely cared for in a nearby public hospital.

4. Adolescents with family involvement may be more likely to be referred to this hospital. Some adolescents were transferred to this medical center's inpatient unit or to the obstetrical service from other hospitals, including the hospital that cares for most of the children in foster care after complex problems were diagnosed. Possibly adolescents with family to advocate for them were more likely to be transferred.

More adolescents alone might be cared for in the ambulatory care clinics than in the inpatient unit of this medical center and in other area hospitals. Because of the brief nature of this study, I was unable to spend much time in such locations. I did add the adolescent HIV/AIDS clinic in an effort to find more adolescents alone. However, even there, most of the patients who required frequent visits to the clinic were older than eighteen; the ones who I met who were younger than eighteen were all living with family.

The Limited Problem of Medical Decision Making and Consent

As stated in the beginning of the last section, I was unable to find a prototypic problem case of an adolescent alone – a person between the ages of thirteen and eighteen, without family or another guardian, who faced an ethically significant medical decision, and encountered difficulties because he or she was not up to the task emotionally or intellectually or legally empowered to give consent. In part, as I have described, this occurred because all the adolescents were involved with parents or other family members.

These cases also failed to present problems concerning consent for at least three other reasons:

1. Parents, patients, and health professionals saw most medical decisions as technical decisions appropriately made by physicians.

2. Some medical decisions were made either without seeking the consent of a legally empowered person or a signature was accepted for consent even though the legal authority of the person signing consent was uncertain or dubious.

3. Adolescents are legally entitled to make some medical decisions themselves, such as decisions concerning pregnancy, the care of their own children, and HIV/AIDS testing.

In addition to medical treatment decisions, there are numerous other decisions, such as when to seek medical care and about compliance with prescribed treatments. However, these are of a different nature, do not involve issues of consent, and raise different ethical issues.

Before this study, I had primarily focused my research on decision making about the aggressiveness of care for critically ill patients in cases identified as ethically problematic because the benefits of prolonging life were in question. In such situations, there is growing consensus that decisions should be made by patients or families, or should be made jointly by patients or their surrogates and physician. However, almost all the decisions I observed as part of this study concerned decisions about providing appropriate care for patients for whom the value of prolonging life was not in question. These decisions were seen as ethically straightforward by the adolescents, their families, and the clinicians, and therefore as appropriately made by physicians alone, based on technical criteria. Therefore, for almost all treatment decisions, including those for procedures for which parents or other guardians were asked to sign specific consent forms, the patients, their parents, and the health care professionals saw the appropriate role of parents or other guardians as one of giving formal permission for physicians to carry out medical recommendations rather than as an occasion for active participation in shared decision making. Although other issues were recognized as in the family domain, such as decisions about when and where to seek medical care, whether to continue a pregnancy, or whether the patients should adhere to medical recommendations after discharge, decisions about what medical procedures to perform or what drugs to prescribe were generally seen as physicians' decisions.

For example, seventeen-year-old Nelson, described earlier as having cancer and being "alone" despite the involvement of his mother, grandmother, and large extended family, had suffered with symptoms for a while before seeking care. He was often tired at work and mentioned his tiredness there; his boss said he should get a medical checkup. He evidently did not discuss his symptoms with his family and didn't seek care. He reported that he had had a number of "spells of sharp pain with each breath," and once had a "spell of breathing hard," but he did not mention these to anyone. One night he woke up severely short of breath. His mother urged him to lie down but he realized that he was seriously ill; he decided he needed to go to an emergency room. His mother reminded him that the last time they had gone to an emergency room at a nearby hospital, the doctors had done nothing to help. Together they decided to take a cab to the medical center with the inpatient unit I studied. Both the choice not to seek health care for a period of time and the decision of when and where to seek medical help were clearly patient or family decisions.

Unlike the decision to seek medical care, the decisions about his treatment once he was in the hospital were seen as physician decisions. The night he was admitted, his condition deteriorated rapidly and he was admitted to the Pediatric Intensive Care Unit (PICU). Soon after, he was diagnosed as having Hodgkin's lymphoma. He recalls waking up in a hospital room a few days later, with his mother and grandmother by his side. He reported that a resident came in and said, "There is something bad and something good to tell you – you have cancer but it is curable." The doctor told them he needed various treatments, including surgery to place an in-dwelling (Hickman) catheter for chemotherapy. He said his mother was nervous but he wasn't scared; he reassured her, he said, because the doctor said his cancer was curable. When I questioned him about who made decisions, he said he would "do anything to cure [the cancer]." Nelson and his family had evidently accepted the physicians' recommendations for treatment without question.

While in the hospital, professional decisions determined his care. Once discharged, however, his decisions and those of his mother regained importance. According to the social worker, both he and his mother have problems complying with medical recommendations and do things that are detrimental to their well being. Feeling that HIV is hopeless, his mother does not take good care of herself, but she thinks Nelson should take care of himself because he can survive. He thinks that if his mother is not doing what she should, he does not have to either. They make contracts with each other to comply with medical recommendations and take care of themselves; neither can stick to them. They both eat poorly, and his mother continues to smoke, although the smoke bothers Nelson.

He goes to medical appointments alone. A note in his chart indicates that his mother has "approved his care"; she is not consulted about his ongoing treatment. His physicians have prescribed a protocol of regularly scheduled chemotherapy, but he sometimes does not come in for his appointments. The social worker says he does not seem to fully understand the importance of the schedule and his mother is less able than he is to organize his care.

In conducting the research on the adolescent inpatient unit, I tried to identify situations in which there were medical treatment decisions that were seen as "ethically complex" by patients, families, or staff. I heard of only three; these did not involve *adolescents alone;* rather, all concerned the care of adolescents with very involved families. In one case, an oncologist father was very involved in decisions about cancer chemotherapy for his daughter. In a second case, a fifteen-year-old AIDS patient, who lived with her very involved aunt, decided to accept the placement of a catheter for TPN (feeding through a central line). In the last case, a thirteen-year-old patient, her mother, and her physicians decided together to try a potentially toxic drug that was FDA-approved to treat cancer but that had not be systematically tested for her condition. I also observed two cases involving care of seriously brain-injured adolescents. Both patients had very involved parents who had previously decided that all measures should be taken to prolong their children's survival; for them, the current admissions involved routine medical decisions.

In addition, there was a significant degree of patient involvement, both by adolescents alone and adolescents with involved families, concerning decisions about pain medication. The staff saw these pain management decisions as psychologically complex but not as ethically complex; there did not seem to be any difference in the way such decisions were handled for patients with or without involved families.

Even though I tried to find decisions conceptualized as *ethically complex* during the period of my observation on the adolescent inpatient unit, I observed none involving adolescents alone. Moreover, both a pediatric fellow in adolescent medicine and a social worker who had spent more than two years working primarily with adolescents reported they had *never* encountered an ethically complex treatment decision for an adolescent alone. Although some of the doctors and nurses who had spent a long time working with adolescents could recount cases, including some of those reported in this volume, all agreed that such cases were rare in the inpatient adolescent unit.

The minimal role played by patients and families in the medical decision making observed for this study, in part, may stem from the types of medical decisions observed. For example, it would be expected that patients and families would be much more involved in decisions about treatment for critically ill patients who could only have a very poor quality of life, for whom the value of promoting survival was questioned, or for whom the burdens of life-sustaining treatment might be seen as outweighed by the small chance of cure. Such decisions are more likely to be made for patients in the intensive care unit than for patients on the inpatient floor.

Patient and/or parental involvement in treatment decisions may also be more common concerning other types of decisions I did not observe. For example, in the outpatient department, where conditions may be less serious and the consequences of delaying medically optimal treatments are less severe, patients and families may be more involved. In addition, patients and parents may play a larger role when decisions are necessary about the long-term management of chronic conditions, for which their knowledge of the individual patients' conditions and broader contexts of the patients' lives may be more relevant. Finally, patients and parents may be more involved in making decisions about participation in experimental trials. A number of the older patients in the HIV clinic were involved in making decisions about such treatments. The only decision I observed about participation in a clinical trial for an adolescent under age eighteen was made for Dushan; it is described shortly.

For the vast majority of cases I observed, both for adolescents alone and for other adolescents, once a patient's condition was diagnosed, there was a clear medical consensus about what to do. If there were disagreements about how to treat, the staff members discussed alternatives and reached consensus among themselves before talking to the patient or family. Patients and families were informed; treatment then generally proceeded to follow the medical decisions made by *physicians alone*. For most of those situations for which a specific consent was needed, a parent or other legal guardian was informed about the medical recommendation as well as about risks and benefits of the treatment. Then they were asked to sign the consent form; in all cases they authorized the medically recommended care.

In some cases, there was no guardian who had clear legal authority to give consent. Even for those cases, however, issues of consent did not impede care for the cases I observed. This is illustrated by the next three vignettes.

As described earlier, when Tameka, a fifteen-year-old with cancer, first sought care, she was living with her grandmother although her mother still had legal custody. Without realizing the seriousness of her condition, Tameka went to an eye doctor complaining that she had had blurred vision for two months. He noticed a large neck mass and referred her to the pediatric clinic, where her eighteen-pound weight loss, episodes of drenching nights sweats, blurred vision, and skin changes were diagnosed as signs and symptoms of lymphoma. Her doctors felt it was necessary to immediately determine if she had Hodgkin's or non-Hodgkin's lymphoma and to start chemotherapy. Her mother was unreachable, so they contacted the risk management office the day after admission; the chart note indicated that risk management's recommendation was that "surgery be performed, as the MGM [maternal grandmother] has given consent which was witnessed." Treatment proceeded without delay. Four days later, the grandmother was officially awarded temporary legal guardianship, which was to last at least until the next court date, scheduled for one month later.

When she learned her daughter was in the hospital, Tameka's mother came to her side. Both mother and grandmother visited her daily; Tameka wanted her mother to stay with her all the time. Her grandmother retained temporary legal custody, but her mother made it clear that she wanted sole custody. For weeks, the doctors were unsure who would be her legal permanent guardian. They explained procedures to Tameka, her mother, and grandmother. Tameka said that she wanted to refuse abdominal surgery, even though the doctor explained that not having surgery could have serious consequences later. Her mother and grandmother, however, did not question the advisability of treatment. They told her to "do what the doctor said." Since the grandmother and mother agreed, the disputes about her custody did not affect her hospital care. It complicated discharge planning, however, because until the last minute it was not clear where Tameka would go when she left the hospital.

Tameka was discharged to her mother's home. Her grandmother, abandoning the custody fight, signed papers relinquishing custody. A month and a half later, Tameka was back in the hospital with an infection, probably due to improper care of the Hickman catheter site. Tameka was supposed to flush the Hickman site on Mondays, Wednesdays, and Fridays to keep it clean. She said, "The procedure wasn't painful but I didn't like looking at the needles." She chose to do it alone rather than have her mother assist. Without her mother's knowledge, she flushed the catheter only on Mondays and Fridays. Despite the seriousness of her condition, she said, "If I didn't change the dressing, I could forget for days that I was sick." Because of both nursing's and Tameka's reservations about Tameka's mother's ability to care for her, she remained in the hospital for weeks rather than return home on IV antibiotics. After completion of treatment with antibiotics, the plan was for Tameka to return home and for her mother to assist her with her Hickman care. The social worker's notes said, "Tameka and her mother are also amenable to a referral for family counseling. Both Tameka and her mother present with many issues as they struggle to become reacquainted with each other."

Treatment without a guardian's consent and treatment with someone signing who was not a legal guardian both occurred in the case of Tammy, the mature sixteen-year-old with asthma, already described. After her mother died of asthma when Tammy was thirteen, she had lived with her sister and then her aunt. Tammy has had asthma since she was five. Even before her mother's death, she had often gone to doctor's appointments by herself; after her mother's death, she always went alone. She made her own decisions about when to take medicine, about the dosages, and about when to come to the hospital. Once, when she was living with her sister, her sister signed for consent for hospital admission, even though the doctors knew she was not the legal guardian. Her regular doctors treated her routinely without consulting her guardians. For example, they had switched her medication a few weeks before without consulting her aunt or sister. While I was conducting the interview, a resident told her she would be going home with a new kind of inhaler. He did not provide any information and she did not ask any questions. Rather than seeing such a change as an occasion for shared guardian/physician decision making, the decision was seen purely as a physician decision.

When I told staff members that I was interested in studying the care of adolescents alone, a number of nurses and residents mentioned Dushan, the thirteen-year-old with AIDS who lived with his stepfather and his stepfather's stepfather. They offered his case as an example of a child who did not have a legal guardian, although, in fact, as his social worker and attending physicians knew, his stepfather, Mr. Paul, clearly had legal custody. A problem did arise, however, when consent was needed for a procedure.

Eight months after the admission with herpes, Dushan was readmitted with a persistent cough and fevers. His physicians ordered a CAT scan with contrast, a procedure ordinarily requiring specific parental consent. When the social worker phoned his home, Mr. Lester informed them that "Mr. Paul was picked up by the police over the weekend." He said he was not sure where his son was at that time. The possibility of finding Mr. Paul and having him give consent over the phone from jail was considered. Instead, according to a chart note, after discussion with the medical and social work leadership, a decision was made "to inform Mr. Lester, who is familiar with the procedure, that his consent is needed. Mr. Lester will be contacted via phone prior to procedure." Early the next week, after Mr. Paul was released from custody, he was encouraged to come to the hospital and sign papers giving his stepfather authority to sign for Dushan's medical care.

Legally, adolescent mothers can make decisions about their obstetrical care and about the care of their infants. Therefore, there is never a problem finding an individual legally entitled to give consent. Moreover, as mentioned earlier, all the adolescents I talked to who had infants admitted to the NICU were *very* involved with their own parents; all planned to live with their families after the baby was discharged from the hospital. In each case that I observed, when consent for treatment of an NICU patient was sought, the staff turned to the adolescent mother, below the age of legal majority, often asking her own mother to witness the consent. This happened even though, in most cases, the father of the baby was acknowledged in the hospital chart and was usually over eighteen, sometimes over twenty-one, years old.

As with the adolescent patients themselves, here again some decisions were seen as appropriate for patient and family decision making, but most of the choices about medical treatment were seen as technical decisions, appropriately made by physicians. For example, decisions about whether to continue pregnancies after prenatal diagnosis of problems were seen as significant decisions for patients and families. Two girls I interviewed specifically mentioned that they had discussed such decisions with their own parents and had made decisions to continue their pregnancies. Staff members reported that young mothers are also often very involved in making decisions about breast feeding and circumcision. One adolescent mother was very upset about a nursing decision, which will be described later. A number of parents of NICU patients, both adolescents and others, were concerned about blood transfusions and considered the pros and cons carefully before, in all cases observed, accepting the physicians' recommendations and signing specific consent forms. However, like the decisions about medical treatment for the adolescent patients, except for blood transfusions, the decisions about medical treatment for NICU patients who were the children of adolescent parents were seen as technical, medical decisions to be made by physicians, not requiring familial participation in decision making.

For example, Jenny, who was described earlier as the seventeen-year-old who gave birth to a baby with the gastroschisis (the intestinal defect), reported having discussed her decision to continue her pregnancy at length with both her parents and Raymond, her boyfriend. While she was pregnant, her physicians had described the baby's defect and general methods of treatment, with the specifics to be decided after the baby was born and the exact nature of the defect was known. She said she did not have any questions for the doctors about the baby's care. She also had not attended childbirth classes; she did not discuss types of anesthesia or modes of delivery with her obstetrician before the birth.

Once Matthew was born, since the defect was large, the pediatricians decided to recommend a two-step procedure for repair, with one operation immediately after birth, followed by a second about a week later. During the first surgery, I talked to the baby's newly assigned pediatric resident and asked how consent for the surgery had been obtained. She said she herself had obtained specific consents herself for both the first surgery and blood transfusions. As the resident described it, "It only took three minutes. I explained it. Jenny asked no questions." Jenny signed the consents; Jenny's mother signed as witness.

When the baby was about two weeks old, however, Jenny was very upset about what she perceived as a poor decision. One evening, she noticed tape marks on Matthew's cheeks. Later that night she talked to Raymond, who said he had previously seen a pacifier taped in Matthew's mouth. Jenny was livid; she said Matthew should have been able to cry if he wanted to and feared that he would choke if he needed to throw up. She came in early the next morning specifically to talk to the head nurse about the taped pacifier. Later, that evening, she asked a nurse if she had taped the pacifier. When the nurse said she had, Jenny said, "You're lucky I don't slap your face." Needless to say, this upset the nurse and the rest of the nursing staff. Although Jenny had no questions or comments about the many treatments her son received, this was a decision she felt she understood and she did not believe it should have been made without her approval.

Another case involved Marisol, a fifteen-year-old girl I was invited to meet because she was identified as an adolescent alone. Marisol was an immigrant from Central America who had come to a public hospital clinic when she was about three months pregnant. A routine ultrasound revealed she was carrying twins; one twin appeared to be anencephalic (lacking a developed brain). She was asked to come back the next day to see a physician who specialized in genetics. He described the twin's problem and said it was lethal. He also explained the second twin was at greater than usual risk for congenital problems and recommended terminating the pregnancy. Marisol said she would return the following day with her mother but she did not come back either the next day or later that month for her regularly scheduled prenatal visits. The clinic staff called her home, but the caller was told that Marisol was not there and that her mother had returned to Central America; later they found out that Marisol had also returned home to care for an ailing aunt. Two months later, when the clinic staff called again, the phone was disconnected. Four months later, when it was too late to terminate the pregnancy, she came back to the clinic and thereafter regularly kept her appointments for prenatal care. The staff was concerned and presented her case at ethics rounds, feeling that she did not really understand the problem she was facing and worried because she was so young, making major decisions on her own.

When I interviewed her, I learned she was not making decisions alone. In fact, although her mother never came with her for prenatal visits, her mother appeared to be the major decision maker. Marisol's mother did not speak English and did not know much about medical procedures. She did, however, know about having babies; she had given birth to Marisol and her sister in their village, at home without medical assistance, less than two decades before. Everything had gone well. Marisol had told her mother what the doctors had said about the twins but her mother did not believe it. Her mother reasoned that if the problems were as serious as they said, Marisol would not feel the babies moving. When she talked to her mother about having amniocentesis and the possibility of abortion, her mother said, "The way they come – that's the way we're gonna get them." It was clear that Marisol, her mother, her boyfriend, and the other members of the family were expecting two live twins without catastrophic problems. They had apparently decided that Marisol should avoid returning to the hospital for prenatal care until it was too late for termination.

After Marisol did return for prenatal care, her obstetrician recommended another ultrasound. Marisol said that she did not want one. She thought the doctors only wanted it so they would know more, and said, "It would be of no use to me"; she didn't think it would change her care. Her obstetrician also talked to her about the management of labor and delivery. During labor, they planned to monitor only the apparently healthy twin and would only do a Cesarian section for that baby's or for Marisol's health. Although this ethically weighty decision was presented to her, she had no comment. Not accepting the diagnosis and probably not really understanding the implications of the management plan, she did not see the decision not to monitor both twins as an issue appropriate for family involvement.

For the birth, Marisol chose to have her mother, rather than her boyfriend, by her side. The first twin was a healthy baby girl. As predicted, the second girl was missing parts of her brain and skull; she had a large mass that resembled a placenta protruding from the top of her head. She also had severe facial deformities. From her chin down, the baby looked normal. The problems had been caused by amniotic band syndrome, rather than a classic neural tube defect; the doctor's predicted terminal prognosis was confirmed.

Marisol's mother saw the second twin at birth; she told Marisol not to look at the baby with the defect. Even though the staff tried to encourage Marisol to see the baby during the twenty-seven hours she lived in the NICU, Marisol followed her mother's advice and never saw the baby alive.

In a few situations I observed, health care providers played more active roles for adolescents alone, in some cases making decisions that they would not have made themselves for other adolescents. Sometimes this happened because the adolescents did not have any involved family members or other guardians; in other cases, it occurred because the patients' families were not able to provide what the adolescents needed. Two such cases are described here.

Sabrina, the fifteen-year-old with sickle cell disease, is described in Case Two as trying to refuse placement in a shelter. Earlier in this chapter, I reported that after her mother had died, Sabrina threatened to commit suicide and was admitted to the inpatient adolescent unit. In addition to her psychological problems, she continued to suffer from her severe leg ulcer, which affected her lower leg bone, a complication of her sickle cell disease. Eventually it was likely to lead to the loss of the use of her leg. Although there were no complex decisions to be made during the current admission about how to best treat her leg medically, because of her psychological and social problems, there were complex issues concerning compliance. Sabrina's doctors advised her to use crutches. Sabrina often refused and eventually claimed to have "lost" her crutches (even though it is hard to "lose" objects as large as crutches on a hospital floor).

Sabrina had been medically cleared for discharge. Ordinarily, compliance issues concerning the use of her crutches would have been handled primarily by her family at home. Although plans were being made for her to go home with her aunt, her aunt had only visited her a few times and did not know Sabrina well. There really was no adult from her family or anywhere else from outside the medical context who interacted with her frequently or who knew her well enough to be involved with making decisions about her use of crutches. While she was a patient the year before, she had become close to the child life specialist, Ellen. At the time of her hospitalization, she seemed to feel closer to Ellen than to any other adult and Ellen seemed to know her better than anyone else. Ellen tried to encourage her to use the crutches as much as she could. Knowing Sabrina well, she also understood how difficult it was for her to use them. In speaking to her physicians, Ellen played the role that would have ordinarily been played by family in expressing and considering Sabrina's feeling and values and making a decision about how hard to push for compliance. Members of the adolescent team, including Ellen and some of Sabrina's doctors, decided to let the crutches remain "lost" for a while, in consideration of Sabrina's overall situation.

The staff also played a more involved role for Dushan, the boy with AIDS who lived with his stepfather and step-stepgrandfather. Although he had *family,* his "father" and "grandfather" didn't visit often while he was in the hospital. Ellen spent considerable amounts of time with him and brought him special foods he liked. She often held his hand when he had IVs placed and accompanied him to procedures. Many members of the hospital staff also brought him presents. Despite attention from many others, no one was as special for Dushan as Ellen. He could recognize her footsteps in the hall and would call out to her whenever she passed. Dushan was scheduled to go home the day before Thanksgiving; because his stepfather was not there on time, Ellen helped him get dressed and packed up his presents. Even after he was all ready, he had to wait a long time until his stepfather arrived.

The adolescent HIV/AIDS team, including his attending doctor, the director of the team, the social worker, and the nurse were also close to him, and did many things they would not have ordinarily done for a patient if his family had been able to do more. They felt obliged to play a key role in the one ethically weighty medical decision about treatment that I observed for an adolescent who had a legal guardian but was, in many ways "alone." Dushan was a candidate for an experimental trial testing a new drug for prophylaxis against an opportunistic infection. The staff talked at length about whether he should be on the protocol. Not only did they discuss the medical benefits for him, but also considered how hard it would be for him to add more pills to the large number of medications he took daily and to have more blood tests, which he hated. They thought that the burdens would be outweighed by benefits, and decided to recommend the trial.

I observed as they tried hard to involve Dushan's step-stepgrandfather, Mr. Lester, in the informed consent process. They tried to explain the benefits and burdens of the new treatment, but Mr. Lester just said they should do what they thought was best. He would only talk about other issues, such as logistic problems trying to obtain some of the medications that Dushan had been taking. Despite their best efforts, they were not able to get Mr. Lester to consider the benefits and the burdens of the experimental treatment. A doctor also explained the protocol to Dushan. He was not happy about the extra blood tests, but he was willing to assent to participation if his doctors recommended it. It was clear that the details of the decision were beyond his capacity to comprehend. The staff felt a special responsibility, knowing Dushan was in many ways alone, and that, in effect, they were making a decision that should have been made by his guardians.

Discussion

My ethnographic research revealed that, at least in the urban hospital settings I studied, very few adolescents were technically *alone* (i.e., without identified, involved guardians). Although many were not cared for by their biological parents, almost all were involved with family members; a few were involved with other people whom they considered family and called by kin terms. I saw only a few adolescents who were in foster care; in all of these cases, the adolescents were also involved with family.

Nevertheless, many adolescents did not have guardians who were able to play an active role in thinking about treatment options and making decisions about their care. Occasionally, guardians could not be reached when decisions needed to be made because they were in prison or had temporarily left the area and did not leave information about how they could be contacted. More often, serious psychiatric or drug problems prevented the adolescents' guardians, whether biological parents or other family members, from being able to participate in decision making. Still others seemed limited in their ability to understand complex medical conditions and treatments. Therefore, even though these adolescents were involved with family, in many ways, they were *adolescents alone.*

Even though many adolescents were in such problematic situations, I was surprised to find that, in the settings I observed, this rarely compromised the making of medical decisions about their care. In general, medical care was not compromised because everyone – patients, their families, and their health care providers – agreed to decisions based on medical recommendations. It also did not cause problems because clinicians were sometimes willing to accept a dubious consent or otherwise proceed to treat even when the authority to treat was unclear.

Although ethically problematic cases concerning medical decision making are rare in the settings I observed, they do occur, presenting especially difficult dilemmas for adolescents alone and their caretakers. In some cases, evaluation of the adolescents will demonstrate that they have the capacity to provide ethically valid informed consent, and therefore discussions about medical care can respect this capacity.

In many cases, adolescents will be found to lack the necessary capacity themselves. However, even when there are no legally authorized guardians, there are often family members, or other adolescents or adults, who can be involved in discussions about care. They may help to make decisions that are in the best interests of the patients by helping to provide information on the values and situations of the adolescents, thus elucidating the broader social implications of treatment choices.

Occasionally, however, there are no involved family members or others present who know the adolescent well or who have the capacity to participate in meaningful ways in discussions about care. In such cases, health care professionals may be the only individuals who know the adolescent well and are thus able to consider the particular interests of the adolescent and bring them to bear in making medical decisions. Decision making by health care professionals carries certain risks. They may make decisions based on their own interests, such as the need to recruit subjects for a clinical trial. Moreover, they may be more likely to "medicalize" decisions, paying more attention to physiological benefits and paying less attention to psychological and social considerations. However, frequently health professionals get to know their patients very well, especially those with chronic conditions requiring frequent ambulatory visits or those who have long stays in the hospital. Their ability to act in the interests of their patients should be acknowledged and utilized.

Since obvious cases of ethically problematic medical decisions for adolescents are relatively rare in the settings observed, it would not appear to be burdensome to develop special mechanisms to foster ethically appropriate decision making, especially for adolescents alone. For example, multidisciplinary ethics meetings can be held to discuss problematic decisions. Usually, even if adolescents do not have the capacity to make decisions themselves, they can provide relevant information. In most cases, family members, fictive kin, or others who know the adolescent well can be invited to participate, even if they do not have legal authority to provide consent. Finally, in those cases in which the adolescent does not have capacity and there are no involved family members or others with the capacity to make decisions in the best interests of the adolescent, health care professionals may be able to play a special role in assuring ethically appropriate decisions about the medical care for the adolescent alone.

Acknowledgments

I wish to thank Jeffrey Blustein, Nancy N. Dubler and Carol Levine and the Project on Decision Making in Medical Care for the Adolescent Alone for their support of this research project and Ann Dill for her helpful comments on an earlier draft of this paper. I also wish to thank the patients, families and health professionals who allowed me to interview them and observe care, especially "Sabrina" and "Dushan," two "adolescents alone," who helped me to learn from their experiences.

Notes

1 All the names and other identifying details have been changed.

PART II

Cases and Commentaries

The cases in the following section illustrate many of the dilemmas that arise when unsupervised adolescents seek services from health care providers. The cases were developed by Diana Bianco when, as a third-year student at the New York University Law School, she worked as an intern on the project called "The Adolescent Alone: Decision Making in Health Care" at The Orphan Project and Montefiore Medical Center. The cases in this section were selected from those presented and discussed at project meetings.

The cases are based on real incidents, although names and other identifying information have been changed to protect confidentiality. The cases present a range of settings, individuals, and dilemmas; the commentaries reflect several disciplinary approaches. Some cases have only one commentary; others have two. Commentary authors may disagree or present a similar position from a different perspective. Sometimes, as in real life, there is no satisfactory solution to these adolescents' problems; there are only more and less ethically justifiable choices.

The intent is to show the often stark reality of these adolescents' lives and the responses from health care providers who try to help within the constraints of the medical, social service, and legal systems. These cases came to our attention because we sought them out; for the most part, youth in similar situations are invisible or unidentified. The presence of a nominal parent or other adult may mask the reality of neglect or unconcern. Yet these adolescents, like others of their age, have hopes and dreams and legitimate claims for attention and resources. By telling their stories, we hope to make concrete the information and analyses of the previous essays and thereby make a place for them in policy, practice, and programs.

Case One: Consent and the Limits of Staff as "Family"

Commentator: Abigail English

Carol was born in Trinidad and lived there with relatives as a young child. When she was nine years old, Carol came to the United States for surgery to repair a heart defect. She contracted HIV from a blood transfusion during the surgery. Six years later, after Carol learned she was HIV-infected through a hospital blood bank "look-back" program, she moved to a large northern city in the United States to live with her mother. She began attending a clinic for HIV-infected adolescents.

Carol's mother beat her, so she ran away constantly. Carol was also raped several times by various men who were living in her mother's home. After the child welfare agency learned that Carol's mother abused and neglected her, they placed Carol in a foster care group home. Carol ran away from this group home and from several others.

At the age of sixteen, Carol went to live with a foster family in a small town. A year later she ran away and returned to the city. At the adolescent clinic, her providers found cigarette burns and whip marks over most of her body, a result of a year of abuse.

By the time Carol turned nineteen (old enough to live on her own), she was sufficiently symptomatic with AIDS to qualify for AIDS-related public housing. Despite her theoretical eligibility, clinic staff questioned whether she had the ability to manage by herself. Over time, the clinic staff had become Carol's "family". She developed trusting relationships with her providers and looked to them for advice and understanding.

Carol talked about her HIV diagnosis freely, almost as if she did not understand the implications of the infection. Carol scored seventy-two on IQ tests, but clinic staff were suspicious that the result was low because Carol had extremely limited formal education. She could not tell time, write, or spell. Carol also had inappropriate social skills; she had little sense of her own and others' privacy. Despite Carol's incapacities, she managed to juggle the demands of the street and the problems of her life with some degree of competence. In addition, the stories she told about her life to clinic staff indicated a degree of savvy and understanding.

Shortly after moving into her apartment, Carol became involved with a young man who had recently been discharged from prison. He moved in with her and began to take over her resources. She seemed to have no notion that he was taking advantage of her.

Soon after, Carol became pregnant and was ecstatic about the news. She reported that she wanted a baby very much, and that having the baby meant everything to her.

Several months into her pregnancy, Carol went to the hospital for a prenatal checkup. (Because she had no clock in her apartment, one of the staff of the clinic provided a wake-up call.) The obstetrical team was very concerned about her pregnancy. She had lost two pounds since the beginning of her pregnancy and, in her seventh month, did not look at all pregnant. They admitted her to the hospital, but she left a day later, saying that her boyfriend needed her.

Carol kept her next appointment with the obstetrical team, but refused hospital admission despite her doctor's recommendations. Carol's providers were worried about her physical condition and wanted to do an echocardiagram and various other tests. They were concerned about the baby's health as well as Carol's. Carol said that she could not be admitted right away because she had to take care of her boyfriend's younger brother. She agreed to be admitted the next day, but never showed up.

During the last three months of her pregnancy, Carol lived in a residential facility for pregnant teens. Six weeks before her baby was born, Carol became very sick and was admitted to the hospital. After a few days, Carol wanted to leave the hospital to visit some friends in the city center. Her providers thought that it was unwise for her to do so, since it would compromise her and her unborn child's health.

Questions to Consider

- Given the clinic staff's primary role in Carol's life, do they have special obligations toward her in terms of her health care decision making and her living situation?
- Does their status as "family" allow the clinic staff to be more paternalistic with Carol than they might be with other patients?
- What steps, if any, should the clinic staff take with regards to Carol's living situation?
- Given Carol's mental capacity, how should the clinic advise her regarding her pregnancy?
- Is Carol competent to make her own health care decisions?
- How large of a role can/should Carol's providers play in her care, given that she is chronologically an adult, but one whose mental abilities and lack of education indicate that she may possess less than adequate intellectual capacity and judgment?
- Did Carol's providers have any responsibility to her "to-be-born" child?
- What should Carol's providers do in response to her desire to leave the hospital prematurely?

COMMENTARY

Carol's case presents a number of important legal and ethical questions. Several significant facts cut across the questions raised in the case description. First, Carol was already an adult – age nineteen – at the time she was living on her own and became pregnant. Second, her intelligence, based on standard measures and indicators, was limited – an IQ of seventy-two and an inability to tell time, write, or spell. Third, Carol's background and experience were characterized by abuse, neglect, and exploitation. Fourth, Carol had a long history of interaction with the health care system, spanning her heart surgery in childhood and her treatment during adolescence for HIV infection. Each of these facts has critical importance in evaluating Carol's rights and responsibilities and those of her health care providers. The two major areas of legal and ethical concern raised by this case are Carol's capacity to make health care decisions and the clinic staff's responsibilities with respect to Carol's health care decisions and living circumstances.

Carol's Capacity to Make Health Care Decisions

Although Carol was a minor, age fifteen, when she began attending the clinic for HIV-infected adolescents, by the time she was living on her own and became pregnant she was nineteen years old and legally an adult. From a legal perspective this fact has overriding importance. As a general matter, adults are legally authorized to consent to their own health care; indeed, their consent is required, with few exceptions. Thus, unless they lack legal or mental capacity or their refusal of care is overridden by a court on some other basis, adults have the right to accept or refuse medical care. Carol's right as an adult to make her own medical decisions is predicated on several factors: the legal capacity to make medical decisions; the mental capacity to make medical decisions; and an ability to give a voluntary, informed consent.

Legal Capacity

Adults are presumed to be capable of making medical decisions and giving an informed consent to specific medical procedures. If an adult had been determined to be legally incompetent and is placed under a guardianship or conservatorship, however, her competence to make medical decisions can no longer be presumed. Rather, that determination depends on the precise terms of the guardianship or conservatorship order. Usually a guardianship of the *estate* would not limited the right to make medical decisions, while a guardianship of the *person* would do so. Even a commitment to a mental facility does not necessarily deprive an adult of the right to make his or her own medical decisions as long as the person retains the capacity to do so. If a person is under a court order limiting the right to make medical decisions, consent must be given by some other person with legal authority to act on her behalf.

Minors are generally presumed to lack the legal capacity to consent to their own treatment unless a specific statute or court decision authorizes them to do so. All states have laws allowing minors to consent to care under specific conditions. Some of these laws allow some minors – such as minors who are "emancipated" by virtue of their living situations or who have been so adjudged by a court – to consent to all care; others allow all minors to consent to specific services, which in some states include HIV testing.

Mental Capacity

In order to be able to give valid consent, a patient must be able to understand the nature and consequences of the treatment. A patient whose mental faculties are so compromised as to be unable to reach an informed decision lacks the mental capacity to give consent. Although an adult is generally presumed to have the mental capacity to give consent, this capacity may be limited – permanently or temporarily – in any one of a number of ways: by mental illness, mental retardation, shock or trauma, physical injury or illness, or substance abuse. If a person's mental capacity is compromised at the time consent is sought, the decision must either be deferred or consent must be obtained from someone with the legal authority to provide it. Unless the individual already has a guardian, conservator, or other person with the authority to make medical decisions (such as someone to whom the patient has given a durable power of attorney for health care), authorization must be sought from a court. In some states legislation would automatically authorize someone other than the patient – such as the parents of an adult who is incompetent – to make such decisions. The existence of such a statute should not be presumed, however. Moreover, third-party consent or court authorization would not be required for emergency care. A patient's refusal of care should not, in and of itself, be treated as evidence of a lack of mental capacity. Rather, the patient's mental capacity should be independently evaluated to determine whether the patient is lucid, rational, and possesses the necessary understanding.

Informed Consent

Ultimately, the patient must have the requisite legal and mental capacity to give an informed consent for any treatment or procedure that requires it. Informed consent requires that the patient be able to understand the risks and benefits of the proposed treatment and give a voluntary consent to proceed. The legal standard for what information the physician must provide to the patient in order for consent to be considered informed varies somewhat among the states. The traditional standard was a community or objective standard – what other qualified physicians in the community would tell their patients – but has shifted in a growing number of states to an individual or subjective standard – whatever information would be material to the patient in making a decision. Generally, the information provided to the patient must include at least a description of the recommended treatment, the risks and benefits of the recommended treatment, the alternatives, the likely result of no treatment, the probability of success, the problems anticipated in recuperation and any other information a qualified physician would provide. Once the information has been provided, the patient must be able to make a voluntary decision about whether or not to proceed. Thus, factors limiting the voluntariness of the patient's decision, including coercion by hospital staff or health care providers, should be carefully evaluated by those clinicians who are responsible for determining whether the patient is able to give or has actually given informed consent.

Evaluating Carol's Capacity

How the clinic and hospital staff should interact with Carol with respect to the many health care decisions that she needs to make depends to a significant degree on her capacity. Does she have the legal and mental capacity to give (or withhold) informed consent to treatment? This requires an evaluation of her capacity in general, as well as an evaluation of her capacity with respect to each of the specific situations in which she is called upon to make medical decisions.

As an adult who has not been placed under legal guardianship or conservatorship, and whose legal capacity to make medical decisions has not otherwise been restricted by a court, Carol is presumed to have the legal capacity to decide for herself. Thus, unless she is determined to lack the mental capacity to make medical decisions, either generally or in a specific situation, Carol's consent is required for whatever medical care she is to receive.

Although Carol has tested low on an IQ test and lacks the ability to read, write, and spell, these facts alone do not demonstrate that she lacks the mental capacity to make medical decisions. Nevertheless, they are relevant to the consent process. Asking her to sign a complicated "informed consent" document, without fully explaining its provisions in language that she can understand, would fail to utilize her actual mental decision-making capacity. Moreover, she has demonstrated "a degree of savvy and understanding" in the way she has managed the demands of life on the street, suggesting that if information is provided to her in a form she can comprehend, she may have the capacity to evaluate that information in a way that makes sense to her.

Nevertheless, some other factors raise concern about her competence: the openness with which she talks about her HIV status; her apparent lack of reservations about her pregnancy despite her HIV infection; and her unwillingness on more than one occasion to comply with medical recommendations. Although none of these factors provides a sufficient basis to conclude that Carol is not competent to make her own medical decisions, they require closer examination.

Carol's open discussion of her HIV diagnosis might reflect a lack of understanding of its implications. However, it might also reflect a belief on her part that the risks of being identified as an HIV-infected person – denial of employment or insurance, for example – were not particularly relevant to her life situation. In fact, her HIV infection has enabled her to receive intense attention and good medical care from the staff at the HIV clinic, as well as subsidized housing.

Carol's enthusiasm at finding out that she is pregnant might suggest an inadequate understanding of the risk that she would bear an HIV-infected infant. On the other hand, she might know other HIV-infected women who have had babies who were not infected, or she might have heard that there is only a one in four chance that the baby will be infected – perhaps even less of a chance if she takes zidovudine (AZT) during her pregnancy. Given the high level of risk she has encountered generally in her life and the high level of risk she is surrounded by in her community, these might seem like reasonable odds.

Finally, Carol demonstrates an unwillingness to accede to the advice of her health care providers on more than one occasion – when she does not return to the hospital to be admitted for tests and, later in her pregnancy, when she seeks to leave the hospital against medical advice. In each of these situations, the staff must evaluate her competence based not on whether they agree with her decision, but on whether her behavior and reasoning demonstrate a lack of mental capacity to decide. Some of the relevant questions are whether her stated reasons for noncompliance – that her boyfriend's younger brother required her care and that she wanted to visit her friends – were reasonable ones and whether the risks she faced for herself and her fetus had been fully explained to her in a way that she could understand. The need to care for a young child seems like a reasonable basis for not remaining in the hospital for further tests, although it does not necessarily explain why she failed to return the next day. Although the desire to visit friends may seem frivolous, it may be Carol's only way of maintaining contact with them. If she is feeling better at the time, it may be difficult for her to understand the level of risk she would incur by leaving the hospital. Thus her "competence" in light of this issue may depend in part on how serious the risk is and how good a job the staff has done in explaining it to her.

Considering all these factors, the facts do not appear to compel a conclusion that Carol is mentally incompetent to make her own medical decisions. However, if Carol's health care providers reached the opposite conclusion and determined that she lacked decision-making capacity, they would be required to seek consent from someone else with legal authority to provide it or from a court.

The Clinic Staff's Responsibilities

Because Carol's social situation is so fraught with problems, it is tempting for the clinic staff to behave as if it is their responsibility to "rescue" her. Nevertheless, it is essential that this impulse be carefully examined in light of both the legal parameters of her situation and basic ethical precepts. In this light, their responsibilities – and rights – might be more limited than it would initially appear.

As already discussed, unless Carol is adjudged incompetent, she must make her own decisions about medical care. With respect to these decisions, it is the staff's responsibility to ensure that her consent (or refusal of consent) is an informed one. Thus, with respect to her pregnancy, the staff must make certain that they have explained the implications of her HIV infection, the degree of risk that her baby will be infected, the risks and benefits of abortion, the risks and benefits of taking AZT during pregnancy, the prognosis for HIV-infected infants, and the treatments available, to mention only a few issues. Similarly, with respect to her refusal to be admitted to the hospital for tests and her desire to be discharged against medical advice, the primary responsibility of the staff is to be sure that she understands the full implications of her actions for herself and for her fetus. Assuming she does, it may also be appropriate for the staff to attempt to determine whether she is being subjected to any undue pressure, perhaps from her boyfriend, that would limit the voluntariness of her decision. If she is under pressure, the staff could offer to discuss the issue with her boyfriend or to assist her in doing so.

As a technical matter, Carol may be capable of making her own medical decisions. However, as a social and psychological matter, she might benefit from some additional support. This help could take a variety of forms – more time spent with her by her health care providers in a process of guided decision making, for example, or encouraging her to identify a competent adult with whom she will routinely consult about her medical care.

With respect to the many difficult issues in Carol's life that do not explicitly involve medical decisions, the role of her health care providers is far less clear. Although in some sense both she and they may feel that they are her family, in reality they are not. They may come and go in her life based on schedules and rotations that have nothing to do with her needs. From the perspective of the ethical principle "do no harm," it is essential that they avoid engendering expectations on her part that they may be unable to fulfill. Thus, their most appropriate role with respect to her situation is to provide comprehensive and appropriate counseling in response to her expressed and perceived needs, while avoiding interventions they have neither the legal right nor the responsibility to make. To cite one example, Carol's boyfriend appears to be exploiting her; based on her past history of abuse, she may be ill equipped to protect herself. Although the staff does not have a legal responsibility to intervene or to solicit outside intervention, they can and should make sure that she is aware of whatever resources may be available to her. These may be alternative living situations or counseling services. She may even require legal services, should her boyfriend become physically abusive, or advice on how to proceed with respect to paternity and custody issues concerning her baby.

Similarly, with respect to Carol's unborn child, the role of her health care providers is one essentially limited to counseling and the provision of information. Let us assume that Carol's situation does not develop into one of the relatively rare, and fairly extreme, circumstances in which late in a pregnancy the courts will order medical intervention over the objections of a pregnant woman in order to save the fetus. In the absence of such circumstances, the role of the medical staff is to make sure that Carol understands their recommendations and the reasons for them. Beyond that, if she chooses not to follow their recommendations, they can override her refusal only by seeking legal intervention based on her presumed incompetence.

Ultimately, what Carol appears to lack is a support system of responsible adults who can provide ongoing care in the manner that some young people can expect from their immediate or extended families, or even from their peers. Although it might be tempting for her health care providers to feel that they can fill this void, the serious limits on the time they can actually spend with Carol, and the areas of her life in which they can actually assist her, suggest that they would serve her better by trying to help her establish such a support system in some other way. To do this successfully would require them to walk a very fine line: becoming sufficiently involved to win her trust while avoiding the danger of doing harm by raising expectations that they cannot meet.

Case Two: Placing an Unplaceable Teen

Commentators: Cathy Cramer, Linda Freeman, and Audrey Smith Rogers

At the age of fourteen, Sabrina was a long-term ward of the foster care system. She had been in more than twenty foster care families and group homes since the age of one. Beginning at the age of ten, she would stay in a family or home for a short period of time and then run away. She had very strong ties to her biological mother, and each time that she ran away she hoped to rejoin her mother. Sabrina's mother apparently encouraged her to run away and then, realizing her inability to take care of her, reneged on her promise. This realization was short-lived; and after Sabrina was in a new home, her mother would urge her to leave again.

The child welfare agency placed Sabrina in a large shelter because they were unable to find another foster care placement for her. Sabrina had sickle cell disease, and the facilities and supervision in the shelter could not meet her medical needs. A chronic leg ulcer grew larger and more painful as a result. By the time Sabrina was admitted to a hospital, she was no longer able to walk and had to be carried by some of the older residents of the facility.

After Sabrina's leg ulcer improved with proper treatment, hospital staff struggled with plans for her discharge. The staff had planned to transfer her to a rehabilitation facility to complete the recovery from her leg ulcer. (That plan became enmeshed in the child welfare agency's reluctance to agree). But Sabrina's mother insisted that she was able to care for her daughter and would bring her to her outpatient rehabilitation appointments. Sabrina's mother was asked to follow through by making concrete plans for discharge to her home, but she never did. At the same time, the rehabilitation facility decided that Sabrina was no longer appropriate for their care. It was also clear that Sabrina's mother was unable to care for her daughter. Because her group home and family foster care placements had all failed, the shelter was the only possible discharge plan. Sabrina's mother exacerbated the difficult situation by insisting that Sabrina had the right to go wherever she wanted. Sabrina adamantly refused to return to the shelter.

By this time, Sabrina had become a difficult, hard-to-manage youngster who acted out in ways that were destructive to herself and to others. She picked at her bandages and failed to comply with her treatment plan. It seemed clear that if the shelter refused to accept her or if she refused this placement she would end up in even less desirable circumstances.

Questions to Consider

- Should the hospital staff force Sabrina to return to the shelter where she was unhappy and did not get adequate medical care? What are their alternatives?
- Does Sabrina have the right to refuse a care plan just as she might have the right to refuse treatment?
- Does an adolescent have the right to refuse care? Under what circumstances? With what restrictions, if any?
- Does it or should it matter that some hospital staff were distressed by Sabrina's increasingly long stay in the hospital?
- Who has the right and who should have the right to make medical and placement decisions for Sabrina?
- What action by hospital staff would be in Sabrina's best interest?

COMMENTARY BY CATHY CRAMER

Relevant Facts

The following facts from this case are particularly relevant in a discussion of who has the right to make medical and placement decisions for Sabrina:

- Sabrina is fourteen years old and has been in foster care since age one. Foster care was designed as a short-term, temporary solution to family problems. Children are supposed to be returned to their parents within twenty-four months of placement. The fact that Sabrina has been in foster care for thirteen years signals that the child welfare agency, which is legally mandated to safeguard Sabrina's "best interests," has not fulfilled its obligations. Either she should have been reunited with her mother after a certain time or freed for adoption at a much younger age.
- Her mother is still actively involved with Sabrina after thirteen years. This suggests that Sabrina is not totally alone, yet she is constantly torn between her mother and the foster care setting of the moment. She might be better off without her mother's involvement, because her mother is unable to care for her and yet causes much of the disruption in her life. The child welfare agency should have acted long ago to bring some permanence and stability to Sabrina's life.
- We do not know the circumstances under which Sabrina was placed into foster care. This is significant, because parents who place their children voluntarily into foster care have different rights from parents whose children are placed by the court due to parental abuse or neglect. For example, a mother who has placed a child voluntarily has the right to demand the return of her child if she disagrees with a placement decision. The agency either has to return the child within thirty days, get a court order to retain custody, or file a neglect petition against the parent.
- Sabrina is only fourteen years old. She has been through tremendous turbulence in her short life. Despite some emotional continuity through her attachment with her mother, she has had no real stability. She has no trusting relationships or apparent ability to foresee future consequences of her actions. Her life experiences, though varied, do not suggest competency for independent decision making, particularly since she keeps going back to her mother, time and time again, only to be disappointed.
- Sabrina has sickle cell disease, a genetic chronic illness that requires proactive measures to remain healthy. The fact that it might have been passed on to her by

her mother might explain her mother's continued involvement with Sabrina after all of these years. Additionally, the fact that she now has a chronic leg ulcer that has progressed to the bone signifies that she and those supervising her have not taken the requisite steps to ensure that she remains healthy.

Discussion

This is not really a case about an adolescent's ability to consent to medical care. Rather, it is a case about foster care placement for a child who has medical problems. It therefore raises different issues from a purely medical case. The major distinction is that the state (through the child welfare agency) and the legal system are additional players in decision making for children in foster care and thus the process is more cumbersome. Although parents retain guardianship rights for their children while they are in foster care, the state has custody rights. Thus, if there is a conflict over placement (or other decisions), the various parties will go to court for a resolution.

Every child in foster care is represented by an attorney who is charged with representing the child's perspective in any court proceeding. The biological parents are also represented by attorneys, as is the child welfare agency. Thus, we do not know whether Sabrina's attorney has been notified of this dilemma and is taking some action. It does not appear that Sabrina's advocate has been particularly effective in the past in helping Sabrina find some permanency or stability, yet this is an avenue that is available to Sabrina. She definitely has the right to make her opinions known, particularly in this case where she may be sent back to a place where her health troubles were exacerbated.

With regard to making health care decisions, Sabrina does not fall into any of the legally sanctioned categories that would allow her to make decisions about her health care without parental or guardian consent. She is not an emancipated minor because she is in foster care. She is under eighteen, not a parent, not married, not pregnant. The types of medical services she requires are not ones that she would be legally sanctioned to consent to on her own (e.g., treatment for sexually transmitted diseases, mental health services).

Sabrina's history also does not make her a good candidate for making health care decisions on her own. She had not taken responsibility for herself in the past; she continued to run to her mother; neglected her physical condition while living in the shelter, and is currently acting out by refusing to comply with the medical treatment plan. But this does not mean that her opinions about her health care should be ignored. They should be considered along with those of her mother, the child welfare agency, the medical provider, and any outside consultant who could be brought in to add insight into the situation. A team approach is the best way to proceed.

If Sabrina's decisions about her health care conflict with those of her mother or the agency, then the matter should be taken up in court. Parents of children in foster care do retain authority to make health care decisions for their child, although the agency has a role, because it is ostensibly guarding the child's "best interest." The child also has a role, although not necessarily a determinative one.

The medical provider's role is quite limited in this scenario. Unlike a medical problem where the individual provider can decide whether the adolescent is competent to make medical decisions and can then decide whether to act on that decision, the medical provider has no authority to decide where Sabrina should be placed. The provider can make recommendations based on her medical condition and perhaps work with Sabrina's (or any of the other party's) lawyers to advance their opinion in court. Ultimately, however, the medical staff cannot direct that any particular action be taken in terms of placement. The medical staff certainly cannot force Sabrina to return to the shelter, although they probably could force her to leave the hospital.

Regarding medical care, the provider needs to consult with Sabrina, Sabrina's mother, and the agency in order to determine the best treatment plan. Although generally adolescents have the right to make their feelings about care known, an individual's competency to make a decision must be assessed by the provider. An adolescent's opinion, depending on the circumstances, should be taken into consideration.

In this scenario, the medical providers have an affirmative obligation to work with Sabrina, her mother, and the agency to come up with an acceptable solution. It is unclear from the facts given why the agency refused to agree to the plan to discharge Sabrina to the rehabilitation facility. It also seems unusual that the facility would decide that Sabrina was "no longer appropriate for their care." Was this because she was healed or because of behavior concerns? In any case, the hospital staff has legitimate concerns about not letting Sabrina languish in the hospital and therefore must work closely with the rest of the team to find an appropriate setting for Sabrina. Perhaps the medical staff could assert a positive influence, given that Sabrina's mother and the agency do not seem to have a good working relationship.

COMMENTARY BY LINDA FREEMAN

Should the hospital force Sabrina to return to the shelter? Of course they should not force her to go – they cannot. As she has done in the past, she can leave the shelter as soon as she is deposited there. They should not want her to go back to the shelter because they know she cannot recover nor stay well in that environment.

What are their alternatives? It is always easier to place an individual case than to create a system to handle many such placements. Individual health care workers have people and agencies who owe them favors, so one can often find room for just this one kid. Such places might be group homes or specialized foster care for behaviorally disturbed children with a temporary contract to remediate the medical problem. A child psychiatrist seeing Sabrina might identify emotional or behavioral problems that could facilitate a transfer either to an acute care psychiatric treatment facility or a longer-term psychiatric care facility. It is a long shot, but the mother may be evaluated by the child welfare agency and found able to respond to intensive case management.

The best plan would be to continue trying to settle her in a foster care home. There is some evidence that even children who have failed in many foster care homes can still eventually find an adequate home and will do better than those who are institutionally placed. In other words, the agency should not give up on her or any other child.

Does Sabrina have the same right to refuse a care plan as she might to refuse treatment? De facto, she seems to have the right to refuse. She refuses care plans by leaving the placement. The medical staff is required only to provide a care plan they think is adequate. They are not obligated to provide a plan that pleases the adolescent or adult patient.

Does an adolescent have the right to refuse care? Under what circumstances? With what restrictions? Since minors have rights to consent based on status, similar rights of refusal based on status should follow. In this case, Sabrina may be a mature minor who understands the risks and benefits of refusing the proposed treatment or care. At age fourteen, studies have shown the medical decision-making capacity of adolescents is not significantly different from adults. Emancipated minors similarly should have this right. Adolescents younger than fourteen or who are not capable of understanding the risks and benefits of the care should be evaluated case by case. As with psychiatric confinement, perhaps a reasonable policy would be examination by two physicians, one of whom is a child psychiatrist or pediatrician with some in-depth understanding of cognitive and emotional development.

Does it matter that the hospital staff were distressed by Sabrina's long stay? I think so. They provide acute care and are neither interested in nor capable of man-aging the emotional and social problems of this child. Staying in an acute care hos-pital is inappropriate and may also be unsafe (infection, etc.), as would returning to a shelter that cannot provide adequate care.

Who has the right and who should make medical and placement decisions for Sabrina? The child welfare agency and the mother (unless her rights were termi-nated) have the right to make medical and placement decisions with recommenda-tions from the medical staff. But given the mother's demonstrated incapacities, the agency and Sabrina herself may make a better decision. As already mentioned, Sabrina should be examined by a child psychiatrist and/or two child specialists to recommend her capacity for decision-making judgment, cognitive ability to under-stand implications of her decision, impulsivity, self-destructive impulses, and so on. A decision made without at least her verbal consent seems unlikely to be useful since she will sabotage it again.

What action by the hospital staff would be in her best interest? Consultation with child psychiatry to evaluate Sabrina and begin a brief crisis-oriented treatment may give her the skills to manage this transition. A longer-term group or individual treatment to help her articulate her grief and anger at the loss of her mother and the loyalty conflicts she seems to experience in her foster homes might also be recom-mended. The hospital staff should also tell the agency that they recommend she have more care, such as that in a special foster care placement.

The staff can also consult with Sabrina about the type of discharge plans they can advocate for her and see if she can agree to any. They can then advocate for these placements. At that point, they will need to establish a relationship with an agency worker to try to influence the agency's decision about her placement.

If Sabrina's condition can justify it, they could recommend temporary nursing home-type placement until her condition improves.

COMMENTARY BY AUDREY SMITH ROGERS*

The key issue in Sabrina's case is the diffusion of responsibility for Sabrina's best interests. Who is responsible? Who should be responsible? Why have the lines been so blurred?

What should be the role and responsibility of the hospital? The mission of an acute care hospital dictates its appropriate role and responsibilities in regard to Sabrina. Its mission is to care for treatable illnesses or conditions, to restore individuals to health, or transfer them to rehabilitative facilities to optimize function. The hospital staff has no primary authority to force Sabrina to return anywhere; they have a responsibility to work with the child welfare agency, which does have placement authority over Sabrina, to ensure that her medical needs are adequately addressed wherever she is placed.

Does it matter that the staff is distressed? What options are open to the hospital? There is an implicit contract between individuals and their health care providers that requires cooperation and honesty. Hospital staff are always distressed when the contract is not honored by individuals who neglect, refuse, or sabotage treatment. Furthermore, disruptive behavior makes caring for other hospitalized individuals more difficult. The hospital should provide counseling to the staff to assist them in understanding the dynamics of Sabrina's situation, developing a strategy for interacting with her, and providing a coordinated and sensitive response to her needs. This could ease the transition from the acute setting.

Does the adolescent have the right to make life decisions? Does the adolescent have the right to refuse medical care? Under which circumstances, if any? Given that an adolescent demonstrates a capacity for understanding and judgment comparable to an average adult's, the youth should be accorded a similar respect for personhood given adults in decisions around care. However, the same qualifying circumstances would hold if an individual refuses care: the person must be of sound mind, not suffering from an affective disorder such as clinical depression, and have a condition for which care would not offer a clear benefit, (e.g., the adolescent's condition is one in which there is no credible chance of significantly prolonging life or one in which there is no serious possibility of restoring an acceptable quality of life). Less dramatic clinical situations must be examined in

* The opinion of the author does not represent the official policy of the U.S. Public Health Service.

the light of risks versus benefits inherent in the intervention, while respecting the individual youth's evolving autonomy.

Does the adolescent have the right to refuse a care plan for placement? A minor for whom the state has responsibility has very limited rights of refusal around placement. Of all objections that a minor might raise, the only one with merit would be the allegation of an unsafe situation. But no one can really dictate the circumstances of his or her childhood, and few have achieved adulthood without wishing the situation were dramatically different.

On the other hand, to make this limitation of choice ethically justifiable, the state has an exacting responsibility to ensure that the minor's safety is guaranteed and that the minor is placed in circumstances that will allow the minor to realize his or her full potential. Society has an obligation to the individual as well as to its own common good to give the minor in its care the capacity to operationalize his/her desires; but society has no obligation to directly fulfill these desires.

What constitutes the *adolescent alone*? Is Sabrina alone? The adolescent alone is a youth who, while still in the position of benefiting from parental or adult-guardian care, guidance, and support, is without such care, guidance, or support. This definition encompasses those youth who are physically apart from parental or adult-guardian supervision and care, as well as those who lack functional supervision and care through parental apathy or antagonism. According to these criteria, Sabrina is an adolescent alone.

Does Sabrina appear to have the capacity for self-determination at this point of development? Sabrina's capacity for sound judgment and understanding seems to be limited, given the absence of a caring and responsible adult in her life who challenges and supports her in achieving critical developmental tasks. This assessment appears to be supported by her adherence to behavior that is not in her own best interest.

What should be the role of a parent – in this case, Sabrina's mother? Although I use the term *parent,* I am, nevertheless, not proposing a structural definition for the role, but rather a functional one that could be assumed by variously configured families or caring adults. The role of the parent has always entailed the preparation of the child to assume a responsible, productive place in society. This preparation has encompassed physical, psychological, intellectual, social, moral, and spiritual parameters. The content and context of the preparation is dictated by the times and the culture. Very few parents perform ideally; most perform adequately.

What are the unreported circumstances around Sabrina's mother? Why has she not been able in thirteen years to stabilize her life enough to provide for Sabrina? What motivates her to stay involved in her daughter's life? Have efforts been made to engage her, to solicit her cooperation? Is she fully competent? What explains her hostility?

With the facts available, it seems clear that Sabrina's mother has failed as a parent. Whatever her motivation (presumably some immature perception of love), her continuing influence in Sabrina's life has been destructive and has resulted in severely restricted placement options for Sabrina. Her manipulation constitutes emotional abuse and her behavior forfeits any parental rights she may claim because she has so consistently failed to fulfill the corresponding responsibilities. Many would readily agree that, on the basis of her reported behavior, Sabrina's mother has forfeited her parental rights. Yet few would want that forfeiture legislated.

What should be the role of the community/society? The child welfare agency? Society has an interest in its children and their growth into responsible and productive adulthood. Through its institutions, society should support the role of the parent in preparing the child to assume an adult role. This means more than assuming that underfunded public agencies will manage the problems caused by inadequate parenting. More than finally providing adequate funding to these agencies, we need to return to the concept of personal responsibility and a personal role in maintaining the fabric of society. We have bureaucratized caring, and in doing so we have lost our souls.

The child welfare agency has been responsible for Sabrina's placements since she was one year of age. Her history of more than twenty different living arrangements for the past thirteen years, continually complicated by maternal interference, speaks either to agency regulations that fail to ensure the best interests of the child or to an incompetent or apathetic staff. The agency should have prevented this mother from interfering in this child's home placements when the pattern started four years ago.

The agency has responsibility for her placement. A minor has no right to reject placement arrangements given that the state has provided a safe and nurturing environment. There is evidence that the shelter is less than safe for Sabrina because her medical condition deteriorated badly while she was a resident there. Yet owing to Sabrina's past disruptive and run-away behavior, there are no other placement options. The agency is obligated to act in Sabrina's immediate interest by increasing her safety in this shelter and to act in her long-term interest by counseling her about her relationship with her mother, the consequences of her actions, and her capacity to assume responsibility for her future.

Options for Sabrina

The child welfare agency should obtain a court order prohibiting contact between Sabrina and her mother. Placement options appear to be limited to the shelter. Assign a consistent and skilled caseworker who can teach Sabrina to trust and who will work with her to reach achievable goals with the long-term objective of another placement; Sabrina should be a partner in this plan.

The hospital should arrange for Sabrina to be followed on a regular basis (ideally, if available) by an adolescent clinic with comprehensive services or other clinic arrangement with comparable services; and by a visiting nurse who can monitor Sabrina's medical condition at the shelter. Sabrina must be engaged beyond the walls of the shelter so as not to feel exiled there.

Case Three: An Adolescent's Contested Wish for a Kidney Transplant

Commentators: Jeffrey Blustein and Susan Coupey

John, age fifteen, was diagnosed with kidney disease when he was very young. He has been receiving dialysis three days a week since the age of three. At the age of six, he received a kidney transplant, which led to his being hospitalized for approximately six months. The transplant exacerbated seizures he had been experiencing, and ultimately the transplant was removed. John remembers this difficult postoperative experience, but the one bright note for him was that he did not have to be on dialysis during that time.

John's mother has serious psychological problems. She has been in and out of psychiatric hospitals throughout John's life. According to hospital staff, John's mother has been unable and unwilling to support him emotionally and psychologically throughout his illness. John's maternal grandmother has served as a surrogate mother to John since he became ill. Whenever John's mother was in the hospital or whenever she disappeared for periods of time, John would stay with his grandmother, who lived in the same neighborhood. John's mother and grandmother argue constantly. John loves both his mother and grandmother very much, although he is particularly attached to his mother. He feels torn by their arguments, and tries not to take sides.

When John turned fourteen, the hospital staff became alarmed that he was missing his clinic appointments. They received no response from his mother after repeated phone calls, so they asked his grandmother to bring him to the hospital. John was ultimately hospitalized because his illness had worsened and hospital staff were concerned he would not get sufficient care at home.

John has been in the hospital for three months. He has unrealistic expectations about his illness and his treatment, saying that he just wants to go home and stay home. The hospital staff finds John fairly immature, with limited capacity to understand the implications of his illness.

Throughout John's stay in the hospital, there has been no way to contact his mother. When she is in touch with his providers, she refuses to acknowledge her son's illness and says she does not want him in the hospital. At the same time, she has not taken any action to bring him home. John's mother does not visit her son for weeks and then suddenly appears to "room-in" for a period of time, sleeping in John's room, as parents are permitted to do. The hospital staff believe that she does not room-in to provide support to John, but does so because she is intermittently homeless and has no other place to stay.

The hospital serves as sort of a haven for John, because as long as he is in the hospital, no decision about where he will live upon release has to be made. John loves his mother and, despite her illness, does not want to be separated from her.

John has been on dialysis for twelve years, so his health care providers are running out of access sites for the needles. There is some question as to how much longer John will be able to continue receiving dialysis. The only alternative for John is a kidney transplant, and he has been on a list to receive one for some time.

John wants a transplant because he does not like the way he looks as a result of the dialysis. He sees other children also on dialysis and thinks they look "freaky." He already feels badly about his body image, because he is in a wheelchair and is somewhat frail. He has trouble keeping up with other children in the ward, and he doesn't want to be hampered any more by the dialysis procedure.

The last time she visited John, his mother refused to consent for either dialysis or a transplant. She has not visited in quite a while, and repeated attempts to contact her have been unsuccessful. John's grandmother thinks John should receive dialysis, not a transplant. She remembers the terrible ordeal of his first transplant experience and is convinced that another transplant will mean death on the operating table or shortly after surgery. John's physician has informed her that the chances of a transplant succeeding are remote, but that the operation is his only chance for long-term survival. John's grandmother says she wants him with her as long as possible, and believes that even if John has only a few more months on dialysis, this is better than losing him to surgery.

Questions to Consider

- What, if any, actions should the hospital staff take with regards to John's family situation?
- Should the hospital contact the child welfare agency and report John's mother to the state for neglect? What other choices do they have?
- How should John's wishes about his future medical care be elicited?
- What legal or ethical obligations do the hospital staff have to respect John's wishes for a transplant once this has been articulated?
- What weight should be given to the wishes of John's grandmother? Why should her input be considered?
- If John's providers decide to honor the grandmother's wishes and give John dialysis instead of a transplant, how will this be conveyed to John?
- Given that John's physicians believe a transplant is his only chance for long-term survival, should they act contrary to his grandmother's wishes?

COMMENTARY BY JEFFREY BLUSTEIN AND SUSAN COUPEY

This case raises a number of difficult questions, including the following: Can one use the "best interests" standard to help decide whether John should get the transplant or continue with dialysis? How much moral weight should be given to John's desire to have the transplant? Who is the appropriate decision maker? What roles should the mother and grandmother play in decision making for John? Or should John be able to consent to the transplant on his own? Do John's caretakers have any special responsibilities with regard to the management of his care because of his age and dependent status?

John is not, strictly speaking, an adolescent alone. However, his mother, whose parental rights have not been terminated, has not given him emotional support during his illness and has not participated in his care. Whatever supervision she has provided him over the years has been erratic at best. She is clearly incapable of providing structure to his life. The grandmother is something of an unknown quantity, although she "has served as a surrogate mother to John since he became ill," which was around the age of three, when he was first diagnosed with kidney disease. She might be able to give John the parenting he needs if she is supported and if the mother's erratic behavior can be controlled. As long as the mother is around intermittently, the grandmother's ability to act as an effective surrogate parent is compromised. Indeed, John's failure to keep his clinic appointments indicates that even with an involved and concerned grandmother, he is not getting the supervision he needs.

Despite John's somewhat chaotic home situation, his renal disease has been adequately managed for about eleven years. With the exception of the short period when he had a transplant, he came to the hospital three times a week for dialysis, apparently took his medications regularly, and complied with dietary restrictions. Now, at the age of fourteen, this situation has changed and hospital staff has become "concerned [that] he would not get sufficient care at home." Whatever the reason – and without further information we can only speculate – it would certainly be morally irresponsible for the hospital simply to send John back home, when there is good reason to believe that this environment is unsafe for him.

The best course of action may be to involve the appropriate state child welfare agency and try to achieve a more permanent and supported living situation for John. If this is done, he can be discharged from the hospital with a reasonable assumption that he will get to his dialysis sessions. This might involve kinship care with the grandmother or a nonrelative foster home. If the mother is amenable to having John live with his grandmother, or can be persuaded to accept this, and the grandmother is willing and able to take John into her home, this would probably be the best arrangement. In the meantime, the staff should help John to establish control of his situation by refusing to allow the mother to stay overnight and putting specific but reasonable limits on her visiting. The object is not to penalize John by depriving him of his mother's company, but to protect him from being overwhelmed by her neediness.

As to who should have the authority or right to make medical decisions for John, we suggest the following principle: parents' authority to make decisions for their children is linked to a substantial degree to the quality of care the children receive from them, and is not merely grounded in biology. On this basis, it seems appropriate for the grandmother to be involved in decision making for John (assuming, for now, that John is not mature enough to make his own decisions). The grandmother is entitled to this by virtue of her ongoing involvement in John's life, her love, and her apparent concern for his well-being. However, the grandmother and John want different things – she wants her grandson to continue receiving dialysis rather than undergo a second transplant; he wants the transplant – and mature or not, John's wish cannot just be disregarded.

The mother, we are told, "refused to consent for either dialysis or a transplant," and of course if John receives neither, he will certainly die in a short period of time. It would be morally irresponsible for John's care providers to honor the mother's refusal for at least two reasons: first, her lack of involvement in John's life disqualifies her from being the one to make decisions of such gravity for him; and second, it would be wrong to let John die when, clearly, he wants to have the chance to lead a "normal" life.

Does John have the capacity to make his own decisions about medical care? We know that the "hospital staff finds John fairly immature," an unsurprising conclusion in view of his nearly life-long dialysis. Typically, youngsters who have been on dialysis from a very early age experience multiple psychological and emotional problems. Transition from one developmental stage to another is complicated by frequent hospitalizations, education is often disrupted, poor body image undermines self-esteem, the normal struggles and confusions of adolescence are exacerbated, and "acting out" behavior is common. Add to this that John is fifteen, in the grey area of middle adolescence, and that his home life is chaotic. Under the circumstances, very likely John's development has been seriously delayed.

Had John had a different temperament or perhaps been less ill, he might have adopted a more parent-like role toward his mother. Fourteen- and fifteen-year-olds are sometimes quite capable of rising above their parents' inadequacies, forming alliances with more stable adults in their social network, and getting on with their lives. However, John did not have such resources of temperament or spirit. Instead, he retreated into a more childlike method of coping with his situation, forming unrealistic expectations about his illness and treatment and saying he "just wanted to go home and stay home."

Body image concerns are paramount and age-appropriate for adolescents. John's dislike of dialysis is certainly understandable and worthy of serious consideration, given its effects on his health and mobility. But John is said to have "limited capacity to understand the implications of his illness." How so? He does not seem to think that his condition is going to improve as long as he continues on dialysis, an accurate conclusion. He knows well enough what life on dialysis is like. Perhaps because of developmental delay he does not appreciate the very real risks to himself of having a transplant, that rejection and death are possible outcomes. In other words, perhaps he has limited capacity to make an informed decision in favor of a transplant.

The grandmother, by contrast, is capable of making an informed decision, and she decides in favor of continuing on dialysis for whatever time is left. We can imagine her reasoning out the pros and cons in the following way. "If John goes for a transplant, there is a very strong likelihood that this will be a terrible ordeal, full of pain and suffering, and that he will not survive. On the other hand, it offers him a (remote) chance of long-term survival. If he remains on dialysis, there is a good chance that I can have him with me for at least another six months (though not necessarily trouble-free months). But then he has no chance of long-term survival." The time element is important here, because the grandmother "wants him with her as long as possible." If the transplant were delayed until John runs out of access sites, then the grandmother might change her mind and opt for it. In fact, even if John is placed on an emergency transplant list, it is likely to be some time before a kidney becomes available, and by then John's access problem might be acute. John's nephrologist should explore this treatment plan with the grandmother. Its advantage is that by placing John on the emergency transplant list now, all his options are kept open. When and if a kidney does become available, the grandmother can reassess her earlier decision. Also, the physician should make certain that the grandmother has a full understanding of the risks and benefits of a transplant.

Since the transplant is not yet urgent, there is time for a series of meetings involving John, the grandmother, the nephrologist, and a facilitator (e.g., a social worker, mediator, patient advocate, or primary care physician). The goal of these meetings is to allow all participants to state their hopes and fears regarding different treatment approaches and to see if they can all agree on a plan. John may choose to acquiesce to his grandmother's wishes, deciding at some level that he needs her support and approval more than he needs to take a big chance on surgery. We think this decision should be supported. On the other hand, John may make his case forcefully enough in the group meetings that the grandmother changes her position and agrees to the transplant. The third scenario is that John and the grandmother continue to disagree, even after all have had a chance to air their views.

In these meetings, the physician should not push strongly one way or the other about the transplant, since the chances "of a transplant succeeding are remote," and dialysis is not going to be able to go on much longer than six months, either. There is no uniquely good or right solution to this problem.

Even if there are grounds for questioning John's maturity to make a decision in favor of a transplant, the hospital has an ethical (but probably not much of a legal) obligation to strongly consider his wishes. His desire is itself not an unreasonable one. A transplant is his only chance for long-term survival and a more or less normal life. He is the one who will suffer the slow, lingering death from dialysis failure if, as his grandmother wants, he does not get the transplant. Moreover, John's desire is not transitory or capricious, and to a degree it is reflective. These two points speak in favor of acceding to John's wish for a transplant. Alternatively, we might use a sliding scale conception of capacity to reach the same conclusion.

John's getting a transplant is neither clearly in his best interest nor clearly against his best interest. In situations like this, the competency standards for valid consent or refusal fall somewhere between very stringent and very lenient. Perhaps John's level of capacity, limited though it is, satisfies these median requirements.

One additional point is that, were John's health providers to go along with the wishes of the grandmother, they would have to give John some explanation for why they are not doing the transplant. They could lie to John about the availability of organs, but this would only cover up one wrong with another.

In these ways, we believe that a persuasive moral case can be made for giving John the transplant and acting contrary to the wishes of his mother and grandmother, if this is what it should come to. The hospital ought to be prepared to seek a court order authorizing the operation, if this should be necessary.

Case Four: Saying "No" to Treatment in Terminal Illness

Commentators: Jonathan Moreno and Kenneth Schonberg

Andy was fifteen when he learned he had rhabdomyosarcoma of the spine (a form of cancer). With his specific form of the disease (alveolar), cure is highly unlikely. He had originally gone to the emergency room because he was having trouble walking, and was admitted to the hospital for additional tests. After he was diagnosed with cancer, he remained in the hospital for a year and a half.

Andy's mother was an alcoholic who had been in and out of substance abuse treatment for years. Throughout his illness, Andy's mother was not available for support or help in decision making. Andy had a six-year-old brother for whom Andy served as a surrogate father. Andy's own father was not at all present in his life. Andy's maternal uncle was somewhat involved in his life, but because he, too, had a substance abuse problem, his involvement was sporadic.

The significant adult figure in Andy's life was a woman he called his aunt, but who was actually a close friend of his mother's. He relied heavily on her for support and had lived with her from time to time. His mother eventually became jealous of his relationship with his aunt-friend and attempted to sabotage it. The relationship between the aunt-friend and Andy's mother fell apart, but the aunt-friend remained close to Andy.

Before his illness was diagnosed, Andy was an athletic, bright young man who enjoyed painting and drawing. According to hospital staff, he was mature beyond his years. Throughout his life, Andy was responsible for his and his brother's well-being. He was thrust into this responsible position in the family at a young age.

Andy tried to make the best of his illness. He used the hospital's resources to improve his quality of life. For example, he visited the Child Life Program daily, painting, drawing, and talking to the counselors. He also took advantage of a summer program where he was employed by the hospital to work with chronically ill younger children.

Andy underwent surgery to remove the tumor, and also had radiation therapy and chemotherapy. None of the treatments was totally effective, and he never went into remission. As his illness progressed, he experienced increasingly severe pain.

Andy's providers openly discussed his illness with him. Because of his mother's lack of participation, the providers discussed Andy's treatment options with him. The doctors actually made most of the day-to-day treatment decisions, although Andy's mother had consented to the surgery and radiation. Andy did not expressly consent to his day-to-day treatment, although his doctors believed he would have let them know if he wanted to refuse treatment.

A significant turning point in Andy's illness occurred when his mother refused to move from her walk-up apartment into a ground-floor apartment available in her building. Because of his illness, Andy was unable to negotiate stairs. If his mother moved into a ground-floor apartment, he could go home. Because of her reluctance to relocate to a new apartment, Andy could never go home again.

In the last stage of his illness, Andy's doctors told him he had to consider whether he wanted to continue chemotherapy. The treatment would not be curative, but palliative care would ease his pain and might prolong his life. If he decided not to have chemotherapy, he would die sooner with more pain. Andy's mother refused to make the decision, nor did she offer him any support. She informed the hospital that Andy could decide without her input. Just as Andy's illness worsened, his mother was hospitalized for alcoholism. His mother's sister, who had previously been uninvolved in Andy's care, appeared at the hospital, wanting to be involved in his heath care decisions. She believed Andy should continue chemotherapy.

Andy consulted with many members of the hospital staff in making his decision. They told him that chemotherapy might ease his pain and discomfort and prolong his life but would not cure him. He spoke with doctors and nurses and a psychiatrist he was seeing about the consequences of receiving and refusing chemotherapy. He also worked with the Child Life Program staff to express his wishes through art. His doctors, along with his mother's sister, wanted him to continue chemotherapy. The woman he called his aunt thought Andy should make the decision, and expressed no opinion of her own. After a couple of weeks, Andy decided he did not want any further treatment.

Questions to Consider

- Should efforts have been made by Andy's providers to involve his mother in his ongoing treatment? How might this be accomplished?
- Is Andy an adolescent alone?
- Should Andy have been asked for consent, or was his assent to his day-to-day treatment sufficient?
- Should Andy's health care providers have intervened at this point? How?
- Did the doctors act appropriately in allowing Andy to make the decision about chemotherapy? Are they now ethically obliged to respect his wishes?
- What roles can/should his biological aunt and his aunt-friend have in his health care decision making?
- Did the hospital staff become a surrogate family to Andy? If so, what rights and responsibilities does this role confer upon them?

COMMENTARY BY JONATHAN MORENO

Although Andy's mother does not conform to any reasonable concept of the model parent, there is no evidence presented that she has been specifically abusive toward him. The worst one can say about her parenting behavior – and this is bad enough – is that she has been neglectful of his emotional needs and in planning for his best possible future. Perhaps her own disease is a mitigating factor, and probably she feels remorseful about her conduct. The brute fact, nonetheless, is that she has not been nearly as involved as she should have been.

Notwithstanding her emotional unavailability to Andy, she is his mother and presumably loves him. Not only does she arguably have a moral right to be informed about his treatment (a consideration that is usually given even to mothers who have lost custody), she may have the capacity to move closer to her son as he faces his last crisis. If a means could be found to support her and involve her in Andy's care, this would be a great benefit for both of them. Certainly denying her information will further reduce the possibility of reconciliation.

If Andy's mother does not respond to telephone calls, the next step is a brief note urging her to call or visit. If she remains unresponsive, an appeal could be made through her sister, who seems interested in Andy and is not known to be an object of his mother's animosity.

For all practical purposes Andy is an adolescent alone. His aunt-friend, in spite of her obvious good intentions, does not have the authority to take full responsibility for him, and neither does his biological aunt. And though the latter is a relative, she does not seem to have as strong an emotional contact with Andy as his surrogate aunt. Although we are informed of his aunt-friend's history of having housed him for a time, she is not now his custodian, and there is no prospect that she will be. Any adolescent whose personal circumstances are so constrained that he or she must be institutionalized for a year and a half with no feasible plan to return home and no regular contact with a parent or legal guardian must be considered to be alone.

Andy's assent to recognized medical treatment is acceptable on the following important conditions: that he understands that he can ask any questions he wants about his treatment, that efforts will be made to modify it if he finds it too difficult to withstand, and that he can ask that treatment be stopped at any time. Active resistance to an intervention by a gravely ill fifteen-year-old should not, and presumably would not, be met by force.

In order to best assure that Andy understands all this, some conversation in which these matters are raised probably needs to take place. Written consent is a formality that is too often a distraction from the important business of planning a course of therapy. Andy's primary physician should undertake a conversation with him about his best possible future and document when the conversation took place and what was said.

There is no reason that a member of the team caring for Andy, preferably a social worker, could not attempt to engage his mother in a conversation about this decision. It is possible that psychological factors are at work here, such as denial or an overwhelming feeling of helplessness, that could be addressed by a skilled counselor. It is also possible that there is some practical reason that Andy's mother refuses to move to a ground-floor apartment, such as a fear for her personal safety if she lives at street level in a crime-ridden neighborhood. In general, the interests of a young patient include going home if at all possible for however long it is practical, and reasonable efforts should be made to satisfy that interest. This is not an invasion of his mother's "privacy," and is not coercive as described, but is an effort to attend to the interests of the child patient.

The normal fifteen-year-old is generally thought to have achieved the same level of moral development as a typical adult. In addition, many, if not most, children this age who have undergone lengthy courses of treatment acquire some sophistication about them. Andy is said to be "mature beyond his years," as evidenced by the fact that he appears to have addressed the issue in a serious fashion with his caregivers, and to have explored his feelings in therapy. The content of his conversations and other means of expression, without which an assessment cannot be made, is not available to us. Still, the elaborate process in which he actively participated gives one reason to believe that he was capable of making the decision.

The doctors' decision to allow Andy to decide about chemotherapy was appropriate given his age and given that they had good reason to believe he was intellectually and emotionally capable of deciding. If they had a sound basis for granting him decision-making authority, then they are ethically obliged to respect his decision. If they were to override his decision, then some new relevant factor must appear if, for instance, having made his decision, Andy becomes depressed or hostile, or undergoes some other kind of personality change. A gravely ill adolescent may express his regrets and second thoughts in ways that are not clear, even to him. Indications of ambivalence after the crucial decision has been made should be carefully explored in therapy, for while they might be consistent with a normal psychological reaction, they might also suggest that the apparent decision was only a *step* in an incomplete decision-making process.

Along these lines, the staff needs to be aware that respecting Andy's decision could be interpreted by him as a sign of rejection; in other words. he may read their acceptance as a message that they are willing to let him die rather than fight for him. But, respecting his decision does not imply passively accepting it if one thinks that Andy is making the wrong choice. His caregivers should surely present their reservations about his decision and may attempt to dissuade him, though they must do so in a way that avoids coercion or manipulation. In any case, they should make it clear to Andy that he has some time to change his mind, and that they will support him.

Andy may ask for the assistance of anyone he wishes to help him make decisions, including his biological aunt or aunt-friend. But it would be artificial and inadequate to limit their role to isolated occasions when specific decisions must be made. They may be encouraged, for example, to attend regular meetings with him and his caregivers to assess his condition and his needs, both medical and psychosocial, and should be encouraged to have sustained contact with Andy – so long as this is acceptable to him, of course.

The hospital staff is a group of devoted professionals composed of caring individuals, but they are not his family. Nor is a so-called surrogate family a family unless they have assumed that role with full understanding of its implications. These implications include an attachment so powerful that no reciprocity is expected. The familial relationship is one that, in the final analysis, must be characterized in terms of sacrifice rather than contract. (Are they prepared to take Andy home with them and take care of him in or out of the hospital? Are they prepared to assume financial responsibility for him? Are they prepared to suffer so that he might benefit, however modestly?) Nor has any legal arrangement, such as adoption, taken place or been proposed in this instance. It is important to be clear about the roles that have in fact been assumed, so as to avoid confusion later.

However, the hospital staff does seem to have become a surrogate family for Andy. As a surrogate family they may be affectionate and caring, but the staff does not have the structure of obligation that is definitive of actual families. Surrogate families are in an odd position, morally speaking, for they do not have the rights that are accorded actual families, such as the right to make medical decisions for Andy if he should lose capacity. But to the extent that the staff has allowed Andy to feel that they are a kind of family to him, they do acquire some measure of moral responsibility toward him, though not to the degree of actual families. For example, if staff members have allowed Andy to project his normal needs for family-like intimacies and relationships upon them (and it would perhaps be cruel of them not to allow a young person in Andy's position to be so engaged with them), then they should not simply disengage from him when, say, their rotation on the unit has ended. For Andy's sake, they should at least put closure on the relationship, making it clear that although they will not see him on the unit every day, they still care about him and are concerned about his illness.

COMMENTARY BY KENNETH SCHONBERG

Should effort have been made by Andy's providers to inform his mother about his ongoing treatment? Our medical team would not undertake the long-term treatment of a fifteen-year-old without a diligent effort to involve a responsible adult in treatment planning and progress. In this instance, until otherwise determined, the adult legally responsible for Andy would have been his mother. Every effort should have been made to keep her informed about his ongoing treatment and to involve her in decisions regarding that treatment.

Should Andy have been asked for consent, or was his assent to his day-to-day treatment sufficient? We would not proceed with treatment of a competent fifteen-year-old without his agreement. Certainly we would not proceed without the agreement of a fifteen-year-old who was "mature beyond his years." Beyond any ethical and legal considerations would be the practical difficulties in treating a fifteen-year-old against his will. The issue of *consent* versus *assent* would be of little importance. For those procedures of such magnitude that they would require a parental (or adult) signature confirming informed consent (in the main for the protection of the institution – not the patient), we would simultaneously seek the signature of the adolescent. For the vast majority of day-to-day treatments, which do not traditionally warrant obtaining a signed consent, the assent of the family and the youth would be sufficient.

Should Andy's providers have intervened when the mother refused to move to a ground-floor apartment necessitating continued hospitalization? Absolutely. Such intervention would be motivated by institutional considerations as much, or more so, as considerations for the welfare of the youth. With some frequency we are faced with young people who are hospitalized for the care of a chronic condition, who no longer need care in an acute medical facility, but are unable to be cared for at home. In all such instances we would seek an alternative placement in an intermediate or chronic care facility. Such placements are not always available but we always try to find them. As already noted, a good deal of the motivation for seeking such placements relates to the major financial burden that accrues to the acute care facility when we retain a patient who is no longer in need of acute care. In addition, for the sake of the young man we would wish to find the "least restrictive environment" in which he might receive ongoing care and rehabilitation.

Was Andy competent to make his own health care decisions? Why or why not? The question needs to be restated. Was Andy competent to make this particular health care decision; that is, to refuse further chemotherapy? The vignette also needs to be restated. A refusal to receive chemotherapy during the early stages of the disease might very likely have resulted in an earlier demise. However, it is unlikely that we would be unable to manage pain adequately in a terminally ill patient. In direct response to the question, I believe he was competent to make this decision.

Either the acceptance or refusal of chemotherapy under the circumstances described would be a reasonable alternative for an adult, a mature minor, or even an immature minor. Under different circumstances, where there was still some chance of cure, one might argue against the option to discontinue treatment, but not at the point when further treatment was admittedly palliative. The vignette strongly suggests that Andy was well able to comprehend the implications of continuing or refusing care. He was competent to make this decision.

Did the doctors act appropriately in allowing Andy to make the decision about chemotherapy? Are they now ethically obliged to respect his wishes? Yes to both questions. Faced with two reasonable choices, to continue or discontinue chemotherapy, this young man, now over sixteen years old, had to be involved in the decision. Absent a conflict with an adult who had legal responsibility for his welfare, his decision should be respected. The decision he reached was a reasonable alternative. It might not have concurred with the decision reached by his aunt but it was neither impulsive nor irrational.

What roles can or should his biological aunt and his aunt-friend have in his health care decision making? His biological aunt and his aunt-friend, as well as many other adults who had become significant in his life (hospital personnel), play the role of advisers to this boy's decision-making process. Absent a legal action conferring guardianship to any of these individuals, it would be inappropriate for the medical staff to confer any greater import or authority to their opinions. Over the course of a year and a half hospital personnel would have had ample opportunity to seek judicial intervention and the appointment of a guardian if there were dissatisfaction with the adult role in decision making. It is even likely that presented with the scenario described, including an alcoholic absentee mother, my own medical team would have early on sought direction from the court. However, having elected not to involve the court, we would not on our own confer a binding authority to any of the significant others.

Is Andy an adolescent alone? Andy is more alone than most older adolescents in that he lacks meaningful parental participation in his decision making. He is less alone than others in that he is surrounded by adults concerned about his welfare, including relatives, adult friends, and certainly hospital personnel with whom he has had over a year to establish meaningful relationships. His decisions were not reached alone.

Did the hospital staff become a surrogate family to Andy? If so, what rights and responsibilities does this role confer upon them? In most instances, if there is no sociopathy, long-term patients become a member of the hospital "family." Close, even extremely close relationships almost always evolve with some members of the hospital staff; in particular nurses, social workers, and child life personnel. The responsibilities are not dissimilar to our responsibilities to all patients—that is, to give them the best of care and the best of advice. However, these responsibilities are made more intense by the length of the relationship, the relative absence of significant others, and the seriousness of the issues under consideration.

Under such circumstances no "rights" accrue magically to hospital personnel, but rather, may be conferred by the adolescent patient as he might select "surrogate parents" from among those caregivers who evolve a special and personal bond. These delegated rights allow no special privilege in the decision-making process except as they affect the deliberations of the patient.

Case Five: Consent and an Informal Guardian

Commentators: Donna Futterman and Peter Millock

Millie was sixteen when she developed full-blown AIDS. At the time, she was living with her aunt, whom she called "Mommy." Millie's mother had died of tuberculosis several years earlier (she also had AIDS). Millie's father was an alcoholic who only sporadically contacted his daughter. Although as her biological parent Millie's father had the legal right to consent to care, throughout her illness it was impossible to discuss her health care with him.

Millie and her aunt had a very close relationship. When Millie learned she had AIDS she turned to her aunt for support and understanding. Her aunt's home, where she lived for some time, was the only supportive environment she had ever known.

Whenever Millie was admitted to the hospital, her aunt, who shared her last name, signed consent forms for her, even though she was not legally entitled to do so. The aunt did not want to seek legal custody of Millie because she had been reported to child welfare authorities for suspected child abuse of her three young children. None of the reports had been substantiated, but the aunt feared reviving these incidents in court. Some of Millie's health care providers were aware that Millie's aunt signed the consent forms illegally, but also knew that Millie's father was uninvolved in her life.

Millie wanted to stay out of the hospital as long as possible. A home attendant and her aunt became the primary caregivers at her aunt's crowded home. As Millie became sicker, the home became increasingly chaotic and tension began to build. Despite other demands on her time, Millie's aunt was very involved in her care, administering her medication and telling her what she could and could not do. Millie started to refuse to take her medication because she was angry at her aunt for trying to "control" her life. Millie's refusal of medication exacerbated her illness. As Millie became more difficult to deal with, her aunt became emotionally abusive to her. After one nasty argument, her aunt said, "I wish you would die so I could get on with my life." Despite the problems, Millie insisted on staying out of the hospital.

As the pressure built, the home became increasingly dysfunctional. The home attendant saw the aunt punch one of her daughters in the face. The home attendant notified Millie's health care providers because she was concerned about Millie's health.

Shortly after this abuse incident, Millie entered the hospital because she was too sick to remain at home. When she went into a comatose state, the issue of a Do Not Resuscitate (DNR) order was raised by the medical staff. Her providers were fairly sure of her wishes, and thought she would want a DNR order. The staff tried to contact Millie's father, because he was the only one who could sign such an order legally. Despite repeated attempts, they were unable to contact him.

Questions to Consider

- Given the circumstances, what should the hospital staff have done regarding the consent issue?
- Was Millie's aunt the ethically appropriate decision maker for Millie's care? What were the alternatives, if any, and the risks and benefits of these alternatives?
- Did the providers have any obligation to intervene in Millie's home situation? Should they have forcibly moved her to the hospital?
- If the staff reported the aunt to the child welfare agency, Millie might have been removed from the only supportive environment she has ever known. How should this factor have been weighed in the clinic's decision regarding Millie's living situation?
- What could be done to help Millie and her aunt with their anger and frustration?
- What should happen with regards to the DNR order?
- Should doctors be authorized to make unilateral decisions regarding a DNR order for adolescents alone?
- Should Millie's aunt be consulted about the DNR order?
- Had Millie been living with a foster care mother, should this mother have the legal or ethical right to consent to a DNR order?

COMMENTARY BY PETER MILLOCK

This commentary addresses Millie's care in light of New York State law. The law in other states may vary. New York State Public Health Law (PHL) §2504 addresses a minor's ability to consent to medical care. This section of the law clarifies that persons who are eighteen years of age or the parent of a child or who have married may consent for "medical, dental, health and hospital services for himself or herself." PHL §2504 states that a pregnant woman may consent for services relating to prenatal care. Since Millie does not fit into any of these categories, she cannot give legally valid consent under PHL §2504.

Other New York statutes authorize a minor to consent for certain listed procedures or for specified disease treatments. These include PHL §2305 (2) for venereal disease, PHL §3123 for blood donation, Mental Hygiene Law (MHL) §§9.13 (a) and 33.21 for mental illness and MHL §§21.11 and 33.21 for substance abuse. None of these addresses Millie's needs.

The "mature minor" doctrine permits minors who demonstrate sufficient maturity to appreciate the significance and consequences of their actions to consent to medical treatment. Several states have adopted, either by case law or statute, a mature minor doctrine. New York does not acknowledge the capacity of a mature minor to render effective legal consent for medical care. The doctrine was endorsed in dicta in *The Matter of Long Island Jewish Medical Center,* 147 Misc. 2d 724 (Sup. Ct., Queens Co., 1990). In that case, Judge Posner ordered a hospital to perform a blood transfusion on an adolescent who was seven weeks short of eighteen years of age, over the wishes of a parent and of the adolescent. The Court "recommended that the Legislature or the appellate courts take a hard look at the 'mature minor' doctrine and make it either statutory or decisional law in New York State." In a footnote, the Court stated: "If the mature minor doctrine becomes law in New York, this court strongly recommends that a hearing be held first to determine whether the minor is mature or not. If he or she is, then that ends the matter. If the minor is found to be immature, then the hearing should continue without the minor's presence." (147 Misc. 2d 724 at 730).

Even if the mature minor doctrine were recognized in New York, it is unlikely that Millie would be found competent to make her own medical decisions. Millie has not demonstrated the ability to hold a job or to provide for her own needs. She has relied on her mother and on her aunt for financial and emotional support. Millie should not be deemed a mature minor merely because her father is irresponsible and cannot be located.

Public Health Law (PHL) Section 2781 permits persons with a "capacity to consent" to the HIV test and for the release of HIV information. PHL Section 2780 defines capacity to consent as "an individual's ability, determined without regard to such individual's age, to understand and appreciate the nature and consequences of a proposed health care service, treatment or procedure, and to make an informed decision concerning such service, treatment or procedure." The decision as to whether a minor has the capacity to consent to an HIV test or to the release of HIV information is made by the health care provider. However, the law does not extend the capacity to consent to decisions about HIV care and treatment.

Under current New York law, Millie's aunt, in her capacity as a close family member, is not authorized to consent for Millie's care. Nevertheless, health care providers routinely turn to family members for consent for incompetent patients. In 1988 the State Task Force on Life and the Law proposed and then Governor Cuomo filed in each of three legislature sessions a surrogate decision-making bill that established procedures authorizing family members or other persons close to patients who lack decision-making capacity to decide about treatment, in consultation with health care professionals and in accord with specified safeguards. Special procedures are set forth for minors and, significantly, the "emancipated minor patient" is recognized and defined as someone sixteen years of age or older and living independently from his or her parents or guardian. Whether Millie's living situation in her aunt's home can be categorized as independent for the purpose of the surrogate decision-making bill is not clear.

Millie's father, her legal guardian, is the only person authorized under the law to render effective legal consent for Millie's drug therapy, surgical procedures, and other treatments. If Millie's father cannot be located (and it is not clear how vigorous the efforts to find him have been), a hospital may refer the matter to the Department of Social Services for the appointment of the appropriate party to consent for medical care. The Department of Social Services' authority is set forth in Social Services Law (SSL), Article 6. SSL §383-b specifically authorizes local commissioners to consent for the care and treatment of neglected children. Millie could be considered "neglected" because her surviving parent has failed to provide her with housing, clothing, or any financial support. However, this process is slow and costly. It entails a lengthy investigation, preparation of a formal report for the Family Court, and a hearing before the court.

Alternatively, the hospital can directly seek judicial review of the situation. Section 233 of the Family Court Act (FCA) permits the court to issue a suitable order for any child within its jurisdiction when the child is "in need of medical, surgical, therapeutic, or hospital care." The Court has relied on this statute to order foot surgery for a minor, notwithstanding her father's objection. (*In Re Rotkowitz,* 175 Misc. 498 [Dom. Rel. Ct. of the City of New York, Children's Ct., Kings Co. 1941]). Hospitals may also seek to have hospital staff or others appointed as guardians for purposes of consenting to surgery under FCA §1012. In one such case, the chief executive officer of Misericordia Hospital Center sought to have himself appointed guardian *ad litem* for a child with spina bifida who needed surgery for which her parents refused to consent. (*In Re Cicero,* 101 Misc. 2d. 699 [Sup. Ct., Sp. Term Bronx Co. 1979].) The court, relying on FCA §1012 and its general equity jurisdiction to act as *parens patriae,* appointed a guardian. The Court justified its appointment by noting that the infant's physical condition was in imminent danger of being impaired and the child had a reasonable chance, with available treatment, of living a useful, fulfilled life.

Millie's aunt may be the appropriate decision maker for Millie because she is the adult most interested in her well-being. However, the hospital staff is not in a position to determine what her role should be. Medical and health-related staff in a facility have no authority, time, or expertise to determine who is best suited to render consent for a minor patient. This case, in which Millie's aunt had a history of reported child abuse, underscores this point. The medical staff might never have known this information, which is critical to an assessment of who should consent for the care of a minor.

SSL Section 413 lists personnel who are required to report suspected child abuse or maltreatment. Physicians, registered nurses, and certain other named hospital personnel must report. Section 414 clearly states that anyone else may report abuse to the registry.

Given the predictable worsening situation in Millie's home, hospital personnel who have been informed of the abusive situation should inform the Department of

Social Services. However, the hospital should not and legally cannot insist on Millie's move to the hospital based solely on nonmedical considerations. Such a recommendation involves nonmedical factors, which cannot be adequately evaluated by hospital personnel. The child welfare agency should review the situation and make the determination based on all the facts, including the presence or absence of a supportive environment. Millie and her aunt may be eligible for respite programs. Community-based AIDS support groups may have volunteers who could assist with housekeeping, transportation, day care, or other problem areas. In addition, if Millie's aunt qualified as a foster parent, funding would be available through the foster care stipend to ease the living situation.

PHL Article 29-B authorizes DNR orders in certain cases. PHL §2967 permits DNR orders when a minor's parent or legal guardian consents and when the consent of a minor with capacity is obtained, provided there is a written determination by a physician and a concurrence by a second physician. If Millie's father cannot be contacted and does not sign a DNR consent, no legally acceptable DNR order can be issued.

Adult patients without capacity and without a surrogate can be the subject of a DNR order under PHL §2966. A DNR order can be issued based on an attending physician's determination that resuscitation is medically futile and a confirmation of such by a second physician. As Millie is not an adult, this provision does not help her.

The legislature may wish to consider whether minors without parents or legal guardians should be afforded the same treatment in law as afforded to adults, provided the minor desires the DNR order. A determination by two physicians and a fully informed adolescent may be a reasonable alternative to the cumbersome court procedures needed to appoint a guardian. A legislative amendment for minors that tracks adult DNR procedures might be preferable to an amendment authorizing one extended family member to consent to a DNR for a minor based solely on the fact that the minor lived in the home of the extended family member, as does Millie. The minor's situation in a home could vary widely from case to case.

The proposed surrogate decision-making bill permits emancipated minors to make decisions about life-sustaining treatment provided an attending physician and an ethics review committee approve. However, the bill does not address the need for surrogates for mature minors. The list of potential surrogates in the bill is appropriate for adults only (e.g., a spouse or son/daughter). Millie's aunt would not be permitted to act as a surrogate even if the bill were enacted.

The question of whether Millie's aunt should be consulted with respect to DNR is complex. The DNR law does not require consultation with relatives. A case-by-case review might be conducted to evaluate numerous issues that bear on the appropriateness of her aunt as a party to be consulted. These issues include the length of time Millie lived with her aunt, the nature of the relationship, the existence of other relationships with relatives, and any conflict of interest between the aunt and Millie (e.g., the possibility of inheritance from the minor). This case-by-case review to establish whether Millie's aunt has an ethical right to be consulted for a DNR order parallels the existing judicial process for guardianship and the Department of Social Services investigative process for a determination of neglected children. Therefore, it may afford no additional benefits to Millie because it too requires time and expense and does not result in a determination of a legally responsible party.

If Millie had been in foster care, the foster care mother or father is not afforded a legal right to consent to a DNR order. Amendments to the DNR law to confer legal rights on foster parents may not be appropriate. Foster parents care for minors for varying lengths of time and with varying levels of attachment. Many foster parents have numerous children. Further, foster parents have a conflict of interest in dealing with the loss of a child because payment for the child from the Department of Social Services will cease when the child dies. Although foster care parents should be afforded the opportunity to discuss a DNR decision with the child and with authorities, the status as foster parents should not, in and of itself, permit the foster parent to execute a DNR.

COMMENTARY BY DONNA FUTTERMAN

The case of Millie, a sixteen-year-old with AIDS, raises many issues that are familiar to clinicians working with HIV-infected youth. In addition to her medical problems, Millie faces significant psychosocial challenges in coping with this disease – in particular, the absence of supportive, functional parents in her life. Her mother died of tuberculosis and AIDS and her father is an absent alcoholic. Millie has found support and a home with an aunt who provides emotional support but lacks legal custody. Millie's life story illustrates the complex and often changing circumstances faced by adolescents who are alone.

Millie should be empowered to be able to consent to and refuse treatments given her age, presumed competence, and the lack of accessible legal adult guardians. However, for a youth faced with such a serious and ongoing medical crisis, it is especially important to have a supportive adult involved in decision making and care. This need will certainly intensify as Millie's clinical condition deteriorates. Millie, in collaboration with her aunt, is certainly the ethically appropriate decision maker. Although we do not know how long they have lived together, the relationship as described is close and supportive and Millie has demonstrated her reliance on her aunt. Her aunt can provide a second voice in decisions about treatment strategies, participation in experimental research, and decisions about the terminal phase of illness. The role of the clinical team is therefore to validate and support that relationship and seek ways to enhance her aunt's role. The clinical care team should seek administrative approval for Millie to provide her own consent. The team should facilitate the involvement of the aunt in the process.

The emotional risk to Millie of reintroducing her father into decision making seems high at this point, but the clinic team should explore with Millie her desires for reconciling her relationship with her father and attempt to facilitate this if Millie wants. Millie (if she is a competent sixteen-year-old) may be eligible to be emancipated from her father, but the emancipation process should not undermine Millie's supportive relationship with her aunt by overemphasizing her independence.

I would explore with the child welfare agency whether her aunt's history of prior abuse reports is truly a barrier to her seeking custody of Millie. If it were a barrier to custody, then perhaps if Millie were competent, her becoming an emancipated minor would be a good idea. If Millie's clinical condition were extremely debilitated or worsening, I would probably treat Millie as functionally able to make her own decisions with input from her aunt.

As Millie's disease progresses, the difficulties and tensions described could occur in any family constellation, even if Millie's aunt were her mother. The lack of a custodial relationship should in no way minimize the role of the clinical team in facilitating the relationship between Millie and her aunt. As Millie's condition worsens, tensions are expected to rise and anger is often directed at those who are closest. This brings up the importance of respite care and the use of a short-term hospitalization to give the aunt and her family a break. This would lessen tensions and give her more time with her own children and would take Millie away from the scene of tension. This might also allow Millie to make treatment decisions on her own and not just in opposition or reaction to her aunt. The clinic team should assertively encourage but not force Millie to be hospitalized for a short period of time and reassure her about their intent to discharge her home quickly. Millie should be provided with counseling that allows her to vent her anger and fears regarding her worsening clinical condition and lack of parental support. Family counseling with the aunt should be offered. Ultimately, Millie's anger may not be resolved. The clinic team and Millie's family will need to adjust to bearing the brunt of this anger without rejecting her.

The clinic team should consider a home visit to make an on-site assessment and better appreciate the conditions in which the family lives. The size, condition, and room arrangement in the apartment (in particular, where Millie's sick room is located) may be major contributors to the tension. If the housing is clearly inadequate, perhaps this could be addressed by an AIDS service agency with a new apartment. At this visit, they should also explore with the aunt the problems that she sees and attempt to help her choose less physical ways of expressing her tensions in an effort to avert further escalation. Explain that Millie's worsening condition is felt by all family members and that an important way to address these tensions is to verbalize what is happening to Millie and explore the fears and imaginings of her own children. Do the children explicitly know what is going on, and are they acting out the tensions and/or family secrets? Explore with the aunt options for allowing the family to address their fears and find other outlets for their tensions.

At this point, a child welfare agency referral seems premature. The aunt should not be threatened with loss of her own kids because she has extended help to Millie, nor should she be made to feel that she has to choose between her family and Millie. However, the aunt should be informed that if her treatment of the children continues or escalates to become more physically abusive, a child abuse report would be mandated. Seeking out assistance from volunteer organizations that could provide some assistance with her kids and provide the aunt with some respite might also help her regain her emotional strength.

The clinic team has already taken an important step because they are aware of Millie's wishes not to be resuscitated. Although Millie might not be able to legally sign a living will, it is important for the clinical team to elicit and document Millie's choices and the fact that she understood the issues in the decision. (It is not clear in this case what is meant by the clinic team being "fairly sure" of her wishes and a prior explicit discussion with documentation would be important.) Her wish not to be resuscitated, although awesome, is mature and realistic given the stage of her advanced AIDS. Although Millie might not be technically able to finalize this choice, her wishes should be respected. I am not sure that the clinic team should seek out her father, since his previous lack of contact has demonstrated his disinterest and his decisions at this point might be in strong contradiction to Millie's wishes and medical reality. In this case, to legitimize a DNR order, the clinic team should seek approval for this decision according to hospital policy (e.g., convene a departmental, ethics, administrative or legal meeting of people who are not on the provider team). If her wishes were not known and the clinical team felt that a resuscitation would be medically futile (i.e., not prolong her life), they should also follow this approach. Clinical providers should not unilaterally make these decisions but should involve interested family members. If the patient is unable to make the decision, the clinicians should consult and seek approval from hospital personnel who are knowledgeable about adolescent clinical/legal/ethical issues but are not directly involved in patient's care. Obviously, the clinical team/physician will have the most insight into the case, but this decision should not unilaterally rest with them because their involvement in the case might cause them to miss key issues.

Millie's aunt should also have input into this decision, as her familial and emotional ties to Millie may give her additional insight. In any case she should know of and understand the clinical decision and should be allowed to offer input and/or concur with the decision. As Millie's condition becomes terminal, participation in decision making is an extremely important aspect of coming to terms with her niece's death.

The issue of foster parents is one in which legal rights lag behind ethical rights. Foster parents have almost no rights to consent, yet those who have longlasting and/or meaningful relationships with their foster children certainly should be considered within the decision-making loop. Being excluded from the final phase, after caring for someone throughout a deteriorating and fatal illness, is unnecessarily cruel if based solely on legal considerations. The act of decision making around the dying process can be an important part of the process of healing and coming to resolution after the death of a loved one. Given the enormous commitment and challenges faced by those who choose to care for nonbiological children, especially those with a fatal illness, every effort should be made to maintain that relationship in the terminal phase of illness.

Case Six: Does "Nonjudgmental" Care Include Prescribing Sex Hormones?

Commentators: Andrew M. Boxer and Michael Clatts

Bob is a sixteen-year-old gay male. He regularly visits providers at a publicly funded health clinic that serves gay, lesbian, and transgendered adolescents. Bob lives on his own, is often homeless, but sometimes stays with friends or lovers for extended periods of time. Bob recently found a doctor who has been providing him with injectable female hormones despite his age. A major reason Bob wants hormones is because "johns" will pay more for a male prostitute who looks like a female. He rejects the pill form because he thinks injections will give him a faster reaction.

Bob recently informed the clinic that he is injecting hormones. They have responded by counseling him about the risks of injection and showing him how to clean his needles and syringe and inject the drug into his muscle. The clinic tries to take a nonjudgmental approach to providing health care to young people and is reluctant to tell him to stop using the hormones, although most of the staff agree that he is too young to understand the implications of this practice. The doctor who is providing the hormones is not associated with the clinic and does not seem to be providing Bob with adequate information or education about the effects of injecting the drug. Thinking the hormones will act even faster if he injects more, Bob frequently does not follow the prescribed dosage. In reaction to Bob's case and a number of similar cases, the clinic is considering dispensing sex hormones to young people so that those who want to use them get appropriate counseling and education.

Questions to Consider

- Is the clinic's nonjudgmental approach appropriate in this situation? What are the strengths and weaknesses of such an approach?
- What are the special ethical issues posed by the administration of hormones to the adolescent alone?
- Would it change the analysis of the case if Bob had undergone extensive counseling and decided he still wanted the hormones?
- What factors should the clinic consider in determining a policy for dispensing sex hormones?

COMMENTARY BY ANDREW M. BOXER

Is the clinic's nonjudgmental approach appropriate in this situation? What are the strengths and weaknesses of such an approach? In general, a nonjudgmental approach to the provision of health care is an important aspect of enabling youth to feel comfortable and safe enough to disclose their concerns, fears, health habits, and self-care practices. Indeed, developing a trusting relationship with a health care provider can set the course of a relationship that will allow the provider (or team) to provide the highest standards of care, including the provision of counseling, education, and information across a spectrum of concerns. In such cases the provider/clinic can link youth to other services to enhance care or to address unmet needs. Such an approach can enhance adherence to medical treatment. A nonjudgmental approach means that "we don't make judgments about you as a person based on your health practices, values, attitudes, or other characteristics." However, a nonjudgmental approach does not mean that the clinic cannot make "judgments" and communicate information to their patients on standards of medical care, on health-enhancing and health-damaging behaviors, or on practices that aid in the prevention of disease and illness.

The clinic staff's reluctance to counsel Bob to stop using sex hormones has greatly compromised their ability to provide adequate health care to him. The clinic appears to be withholding information, guidance, and recommendations on the use of a set of drugs that have the potential to cause significant physical harm and increase medical risks for other illnesses. They believe that a refusal to prescribe such hormones will force adolescents to seek them in alternative ways and may pose greater risk than administering the hormones through the clinic. This ambivalence or reluctance to discuss their assessment of this situation with him will probably also alter his perception of the staff in some ways. Bob wants the female hormones to feminize his body to enhance its value as a commodity. Bob informed the clinic that he is injecting sex hormones. The clinic does not appear to discuss this or his prostitution among themselves or with Bob. Their nonjudgmental approach could be useful in opening a dialogue with him about his concerns and need to prostitute, and his wish to enhance his market value to his johns. Such discussion could open the door to a counseling situation where Bob could further discuss his strategies for coping.

The clinic staff's concerns about his use of the hormones, if communicated effectively, could enhance their relationship with him and their commitment to his care and well-being. The clinic staff could tell Bob about the dangers and risks of sex hormones without "telling him to stop" using the hormones, and could thereby empower him with the decision-making capability. They could even support Bob in formulating all the advantages. Providing Bob with education and information on safer needle practices and injecting behavior could also be an important part of the clinic's responsibility in providing him with sex hormones.

In this example the nonjudgmental approach to the provision of adolescent health care has been confounded. The prescription of sex hormones (which carry significant health risks) to enhance economic survival is contrary to ethically sound standards of medical care. There are also legal risks posed by the provision of sex hormones in this particular case; such risks may jeopardize this publicly funded clinic's very existence. If Bob told the clinic that he wanted a prescription for methamphetamine because he discovered that this drug made him feel much clearer and function more effectively in his daily life, should the clinic prescribe this drug based on the fear that he will get the drug on the street if they do not provide it to him?

What are the special ethical issues posed by the administration of hormones to the adolescent alone? The ethical issues posed by the administration of sex hormones include the adolescent's decision-making capacity and his or her ability to make decisions that may carry irreversible effects. Additionally, the adolescent alone may be more likely to seek out the hormones through alternative means. On the other hand, in many ways the ethical issues of administering hormones are no different for the adolescent alone than for other groups of adolescents. The issue is the use of sex hormones for nonmedical problems (to enhance economic gain). This includes teens who desire to take such hormones for enhanced athletic prowess, as well as those who want to take sex hormones because of gender dysphoria.

To consider the first two instances, in which sex hormones are requested for non-medical problems, the potential health risks for long-term and continuous use of hormones would far outweigh any possible advantages and gains. In fact, in such cases there are no known direct benefits to health. The use of sex hormones, both estrogens and anabolic steroids, can potentiate many complex adverse effects, including irreversible ones such as infertility and cardiovascular disease. The long-term and continuous use of estrogens, for example, has been associated with thromboembolic disease, increased risk for elevated blood pressure, as well as glucose and calcium abnormalities. Anabolic steroid use has been associated with edema, with and without congestive heart failure, particularly in patients with histories of preexisting cardiac, renal, or hepatic disease. The administration of sex hormones during or prior to puberty can also detrimentally affect normal growth and development. There are also many unanswered questions regarding the impact of long-term use of sex hormones. It would be contrary to current standards of care to prescribe sex hormones in this case, and it is unethical because of the risks of health damage and the lack of any potential medical benefits. In cases where there are medical conditions requiring the administration of sex hormones, a detailed medical history is requisite, as is close, ongoing medical monitoring and cyclic dosing to lower the risk of adverse effects.

In the case of gender dysphoria the ethical issues for the adolescent alone may be more complex. The term *gender dysphoria* describes a group of individuals who express varying degrees of dissatisfaction with their anatomic gender and the desire to possess the secondary sexual characteristics of the other gender through reassignment surgery or hormone therapy. These individuals report varying levels of psychological distress related to their subjective sense of gender identity, which is discrepant with their anatomical sex. Standards of care have been established for gender dysphoria, although they are premised on adults; these include the provision of counseling or psychotherapy. Most health care providers will not provide sex hormone reassignment therapy to minors. Commonly reported concerns include the fact that adolescence is a time of *identity crisis* (although a defining criteria for gender dysphoria includes establishing the long-term presence of discrepant gender identity/anatomical sex), and teens might not understand that the effects of hormone therapy may be health-damaging or irreversible. Most teens with gender dysphoria cross-dress. One alternative has been to support the adolescent's decision to cross-dress continuously and to encourage the youth to live a life in a way that is congruent with their gender dysphoria as a treatment or precursor to surgical sex reassignment. This procedure requires the adolescent to be able to understand the possible adverse and irreversible effects of such treatment; it also assumes that the adolescent has no preexisting psychopathology that would compromise competence or impair thinking.

Would it change my analysis of the case if Bob had undergone extensive counseling and decided he still wanted the hormones? Regardless of whether Bob had undergone extensive counseling, the prescription of sex hormones would not be ethically justifiable or medically warranted. The provision of counseling to Bob is a critical part of his care; he needs to learn about sex hormones, how they work, the risks that may be incurred, and about safer needle practices. This counseling should occur regardless of whether the clinic dispenses sex hormones. Bob is someone who would obviously benefit greatly from a supportive, nonjudgmental relationship with a caring adult who is not interested in him as a commodity.

What factors should the clinic consider in determining a policy for dispensing sex hormones? The clinic needs to determine if the benefits of dispensing hormones are greater than the risks; whether adolescents who are denied sex hormones from a medical provider are at greater risk in seeking the drugs on the streets than they would be if they were prescribed such drugs in a clinic. In addition, the clinic needs to consider the legal as well as medical risks for dispensing hormones. The purposes for which adolescents request sex hormones is a critical factor in determining a policy for dispensing them. Dispensing sex hormones also sanctions them. The agency may wish to consider alternatives to prescribing sex hormones. This includes creating a supportive environment for the provision of counseling and education on sex hormones, including education about safer needle use. Such individual counseling could also be supplemented with youth group discussions among teenagers who either use sex hormones or desire to do so. The purposes of such a group would be to provide a safe environment in which adolescents could discuss the risks and benefits of sex hormones; learn more about such risks and benefits from nonjudgmental health care staff; and hear about the experiences and concerns of other youth who have used them.

COMMENTARY BY MICHAEL CLATTS

The circumstances upon which this case is predicated are somewhat specious. It is true that male street youth sometimes take on the persona of a female in order to exploit a particular niche in the street economy. Similarly, female street youth sometimes attempt to "look like boys." In both contexts, this is a situational strategy, one that varies from day to day or even from one part of the day to another. The use of these strategies is not limited to youth who identify as gay, lesbian, or bisexual. Some street youth seek to make more dramatic and permanent changes in their presentation of self, including cross-dressing, the use of particular speech patterns and linguistic markers, and alterations in their body through the use of sex hormones, and in some cases, surgery. Often these changes are also associated with profound changes in the kinds of social relationships that these youth seek to cultivate – changes that are not evidenced by youth who alter their appearance for situational economic purposes. Street youth who change their physiobiological "self" are seeking to make a permanent change in their identity, usually in response to profound internal forces with which they have struggled for many years. One phenomenon should not be mistaken for the other, nor should the latter be trivialized simply as a response to the shifting vagaries and vicissitudes of the street economy.

These concerns notwithstanding, this case study nevertheless raises a number of important ethical issues with which front-line service providers working with street youth are routinely confronted. I have tried to respond to the issues posed by the case study based on my experience with street youth but also in the context of what I know about the social service and health care delivery systems to which street youth have access. That is, I have tried to respond in the context of what I know to be possible in nonabstract, real-world contexts in which street youth live, rather than by what might be the proper ethical response in an ideal world or even in an institutional environment in which both the capacity and the duty to intervene are quite different.

Is the clinic's nonjudgmental approach appropriate in this situation? What are the strengths and weaknesses of such an approach? In my view, the clinic's approach is appropriate. Unfortunately, if Bob does not obtain the hormones from the clinic, he is likely to obtain them elsewhere – either from the street economy or from a doctor who is willing to "look the other way." In either case, he is likely to have to "work" in the street economy in order to obtain the money with which to purchase the hormones, the equipment needed to inject them, and the knowledge of how to do so. His participation in the street economy, like that of street youth in general, is likely to involve the exchange of sex for money or goods – an exchange in which Bob's participation will not be truly voluntary. He will have little or no effective control in terms of risk reduction, and hence will almost certainly be exposed to a host of health risks, including HIV infection.

Whether Bob obtains hormones from an unscrupulous physician or from an even less scrupulous street vendor, the exchange is likely to be predicated upon profit and is unlikely to be a context in which he will be adequately educated about either the risk of injecting hormones or the proper and safe use of the hormones. Moreover, neither context is likely to be one in which he will be helped to make healthy choices about the expression of his sexuality. Inasmuch as the *duty to warn* is of paramount importance in any case in which there is a threat to health, I would argue that if providing Bob with hormones is the best way to ensure that he gets adequate health education and support, then this is the ethically responsible course of action. Indeed, given the fact that these youth are so alienated from health services, I would raise ethical concerns about not doing so, particularly if this would in any way jeopardize the relationship that the clinic had established with him.

What are the special ethical issues posed by the administration of hormones to the adolescent alone? This question is complex. Many street youth like Bob can and do make decisions about their lives that exceed the usual expectations about someone of their chronological age. Certainly, many of these youth are involved in adult behaviors. Thus, in terms of experience (which is the foundation for the capacity to exercise judgment), many of these youth are "older" than their chronological age. On the other hand, the circumstances that characterize these youths' lives often serve to impede or impair emotional and cognitive development. As a result some of these youth are "younger" than their chronological age. Given this kind of dynamic, it is all the more difficult to strike a reasonable balance between the impulse to protect and the very real danger of acting paternalistically. When issues of sexual identity and its proper expression are added to the equation, the picture becomes all the more complicated.

Concern about Bob's chronological age and maturity notwithstanding, the central issue that remains is Bob's right to define himself – however temporary, shortsighted or seemingly immature that articulation (decision) might be by someone else's standards. The fact that Bob has chosen to exceed the appropriate dose suggests that he feels some degree of urgency about this change, a sign that I would take to be reflective of substantial resolve on his part. First and foremost, and certainly with respect to ethical responsibility, I believe that it is the service-provider's obligation to support that resolve. I would add that simply as a practical matter, albeit one with important ethical implications, not supporting his decision is unlikely to prevent his use of hormones and is likely to accomplish little more than alienating him from the clinic (and probably health services in general).

This is, in fact, very common in the experience of street youth, particularly gay, lesbian, bisexual, and transgendered youth who face overwhelming problems in accessing health care, drug treatment, and housing. Alienation from these critical services is placing these youth at exceptional risk for HIV infection and other poor health outcomes – a fact that is readily apparent in the morbidity and mortality patterns of this population. Moreover, the emotional damage and internalized rejection that results when youth are turned away by service providers because of their sexuality is incalculable. In my view, this is the greatest single danger in this situation. Our primary ethical responsibility is to assist Bob in making decisions that will minimize risk to his health and well-being. This does not mean making the decision for him, even if his decision is contrary to our own "better" judgment and that of standard medical practice.

Would it change my analysis of the case if Bob had undergone extensive counseling and decided he still wanted the hormones? If the clinic is going to dispense the hormones, then they have an ethical responsibility to attempt to provide Bob with education about their proper use. I do not think that it is useful to do a lot of second guessing about what Bob will do with this information or whether he has a complete understanding of the implications of injecting hormones. Despite the gratuitous rationalism that pervades much of public health discourse, the simple fact is that few of us make decisions simply on the basis of external facts alone, which ultimately are often only "frequency interpretations" about partial truths, anyway. Consciously or unconsciously, we all weigh potential risks and benefits in the context of a complex and dynamic series of competing needs and goals, both short- and long-term. The clinic has the obligation to provide Bob with as much education and counseling as he is willing to accept and at a pace that he is willing to accept it. However, the provision of hormones (and proper injection equipment) should *not* be predicated upon requiring Bob to undergo extensive education or counseling if such coercion would functionally create a barrier to utilization of services.

What factors should the clinic consider in determining a policy for dispensing sex hormones? Whether the clinic should dispense hormones in general, and whether it should dispense them to Bob in particular, are different questions. I would strongly discourage the development of a "one-size-fits-all" approach to the formulation of service-delivery policy because I do not think such an approach provides adequate flexibility to front-line service providers, particularly those working with street youth. I recognize that, in theory, such policies can help to direct service-delivery practices and to safeguard ethical standards. Particularly in a context in which staff have limited training or are being asked to juggle very complex and potentially serious decisions, such policies can be extremely important. More often, however, such policies are used to mask inequities in power that are rooted in prejudices about class, sex, gender, and race. Structuring the therapeutic process by reference to some kind of agency standard (policy) serves to fit the youth to the "needs" of service policy rather than the service policy to the "needs" of the youth. Such an approach creates barriers to services, exacerbating the messages of failure and blame with which these youth have been inundated and from which they suffer greatly. Minimally, one-size-fits-all policies often result in our failure to really listen to the needs that street youth themselves identify as important – a fact that is unlikely to result in positive health outcomes.

Policies are useful guides, but no matter how well-intended, clearly stated, or carefully nuanced, they should not be used to replace the judgment of a well-trained service provider (outreach worker, nurse, physician, etc.). Hence, staff development and staff support are the keys to providing effective and ethically responsible services to street youth. In framing service-delivery policies, including ethical standards, it is important to recognize that the needs and capacities of different individuals will vary, should be respected, and should be accommodated. Providers should be given guidance, not a rule book, and the decision of whether the clinic should dispense hormones should be made on an individual basis.

Rather than *policy*, I would prefer to approach the question by reference to service-delivery principles that can be used to guide a hierarchy of goals that serve to maximize the protection of health and well-being while minimizing abrogations of personal freedom and responsibility. In my view, the first of these goals is safeguarding a youth's health in whatever way is possible given the resource limitations of the agency and a youth's own willingness and capacity to understand, accept, and respond to intervention. Given what we know about the street youth population, it is reasonable to assume that failing to provide hormones and injection equipment may serve to "force" youth to obtain access to these materials through alternative means. It is very likely, at some point or another, that these alternative means will include obtaining them from the streets. As already described, since it is well-documented that this is a context in which street youth may be forced (by necessity) to use drugs, hormones, and drug injection equipment in an unsafe manner (i.e., drug sharing, needle sharing, contaminated hormones, etc.), the paramount goal of policy should be that of averting a situation in which youth will have no other choice than to depend on the street economy to gain access to hormones and injection equipment – a situation that will pose high risk for HIV infection.

The service-delivery principles just described are consistent with what has become known as the Harm Reduction Model (Strang, Heathcote and Watson 1987; Newcombe and Parry 1988; Buning 1990; Newcombe 1990; Sorge 1991; Springer 1991; Strang and Farrell 1992; Clatts et al. 1996). First developed in England in the mid-1980s as a strategy with which to reduce the harm associated with risk for HIV infection among out-of-treatment IV drug injectors, the Harm Reduction Model has since been extended to a wide number of at-risk population and clinical applications. For the purposes of this discussion, two salient features of the Harm Reduction Model can be identified: First, as a public health strategy, the Harm Reduction Model is predicated upon the recognition that some behavioral outcomes have greater importance than others. Specifically, the Harm Reduction Model prioritizes the prevention of HIV transmission. Second, as a strategy by which to achieve reduction in the transmission of HIV, the Harm Reduction Model is based on the recognition that public health goals must be tailored to the specific needs and real-life capacities of the individuals to whom they are directed. In the context of services to a youth such as Bob, for example, the principal public health goal is one of providing risk-reduction choices, rather than one that seeks to impose a uniform code of behavior or one that uses adherence to a particular code of behavior as a condition for access to services. In the Harm Reduction Model, the task is to provide risk-reduction education and tools that will enable an individual to make the most health-promoting choices possible in a particular place and time. It contrasts with approaches to service delivery that are predicated upon failure, blame, and deviance, particularly so-called *incentive* strategies for behavioral change that rely on coercion, penalty, and criminalization.

References

Buning, E. (1990). The role of harm reduction programmes in curbing the spread of HIV by drug injectors. In J. Strang and G. Stimpson (Eds.), *AIDS and Drug Misuse: The Challenge for Policy and Practice in the 1990s.* London: Routledge.

Clatts, M. C., W. R. Davis, M. Bresnahan, E. Springer, G. Backes, and C. Linwood (1996). The Harm Reduction Model: An alternative approach to AIDS outreach and prevention among street youth in New York City. Forthcoming in *New Public Policies and Programs for the Reduction of Drug-Related Harm.* Toronto: University of Toronto Press.

Newcombe, R. (1990). The reduction of drug-related harm: A conceptual framework for theory, practice and research. Paper presented at the First International Conference on the Reduction of Drug-related Harm, University of Liverpool, Liverpool, England.

Newcombe R., and A. Parry (1988). The Mersey Harm Reduction Model: A strategy for dealing with drug users. Paper presented at the International Conference on Drug Policy Reform, Bethesda, MD.

Sorge, R. (1991). Drug policy in the age of AIDS: The philosophy of "harm reduction." National Alliance of Methadone Advocates Educational Series no. 2, Reprinted from *Health PAC Bulletin, 20* (3), 4–10.

Springer, E. (1991). Effective AIDS prevention with active drug users: The Harm Reduction Model. *Journal of Chemical Dependency Treatment, 4* (2), 141–157.

Strang, J., and M. Farrell (1992). Harm minimization for drug users: When second best may be best first. *British Medical Journal, 304,* 1127–1128.

Strang, J., S. Heathcote, and P. Watson (1987). Habit moderation in injecting drug addicts. *Health Trends, 19* 16–18.

Case Seven: An Adolescent's Decisions about Reproduction and HIV Transmission

Commentators: Francine Cournos and Nancy Dubler

Renee, a seventeen-year-old Haitian female, came to the United States after spending time in a refugee camp, where she was raped at age sixteen. At the camp, she tested HIV positive and, at the same time, learned she was pregnant. Because she was a minor and had no family in the United States, she was placed in foster care.

During her pregnancy Renee's doctors urged her to begin taking zidovudine (AZT), but she was reluctant to do so because she wanted a "pure" baby. She believed that her child would be harmed by the medicine.

Renee never missed appointments with her providers and, aside from the disagreement about AZT, had always adhered to her doctor's recommended treatment. After Renee had been seeing the same health care providers for some time, she told them that she heard voices, including voices telling her to kill her baby. She also told them that she believed voodoo magic was responsible for the voices. After these revelations, her providers became concerned about Renee's mental health.

Renee plans on leaving her foster care home as soon as she is legally allowed to do so. She wants to move into her own apartment and take care of her child.

At her doctor's suggestion, Renee wants to start using the contraceptive Depo-Provera after her baby is born. Her foster care mother is opposed to Renee's sexual activity and has expressed this to Renee's providers. She believes the correct way to deal with Renee's sexual activity is not to give her birth control, but to convince her to be abstinent.

Questions to Consider

- What are the ethical responsibilities of Renee's providers at this point, given her reluctance to take measures that might benefit her child?
- How can Renee's providers best deal with her questionable mental health status?
- What obstacles do cultural issues present in Renee's care? How do these issues affect her providers' assessment of her mental health status?
- How might providers address Renee's intention to care for her child independently once she "ages out" of foster care?

- Is Renee competent to consent to her own health care?
- How can Renee's doctors help her make decisions about birth control, given her foster care mother's strong feelings about it?

COMMENTARY BY FRANCINE COURNOS

The most significant point Renee's case illustrates is the importance of establishing a meaningful dialogue between a patient and her health care providers. The positions taken by both Renee and her foster mother can only be considered starting points for future discussion. What each of them says only represents their first impulses. It is the understanding of what underlies these initial statements that will permit caregivers to work with Renee and her foster mother effectively.

Renee's Reluctance to Take AZT

Renee's initial statement about wanting a "pure baby" needs to be viewed from multiple perspectives: her individual life experience; the events that led to separation from her family and country, and to the rape; Haitian beliefs about purity, illness, and medication; and Renee's current concerns about her HIV status and becoming a mother. Because the baby is a product of rape, some of her concerns about purity might reflect the idea that she holds the rape itself to be a contamination. How traumatized was she by this event? Was the rape considered the likely source of her HIV infection? Has anybody worked with Renee to help her understand and integrate the psychological impact of the traumatic experiences she has lived through? That's where I would begin.

Renee's awareness of the facts concerning AZT will be the easiest area to explore. As background, it will be important to know the extent of Renee's formal education and ability to understand English. Previous information about HIV and AZT may have been presented in a way that confused her, upset her, or left her with distorted ideas. For example, perhaps she was told about percentages and mathematical probabilities, which she failed to comprehend. Or it could be that the informed consent process frightened her about the toxicity of AZT.

Adolescents can have difficulty maintaining a future orientation. Renee could be focused on the immediate implications of taking AZT, not the long-range potential benefits to her baby. Renee must grapple with the strange and frightening task of trying to link the life-affirming state of pregnancy with the reality of a fatal transmissible illness. Does Renee have any symptoms of HIV disease? If not, it may take more effort to persuade her that despite feeling well, she still needs to take a potent medication. Renee may have met other girls who were HIV-infected and who had healthy babies without taking AZT, or who had unhealthy babies despite taking it. Even a single such experience could have a powerful influence on her decision.

Other elements of Renee's thinking are, and will probably remain, totally outside her awareness. Nonetheless, clinicians who are familiar with the importance of unconscious fantasies will be less inclined to take what Renee says at face value. For example, Renee might not have digested the seriousness of her HIV infection, and the idea of a "pure" baby might be linked to her own wish to be *pure,* that is, uninfected. Taking AZT then becomes an unwelcome admission of illness. On the other hand, to the extent that Renee worries about becoming ill and dying, she may fear that no one will be available to take care of her baby. This could encourage the fantasy that it would be best if she and the baby died together, in which case her motivation to ensure the baby's health would be diminished.

If the informed consent process, both its conscious and unconscious elements, is viewed as something that takes place over time with multiple opportunities for discussion, there is a good chance that Renee will change her mind and go along with the AZT, especially since she's a generally cooperative patient. However, if despite all efforts she still refuses the medication, I would not be in favor of obtaining a court order or another form of permission to administer it over Renee's objection for the following reasons:

1. Although the short-term benefits are clear, the long-term risks of taking AZT during pregnancy are unknown. Most babies of HIV-infected mothers will be born uninfected. AZT is a toxic drug that, while it reduces the transmission of HIV from mother to child, could have long-term toxic effects that won't be seen for many years. It is possible that Renee could give birth to a healthier baby without the AZT than with it. (That is, one that has neither been HIV-infected nor exposed to AZT.)
2. Other than in locked involuntary settings, it is extremely difficult to force patients to follow medication regimens to which they are opposed. How will anyone force Renee to take her medicine several times a day, after day over a period of months? Even watching people put medication in their mouths does not guarantee they receive it. They can "cheek" it (hide it in their mouths and spit it out later), or even swallow it and then induce vomiting. These behaviors are commonly observed in psychiatric units when patients are given medications they do not wish to take.
3. In any case, even if Renee refuses AZT now, maybe she will accept it closer to the time of delivery, which can still prove helpful. Other measures could also reduce the risk of vertical transmission of HIV from Renee to her baby, such as persuading Renee to avoid breast feeding.

Renee's Mental Health Status

Renee needs a careful psychiatric evaluation if her questionable mental health status is to be dealt with successfully. This includes an overall assessment of her mood, thinking, intellectual ability, and functioning in daily life. Renee's complaints need to be understood in the context of her cultural background as well. Believing in voodoo, the power of roots, and other forms of magic are common in Haiti.

Hearing voices is aberrant in most cultures. But not everyone who reports hearing them is talking about the same thing. For example, some people will go on to clarify that the voices are inside their own heads, and they know they are not real. A thorough medical evaluation is necessary as well, since metabolic abnormalities, medication side effects, and even HIV itself can sometimes produce psychotic symptoms. In any case, "hearing voices" is not a diagnosis, and no plan to treat her mental health condition can take place without one.

We also need to assess Renee's thoughts about whether she would act on what the voices tell her. People with psychotic symptoms vary considerably in how they respond to command hallucinations. Even if Renee worries about acting on her voices, and even if the voices do not remit either spontaneously or with antipsychotic medication, it is possible to teach her that the voices are really her mind playing tricks on her, and that not responding is the best course. As patients gain a better understanding of psychotic illness, they can learn to maintain an observing ego that views the psychotic symptoms with some objectivity.

Aging Out of Foster Care

Again, although Renee states she plans to leave foster care as soon as she is legally allowed to do so, that may not represent her true position. If she really wanted to leave, she could run away, as so many foster children do. Once Renee has a baby, it will be even easier for her to leave home. She will achieve the status of an emancipated minor, and may be eligible for a variety of government benefits.

Every adolescent who has been abandoned will have conflicted feelings that involve wishes to be independent and desires to be taken care of. This can only be addressed by an ongoing dialogue about the issues. Nor are Renee's only options remaining in foster care or living totally independently. She may be able to find a special program for adolescent women and their children, or one geared to families affected by HIV. A year from now, when she is ready to leave foster care, she may be on a complex regimen for her HIV infection. This could also change her view of her situation.

Renee's Competency to Consent to Her Own Health Care

Even if Renee is currently psychotic, it does not automatically mean she is incompetent. Competence should be narrowly focused on the specific medical decisions Renee is being asked to make. What does she understand about the medical risks and benefits? Are her decisions rational? Are they a reasonable reflection of her values?

I believe the sliding-scale concept of capacity makes sense to clinicians and is intuitively invoked by them. This view of capacity suggests that the greater the benefits and the less the risk, the lower the level of capacity a patient will need to consent to a treatment. Conversely, the less the benefits and the greater the risk, the higher the level of capacity a patient needs for informed consent. So, for example, we demand little capacity when a patient consents to take penicillin for pneumonia, but we require considerably more capacity when a patient consents to a heart transplant. These principles also apply to refusal and were part of my own reasoning with regard to Renee's refusal of AZT.

In summary, although legal and ethical principles provide the crucial framework in which clinicians operate when they seek consent to treatment, in the vast majority of instances, clinicians will resolve dilemmas through negotiations with the patient and family. In most cases, invoking formal procedures should remain the last step after all negotiations have failed.

Will the foster mother accept Renee using the contraceptive Depo-Provera? Again, the foster mother's initial statement of opposition is a starting point. We need to begin by learning more about Renee's relationship with her foster mother. How do they get along in general? What is the foster mother's cultural and religious background, and how does it differ from Renee's? How did Renee get along with her own mother, and where is her mother now? Does Renee think that having the relationship with her new foster mother is disloyal to the biological mother she left behind? Is there a father or a foster father? Are there siblings? This background is essential to negotiating a solution to the disagreement between Renee and her foster mother.

Beyond that, caregivers can point out to the foster mother that Renee can take a contraceptive while they simultaneously work with her to encourage abstinence from sexual activity. The foster mother can be reminded that Renee's pregnancy resulted from a rape, and that Depo-Provera will prevent Renee from getting pregnant again against her will.

If, however, the foster mother maintains her position, taking birth control should be Renee's choice. Seventeen-year-olds outside the foster care system can often make such a choice without parental consent. This is as it should be, since it is unrealistic for parents to control their adolescents' sexual activity, and since pregnancy has its greatest impact on the teenager, not her mother. Renee will also need to understand that Depo-Provera is not enough. She must be encouraged to take responsibility for informing her sexual partners of her HIV status and for using condoms.

COMMENTARY BY NANCY DUBLER

Decisions about how to manage or whether to maintain or terminate a pregnancy are intensely personal. In my personal lexicon of values, such decisions should be informed by a woman's philosophical and religious convictions, an evaluation of her life's plan, her ability and willingness to care for the infant and child in the present and for the future, the wishes of her partner – if her partner will be involved in the rearing of the child – and the advice of her physician or midwife. The consideration of these, and many other factors, should precede the decision to become pregnant, or if the pregnancy is not planned, the decision of whether to terminate. But we all know that this paradigm of planning is not the norm.

Conscious planning and reasoning about pregnancy present a rational ideal. But neither the ideal of the rational plan nor the process of conscious and thoughtful evaluation accompany many, or perhaps most, pregnancies. For many women, a romantic ideal displaces any rational process. Barely formed notions of appropriate natural events or ideas of predestination predispose women to risk pregnancy and to carry to term.

Many women, especially young women, may lack a fully formed personal philosophy governing moral obligations and options. And religion, if relevant to their lives, may reinforce the disinclination to use contraception or consider abortion. For many teenagers the basic physiology of intercourse, pregnancy, and birth may be unclear. For others the desire to love someone, and more importantly, the desire to be loved, encourages bearing a child.

Legislators and courts in this country have made the decision that, largely without regard to age, women can decide how to manage their bodies and pregnancies. Except for certain states that require parental or judicial consent before abortion, use of contraceptives, management of pregnancy, and birth are governed by the individual woman's choices. Renee's choices are supported by the same laws and logic. There do not appear to be any reasons in her case to deny her the protection for her decisions. She is likely no more or less prepared than most of her cohorts.

In addition to personal values, the advice of caregivers should be part of any woman's calculus about her medical care during pregnancy. In this case, Renee's doctors urged her to take AZT. This recommendation could be based on an assessment of her needs, the best interest of the fetus, or both. If her T cell count were under 500, the standard medical protocol would provide AZT for her benefit. But there is a likely second reason growing out of the results of a National Institutes of Health study – AIDS Clinical Trial Treatment Group #076 – of perinatal transmission. The study showed a decrease from 25 percent to 8 percent transmission of HIV to infants when their mothers took AZT in the last trimester and during the birthing process and, when the baby continued to receive AZT after birth. Given the study, despite its limitations, the U.S. Public Health Service and many medical practitioners are recommending that pregnant women who are HIV positive be offered AZT. Renee refused.

The obligation of the obstetrician in this case would be to argue as forcefully as possible for the regimen that she thought most appropriate for the mother and the baby. AZT might be problematic for a woman if it were not yet required for her own health, as premature intervention might lead to resistance that would make the drug less effective for her in the future. AZT is a drug with side effects, and taking it at any time is not a simple matter. There are therefore supportable reasons why a woman might refuse AZT.

Were the data absolutely clear that AZT always prevented transmission of HIV infection and posed no harm or adverse side effects to the pregnant woman, a "nightmare" scenario would emerge, at least for me. Whereas I am committed to supporting a woman's right to control her body and her pregnancy, I am troubled by the irrational use of that right if it results in preventable harm to the fetus at no cost to the mother. Even in this case I would probably opt not to overrule the mother's refusal by force, but I would struggle with the emptiness of a legal doctrine that produced such a troubling and indefensible result. It would be morally unconscionable for any woman to risk the health of her fetus when the proposed intervention posed no danger to her. However, it is, at present, legally difficult to overrule her decision. The need to protect the autonomy of women should permit this harsh rule to remain as law.

Despite the moral and legal complexities that surround a woman's right to control her body and her own pregnancy, the physician's ethical and legal obligation is, as always, to argue as forcefully as possible for the plan she thinks is the best. This process of discussion and deciding should begin with a statement of the risks and benefits to the woman and the fetus of the alternative interventions. This measured presentation is required by the ethical precepts underlying, and the law interpreting, the right of informed consent. The discussion should be followed, however, by the doctor's offering her best advice; the doctrine of informed consent does not require abandoning the patient to solitary decision.

The physician also has the obligation, especially given the youth of her patient, to try and probe into the patient's objections and address her fears. Refusals of care can be generated by fear, lack of trust or confidence in the physician or the health care system, and misunderstanding. Any refusal of what a physician thinks is needed care is troubling. The refusal by a young person who is alone and who has experienced dislocation and violence calls for additional sensitivity and attention. This refusal should indicate the *start* of a discussion, not its end.

One might question whether, in general, Renee has the capacity to provide or to withhold consent. The health care system has accepted her consent for her own care until this point, thus indicating its comfort with her capacity to consent. Contesting her capacity would indicate that a careful assessment of her abilities was triggered only by her refusal – a seemingly inconsistent but arguably defensible policy. As long as a patient agrees with care providers, it is in no one's interest to contest the decision. As soon as the decision contravenes medical advice and the risk of negative consequences looms, there is an ethical responsibility to reexamine the individual mechanisms of deciding in addition to each decision. Uncertainty demands and justifies a more focused examination of capacity.

Many practitioners consider providing contraceptives for sexually active teenagers legally and morally uncontroversial. This attitude prevails despite the objections of some citizens, politicians, legislators, parents, and religious counselors. The combination of federal and state law, in every state, is clear – adolescents have rights under Title 10 of the Family Planning Act and under U.S. Supreme Court decisions to receive contraceptive advice and devices without parental consent and over parental objection.

In this case the objecting adult is the foster care mother. Even assuming that she is loving and caring, which not all foster parents are, she has no legal right to interfere with the youngster's decision to prevent pregnancy. Nor does she have the moral authority to impose her personal sexual and religious values on her foster child. Indeed, most persons would applaud as responsible the decision by a sexually active young woman to use contraceptives. Unless Renee were willing to choose abstinence, which she clearly is not, the withholding of contraceptives would merely put her at risk for a new and unwanted pregnancy. The state, which has official legal custody of Renee, also has no legal, and I would argue no moral, right to interfere with her decision to use contraceptives. Religious fundamentalism aside, there are no good arguments for denying this young woman Depo-Provera.

Depo-Provera is less controversial than alternative long-acting contraceptives such as Norplant. It is relatively time-limited, a few months versus five years. It ends its effectiveness naturally without requiring a physician's intervention. Even if there are side-effects, they will be for a relatively short time. Given the possibility of a youngster changing her mind about her desire to use contraceptives, this particular intervention is time-limited and far more effective than the pill or other contraceptives that require conscious use either daily or before any sexual encounter.

Renee's physicians can and should support Renee in her decisions in any way that she chooses, but one. It is neither morally permissible nor ethically advisable for the physician to lie to the foster mother even if Renee so requests. The justifications for lying are few and do not include the desire to avoid mere discomfort with a parent or foster parent. The analysis might be different if a threat of violence or retribution existed.

Part of the task of treating adolescent patients is providing them with the support they need to navigate discussions with parents and guardians. Duties of confidentiality are owed to these patients, unless they threaten to harm themselves or others. In such cases, whether or not the patient is an adolescent, most caregivers would breach confidentiality to lessen the possibility of harm.

Renee's admission that she hears voices, however, is, as a learned professor of mine once stated, "like the thirteenth ring of the cuckoo clock . . . not only is it wrong in and of itself, but it casts doubt on all that went before."

All of the analysis thus far has been premised on the supposition that Renee is a healthy teenager – or as healthy as one can be who has been uprooted from her home, experienced rape, and been relocated into the home of strangers. The mention of voices requires that we reexamine her decision-making capacity and consider the possibility that mental illness, rather than youthful consideration, is the basis for her choices. The fact that Renee is seventeen does not argue for the necessity for an alternative decider. The fact that she hears voices does.

Many adolescents have the emotional and intellectual capacity and the judgment to make decisions about their own care. Many have no clear alternative decider and are forced by circumstances to rely on their own values and reasons. Like Renee, they are actually or functionally alone and have no adult person who is committed to fostering best interests. For these teens the best solution is a knowledgeable and caring physician or provider who can guide the care plan. But this freedom to decide is based on the premise of developing decisional capacity; mental illness calls that assumption into question. Hearing voices connotes at the least disorientation, and perhaps full blown incapacity, making us question her first decision to refuse AZT as well as her future capacity to care for her infant.

Had she already given birth, were there a child to protect, the admission that voices told her to harm the child would trigger a very close examination of her mental health, a referral to the child protective agency, and perhaps the removal of the child. The child abuse reporting laws require only the "suspicion" of abuse – one need not wait for the harm – to act. The urgency of action might be lessened if Renee was planning to stay in a foster care setting where other adults would be present to monitor her behavior with the infant (although that would present a huge burden for the foster parents). Absent ongoing support, the physician would need to be quite certain that she would not harm the infant before releasing the child to her custody. Further complicating the picture is the fact that the obstetrical service cedes authority after birth to the pediatric service for the care of the child. This information about her "voices" must be passed from one set of care providers, with a history of patient interaction, to a new service, where care providers will be strangers. Clearly the obstetrical service must remain involved and supportive.

Effective monitoring in the foster home would require that the foster mother be told about the voices. Notions of confidentiality would normally preclude breaking confidence. Here fear of harm to the infant would justify the breach. If Renee were to stay in foster care, if her foster mother were aware of the danger, and if she was prepared to work with Renee and her caregivers, maybe, just maybe, a report to the child protective agency would not be required. This scenario, however, places a huge responsibility on the foster mother, whose ability to manage a complex situation is uncertain.

At this point the only justifiable plan of care would be the referral of Renee to a mental health professional for a full work-up and evaluation. If the result of that examination convinced the consultant and the primary care provider that no danger existed to the child, then no further action would be required. Were there lingering questions about the patient's mental stability, then a referral to the child protective agency would be mandatory.

Central to this mental health consult is the nature of Renee's religion and the particular ways in which her religious experience might be felt by and expressed by her. Were the image of killing a child part of the mythology and imagery of voodoo, it might have a very different meaning in an examination of her mental health than if the concept were unknown in her culture. Some knowledge of the cultural and religious context of her belief system is a necessary foundation for any examination of her mental health.

Renee is a battered, abused, and dislocated teenager who may or may not be capable of making decisions about her care and the care of her fetus. In her case, as in the case of so many youngsters, there is no ready alternative person as a decider. If Renee is not capable of deciding about her care, the only alternative the legal system provides is the bureaucratic option of foster care. In most locations, foster care agencies have been unable, in general, to focus on the needs of any particular child. There is no reason to think that this case will be exceptionally well handled. Renee is functionally alone to confront medical decisions about herself and her child.

In cases involving adolescents alone there is only one dependable source of help – the medical care providers. Despite the thoroughgoing attack of the last three decades on paternalistic physician behavior, the care and treatment of the adolescent alone may justify and require a paternalistic approach. However sophisticated and worldly the teen, there is just so much wisdom, experience, and knowledge that the youngster could have amassed by her second decade of life. The physician or care provider should assume that discussion, direction, and support will be needed to arrive at the correct answer for this patient. Is this paternalism? Not in its usual form – dictating and imposing a care plan. Is it morally defensible? Yes, in order to replace the consultation and support that are developmentally appropriate and that a loving and involved family supplies.

Renee's case is complicated but common. Pregnant teenagers abound; many have encountered violence and abuse in their past. Many are functionally alone and have only the physicians and care teams on whom to depend. These providers must protect the rights of the young woman to make decisions about her body and to have her confidences protected. They must be comfortable that she has, in general, the capacity to make decisions about her health care. If her capacity is questioned they must be able to resolve doubts about her ability or mental health and be prepared to act if she is in danger of harming herself or another.

Despite a general queasiness about providing advice and direction, the absence of alternative involved adults leaves only the physician to act. Without this support the youngster is truly alone, abandoned yet again in the struggle with life's complexities.

Case Eight: Family and Culture in HIV Care for a Latino Adolescent

Commentator: Luis H. Zayas

Victor, a Latino gay-identified sixteen-year-old, ran away from home when two men he met in his village offered to take him to the city. Victor had been living with his mother and her boyfriend, both substance abusers. Initially, the two men let Victor stay with them, gave him money, and took him to expensive restaurants. Several months after he arrived in the city, his relationship with the two men ended, and he found himself homeless. Although he had an aunt and a grandmother in the same city, they were neither willing nor able to take responsibility for him.

Neither Victor's aunt nor his grandmother speak English. Both are aware that Victor is HIV-infected and gay, but they have only spoken to Victor about these issues on one or two occasions. They are uncomfortable talking about his homosexuality and his HIV status with him or with anyone else. Victor's aunt was initially reluctant to participate in Victor's health care because she could not understand "why he did this to himself." She believed he was being punished for his homosexuality. Nevertheless, Victor's aunt took him to an adolescent health clinic out of concern about his health. After several visits to the health clinic with Victor, his aunt felt overwhelmed by the type of care his illness might eventually require. Language presented an additional barrier for his aunt because when they visited his health care providers, Victor had to translate for her. Over time, his aunt stopped accompanying Victor to the clinic.

After getting permission from Victor, clinic staff contacted his mother, who said she could not take care of him because she was entering a drug rehabilitation program. She also said she was willing to relinquish responsibility for him and wanted no part in his health care decision making. She told one staff member that "he is old enough to take care of himself – he always has been on his own."

Clinic staff have considered involving the child welfare agency in Victor's case because he is a minor. Victor has told them that if "the authorities" try to return him home or put him in foster care he will run away and no one will ever see him again.

Aside from his threat to run away, clinic staff find Victor mature, responsible, and fairly in touch with his feelings and his situation. He seems to understand the implications of being HIV-infected, and tells his providers that he practices safe sex.

Victor moves from place to place, although he is resourceful enough to avoid sleeping on the street. Sometimes he stays with his grandmother or aunt, other

239

times with friends. Victor keeps his medical appointments, and has come to rely on the clinic staff for support and friendship.

Questions to Consider

- What, if any steps, should Victor's providers take to increase his family's participation in his health care?
- How can clinic staff deal with the cultural and language barriers faced by Victor's aunt and grandmother?
- How should the trusting relationship between Victor and the clinic staff be used by the staff to best help Victor during the course of his illness?
- Do the clinic staff have an ethical obligation to involve the child welfare agency in Victor's care? Why or why not?
- Is Victor competent to make his own health care decisions? How can this be determined?

COMMENTARY

The information available on Victor raises as many questions as it answers. The first question is: what do we know about Victor's family history? There is considerable ambiguity about this in the case description, yet this knowledge would be quite valuable to clinicians and advocates for Victor. His mother's substance abuse may have been one of the stigmas Victor carried with him in his extended family. How other members of the family associated him with his mother's behavior would affect the kind of support or lack of it that he may have grown up with, and whether there were alternative sources of nurturance for him. How many siblings did he have? What role did he play with them? Often, Hispanic families parentify the oldest child in a culturally normative way; youngest children may become the responsibility of older siblings. What was Victor's place in this family?

Victor's aunt and grandmother view homosexuality in negative terms, overshadowing their filial relationship. But to their credit, aunt and grandmother have tried and continue to be connected to Victor. As a family therapist, I would urge working with the aunt and grandmother within the context of their home. Developing an alliance with them is essential. My sense is that discussing homosexuality and HIV infection with Victor is not only painful but embarrassing to them, particularly in light of the strong role boundaries that exist in traditional Hispanic families. I would not urge the discussion with the aunt and grandmother to include Victor. First, I would gain Victor's trust and his consent to act as an advocate for him with his aunt and grandmother, assuring him that he has a major role in this, that he can say no to the plan, and that we will go over what I can and cannot cover with his aunt and grandmother. The purpose of this approach would be to avoid forcing aunt and grandmother to have to confront Victor and feel threatened by the potential breach in the boundaries that they may be operating by that clearly distinguishes what kinds of issues can be discussed between adults and children in Hispanic families. Thus, I would be operating within a cultural framework that both Victor and his family could understand. Although not including Victor initially may be contrary to our emphasis on integrating the adolescent in his or her health care, it does not exclude Victor or overshadow what input he can have on his care. It is also a means to the goal of having Victor take more control of his own care.

I would make home visits to meet with the aunt and grandmother. Since Spanish is the dominant language, I would meet with them myself or closely supervise a skilled native Spanish-speaking caseworker who could handle sensitively the cultural values in the encounter as well as the issue of the family's reaction to homosexuality and HIV infection. Taking into account the aunt's obvious initial willingness to help Victor, these sessions would help gain their trust and offer opportunities to answer questions and eliminate stereotypes and misunderstandings about homosexuality and HIV infection in a nonthreatening forum in which the aunt and grandmother's relationship with Victor or the family roles and hierarchy are not compromised.

This approach would also serve as a conduit to repairing their relationship with Victor and connecting them to the health providers. The clinic must be prepared to meet Victor's family more than halfway, such as providing a Spanish-speaking physician to oversee Victor's health care. The physician will have to be sensitive to family and cultural dynamics, and be ready to include the family's caseworker at any time. If a Spanish-speaking provider is not available, then a *trained* translator must be made available. I emphasize trained because of the error commonly committed by clinics serving Hispanics and other non-English-speaking patients when they enlist anyone – from a child in the family to a janitor or fellow patient – to translate. The clinic and the health care system must be prepared to make this kind of commitment. Again based on what we have seen of the aunt's willingness to help Victor until it takes too much effort, I would urge the clinic to try increasing the family's participation in Victor's health care by providing transportation, adjusting appointments to meet the family's own schedule, and using other means to facilitate their participation (e.g., providing child care on site in case the aunt has small children who must accompany her). Both the aunt and the grandmother have not totally given up on Victor, judging by their willingness to have him stay with them occasionally. It suggests to me that the stigma of homosexuality and HIV infection can be overcome with this family. Emphasizing their solidarity and past willingness to help Victor would be an essential intervention.

This leads me to the fact that Victor's mother has relinquished responsibility for him. Child welfare agencies often have very limited resources for dealing with HIV-infected homosexual teens – resources that are often unacceptable to adolescents who are used to living on their own and making their own decisions. Therefore, I would not contact the agency. Although we may have an ethical or legal commitment, a creative solution could be fashioned to meet the "letter of the law," so to speak. My emphasis on family solidarity and support would lead me to create an arrangement whereby the aunt and grandmother might assume some type of guardianship role with Victor that would give him considerable freedom to manage affairs for himself. This would require, however, commitment by Victor, the family, and the clinic. Since Victor seems to derive considerable support and nurturance from the clinic and its staff, he could be assisted in his decision making, which would then be followed by some discussion with his aunt and grandmother so that they are informed, at the very least. Viewing the clinic's willingness to support them, the aunt and grandmother would be likely to assume such a responsibility, which would not be an undue burden. Because Victor moves from place to place, one part of this agreement is that he should inform them of his whereabouts at any given time and that the aunt and grandmother accept this without intrusion. At a nominal level, the family might be designated as proxies for Victor as his health deteriorates. I am hopeful that such an arrangement might lead them to work more closely.

Victor's threat to run away when the child welfare agency is mentioned should be taken very seriously. More than just a threat of running away and disappearing, his comments lead me to be highly concerned with the potential for suicide. Feeling desperately alone and beleaguered may lead Victor to taking his life. Because of the stigma attached to homosexuality in our culture, gay adolescents are subject to family rejection, ridicule by peers and others, and exclusion. Combined with their developmental confusion about their sexual orientation, depression and suicidal ideation or attempts are common in their biographies.

With a guardianship arrangement, Victor, his family, and the staff could perhaps obtain some emancipated minor status that would permit Victor to get his own public assistance and Medicaid. Even if it must be obtained through the family, arrangements could be made for Victor to manage these himself.

Victor seems to be making competent health care decisions. He keeps his appointments and practices safe sex, which is more than can be said about many adults we see. His relationship to the staff seems strong, and may be used as a foundation for engaging him with other institutions and community-based agencies. His clinicians, both biomedical and psychosocial, should recognize these strengths and help Victor solidify them. These strengths may also need to be pointed out to the aunt and grandmother, so that they too see Victor as a competent adolescent.

Case Nine: Consent By Antisocial Adolescents: Defining the "Least Bad" Option

Commentator: Michael Pawel

Since he was discharged from a residential treatment center six years ago, Kevin has been living in a foster care group home. Now seventeen, he has lived in a variety of psychiatric hospital and foster care settings continuously since he was abandoned by his aunt at age five. His mother is believed to have died of AIDS. Kevin's only known relatives are his aunt and his father. His aunt lives with her own young children, telephones Kevin occasionally, and visited him once on Thanksgiving. His father is incarcerated for an extended period for dealing illegal drugs; he telephones Kevin from prison about once a month.

Kevin has been diagnosed with a variety of mental illnesses, including attention deficit hyperactivity disorder, personality disorders, and conduct disorder. He has demonstrated major problems in impulse control and social judgment. He fights frequently and flies into tantrums at the least provocation. He walks out of classrooms when he cannot answer questions and feels "picked on." He smashes his own and other people's belongings when prevented from making a phone call or getting a snack. His intelligence is in the dull to normal range; he reads at a fourth-grade level.

The facility psychiatrist prescribed medications for Kevin, in an effort to control his distractibility, hyperactivity, and impulsive aggressiveness. Initially, Kevin refused to take any medication, and was unwilling to discuss possible benefits or side effects. He says that he is not "retarded" or "mental" and is not a "junkie."

Kevin became involved in an assault sufficiently dangerous that the victim wants to press charges. A staff member reminded Kevin of his refusal to take medication, and suggested that if he would agree to take medication, this action against him might be dropped.

Kevin agreed to take medication, began to do so, and appeared to staff to be making a better adjustment. However, when his father telephoned and learned that Kevin was taking medication, he demanded of both Kevin and the social worker that the medication be stopped because he "will not have his son on drugs."

Despite his father's disapproval, Kevin said he wanted to continue the medication, which he believed was helping him. When his father telephoned again, Kevin refused to speak to him. The father was enraged and told the social worker, "It is crazy to let children make decisions like that. I'm his father. Put him on the phone."

Questions to Consider

- Should Kevin's refusal stand unchallenged? If not, who else can or should be involved in the risk–benefit decision-making process?
- Kevin's father's parental rights have not been terminated, so he has standing as legal guardian to consent to (or refuse) treatment for Kevin. What is the appropriate response to his refusal of treatment?

COMMENTARY

Apart from its practical urgency, what makes the issue of consent to treatment by adolescents so interesting is its complexity – which is to say that it offers no clear answers. This suggests that from one, perhaps perverse, point of view, the most fascinating aspect of the consent problem is its application to behaviorally disruptive teenagers. Kevin is one such adolescent, and his behavior is typical of this group. In considering this group, all the already unsatisfactory options begin to appear even worse. This case, which presents a small but representative sample of the issues that arise routinely in the care and treatment of seriously disturbed adolescents, suggests some of the complexity and ambiguity that arise when theoretical pronouncements about autonomy and competence are juxtaposed with real-life problems.

The landmark book *Beyond the Best Interests of the Child* (Goldstein, Freud, and Solnif 1973) proposed that one aspect of surrogate decision making, assignment of child custody, would actually be most benevolent if implemented not as a Quixotic quest for perfection ("the best interest"), but as a rapid assessment of the much less grandiose "least detrimental available option." When it comes to consent for treatment by teenagers, particularly for those who are actively antisocial or severely psychiatrically impaired, the realities of the situation argue for the acceptance of a parallel standard, that is, for the least detrimental available consent mechanism. This rather deflated conclusion arises from the observation that, in fact, none of the options is really very good.

Consider the possibilities: First, of course, is the option of full autonomy – consent by the adolescent him- or herself. Without reviewing the whole argument about age of consent, it suffices to say that defining such an age proceeds from the obvious differences in cognition between neonates and "mature" adults, and the equally obvious assumption that the transformation from the former to the latter occurs slowly and unevenly, in a pattern and to a degree that is variable from one person to another, over a fairly long period of time. If this complex developmental process is grossly oversimplified into a beginning, a middle, and an end, adolescence is the middle, and therefore, the most confusing stage.

There is substantial variability among all individuals, and certainly among all teenagers, in the extent of their cognitive, emotional, and social, as well as their physical development. The view that antisocial behavior represents a developmental *lag* in some of these areas has been clearly articulated for at least a half century. Most of the serious street crime we dread is infantile behavior by individuals with some physical maturity and access to sophisticated weapons.

The fundamental areas in which antisocial adolescents are developmentally behind the norm are implied by the nature of the behavior that defines them as delinquent. Although they are by no means necessarily lacking in the global entity we refer to as *intelligence,* the overwhelming majority have significant deficits in language, extremely rudimentary resources of general information, and very little ability to abstract (which requires linguistic skills and some knowledge base). This implies, among other things, that their sense of time is very primitive. A promise that is not kept within a few minutes ("now") is considered broken; a person who is absent has left. There is little difference between "not now" and "never," between "yesterday" and "a long time ago." This has profound implications for understanding causality, since both the past – meaning anything more than a few minutes ago – and the future – meaning anything that isn't now – are routinely discounted as irrelevant.

In this context, it is difficult to develop such fundamental emotional traits as basic trust ("Mother will come back soon") or empathy ("Why are you still upset because I hit you this morning?"). If every absence might as well be forever, what distinguishes death from "going upstate"? Why is killing different from sending someone "down south," given that geographical distance is an obscure concept?

Even in an ideally benevolent environment, an individual with this world-view is subject to constant danger and frustration and is likely to be frequently enraged. In the real world, the levels of hatred, fear, and self-destructiveness are often beyond most of our belief. Coupled with minimal coping skills (impulsivity is another name for inability to tolerate frustration and delay; poor social judgment follows from the inability to recognize other people's feelings), and, sometimes, with actual distortions in perception of reality, this set of traits defines an individual almost completely unqualified to exercise competent autonomous judgment about complex choices, or the risks and advantages of competing life decisions.

On the other hand, consideration of other potential decision makers is almost equally disconcerting. Although a bizarre alliance of the politically correct left and the religious right has coalesced around the mythology of a near-sacred entity referred to with reverence as *The Family,* this poorly defined grouping does not, in fact, offer much hope as a candidate for ethically appropriate decision making. We know that abandoned or *thrown-away* children are all too common, and those families who choose to assert their connection with the most poorly functioning children are often more vicious than the ones who simply leave the child alone. Although the fact is often ignored, torture, rape and murder are commonplace family events. In our professional work, we routinely encounter parents and other relatives who frankly or covertly want their children to suffer as much and/or die as soon as possible. This is not surprising because many of the parents of asocial children are the same group at a later (and not necessarily more mature) phase in the life cycle, and they exhibit essentially unchanged rage and incapacity for empathic concern.

If we turn from the biological family to the foster care system, we again find little cause for reassurance. A bureaucracy responsible for tens of thousands of youngsters of all ages cannot possibly make sensitive individualized management decisions. Even if all of its employees were paragons of virtue and conscience (which is unlikely to happen in our lifetimes), a politically sensitive public agency cannot delegate policy-making authority to hundreds or thousands of individual civil servants. Instead, it must make blanket policy decisions – like mandatory HIV testing for children in foster care – that are invariably wrong for many of its charges even when they are adequate for the majority. A child welfare agency policy that was clearly "right" for 90% of its charges would, by definition, still be "wrong" for some children.

Furthermore, no child welfare agency's sole concern is the welfare of the children in its care. Sometimes, every candid bureaucrat will concede, the bureaucracy must think first of its own welfare. The risk–benefit ratio for a commissioner weighing a course that might make 1000 children somewhat more comfortable, but might also, if it failed, cost him his job, would, at best, be very close. In the real world, bureaucratic decisions about health care consent will be made with one eye on the courts and the other on the media. It would be extraordinary for the casework jungle to withhold consent for a treatment that was strongly advocated by the medical caretakers, regardless of the point of view of the child – even though the same bureaucracy might routinely advocate that children with broken bones wait many hours for obviously indicated medical treatment because no one authorized to sign a consent is available – and it is contrary to policy to sign blanket advance consents.

Of course, the ultimate bureaucratic device for evasion of responsibility is resort to the court system, with every possible participant represented by an attorney, and the attorneys' presentations judged by another attorney who has never met any of the participants, according to a set of general rules written and interpreted by other attorneys who could not foresee the particular circumstances of the case. The court system serves the purpose of absolving anyone of personal responsibility, and is thus the dream of those whose ideal is to make no decisions at all and the nightmare of anyone with serious ethical concerns.

Finally, then, we are thrown back on the medical treatment system (or health care providers, themselves) as potential treatment decision makers. This, of course, poses the basic structural problem of the absence of formal checks and balances: the proposer and the decision maker may be the same person. The practical consequences are clear: a blank check for any designated *treator* to do anything that could be called treatment to anyone who could be categorized as an antisocial child. In some situations, particularly in the area of psychiatric intervention, the results could be horrendous.

More insidiously, if less obviously, this would also legitimize withholding of care by providers who, for whatever financial or strategic marketing reasons, do not choose to involve themselves with populations they consider undesirable. Most of us are aware of major medical centers that have made their adolescent care so user-unfriendly for nonprivate patients who cannot readily document parental consent that they have, in practice, eliminated this group from their patient population.

The patient, the family, the caretakers, and the state are all clearly incapable of making competent ethical consent-to-treatment decisions for antisocial adolescents. How, then, should these decisions be made? The present process at its best seems to suggest a reasonable model. Briefly, for most decisions, the provider plus at least one of the other three (preferably the patient) should be sufficient to determine a course of action, while, for the most critical decisions, two of the three non-provider participants might be required.

In general, if a responsible medical provider and the patient him- or herself agree on a course of treatment, that should be sufficient. In the case example of Kevin, decisions about medication management should probably be made in this way if at all possible. Alternatively, the provider might obtain the consent of the family or the state, particularly if it appears that the patient does not demonstrate competent grasp of the severity of the adverse consequences of treatment refusal. For decisions involving substantial risk or cost (in terms of pain or suffering as well as of money), the provider should have the consent of the patient and the family, or the patient and the state, or, at the very least, the family and the state. Decisions regarding reproduction and exposure to life-threatening substances (e.g., alcohol and tobacco), seem to fall into this category, and are generally handled with this dual-consent approach (the state arbitrarily withholds consent for individuals below a certain age).

Numerous objections can be raised to this process. However, it does seem to reasonably meet the requirement suggested at the beginning of this discussion: to define the least detrimental available option. It is offered, therefore, in that spirit, as a basis for further consideration.

References

Goldstein, J., A. Freud, and A. Solnit. (1973) *Beyond the Interests of the Child.* New York: Free Press.

PART III

Ethics Guidelines for Health Care Providers

Ethics Guidelines For Health Care Providers*

Jeffrey Blustein, Nancy Dubler,
and Carol Levine

Introduction

Youth in American society are both romanticized and demonized. With few exceptions, however, they are seen in a family context, struggling for independence, fulfilling their family's hopes and dreams, or bitterly disappointing them. A growing number of young people do not have a supportive and trusting relationship with an adult in a birth, foster, adoptive, or chosen family. Through a variety of circumstances, these young people are literally or functionally *alone.*

Their needs are complex and urgent. For these adolescents, the transition to adulthood is often marked by insecurity, instability, and outright danger. Most have experienced traumatic childhoods that have brought them to adolescence with a host of prior losses. In conventional adult terminology, they are sometimes called *hard to reach* or even *unreachable.* Yet they must not be ignored or abandoned. Although many of their most pressing needs lie outside the health care arena, their contacts with supportive health care providers may offer a rare opportunity to obtain acceptance and support.

These adolescents, like adolescents generally, need both routine and specialized medical care. The HIV/AIDS epidemic has brought a new urgency to care for these young people (American Academy of Pediatrics 1993). Among people in the United States infected with HIV between 1987 to 1991, one of four was younger than 22 (Rosenberg, Biggar and Goedert 1994). Young gay men and young heterosexual women are particularly at risk.

The *adolescent alone* occupies an ambiguous legal status, which can present particularly thorny problems with respect to issues of consent and confidentiality in health care. A variety of legal provisions may justify the provision of care to the adolescent alone based on his or her own consent in specific circumstances. These

* These guidelines are a product of the project *The Adolescent Alone: Decision Making in Health Care in the United States.* They were designed as a self-contained document. Therefore, the guidelines reflect, and in some cases repeat, themes, information, and arguments found elsewhere in this book.

include the emancipated minor and mature minor doctrines, as well as specific state medical consent laws. However, these doctrines are not accepted everywhere, and consent statutes vary from state to state. Moreover, health care providers and institutions interpret the doctrines inconsistently (Holder 1995; Oberman 1996). Even when consistently understood and interpreted, the laws do not address the broad range of ethical issues presented by care of the adolescent alone. These guidelines are intended to help fill that gap.

Ethics guidelines for clinicians are useful in areas where providers encounter complex and ambiguous choices in their contacts with patients, where the law is unclear or inadequate, and where there is no political consensus to support a change in the law. In such cases, clinicians tend to fall back on feelings and intuition, which are not necessarily a reliable guide. Guidelines encourage consistency and contribute to the equitable distribution of medical services. They also help reduce the chance of arbitrariness or bias in decision making. They are *not* rules or regulations, the violation of which may be punished by the state and, in some situations, be the basis for civil lawsuits by private individuals. Rather, they present salient ethical principles and practices that should be considered in individual decision making. Although these guidelines are intended to be flexible and to encourage reflection, they do recommend the outer bounds of permissibility and the inner bounds of ethical requirement.

For the purpose of these guidelines we define adolescence as ages ten to twenty-one. This covers early, middle, and late adolescence, which have significant developmental distinctions. For some youth, particularly those who have had to fend for themselves at an early age, adolescence may begin as early as ten. By age eighteen persons are able to give legally valid consent in all states. In some states the age of majority may be younger than eighteen, if so defined in statute, or if the young person fits into a legal category of "emancipated" or has been deemed a "mature minor" by a court (Holder 1985; N.Y. State Task Force 1992). On the other hand, the developmental maturity that supports independent action may not occur until well past the age of eighteen, making the ethical issues salient at older ages (Holder 1995).

Characteristics of Adolescents Alone

The prevailing legal and medical paradigm is that parents are empowered to make medical decisions for their children because they are assumed to be in the best position to determine the best interests of their child; they know and love the child; and they can interpret medical options in light of their family history and values. Moreover, they have to share the consequences of the decision, which may affect not only one youngster but also siblings and other family members. Parents (through public or private insurance) are also the primary source of payment or eligibility for medical care. For the majority of families, and for the majority of decisions, this paradigm works well enough.

The paradigm, however, has clear limits. First, it is best suited to infants and young children, not adolescents. A second limitation is that adolescents need some medical services for which parental consent or even notification may present serious barriers. The most common examples are treatment for sexually transmitted diseases, reproductive health, and drug and alcohol abuse treatment (Holder 1985; N.Y. State Task Force 1992; Holder 1989; Holmes 1989). Accordingly, state laws, federal statutes, and medical practice have carved out exceptions to parental consent for these sensitive area (English 1992a). More recently, many jurisdictions have added treatment for HIV infection and AIDS (Ad Hoc 1991; English 1995; Futterman, Hein and Kunins 1993; Lindegren et al. 1994).

A third limitation is that the model of parental decision making assumes the presence of at least one parent who has a stable, nurturing, and supportive relationship with the child. Clear-cut cases of abuse or medical neglect have always been an exception to the family paradigm (Holder 1995; English 1992a). Other cases have involved parents whose religious beliefs or preferences for nontraditional medicine brought them into conflict with conventional medical practice.

Beyond these limits, the paradigm itself bears little relationship to reality for a growing number of teenagers. Some are literally alone, because their parents are ill or have died of AIDS or other diseases. By the year 2000 more than 50,000 teenagers (ages thirteen to eighteen) will have lost their mothers, typically single parents, to AIDS in the United States (Michaels and Levine 1992). Although younger children are most often taken in by an extended family member, teenagers are hard to place and frequently move from one temporary residence to another. In most of these informal arrangements, no one has legal guardianship.

Some adolescents are functionally alone, because their parents are suffering the effects of drug use or mental illness. Some are among the estimated two million temporarily or permanently homeless youth who live on city streets and are called runaways, throwaways, or street kids (Mackenzie 1992; English 1991; Ryan and Irwin 1992; National Network of Runaway and Youth Services 1991). Some are among the 440,000 youngsters, perhaps a third of them adolescents, in foster care, where they may have both living birth parents and foster parents but no significant emotional or trusting connection to any of them (Pinkney 1994). (Although these guidelines do not specifically address adolescents in foster care, they can be useful for physicians treating this group of youth.) Some adolescents alone are not estranged from their families but are living apart from them for economic or other reasons.

Some adolescents do not appear to be alone; that is, several adults may claim to represent the young person's interests but have neither legal guardianship nor continuous relationships. The involvement of many adults, none with clear parental authority or responsibility, may create conflict or ambivalence rather than support.

Because of the circumstances that have brought these young people to adolescence without a sustaining adult presence, they may have special strengths as well as vulnerabilities. They may be more self-reliant than other youth, more experienced in finding resources to survive day by day. On the other hand, they may be more mistrustful, of their own peers as well as adults. Although many have the same aspirations as their peers, they may be unable to identify and utilize resources to attain longer-term goals. It is part of normal adolescence to feel immortal (Quadrel, Fischhoff, and Davis 1993), but some adolescents alone have experienced so much emotional and physical trauma and loss that they may feel that their future holds little promise. They are also more likely to engage in risky behavior (Mackenzie 1992; Ryan and Irwin 1992; Quadrel, Fischhoff, and Davis 1993). Risk taking, typical of adolescence, assumes a more ominous meaning when it includes survival sex and street drugs (Mackenzie and Kipke 1992; CDC 1992). Despite their resiliencies, life for many of these adolescents is fearful and fear-ridden.

Youth who are most alienated from adult guidance often have the least access to care (Ad Hoc 1991; National Network of Runaway and Youth Services 1991). They do not have private health insurance of their own. Medicaid is difficult if not impossible to obtain on their own (Cheng and Klein 1995). They will not or cannot use their estranged parents' insurance, even if it technically covers them (Ad Hoc 1991; National Network 1991). Moreover, they typically do not trust health care providers in general or any system that is likely to place limitations on their independence or that is inflexible in its approach. As a result, most medical care is delivered sporadically in hospital emergency rooms or in specialized adolescent clinics. The erratic nature of these contacts makes each one especially important as an opportunity to establish trust and continuity in care.

Basic Principles

There are several basic principles regarding health care for adolescents:

1. Health care providers have a moral obligation to respect each adolescent as a unique person and to support his or her developing autonomy.
2. Health care providers have a moral obligation to promote the well-being of their patients and to minimize harm.
3. Because of the need for beneficent guidance, health care providers should work with adolescents to identify a supportive and responsible adult who will assist them in decision making.
4. Health care providers have a moral obligation to treat adolescents fairly–that is, to avoid discrimination on the basis of economic, social, or familial circumstances, sexual orientation, race or ethnicity, or other personal characteristics.

We will examine these principles in more detail.

Support Adolescents' Developing Autonomy

The ethical principle of respect for persons acknowledges the value of individual self-determination, a value based on the philosophical concept of autonomy. Central to this principle is the notion that individuals are, or have the potential to become, autonomous decision makers who should be free to make their own decisions and who should control their own destinies (Buchanan and Brock 1989). In the medical context, this translates into the right of the patient to determine the course of his or her own medical treatment.

The principle of respect for persons has a special relevance for adolescents. Although among adolescents autonomy may not yet be fully developed, the principle supports those conditions that nurture it (Moreno 1989). As part of normal development adolescents struggle to establish a secure identity, independent of their parents and other adults. (Petersen and Leffert 1995). In this quest they often adopt unconventional styles, behaviors, and attitudes that adults may find foolish, embarrassing, or unnerving. Because of traumatic childhood experiences and current life situations, some adolescents alone may experiment in even more extreme ways than adolescents who have grown up in a secure and loving family environment. Regardless of how they present themselves to health care providers, they should not be stereotyped or treated in a dismissive or demeaning way (Mackenzie 1992).

The right of autonomous persons to make their own decisions undergirds the doctrine of informed consent. An essential aspect of informed consent is the ability to comprehend the information about the benefits and risks of medical treatment (Beauchamp and Childress 1994). This ability is impaired by anxiety and a lack of control (Dorn, Susman, and Fletcher 1995). Health care providers should commit the time and energy necessary to establish a trusting relationship and to communicate effectively with all adolescents so that they can fully understand the choices before them. In the case of adolescents alone, this may require explanations that translate medical language to slang or *street talk,* as well as providing information about basic biological functioning (English 1991; Ryan and Irwin 1992; National Network 1991). The informed consent process should be an educational experience through which a physician provides wise and directive counsel as part of a process of partnered decision making.

Promote the Well-being of Patients and Minimize Harm

The principle of beneficence (Beauchamp and Childress 1994) requires people to promote good and prevent harm for others. It sometimes encompasses, as well, the notion that people must refrain from harming others. Because physicians care for persons who are sick and often limited in significant ways by their illness, physicians have a special obligation to help patients further their important and legitimate interests.

Although the principles of beneficence and respect for persons sometimes conflict, both of them impose a moral obligation to identify and take into account the special vulnerabilities associated with adolescence. Patients generally, not just adolescents, function better in some areas than in others, whether due to cultural background, educational level, medical condition, or experience with the health care system. Some of the vulnerabilities associated with adolescence generally are an excessive concern with body image, undue deference to negative peer pressure, and difficulty in evaluating long-term consequences of actions (Moreno 1989). Age, too, is often a major determinant of the equality of the relationship. Some adult patients may be on relatively equal power relationships with providers in terms of educational level, experience, and self-confidence. When patients are elderly or adolescents, their age tends to put them at a power disadvantage. In the case of adolescents, the power disadvantage is increased because of their ambiguous legal status.

Providers should not exploit these vulnerabilities but should work with patients to find ways of compensating for them. Even more than typical adolescents, adolescents alone need advocates to protect and promote their well-being.

Identify a Supportive and Responsible Adult to Assist Adolescents in Decision Making

Most adults consult with other persons significant in their lives before making weighty medical decisions. Adolescents also need the support of a trusted person. Adolescents alone do not have someone who automatically fills that role, but that does not obviate the provider's responsibility to search, in cooperation with the adolescent, for the best possible outside adviser. Health care providers should explore whether there is a way of involving an adolescent's parent in his or her care that can be beneficial to both the parent and the adolescent. If not, there may be an extended family member, an older sibling, a youth counselor, or community leader. Health care providers should discuss with their patients the qualities young people feel are important in an adult adviser.

Members of the health care team (e.g., social worker, psychologist, chaplain) may also offer valuable assistance and develop special relationships with the adolescent. Even so, they do not substitute for a long-term relationship in a nonmedical context (see guideline 9).

Treat Adolescents Fairly

The principle of justice is frequently the point of reference for discussions of access to health care as a matter of social policy. Justice requires that in comparison to others, people who are situated equally should be treated similarly. More precisely, people who are similar in ethically relevant respects should be treated similarly, and people who differ in ethically significant ways should be treated differently. Thus, the principle of justice forbids discrimination on the basis of such factors as race, sex, and religion, when they are morally irrelevant in a particular context (Beauchamp and Childress 1994).

This discussion does not address the question of whether it is just to treat adolescents in general differently from adults or whether our health care system as a whole is just. It is designed, rather, to address the inequity of some adolescents being treated unfairly in comparison with others of a similar age and capacity. This is a matter of special importance in the treatment of adolescents alone, many of whom are poor, gay or lesbian, or members of minority groups. Justice requires that these factors not be used as a basis for denying or limiting care to these adolescents.

Guidelines

Capacity and Informed Consent

1. Health care providers should assess an adolescent's capacity to consent in light of the specific decision and the young person's developmental characteristics, life situation, and medical history.

As used here, *capacity* refers to the ability to make an ethically valid decision on the basis of relevant information; that is, to recognize the importance of the issue, consider the information in terms of personal preferences and values, and communicate the result of the process in the form of a decision (Arras and Steinbock 1995). Capacity differs from *competency,* which is a legal definition that normally makes a sharp distinction between a person who is *competent* and one who is *incompetent* (Beauchamp and Childress 1994; Cournos et al. 1993). Because we are concerned with the power of adolescents alone to give ethically valid and legally accepted agreements to their medical care, we use *consent* rather than *assent.* The latter term is often used, especially in research, to describe a minor's agreement to proceed when an adult's consent or permission is required (Holder 1985; Committee on Bioethics 1995).

The notion of decision-specific capacity has long been the standard for adults of fluctuating, diminished, or uncertain capacity, to permit them to exercise choice in some areas but not necessarily all. It is based on a balancing of the principle of respect for persons (patient autonomy) and beneficence (promoting welfare) (Figure 1) (Buchanan and Brock 1989).

Adolescents over the age of fourteen, except those with severe mental or developmental deficiencies, have the cognitive abilities necessary for capacity to give ethically valid informed consent (Brock 1989). The determination of an adolescent's capacity to provide informed consent in a specific decision-making context should consider several factors beyond age. Among the factors to be weighed: the adolescent's cognitive skills, moral development, life experiences, strengths and vulnerabilities, and current functioning (Gittler et al. 1990; Sigman and O'Connor 1991).

The idea of decision-specific capacity for adolescents is challenged by those who believe it is too broad and also by those who believe it is too narrow. Ross, for example, argues against health care autonomy for minors under the age of emancipation ("children" in her view) because, she believes, it "places the emphasis on short-term autonomy" instead of giving children a "protected period" in which to develop their potential for self-control and other characteristics that advance life-

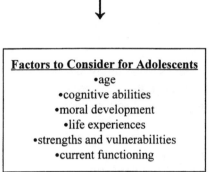

Decision-specific Capacity: The capacity to make health care decisions is relative to the nature and demands of the particular decision-making task.

Factors to Consider for Adolescents
•age
•cognitive abilities
•moral development
•life experiences
•strengths and vulnerabilities
•current functioning

Routine Level of Scrutiny
•well-accepted treatments
•low risk, high benefit
•trivial or reversible consequences of treatment or nontreatment

Heightened Level of Scrutiny
•controversial treatments
•high risk, low or ambiguous benefit
•short- or long-term negative consequences of treatment or nontreatment

Figure 1. Decision-making capacity.

long autonomy. In her view, parents' interests in "raising a family according to their own vision of the good life" extend to overriding their children's short-term autonomy. Although this argument presumes the existence of a strong parental role, the authority given to parents might well be extended in their absence to other adults, such as health care providers (Ross 1995).

Clatts, on the other hand, sees an inherent ethical conflict in the formulation of decision-specific capacity. "Either youth have capacity to make decisions or they do not. Either they have rights over their own bodies or they do not." In this view, the nature of the treatment should not determine the level of scrutiny of capacity.

No one can foresee the future. Just because decisions may have serious long-term consequences in no way diminishes an individual's rights to exercise decision-making authority over what happens to him or her, even if the outcomes are negative. Adolescents are no different in this regard, Clatts asserts. The only instance that would warrant overriding an adolescent's decision-making authority would be an intrusion on the rights of others. Such is not the case in the vast majority of medical decisions (Michael Clatts, personal communication).

While recognizing the objections, we believe that the concept of decision-specific capacity has great utility and steers a middle course between these views. If providers deny patients the right to make decisions for which they have capacity, they fail to respect them. If they permit them to make decisions for which they lack capacity, they abandon them.

There is an important distinction to be drawn between judging capacity in adults and in adolescents. Although both principles of respect for persons and beneficence are important, their relative weights vary. Among adults, the principle of respect for patient autonomy has significantly greater moral weight than beneficence, whereas among adolescents, this is not the case.

2. Health care providers should not impose higher standards for determining capacity for adolescents alone than they do for adolescents generally.

This guideline addresses a question of fairness. Some providers may be comfortable with giving broad decision-making authority to their adolescent patients but hesitate when faced with an adolescent alone. In the typical case, there is a parent or parental substitute in the youth's life who, it is assumed, will act as a brake on unwise decisions and encourage sensible ones. The capacity of an adolescent alone who lacks such a back-up person should not be assessed by a more demanding standard than that deemed appropriate for adolescents who are not alone but who are otherwise comparable. The fact of being alone can certainly be a negative factor in the young person's developing capacity and autonomy. It can also be a positive factor. Some adolescents alone are themselves the responsible persons in households where the parent is too ill to function and where there are younger children who need care. They arguably have more decision-making capacity than an over-protected adolescent in a family that restrains independence. Adolescents alone may need special assistance in following through on their decisions, but that need should not be equated with lack of capacity to make the decision.

3. For all adolescents, a heightened concern about capacity is necessary when the decision under consideration involves long-term negative health or life consequences.

On the basis of the decision-specific nature of capacity, adolescents' decisions that adults may think are wrong or ill-advised, the result of a failure to appreciate long-term consequences or that represent capitulation to peer (or adult) pressure, are more tolerable if the consequences are trivial or easily reversible. Furthermore, adolescents' decisions about well-accepted treatments that have great benefit for the patient and present little risk require less capacity than decisions that are ambiguous, controversial, or associated with short- or long-term negative consequences. For example, consent to antibiotic treatment by an otherwise healthy adolescent with a streptococcal infection requires a less rigorous assessment of capacity than that of a youth with leukemia who consents to a new regimen of chemotherapy when all previous attempts have failed. Adolescents alone are no different in this regard. Because this guideline brings to a specific context the general concept of decision-specific capacity, it will evoke the same criticisms discussed earlier.

4. *Health care providers should be aware of the most expansive legal definitions of capacity in their jurisdictions that might provide the basis for the adolescent's legally valid consent.*

A leading expert on the legal rules governing medical care provided to minors asserts: "Regardless of statutory authority . . . it has been at least forty years since any court in the United States has allowed parents of a child of fifteen or older to recover damages from a physician for treating their adolescent without their consent, when consent was given by the child" (Holder 1985). In addition to the patient's consent and his or her age (fifteen or older), Holder notes that her statement applies to cases when the care given was uncontroversial and solely for the benefit of the patient.

Despite the reassuring legal record, providers remain concerned about their potential liability (Sigman and O'Connor 1991). It is particularly important for providers who work with the various categories of adolescents alone to learn about federal, state, and local laws that provide the strongest support for treating adolescents on the basis of their own consent. Many who are relatively unfamiliar with these sources will be reassured by the degree to which adolescents are even now authorized to make decisions about their medical care. In those relatively infrequent instances when the law does not authorize adolescent consent, there may, nonetheless, be a strong ethical obligation to provide routine ambulatory or clinic care. Consent for surgery or other major interventions may be governed by the hospital's risk-management policy.

5. *If an adolescent demonstrates capacity to provide ethically valid informed consent, discussions about medical care should respect this capacity, even if formal legal consent to treatment must be obtained from an adult.*

If the adolescent has demonstrated capacity to consent to care, it is ethically justified to regard him or her as the main decision maker. Health care providers should engage the adolescent in a discussion of the benefits, risks, and consequences of treatment and the alternatives. Just as with adults, however, who have varying degrees of emotional stability and intellectual sophistication, the discussion should be carried on in terms that are appropriate to the young person's cognitive level, knowledge, and age-appropriate concerns. Even when consent from an adult is legally or administratively required, health care providers still have the responsibility to engage in this discussion.

Adolescents and adults alike value the affirmation that they are able to make their own decisions. Furthermore, in decision making, one learns by doing.

Adolescents, particularly those who are alone, may never have felt any control over their lives. The opportunity to make choices, and to have them respected, is an important step in developing the fully mature ability to make wise choices.

The Right to Refuse and Demand Care

6. An adolescent's refusal of recommended treatment should initiate an extensive discussion with the teen and a consideration of mutually acceptable alternatives.

Health care providers are understandably concerned when any patient refuses to accept their carefully considered recommendations for treatment. An adolescent's refusal often evokes a strong paternalistic impulse. And so it should. The alternative – simply accepting at face value the rejection of what the provider deems to be beneficial care – is an abdication of ethical responsibility. However, the provider's response should in all but the most extreme cases stop short of outright coercion or force (Figure 2).

In life-threatening or health-impairing emergencies in which capacity to consent is impaired, health care providers should, as they nearly always do, opt for treatment even over objections. This is true for both adults and adolescents (Iserson, Sanders, and Mathieu 1986). For adolescents with chronic or terminal conditions, where life-threatening emergencies can be anticipated, a youth's decisions about the level of treatment in these situations should be determined in advance (Leiken 1993). In nonemergency situations, a refusal of care should initiate a new and more focused discussion (Fleischman et al. 1994). Among the factors that should be explored are: possible misunderstandings, the youth's emotional state, consequences of failing to treat or postponing treatment, alternative treatments that may be more acceptable, the risk of alienating the adolescent from care if the refusal is not taken seriously, and the duration of the treatment. Some refusals may reflect the adolescent's failure to understand the facts, concern about body image, excessive concern about peer judgments, hopelessness, fear of pain, poor ability to think in terms of future consequences, or panic. In other cases the adolescent may simply be asking for more time, or more attention, before consenting. Adolescents alone may need more patience and support than other adolescents because of their prior history and lack of trust.

A chronic condition presents special problems. The prime characteristic of a chronic condition is that it requires the cooperation of the adolescent patient for the long haul. This sort of cooperation over time precludes the sort of intervention-over-objection that might be contemplated by acute care providers.

7. An adolescent's request for a treatment that the health care provider judges to be inappropriate or dangerous should initiate the same assessment and serious discussion as a treatment refusal.

Some adolescents, including adolescents alone, are quite knowledgeable about treatments that in their view will improve their appearance, enhance their ability to compete with their peers, or ease their psychic pain. Examples include plastic

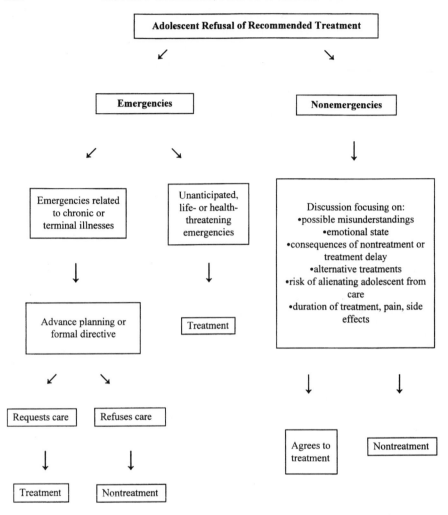

Figure 2. Refusal of treatment.

surgery, hormones, and psychoactive drugs. There are legitimate and beneficial uses for all these therapies. But hormone administration for an endocrine deficiency is different from hormone administration to an adolescent boy so that he will develop feminizing characteristics, whether for sexual identity or other reasons. Health care providers should treat requests, sometimes issued in the form of demands, for such treatments in a nondisparaging and respectful way. This does not mean that health care providers are morally obligated to provide this care. In fact, they may be morally (as well as legally) obligated to refuse to provide it, even though there may be a risk that the adolescent will seek and obtain the care under worse circumstances.

Some of these requests are indications of serious problems in the young person's life and should be the occasion for opening a dialogue about the long-term risks of the treatment, the reasons it is desired, and alternatives. Even if the adolescent persists and finds a practitioner who will accede to the demand, the original health care provider should keep the lines of communication open so that the youth may be willing to come back should side effects or a change of mind occur.

Confidentiality

8. Health care providers have a moral obligation to protect the privacy and confidentiality of their adolescent patients and to set out clearly at the outset of the relationship the limited conditions under which confidentiality may be breached.

Adolescents' fears that private information about their lives and medical care will be disclosed to others are among the main reasons that adolescents do not seek medical assistance in a timely fashion. When adolescents alone have a medical problem, they may fear the repercussions from foster parents, absent parents, or another authority. This fear may act as a barrier to care. It is important that these fears be dealt with immediately. Without the assurances of confidentiality accurate information is less likely to be shared, and needed care may be forgone.

Confidentiality has special developmental significance for adolescents (Blustein 1996). It is intimately connected to efforts to establish a separate identity, to experiment with various behaviors, and to protect themselves from parental or peer abuse, ridicule, or ostracism. Adolescents may value confidentiality even more than adults and yet may have less capacity to assess the likelihood of a breach and the possible consequences. Therefore confidentiality and its limits must be addressed explicitly (Figure 3).

In the case of adolescents alone, breaches of confidentiality may carry additional risks and may be especially counterproductive. Breaches of confidentiality could result, for example, in youth being returned to the abusive homes from which they fled, exacerbating the problems that led them to their current difficult situation.

At the outset of a relationship health care providers should assure a youth that confidentiality will be protected except in certain, limited circumstances. They should also be assured that, should such a circumstance arise, the health care provider will inform them who will be told and what will be disclosed. The disclosure may be to some adult relative, a social service agency, or in extreme circumstances, a court. The youth should be assured that he or she is not being abandoned and that the provider will continue to provide support after the disclosure. One circumstance requiring disclosure is a serious intent to commit suicide (English 1992; Setterberg 1992). Another is an acute and complex disease, such as leukemia, that requires extensive treatment over time and explicit adherence to a medical regimen. A similar situation is a chronic disease such as juvenile diabetes that requires frequent monitoring.

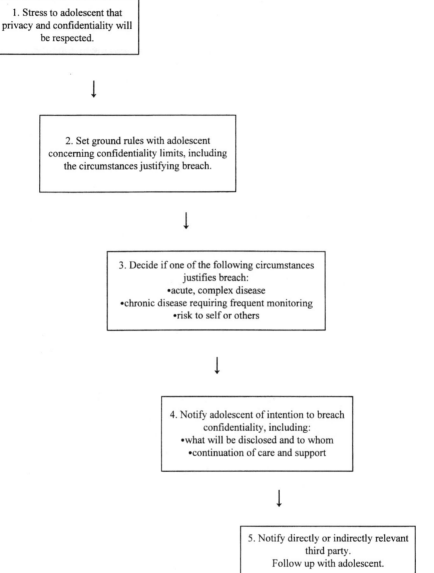

Figure 3. Confidentiality.

Other circumstances in which disclosure may be necessary involve risk to others. These may be threats of violence to a specific individual. A particularly controversial circumstance is the case of an HIV-infected adolescent who knowingly and consistently places a regular sexual or needle-sharing partner at risk without informing him or her.

Within the group that considered these guidelines there was a sharp disagreement between those who consider that a breach of confidentiality in such circumstances would be counterproductive and would further alienate a disaffected youth, and those who thought that the interests of the unknowing, uninfected partner weighed more heavily in the ethical balance. Assuming that an identifiable and uninformed person is at real (not just assumed) risk and that all best efforts at counseling the HIV-infected adolescent and offering assisted notification have failed, the authors opt for the same standards that apply to adults: notification, with ongoing support and follow-up for both partners. Partner notification depends on the willingness of the infected person to provide the names and addresses of the partner at risk. In some cases the infected person will provide this information but will not tell the partner or bring him or her in for counseling. Sometimes third-party notification is more acceptable to the infected person; sometimes it is not. If notification is ultimately the decision, this difficult task need not, perhaps should not, be done by the health care provider directly. Most providers are not trained to provide the necessary counseling and referrals. Public health systems have trained counselors to provide this service, without naming the source case. Partner notification programs allow health care providers to honor their responsibilities to patients as well as fulfill their public health duties.

Limits of the Health Care Paradigm

9. When treating an adolescent alone, health care providers should be very clear about the boundaries of their responsibility and the limits to their caring.

In treating an adolescent alone, it is the natural inclination of many care providers to expand their role to meet many of the youth's unmet needs. For many adolescents alone, their relationship to the providers is the closest experience to being in a family that they have had. Although providers may feel as if they are acting like a family, it should be clear to them and to the adolescent that they are professionals with the skills–and limits–of professionals.

The notion of binding ties and permanent commitments that is the core of the idea of *family* does not characterize the provider–patient relationship. It would be a disservice implicitly to suggest or support a youth's fantasy of unbounded care unless the provider is truly willing to become the substitute parent (i.e., legal guardianship or adoption). Fulfilling the role and responsibilities of trusted advisor and medical counselor is ultimately the best a health care provider can do for an adolescent alone.

Acknowledgments

The project from which these guidelines are derived, *The Adolescent Alone: Decision Making in Health Care,* was supported by grants from the Fan Fox and Leslie R. Samuels Foundation and the American Foundation for AIDS Research. A multidisciplinary working group of scholars, clinicians, and activists met for two years to discuss commissioned papers, presentations by experts, including adolescents, and clinical studies. The guidelines represent consensus statements developed by this working group.

The following are signatories to these guidelines. Although those whose names appear here endorse the guidelines as a whole, there are differences of opinion with respect to individual recommendations. Organizations are listed for identification only: Elizabeth Alderman, M.D., Director, Adolescent Ambulatory Service, Montefiore Medical Center, Bronx, NY; John D. Arras, Ph.D., Porterfield Professor of Biomedical Ethics, Department of Philosophy, University of Virginia; Diana M. Bianco, J.D., attorney, Oregon Advocacy Center, Portland OR; Andrew M. Boxer, Ph.D., Assistant Professor, Department of Psychiatry, University of Chicago; Michael C. Clatts, Ph.D., Principal Investigator, Youth At Risk Project, National Development Research Institutes, New York, NY; Susan M. Coupey, M.D., Professor of Pediatrics and Associate Director, Division of Adolescent Medicine, Albert Einstein College of Medicine/Montefiore Medical Center, Bronx, NY; Francine Cournos, M.D., Professor of Clinical Psychiatry, College of Physicians and Surgeons, Columbia University, New York, NY; Sheryl Dicker, J.D., Executive Director, Permanent Judicial Commission on Justice for Children, New York, NY; Barbara Draimin, D.S.W., Director, The Family Center, New York, NY; Abigail English, I.D., Project Director, Adolescent Health Care Project, National Center for Youth Law, Chapel Hill, NC; Linda N. Freeman, M.D., Assistant Professor of Social Work, Columbia University, New York, NY; Donna Futterman, M.D., Associate Professor of Pediatrics and Director of the Adolescent AIDS Program, Albert Einstein College of Medicine/Montefiore Medical Center, Bronx, NY; Neal D. Hoffman, M.D., Assistant Professor of Pediatrics and Medical Director of the Adolescent AIDS Program, Albert Einstein College of Medicine/Montefiore Medical Center, Bronx, NY; Betty Wolder Levin, Ph.D., Associate Professor, Department of Health and Nutrition Sciences, Brooklyn College, Brooklyn, NY; Peter J. Millock, J.D., Nixon, Hargrave, Devans & Doyle, Albany, New York; Jonathan D. Moreno, Ph.D., Professor of Pediatrics and of Medicine, Director of the Division of Humanities in Medicine, SUNY Health Science Center at Brooklyn, New York; Michael A. Pawel, M.D., Executive Director, August Aichhorn Center for Adolescent Residential Care, New York, NY; William Ruddick, Ph.D., Professor of Philosophy and Codirector, Philosophy & Medicine Program, New York University; S. Kenneth Schonberg, M.D., Professor of Pediatrics and Director, Division of Adolescent Medicine, Albert Einstein College of Medicine/Montefiore Medical Center, Bronx, NY; Luis H. Zayas, Ph.D., Associate Professor, Graduate School of Social Service, Fordham University, Tarrytown, NY.

We wish to acknowledge the contribution made by the following persons to the collaborative work. This acknowledgment is not meant to imply their or their organization's endorsement of the guidelines: Audrey Smith Rogers, Ph.D., Epidemiologist, Pediatric, Adolescent, and Maternal AIDS Branch, Center for Research for Mothers and Children, National Institute of Child Health and Development, Bethesda, MD; Susan F. Newcomer, Ph.D., Statistician, Demographic and Behavioral Sciences Branch Center for Population Research, National Institute of Child Health and Development, Bethesda, MD.

Special acknowledgments are due to Diana Bianco, Staff Attorney at the Oregon Advocacy Center, Portland, Oregon, and research assistant on this project while she was a student at New York University Law School, for her substantive and administrative contributions to the project meetings, and to Ben Munisteri of The Orphan Project staff for his editorial and administrative assistance. Thanks also to Cheryl Fried and Dillan Siegler for research assistance and to Linda Farber Post for graphics assistance.

References

Ad Hoc Committee on Adolescents and HIV (1991). *Illusions of immortality: The confrontation of adolescence and AIDS.* Albany, NY: New York State AIDS Advisory Council.

American Academy of Pediatrics (1993). Adolescents and human immunodeficiency virus infection: The role of the pediatrician in prevention and intervention. *Pediatrics, 92,* 626–630.

Arras, J. C., and S. Steinbock (1995). *Ethical issues in modern medicine* (4th ed.). Mountain View, CA: Mayfield Publishing Co.

Beauchamp, T. L., and J. F. Childress (1994). *Principles of biomedical ethics.* (4th ed.). New York, NY: Oxford University Press.

Blustein, J. (1996). Confidentiality and the adolescent: An ethical analysis. In R. Cassidy and A. Fleischman (Eds.), *Pediatric ethics: From principles to practice.* Newtown Square, PA: Harwood Academic Publishers.

Brock, D. W. (1989). Children's competence for health care decisionmaking. In L. Kopelman and J. Moskop (Eds.), *Children and health care: Moral and social issues.* Norwell, MA: Kluwer Academic Publishers.

Buchanan, A. E., and D. W. Brock (1989). *Deciding for others: The ethics of surrogate decision making.* New York: Cambridge University Press.

Centers for Disease Control and Prevention (1992). Health risk behaviors among adolescents who do and do not attend school – United States. *MMWR, 43,* 129–132.

Cheng, T. L., and J. C. Klein (1995). The adolescent viewpoint: Implications for access and prevention. *JAMA, 273,* 1957–1958.

Committee on Bioethics (1995). Informed consent, parental permission, and assent in pediatric practice. *Pediatrics, 95,* 314–317.

Cournos, F. et al. (1993). Report of the task force on consent to voluntary hospitalization. *Bull Am Acad Psychiatry Laws, 21,* 298.

Dorn, L., E. Susman, and J. Fletcher (1995). Informed consent in children and adolescents: age, maturation and psychological state. *Journal of Adolescent Health, 16,* 185–190.

English, A. (1991). Runaway and street youth at risk for HIV infection: Legal and ethical issues in access to care. *Journal of Adolescent Health, 12,* 504–510.

English, A. (1992a). Legal aspects of care. In E. McAnarney, et al. (Eds.), *Textbook of adolescent medicine.* Philadelphia, PA: W. B. Saunders Co., 165–171.

English, A. (1992b). Legal and ethical concerns. In S. B. Friedman, M. Fisher, and K. Schonberg (Eds.), *Comprehensive adolescent health care.* St. Louis, MO: Quality Medical Publishing, 95–99.

English, A. (1995). Guidelines for adolescent health research: Legal perspectives. *Journal of Adolescent Health, 17,* 277–286.

Fleischman, A. R., et al. (1994). Caring for gravely ill children. *Pediatrics, 94,* 433–439.

Futterman, D., K. Hein, and H. Kunins (1993). Teens and AIDS: Identifying and testing those at risk. *Contemporary Pediatrics* (August), 68–93.

Gittler, J., et al. (1990). *Adolescent health care decision making: The law and public policy.* Washington, DC: Carnegie Council of Adolescent Development.

Holder, A. (1989). Children and adolescents: Their right to decide about their own health care. In L. Kopelman and J. Moskop (Eds.), *Children and health care: Moral and social issues.* Norwell, MA: Kluwer Academic Publishers.

Holder, A. R. (1985). *Legal issues in pediatric and adolescent medicine* (2nd ed.). New Haven, CT: Yale University Press.

Holder, A. R. (1995) Adolescents. In W. T. Reich, (Ed.), *The encyclopedia of bioethics (Vol. 1).* New York, NY: Simon & Schuster Macmillan, 63–71.

Holmes, R. (1989). Children and health care decision making: A reply to Angela Holder. In L. Kopelman and J. Moskop (Eds.), *Children and health care: Moral and social issues.* Norwell, MA: Kluwer Academic Publishers.

Iserson, K. V., A. B. Sanders, and D. Mathieu (1986). *Ethics in Emergency Medicine* (2nd ed.). Tucson, AZ: Galen Press.

Leikin, S. (1993). The role of adolescents in decisions concerning their cancer therapy. *Cancer, 71,* 3342–3346.

Lindegren, M. L., C. Hanson, K. Miller, R. Byers, and I. Onorato (1994). Epidemiology of human immunodeficiency virus infection in adolescents, United States. *Pediatr Infect Dis J, 13,* 525–535.

MacKenzie, R. (1992). At-risk youth. In E. McAnarney et al. (Ed.), *Textbook of adolescent medicine.* Philadelphia, P.A: W. B. Saunders & Co., 237–240.

Mackenzie, R. G., and M. C. Kipke (1992). Substance use and abuse. In S. B. Friedman, M. Fisher, and K. Schonberg (Eds.) (1992). *Comprehensive adolescent health care.* St. Louis, MO: Quality Medical Publishing, 768.

Michaels, D., and C. Levine (1992). Estimates of the number of motherless youth orphaned by AIDS in the United States. *JAMA, 268,* 3456–3461.

Moreno, J. (1989) Treating the adolescent patient: An ethical analysis. *Journal of Adolescent Health Care, 10,* 454–459.

National Network of Runaway and Youth Services (1991). *To whom do they belong?: Runaway, homeless and other youth in high-risk situations in the 1990s.* Washington, DC: The National Network.

New York State Task Force on Life and the Law (1992). *When others must choose: Deciding for patients without capacity.* Albany, NY: The New York State Task Force on Life and the Law.

Oberman, M. (1996). Minor rights and wrongs. *The Journal of Law, Medicine and Ethics, 24,* 127–138.

Petersen, A. C., and N. Leffert (1995). Developmental issues influencing guidelines for adolescent health research: A review. *Journal of Adolescent Health, 17,* 298–305.

Pinkney, D. S. (1994). America's sickest children. *American Medical News* (10 January), 16.

Quadrel, M., B. Fischhoff, and W. Davis (1993). Adolescent (in) vulnerability. *American Psychologist, 48,* 102–116,

Rosenberg P. R. Biggar, and J. Goedert (1994). Declining age at HIV infection in the United States. *The New England Journal of Medicine, 330,* 789–790.

Ross, L. (1995). Arguments against health care autonomy for minors. *Bioethics Forum, 11,* 22–26.

Ryan, S. A., and C. E. Irwin. (1992). Risk behaviors. In S. B. Friedman, M. Fisher and K. Schonberg (Eds.), *Comprehensive adolescent health care.* St. Louis, MO: Quality Medical Publishing, 795.

Setterberg, S. (1992). Suicidal behavior and suicide. In S. B. Friedman, M. Fisher, and K. Schonberg (Eds.), *Comprehensive adolescent health care.* St. Louis, MO: Quality Medical Publishing, 862–867.

Sigman, G., and C. O'Connor (1991). Exploration for physicians of the mature minor doctrine. *Journal of Pediatrics, 119,* 520–525.

Index